ANONYMOUS AMERICANS

Explorations in
Nineteenth-Century Social History

edited by
TAMARA K. HAREVEN
Clark University

PRENTICE-HALL, INC., Englewood Cliffs, N.J.

C 13–038398–8   P 13–038380–5

Library of Congress Catalog Card Number: 77–143813

Current printing (last digit):

10   9   8   7   6   5   4   3   2   1

Prentice-Hall International, Inc., *London*
Prentice-Hall of Australia Pty. Ltd., *Sydney*
Prentice-Hall of Canada Ltd., *Toronto*
Prentice-Hall of India Private Limited, *New Delhi*
Prentice-Hall of Japan, Inc., *Tokyo*

Printed in the United States of America

You remember the old fable of "The Man and the Lion," where the lion complained that he should not be so misrepresented "when the lions wrote history"—Letter of Wendell Phillips to Frederick Douglass (Boston, April 22, 1845).

Contents

Preface

The essays in this collection explore the experience of those groups in American society which have largely escaped traditional historical inquiry. They were chosen for the kinds of questions they raise and for the fresh insights they provide into the experience of laborers, slaves, freedmen, and immigrants, as well as the members of the middle classes. The essays are not limited, however, to "inarticulate" Americans or to "history from the bottom up." [1] Nor do the contributors advocate tipping the balance of American social history to an exclusive treatment of lower classes and minority groups. They call, instead, for an integration of neglected experiences into the broader field of American social history, and for an incorporation of forgotten dimensions that are not necessarily restricted to certain groups or classes. To use a musical analogy, these essays provide contrapuntal variations to the constant theme of change and continuity in history.

Until very recently, American social history was written from the perspective of the dominant culture. It dealt with elites rather than common people, with institutions rather than social processes, with attitudes rather than experiences. Large segments of the population were ignored or frequently subjected to stereotyping. Common dimensions of human experience such as family life were largely absent. The habitual lumping of "social" with intellectual history, or its identification with "reform," made American social history an index of upper-

and middle-class standards and values. "Progress" was measured in the linear progression of "uplift" and social service. Social problems were rendered from the perspective of the leader, the custodian, or the caretaker. Consequently, historical discussion focused on unions rather than on laborers, on social welfare rather than on the experience of the poor, on institutions rather than on the people they purported to serve.[2] Social conflict was interpreted either as social disintegration, or as class conflict from a Marxist perspective.

With some exceptions, traditional American social history was static and nonspatial, and at best it discussed social customs and institutions. Arthur M. Schlesinger, who with Dixon Ryan Fox edited the multivolume *History of American Life* series, criticized the limitations of this series as well as the general state of social history before his death: "Much of it is still of taxonomic or descriptive variety, consisting of catalogues of facts grouped in appropriate categories and treated for their own sake instead of in relation to other developments of the times." It still fell short of what Schlesinger considered the major goals of social history: "to grasp and depict both the inner and outer life of society and to integrate the two." [3] Although process is valued as a dominant characteristic of American culture, and change is the underlying force in history, traditional history rarely includes a discussion of process. With few exceptions, one reads about cities, rather than the process of urbanization; about immigrants, rather than migration; about ideals of success, rather than those of mobility; about structure, rather than relationships.[4] All movement has been treated as *terminal,* for somehow historians have implied that human experience stopped whenever historical discussion came to a halt.

Because of the emphasis on social classes in a narrow, structural approach, more subtle relationships escaped attention. Generations were treated as chronological sequences, rather than as stages in the life cycle. What effect did the complexity of age groups *within* a certain historical period have? How did stages of human development influence certain cultural contexts? In what ways did economic change, social upheavals, mobility, and migration affect the relations between fathers and sons? And how did family behavior, in turn, influence the experience of larger social groups? [5]

As early as 1940 Caroline Ware challenged her colleagues to ex-

plore American history "from the bottom up." Why did her call go
unheeded for so long?[6] The common excuse for omissions in traditional social history has been the unavailability of sources. True, there
has been a dearth of sources for the history of the inarticulate and the
non-heroes in America. The experience of silent participants seeps
through fragmentary documents only and is often presented through
the biases and perceptions of the recorders or compilers. Even the U.S.
Census, a relatively neutral source, is slanted by the peculiar biases and
omissions of the census taker. Historians presently engaged in the effort
to recapture the experience of the anonymous are not oblivious to these
limitations of sources. They are determined, however, to ask new questions of traditional materials, as well as to develop methods that would
enable them to explore often untapped sources, such as Census manuscript schedules, school records, marriage and birth certificates, wills,
and tax records.

The techniques of the social sciences, especially the use of com-
puters, now enable historians to study vast numbers of hitherto anonymous people and to analyze quantities of materials in search for
information about social processes such as migration, mobility, and
assimilation. Similarly, the use of anthropological and psychological
theory has deepened our perception of human experience in the past
and provided conceptual frameworks for the treatment of the sources
of cultural history in the context of a total society.[7] The combined
impact of the social sciences has stimulated much scholarly effort in
three emerging areas: structure and process, the "new urban history,"
and the history of the family.[8] Oscar Handlin, Stephan Thernstrom,
Sam B. Warner, and more recently, John Demos, Philip Greven, and
Kenneth Lockridge have clearly shown that the work of current social
historians owes as much to the asking of new questions of traditional
sources as to methodological inventiveness and the use of previously
unexploited sources.

Recent social historians were not the first to apply social science
methods to historical analysis. The "new social history" actually dates
back to Frederick Jackson Turner, Charles Beard, and James Harvey
Robinson's "New History." [9] Even the professed interest in the experience of common people is not unique, as Caroline Ware pointed out
in 1940:

The attempt to write history from the bottom up started a generation ago with the study of the frontier; it has recently been extended into the study of local communities and culturally homogeneous regions. In the still unexplored history of the non-dominant cultural groups of the industrial cities lies the story of an emerging industrial culture that represents the dynamic cultural frontier of modern America.[10]

It is this aspect of the experience of common people that the social historians are now concentrating on. For although the New History of the Progressive Era advocated incorporation of all social sciences into the study of total societies, its historians primarily used the sources articulated by the upper classes. Moreover, their concern with the application of social science to historical inquiry emanated from a commitment to scientific history. Recent historians, however, in Stephan Thernstrom's words feel that they "ought not so much to make urban social history more scientific and rigorous as to make it less elitist and formalistic." [11] Both the old "New History" and the current social history share what Morton White referred to as "cultural organicism"—the historian's reaching out into the entire social space. Thus, the application of the social sciences to historical phenomena reflects a certain view of society as a whole, expressed in a concern for experience, process, context, and function.[12]

Not unlike the New History school, these new social historians are present-oriented, and they are frequently driven to understand the past by the crises of the present. Rather than cripple historical perception, this concern for the present will yield a richer, more lively past. The commitment of the new social historians to historicity is perhaps even more intense than that of traditional historians because the former strive for a total exposure of the past in all its complexities, as interpreted and experienced by all social groups respectively. Their concentration on common laborers, the poor, immigrants, and blacks does not suggest a commitment to class, but an effort to redress the historical balance in order to provide a total picture of society. As Richard Hofstadter remarked, the predominant characteristic of the new social history is in "the rediscovery of complexity in American History." [13]

Methodologically, the essays in this collection fall into two broad categories: those employing the quantitative method, and those interpreting the sources of cultural history. Joseph Kett studies the transition from childhood to adulthood in rural New England; Stephan Thernstrom and Peter Knights investigate migration patterns; Martyn Bowden traces popular perceptions of the American desert and their impact on the westward movement; David Grimsted discusses the symbols of melodrama as an expression of the frustrations and aspirations of its audiences; Lawrence Levine explores music as a source for the study of the slave experience; Leon Litwack presents a new perspective on the Negro's adjustment to freedom; Paul Worthman compares the economic and social advancement of black and white laborers in rapidly industrializing Birmingham, Alabama; Timothy Smith traces lay leadership in immigrant congregations in the United States from their European predecessors; Gerald Grob approaches the mental hospital from the perspective of the inmate as well as that of the custodian. And although Grob's essay is more heavily focused on the institution, the article attacks the fallacies of writing history strictly from a middle-class perspective. Finally, Richard Sennett examines the reaction of middle-class suburban families to the outbreak of violence in Chicago.

In addition to offering fresh information and new interpretations on their respective subjects, the authors of these essays address themselves to such broad historical problems as the forces of continuity in periods of rapid social change, alternatives to elite leadership, the relationship between ideology and social experience, environmental perception, cultural pluralism in a conformist society, the dynamics of resiliancy in oppressed minorities, and class definitions of social deviancy.

This collection is exploratory, rather than exhaustive. Together these essays will not produce a profile of nineteenth-century American society. Rather, each essay is designed to stimulate the reader into considering the historical processes of the period from a different perspective.

With the exception of Richard Sennett's article, all the essays were written especially for this collection.

ACKNOWLEDGMENTS

Stephan Thernstrom responded to the proposed collection with enthusiasm, and followed its progress with scholarly advice and friendly encouragement. The contributors struggled with heavy schedules to meet deadlines and invested beyond their respective essays. Barton Bernstein provided valuable advice at the planning stages. George Billias volunteered his help in a difficult situation. John Demos, William Koelsch, and Paul Prucha provided constructive criticisms for several essays. William Koelsch especially subjected the Preface to critical scrutiny. James Mooney and the staff of the American Antiquarian Society were extremely helpful in the selection of pictorial materials.

Robert Fenyo, history editor of Prentice-Hall, Inc., welcomed the project from its inception, and considerably eased my task with unfailing support and with his special talent for transforming work routines into pleasant occasions. Barbara Van Osten provided efficient management. Dorothy Green of the College Book Production Department steered the manuscript through production with expertise, precision, and remarkable patience. Beverly Baxter adjusted busy schedules to type revisions, and Donna Soliday was ready to help as usual. Terrance Coyne and Graham Moodie at Clark University were avid proofreaders.

Perhaps the most important debt is to our students whose interest confronted us with the need for such explorations. I am especially grateful to the students of the Clark University Urban History Seminar of 1969, whose insightful discussions of certain essays considerably improved the manuscript.

TAMARA K. HAREVEN

Monhegan Island, Maine

FOOTNOTES

1. For a formulation of this approach, see Jesse Lemisch, "The American Revolution Seen from the Bottom Up," in Barton J. Bernstein, ed., *Towards a New Past: Dissenting Essays in American History* (New York, 1968).

2. In his assessment of the current state of social welfare history, Robert H. Bremner stressed the need for "not only individual biographies of social welfare leaders but collective biographies of such groups as the aged, orphans, widows, paupers and the unemployed. . . ."—"The State of Social Welfare History," in Herbert J. Bass, ed., *The State of American History* (Chicago, 1970), 95.

3. Arthur M. Schlesinger, *In Retrospect: The History of an Historian* (New York, 1963), 200.

4. Eric E. Lampard's plea to historians to study the process of urbanization has not yet been answered. See "American Historians and the Study of Urbanization," *American Historical Review,* 67 (October, 1961), 49–61; also "Urbanization and Social Change: On the Broadening of the Scope and Relevance of Urban History," in Oscar Handlin and John Burchard, eds., *The Historian and the City* (Cambridge, Mass., 1963), 225–47. Stephan Thernstrom's emphasis on process in his studies of mobility and migration calls for a reassessment of traditional immigration history, since Thernstrom places immigration from abroad into the larger context of local rural-urban migration. The field is still wide open, however, for comparative studies of migration patterns and the interaction of various racial and ethnic groups among themselves and with the larger society. See, for example, Rudolph Vecoli, "Ethnicity: A Neglected Dimension of American History," in Bass, ed., *The State of American History,* 70–84.

5. These questions have remained largely unanswered. Stephan Thernstrom's pioneer study of Newburyport provides the first attempt to compare the degree and nature of mobility over several generations within the same families: *Poverty and Progress in a Nineteenth Century City* (Cambridge, Mass., 1964); Richard Sennett studies the relationship between family structure and the adjustment to the world of work: *Families Against the City* (Cambridge, Mass., 1970). Herbert Gutman, University of Rochester, is currently engaged in a large-scale study of black family structure in the nineteenth century. Sam B. Warner is studying family structure in several Michigan counties. With these two exceptions, the study of the family in the process of urbanization still awaits historical investigation. The most profound studies of the family are for the colonial period: John Demos, *A Little Commonwealth: Family Life in Colonial Plymouth* (New York, 1969); and Philip Greven, *Four Generations: Population, Land and Family in Colonial Andover* (Ithaca, N.Y., 1970). For a long time Oscar Handlin and Bernard Bailyn stood virtually alone in their emphasis on the importance of the family for the understanding of historical processes. See Handlin's *The Uprooted* (New York, 1951) and Bailyn's *Education in the Forming of American Society* (Chapel Hill, N.C., 1960). The work of Stephan Thernstrom, John Demos, and Richard Sennett was partly sparked by the insights of Handlin and Bailyn. Curiously, a recent volume summarizing the state of American history makes no reference to the family: Bass, ed., *The State of American History, passim.* To some extent, the family still is a neglected field of social history. In his lament of the current state of social history, Samuel P. Hays calls for the application of a broad structural approach encompassing the experience of the majority of silent participants in historical processes. Yet Professor Hays does not mention the family as a significant aspect of social history. See his "A Systematic Social History," in George Billias and Gerald Grob, eds., *American History: Retrospect and Prospect* (New York, 1970).

6. Caroline Ware, ed., *The Cultural Approach to History* (New York, 1940), 8–9. The essays in her collection were based on a special session of the American Historical Association devoted to the formulation of an interdisciplinary, cultural approach to history. The papers covered such subjects as nationality groups in the U.S., the peasant family, local history, population studies, and the uses of new sources for social history.

7. On the use of the quantitative method in historical analysis, see William O. Adelotte, "Quantification in History," *The American Historical Review,* 71 (April, 1969), 803–25. See also Don K. Rowney and James Q. Graham, Jr., *Quantitative His-*

tory (Homewood, Ill., 1969). On the application of sociological methodology to history, see Seymour Martin Lipset and Richard Hofstadter, *Sociology and History: Methods* (New York, 1968). The best example for the impact of psychological theory on social history is Demos, *A Little Commonwealth.* The influence of anthropology on the "new social history," although evident in John Demos' work, is most pronounced in Kenneth Lockridge, *A New England Town* (New York, 1969).

8. The structure and process approach is defined by Samuel Hays thus: "Social History is concerned with structural changes in society over long periods of time. The crucial concept is *social structure,* those patterns of human interaction which relate some people and differentiate others, which reflect characteristics held by some in common and by others in distinction. The historian is uniquely concerned with *long-run social change.* . . . While other disciplines emphasize structure, only history focuses on large-scale changes in structure over long periods of time"—"Systematic Social History," in Billias and Grob, eds., *American History.* The "new urban history" is best exemplified in Stephan Thernstrom and Richard Sennett, eds., *Nineteenth-Century Cities: Essays in the New Urban History* (New Haven, 1969). Most of these scholars apply the quantitative approach to an analysis of patterns of mobility and migration, as well as cultural traditions and ideology. As Thernstrom points out, these studies constitute the building blocks for a more general theory of urban social history: "Analysis of the relationship of those variables in a particular urban setting in a particular historical epoch and then of variations over time from place to place, within and without the culture, will supply a basis for generalizations of increasing breadth and abstraction and eventually, perhaps, permit the construction of a general historical theory of urbanization"—Thernstrom, "Reflections on the New Urban History," paper presented at the Conference on New Trends in History sponsored by *Daedalus* and the Ford Foundation (Rome, June 17–20, 1970), p. 4. The history of the family draws on the techniques of demography, on the one hand, and on anthropological and psychological theory, on the other. For a discussion of the current state of progress in this field see above, note 5.

9. On the New History, see Richard Hofstadter, *The Progressive Historians* (New York, 1968), and James Harvey Robinson, *The New History* (New York, 1912).

10. Ware, *The Cultural Approach to History,* 73.

11. Thernstrom, "Reflections on the New Urban History," 2.

12. Morton White, *Social Thought in America: The Revolt Against Formalism* (New York, 1959).

13. Hofstadter, *Progressive Historians,* 442.

Contributors

Martyn J. Bowden, Associate Professor of Geography, Clark University

David Grimsted, Associate Professor of History,
University of Maryland

Gerald N. Grob, Professor of History, Rutgers University,
New Brunswick

Tamara K. Hareven, Associate Professor of History, Clark University,
Editor of this volume

Joseph F. Kett, Associate Professor of History, University of Virginia

Peter R. Knights, Assistant Professor of Journalism,
University of Illinois, Champaign

Lawrence W. Levine, Associate Professor of History,
University of California, Berkeley

Leon F. Litwack, Associate Professor of History,
University of California, Berkeley

Richard Sennett, Assistant Professor of Sociology, Brandeis University

Timothy L. Smith, Professor of Education and History,
    Johns Hopkins University

Stephan Thernstrom, Professor of History, University of California,
    Los Angeles

Paul B. Worthman, Assistant Professor of History,
    University of California, Los Angeles

The home circle. By B. W. Tilburn, 1889, Littleton, New Hampshire. From the Library of Congress Collection.

"Gwine to de Field"—James Hopkinson Plantation, Edisto Island, South Carolina. By H. P. Moore, 1862. Reproduced from The Philadelphia Photographer, *April 1865.*

Frederick Warren, City Marshal of Worcester, Massachusetts, with prisoner. By Moses Sanford Chapin, about 1850, Daguerreotype. Reproduced by permission of the American Antiquarian Society, Worcester, Massachusetts.

Silverton Railroad: transferring passengers at Red Mountain. By Ralph W. Andrews. Thomas McKee collection, Denver Public Library. Reproduced by permission of the Denver Public Library.

"Election Returns." By J. M. Brooks, in Antony's Photographic Bulletin, *August 1896, Vol. 27, p. 262.*

Class picture, H. C. Young's school, Greenwich, Connecticut, February 6, 1852. From the Stober Collection. Daguerreotype in Rare Photographic Images, Parke-Bernet Galleries, New York, 1970, Catalog No. 84.

Italian Family seeking lost baggage, Ellis Island. By Lewis W. Hine, 1905. Reproduced by permission of the George Eastman House, Rochester, New York.

JOSEPH F. KETT

Growing Up in Rural New England, 1800–1840

𝄢𝄢𝄢𝄢𝄢𝄢𝄢𝄢𝄢𝄢𝄢𝄢𝄢𝄢𝄢𝄢𝄢𝄢𝄢𝄢𝄢𝄢𝄢𝄢𝄢𝄢𝄢𝄢𝄢𝄢𝄢𝄢𝄢𝄢𝄢

A concern with the adolescent has been a distinctive feature of twentieth-century social thought. Psychologists and others have written books on the teen years as frequently as nineteenth-century theologians turned out concordances of the Bible. Whole journals have been devoted to the psychological and social significance of adolescence. Professional writers on youth have enjoyed successful careers, while youth culture has become so pervasive that it is often dominant over adult culture. All of this presupposes the existence of typical adolescents, so that one can generalize from the experience of a sample group to that of untested groups. We assume that street-corner society in Brooklyn is like street-corner society in Cicero, that the Grosse Point teenager shares common experiences with the Mamaroneck teenager. Few early adolescents work; the great majority attend school of a special type, the high school. There they are segregated by age with peers, exposed to similar subjects, and expected to engage in carefully regulated and age-graded pursuits, whether cheerleading or sports, proms or debating.

Nothing remotely resembling this pattern existed in early nineteenth-century America. The experience of growing up differed, often profoundly, from one youth to the next. There was no set age for leaving school, leaving home, or starting to work. Variations among regions were at least as deep-seated as those among classes or individuals.

1

The dominance of regional variation arose from two sources: the differing character of work demands and opportunities in settled and in frontier areas, and the immense discrepancy among the kinds of schooling available in the Northeast, the South, and the West. These variations often had an intensely personal application. The boy who started to grow up in New England might find himself at the age of ten in Ohio and at fifteen in Michigan. His attachment to his family would be the only constant factor as he was ruthlessly ushered from one setting to the next.

The pattern of random experience, however, could extend just as readily to the family itself. Families were constantly being disrupted by the death of one or both parents, not simply because of higher mortality from disease, but also because of the length of time which usually elapsed between the birth of the first and the last child. A man who fathered his first child at 25 might not father his last until he was 40 or even 45. It was a statistical probability that the father would be dead before the youngest child reached maturity. The frequency of being orphaned in the early nineteenth century had a personal as well as a demographic significance, for it meant that the plans laid by youth were subject to drastic shattering by chance.

All of these factors make it difficult to reconstruct the experience of growing up in the early nineteenth century. Even if we confine our attention to New England between 1800 and 1840 and exclude from consideration sons of the very rich and the very poor, we only assuage the problem. The most typical experience of any child in the early nineteenth century was coming into contact with death before he reached the age of five. Although writers in the period did not produce a significant body of literature on the teen years, they did often talk of childhood and youth, indicating that they were conscious of some model experiences, and thereby tempting the historian to explore the nature of growing up.

FEMININE CONTROL IN
THE EARLY YEARS

Very early in the nineteenth century a consensus emerged in published literature to the effect that the first five or six years of childhood were primarily the mother's responsibility. These were the years of "infancy," not in its modern connotation of reference to suckling babes, but used more broadly to indicate the years of maternal control of the child. The same literature which affirmed the preeminent role of the mother insisted on two corollaries: the need to pay attention to little children, and the superiority of moral suasion over corporal punishment in discipline.[1]

In all likelihood, the simple conditions of farm life did more to reinforce than to frustrate the accomplishment of the prescribed regimen. Although mothers were busy managing large families and cooking meals for husbands and field hands, they could expect and command assistance from older daughters for these tasks. During the winter, moreover, the workload for all parties eased and more time could be found for children. In the summer, especially in the busy hours before noon (the time of the principal meal), children under eight were usually sent to district schools, which functioned virtually as nurseries in the planting, haying, and harvesting seasons. Summer schools, which usually served three- to eight-year-olds, were taught by women, and never acquired the unsavory reputation for disorder which marked the winter schools. The absence of older boys in summer sessions meant that discipline for younger children could be mild, an extension of approved family discipline.

DISTRICT SCHOOL AND DISCIPLINE

The first of many jarring discontinuities involved in the experience of growing up usually came not in "infancy" but between the ages of six or eight to twelve, and was an outgrowth of new experiences in school, work, and, often, religion. After the age of eight or nine, boys customarily attended only winter schools, being kept at home to work on the farm in summer. The transition to winter school was, in a fundamental way, abrupt.

District schools in the winter bore little resemblance in either composition or discipline to summer sessions. Prior to the 1840's, the former were usually taught by men of all ages and temperaments. Some were college students, some academy students, and others were local farmers who had advanced to the rule of three, if little beyond.

Differences among the pupils were even greater. Most winter schools included "large boys" of 16 and 17, and many had young men of 18 or 20. The majority of pupils, however, were between 8 and 15. Sometimes efforts were made to seat the smaller children separately, but they would still be in the same room with older boys, since no effective grading system existed outside of large cities before 1840.[2]

Available evidence suggests that disorderly conditions were the norm in winter schools. Even progressive educators and reformers attached primary importance to the establishment of order. School was occasionally broken up by the "carrying out" of the schoolmaster. Although such complete dismantling was rare, chaos, or a measure of order purchased by brutal discipline, was common. Discipline itself consisted in a combination of corporal punishment and humiliation, especially the latter. There was nothing in theory to exempt younger boys from this regimen, but in practice schoolmasters had to focus on the teenagers who, by all accounts, made the most trouble. This preoccupation gave a random quality to the kind of discipline experienced by the younger boys. But such discipline could be as unsettling as systematic chastisement. Autobiographers frequently commented on the shame they felt when they were first singled out for correction, for severe discipline occasionally administered was likely to produce a more profound sense of shame and guilt than the daily drubbing to which the older boys became inured.[3]

EARLY PIETY

If the years of seven and eight were significant as the time when most boys started to attend winter schools, these years had importance in other respects as well. At about the age of seven a boy was expected to begin work on the farm. How much he would do was dependent on a host of factors including his size, the number and age of his male siblings, the health of his father, and the size of the farm. Whatever the variables, however, direction in his daily routine now came both at school and work from older boys or men.

The third experience which occurred with some regularity between the ages of eight and twelve was the commencement of religious anxiety. Religious instruction began earlier, just after infancy, but most autobiographers traced the start of personal religion to the period between eight and twelve. At times, especially among girls, religious conversion took place this early, but the expectation, at least up to the 1840's, was that conversion would come later. At eight or nine children were expected to evince no more than "early piety" and to become subjects of "hopeful conversion." [4] Early piety usually involved lying awake most of the night in anxiety about salvation, a morbid fear of death, and a tendency to meet together with peers, sometimes in district schools, in prayer meetings. This is the syndrome which emerges in autobiographies of evangelicals, and considerable evidence points to its spread among those who never went on to become ministers.[5] Some of it was undoubtedly due to the intense desire of most boys between eight and twelve for peer group acceptance. Contemporary skeptics put forward a version of this argument, attributing early piety to mere "sympathetic enthusiasm," but there was also an aspect of solitary introspection to it not explicable in terms of any current developmental model.

Although peer group pressure is not an altogether satisfactory explanation for the prevalence of morbid piety among children in early nineteenth-century New England, other leads are available. The kind of regimen of guilt and shame to which most schoolchildren were exposed could produce feelings of inadequacy which led to juvenile religious anxiety. Early nineteenth-century New England Calvinism, moreover, took a paradoxical approach to childhood. Children were told that they were damned unless converted, that they had to repent, but that they could not do so without divine aid. Finally, they were told that such assistance was not likely to come before the age of 17 or 18.[6] The approved practice in much of New England before 1840 was to usher children into religious anxiety but not to let them out. To take an apt if anachronistic analogy, children from 8 to 17 or 18 were put into a kind of moral pressure cooker.

CHILDREN OF THE WEALTHY

There were, naturally, differences among classes in the experience of growing up. Children of moderately wealthy or well-educated parents were less likely to be exposed to the district school's winter session. Instead, they were sent to private schools or academies where classes were smaller, the curriculum much more difficult, and discipline more regular. The regimen of moderately wealthy children was not softer but more consistent, for all academies stressed punctuality, and, at least within a given term, regular attendance. After 1840 the school reform movement had the effect of bringing practices in public schools more in line with those of private schools, but the gap in the previous period between the discipline of boys who, for whatever reason, never went beyond district schooling, and those who were exposed to private schools and academies was substantial. In a general way, this represented a class difference.[7]

The years from eight to twelve comprised a unit in the lives of most boys, marked primarily by the commencement of work and winter schooling and often by the start of religious anxiety. Neither idleness nor leaving home was an ingredient of this unit. An artisan's son was likely to work in the shop, close to his father or an older brother. A farmer's boy would follow the plough and perform odd jobs around home. Both would be sent to district schools in the winter. There were exceptions, coming, oddly enough, at opposite ends of the social ladder. Children of poor people were often sent away to work, because they could not easily be incorporated into the family routine. When the father did not own his own shop or farm, it was difficult for him to find a suitable place for his son close to home, even though such a father would need all the money a son could earn. Similarly, children of ministers or of wealthy parents were often sent away to school at extremely early ages. Wealthy mill owners and manufacturers, who were not, as a rule, great believers in prolonged schooling, often put their sons into the family factory at eight or nine, making them child laborers. Length of dependency did not correlate neatly with rising social class. In fact, there seems to have been an inverse correlation. Children of wealthy parents were thrust out into the world at an earlier age than sons of middle-class farmers. Thus, one encounters 16-year-old sons of merchants traveling to St. Petersburg as supercargo and being taken in as partners of the firm at 19.[8] In the course of the nineteenth century a reaction to this did take place, and by 1900 the sons of the rich usually enjoyed a more protected and sheltered upbringing than did the sons of the middle classes. But this reaction had little effect before 1840.

DEPENDENCY AND DISCONTINUITIES

It is difficult to say exactly when the period of total dependency ended, simply because youthful experiences in the early republic were not determined in any precise way by numerical age. Still, sometime after the age of 12 and before the age of 15 or 16, middle-class boys passed into a new stage of semidependency. Sons of artisans and small manufacturers were likely to be apprenticed, sometimes to their fathers, sometimes to relatives, sometimes outside the family altogether. Those who were not apprentices in theory were usually apprentices in fact, having entered machine shops or mills to learn the routine. The pattern does not seem to have involved continual employment at the same position until 21, but rather a moving about from job to job or apprenticeship to apprenticeship. Thus, while tradition sanctioned a lengthy apprenticeship to occupy the remaining years of minority, social conditions facilitated short-term apprenticeships with frequent removals.[9]

Sons of farmers experienced a different pattern. They were likely after the age of 12 or 14 to be withdrawn from winter schooling and encouraged to seek employment or possibly advanced schooling away from home during the winter. Late spring, summer, and early fall would find them back on the farm again, thus completing the cycle of homeleaving and homecoming. Although there was an element of regularity in the summer employment of farm boys, their winter occupations had little consistency. Some clerked in country stores, others went to academies, others found employment in such winter work as lumbering. Although many stopped attending winter school between 12 and 14, there was nothing to stop them from resuming attendance at 16 or 17.[10]

Whether one is discussing sons of artisans or small manufacturers or sons of farmers, there were certain discontinuities which beset the life experiences of teenagers in early nineteenth-century New England regardless of occupation or parentage. The first of these was between school and work. In the twentieth century work normally follows a period of schooling, but in the early nineteenth century the relationship was less definite. Many apprentices had the right to a month or two of annual schooling stipulated in their contracts with

masters, and farm boys often managed to snatch a few months of
schooling in the winter. Two aspects of the school experience of teenagers might be noted. First, prior to the middle of the century, there
seems to have been little understanding that teenagers might need a
type of discipline different from that given to younger children. If
there was any difference of emphasis in pedagogical thought, it was
that older boys were more unruly and hence greater effort had to be
made to break their wills. Second, in virtually all types of school (including colleges), few efforts were made before 1840 to segregate pupils
by age. Pupils of 15 or 16, both in academies and common schools,
were likely to be grouped with much younger children in classes and
exposed to a more severe version of the same type of discipline experienced by the eight- or nine-year-olds. Quite obviously, the adult roles
which teenagers often played in one part of the year were followed by
demands for childish submission during the rest of the year.

The major educational innovation of the late eighteenth and
early nineteenth century, the New England academy, dramatically accentuated these tendencies. Although the academy offered a valuable
opportunity for intermediate education between the district school
and the college, academy students were subject to many of the same
anomalies as district school pupils. One encountered in academies, as
in winter district schools, students of eight or nine to 20 or 25 years of
age, with the concentration falling in the 10- to 20-year-old category.[11]
Teenagers were constantly matched first against children and then
against mature men.[12] We sometimes indulge in a stereotype of nineteenth-century boyhood which postulates that boys were then exposed
much more than now to the company of adults. The stereotype has
an element of truth, but older men were also periodically classified
with children. Like the experience of work, the academy experience
presented boys with alternating demands, now for childish submission, now for adult responsibility.

The fact that many boys had already worked for a number of
years before attending academies accentuated the anomaly. This ac-
counted for the unusual age distribution of academy students; for
some attendance at the academy was the first departure from home, for
others it represented a respite from job demands. Moreover, for nearly
everyone, attendance at academies did not exclude the performance of

useful work during part of the year. Attendance usually fell off in the winter as students went out to teach or labor, and again in the summer, when any strong male, boy or adult, could command high wages on the farm. The academy was a form of seasonal education to complement the seasonal labor pattern of an economically active but preindustrial society. Academy pupils thus experienced the same odd shifting from dependent to independent to dependent status which characterized the lives of boys who never attended school beyond the age of 12.

The critical constituent of the teen years was, therefore, an endless shifting of situations—home to work, work to school—in a society in which discipline was determined not so much by numerical age as by situation. Flogging was much less common in academies and colleges than in common schools, yet pupils in the latter were often older than students in either of the former. Similar factors dominated the experience of work. Because of rapid economic change in New England in the early nineteenth century, boys often had to give up one type of employment to learn a new trade; one could be nearly self-sufficient at 14 and an apprentice at 16. This was especially true of farm boys, who often did not enter apprenticeships until their late teens after years of semi-independent manual labor in winters, but it was also at least partly true of sons of artisans. Although the institution of apprenticeship no longer existed in its Elizabethan form, it still involved a master-dependent relationship, with the latter receiving low wages for the duration. The pattern of discontinuity was not only horizontal, between work and school, but vertical, between types of work and types of schooling.[13]

A second tension in the lives of teenagers was between their desire for ultimate independence and the fact of their semidependence. Because of the new economic opportunities created by the beginnings of industrialization and by territorial expansion, many teenagers were largely self-supporting. Even those who sought higher education in the academies could probably earn enough in the winter and summer months to pay the meager tuition demands. There were even instances of boys becoming factory overseers at 16 or 17. But traditional assumptions about maturity persisted, assumptions which thus ran counter to the new economic forces. Although the latter made possible an earlier independence than ever before, the former still provided that a boy became a man at the age of 21. Before that age he was conceived of as a piece of property under obligation to work for his father. Even where there were more sons than could possibly be settled on family land, as was often the case in New England, fathers could usually use their sons' labor in the late spring, summer, and early fall. There was no easy or consistent resolution of this problem. A few boys simply left home at 15 or 16, never to return; a few stayed on the farm until 25 or later. For most, however, the critical period came between 17 and 21. By the age of 17, many youths had acquired enough capital to launch themselves in the world, and saw that there was no future for them on the farm. If a father resisted his son's demands for independence, the likeliest solution was for the son to make a cash payment to the father in lieu of his services, thus in effect ending the contractual relationship.[14]

A final, and central, ingredient of the teen years in the early nineteenth century was religious crisis, which was often followed by conversion. Evangelical clergymen involved in the Second Great Awakening in the early 1800's noted time and again the frequency of religious conversion among "youth" or the "young people." There had been some foreshadowing of this in the Great Awakening of the eighteenth century, although young converts at that time were more likely to be in their late 20's than in their teens. In the early nineteenth century, by contrast, a pattern of teenage conversion began to emerge. It is impossible to compute the average or median age of conversion, and it would be pointless, since some individuals experienced a religious crisis in their teens without going through conversion, and others experienced conversion without a religious crisis. A huge number of published autobiographical conversion narratives of the nineteenth century, however, point to the predominance of conversions between the ages of 15 and 21.[15]

TEENAGE CONVERSIONS

Conversion narratives emphasized three themes. Two were traditional—the idleness and sinfulness of the convert's past life and the appeal of conversion as a decisive break with the past. But a third theme was relatively novel in the early nineteenth century: the importance of a sudden, quick transformation. Although seventeenth-century Puritans had emphasized a gradual conversion experience, the distinctive feature of early nineteenth-century thought, encapsulated in the doctrine of regeneration or rebirth, was that one could experience the turning point in an instant.[16]

Given this rhetoric of the Second Awakening, it is possible to locate at least one factor in the experience of middle-class New England boys which would dispose them to evangelical conversion. Enough has been said to indicate that the need to make choices was, perhaps as never before, incumbent on every youth. The beginnings of industrialization, the spread of commercialization, increasing pressure on the available land, and proliferation of educational opportunities for teenagers gave the experience of maturation novel dimensions. But the religious dimension of choice was no less important. In seventeenth-century Massachusetts the principal sects had been Congregationalism and Anglicanism. Dissenters such as Baptists and Quakers could be isolated in places such as Rhode Island. From 1750 on, however, the number of dissenters increased, and arguments and even fistfights among dissenters and between dissenters and the orthodox became more common. By 1820 even small villages in New England were likely to have, besides the "standing order," a number of free-will Baptists, Methodists, and Universalists.[17]

The extravagant claims of each sect only further necessitated the importance of making a choice. In his autobiography, Joseph Smith, who had grown up in Vermont but moved to western New York state—the so-called burnt-over district which was to be the scene of extraordinary religious commotion in the years 1820–1845—drew a revealing portrait of small-town religious excitement:

> Indeed, the whole district of country seemed affected by it, and great multitudes united themselves to the different religious parties, which created no small stir among the people, some crying, "Lo, here!" and others, "Lo, there!" Some were contending for the Methodist faith, some for the Presbyterian, and some for the Baptist. . . . During this time of great excitement my mind was called up to serious reflection and great uneasiness. . . . In process of time my mind became somewhat partial to the Methodist sect and I felt some desire to be united with them; but so great were the

confusion and strife among the different denominations that it was
impossible for a person young as I was and so unacquainted with
men and things, to come to any certain conclusion who was right
and who was wrong. . . . In the midst of this war of words and
tumult of opinions, I often said to myself, what is to be done? Who
of all these parties are right; or are they all wrong together? If any
one of them be right, which is it, and how shall I know it? [18]

Smith, only 15 at the time, resolved his crisis with the discovery of the
Book of Mormon and the launching of a new religion. While his
resolution was atypical, the kind of anxiety he expressed at confronta-
tion with religious choice found expression elsewhere.

In one sense religious choice was part of the larger pattern of
choice; in another sense it held forth to the convert the lure of finality.
Although many lapsed after making a religious identification, in theory
religious choice was absolute. Therein lay part of its appeal to the
young, for it was the choice to end all choices in a society in which
young people were subjected to an apparently endless sequence of role
changes.

THE TURBULENCE OF ADOLESCENCE

In the twentieth century a variety of factors have conspired to
make the teen years difficult. The evidence indicates that they were also
turbulent in early nineteenth-century New England, but for different
reasons. The significance of adolescence today lies in its following a
protected and sanitized period of childhood and in the forced economic
inactivity of teenagers. Neither of these conditions was present in the
early nineteenth century. Although attitudes toward childhood were
changing in the direction of sentimentality, social conditions scarcely
permitted sealing off the cares of adulthood from the life of the child.
One might illustrate this by taking so simple yet pervasive a concern
as death. People generally did not die in hospitals in early nineteenth-
century New England, but in homes, right in front of the family. Although intense religious anxiety often marked the teen years, religious
concern, the so-called early piety, was expected to begin before the
age of 12. In the experience of work, a farm boy of nine or ten toiled

in the field alongside his older brother of 14. Many aspects of adolescent life were thus simply extensions of patterns launched in late childhood.

Although adolescence as we know it did not exist in 1820, boys did experience an intermediate period between childhood and adulthood. An opposing view is sometimes presented. The period of dependency, it is asserted, was very short in the early nineteenth century. Boys left home and became men at 15, if not earlier, and thus scarcely experienced a period of youth. It is true that the period of total dependency was brief, but the intermediate stage of semidependency was often lengthy. However, even the period of semidependency was getting shorter after 1750. Research on the seventeenth century has indicated that boys commonly stayed around the homestead until their middle 20's.[19] Between about 1750 and 1820, pressure on the land and availability of attractive alternatives to following the plough were operating to end the period of semidependency in the late teens. But the very fact that the period of semidependency was shortening made it even more turbulent. As long as young people were not expected to make important decisions until they reached 21, semidependency had more chronological than psychological content; it was long but not critical. One could have dependency without youth, without a time of erratic indecision. In this sense, youth hardly existed in the seventeenth century, even though the period of semidependency was long. It did exist by the early nineteenth century, largely because of the contraction of the outer limits of semidependency.[20]

What effect did the kind of experience described have on the attitudes of those who went through it? It would be ridiculous to suppose that it had any uniform effect; personalities differed as much in the nineteenth century as they do in the twentieth. But Americans born between 1800 and 1840, especially those born in New England, were more prone than any previous generation to assign importance to boyhood and youth. Two themes in their romanticization of boyhood did have a traceable connection to the actual experience of growing up: the idea that such a boyhood was free, and that it encouraged initiative or individualism.[21] It was free, not because parents or teachers were indulgent, but because the social institutions which came to bear on youth had a loose and indefinite character. An economically active but largely preindustrial society allowed boys, and adults, a footloose life. The cycle of the seasons rather than the time clock or an office manager regulated the routine of work. Home authority could be severe, when one was home, but a great deal of time was spent outside the home. Discontinuity of experience, frustrating in one respect, was liberating in another, since it meant that no single regimen had to be submitted to for long.

Finally, the experience of growing up in New England between 1800 and 1840 did encourage initiative. There were abundant opportunities but no fixed experiences which automatically led the young to success. One had to respond to and make the best of a complicated situation. What writers in the late nineteenth century had to say about the early initiative nurtured by a rural boyhood certainly had its fanciful elements. Whole segments of society—Negroes, women, paupers, and immigrants—were excluded from even the opportunity of making a choice, and the mere presence of choice did not ensure that those who could choose would make the right choices. Moreover, an ability to make choices was a precondition, even if not a guarantee, of success in life.

FOOTNOTES

1. John and Virginia Demos, "Adolescence in Historical Perspective," *Journal of Marriage and the Family*, XXXI (November 1969), 632–633; Bernard Wishy, *The Child and the Republic: The Dawn of Modern American Child Nurture* (Philadelphia, 1968), Part I.

2. Warren Burton, *The District School as It Was* (Boston, 1833), 118–123; George Moore, Diaries, ms., 4 vols., Harvard College Library, I, *passim*.

3. John T. Trowbridge, *My Own Story with Recollections of Noted Persons* (Boston, 1903), 40–42; Heman Dyer, *Records of an Active Life* (New York, 1886), 9.

4. Elias Smith, *The Life, Conversion, Preachings, Travels and Sufferings of Elias Smith* (Boston, 1840); *Autobiography of Adin Ballou* (Lowell, Mass., 1890), 31; Raphael Pumpelly, *My Reminiscences* (2 vols., New York, 1918), I, 14–15.

5. Henry C. Wright, *Human Life: Illustrated in My Individual Experiences as a Child, a Youth, and a Man* (Boston, 1849), 96; Catherine E. Beecher, *Religious Training of Children in the School, the Family, and the Church* (New York, 1864), 133–136; Joseph Packard, *Recollections of a Long Life*, ed. Thomas J. Packard (Washington, D.C., 1902), 48.

6. Packard, *ibid.*, 48.

7. *Reminiscences of Neal Dow: Recollections of Eighty Years* (Portland, Me., 1898), Chap. 2; Octavius B. Frothingham, *Recollections and Impressions, 1822–1890* (Boston, 1891), 20.

8. J. D. Van Slyck, *New England Manufacturers and Manufacturing* (2 vols., Boston, 1879), II, 693, 700.

9. *Ibid.*, I, 371–372, II, 641–642; Thomas V. Sullivan, *Scarcity of Seamen* (Boston, 1854), 5–6.

10. Richard C. Stone, *Life-Incidents of Home, School and Church* (St. Louis, 1874); *Memoir of the Life and Religious Experience of Ray Potter* (Providence, 1829), 22–23.

11. *Catalogue of the Officers and Students of Phillips Exeter Academy, 1783–1883* (Boston, 1883). The same pattern prevailed at other academies.

12. Hiram Orcutt, *Reminiscences of School Life: An Autobiography* (Cambridge, Mass., 1898), 25–26.

13. Van Slyck, *New England Manufacturers*, II, 519, 554–557, 606–608, 617.

14. For examples of buying time, see Van Slyck, *New England Manufacturers*, I, 264–266; Jason Whitman, *A Memoir of the Rev. Bernard Whitman* (Boston, 1837), 34. The assertion that the critical period came between 17 and 21 is based partly on this author's strong impression gained from autobiography and partly on two surveys I have made. The first is from Van Slyck, *New England Manufacturers*. I have charted the early careers of 200 of the 350 manufacturers listed. All were born between 1785 and 1840, with the great majority between 1800 and 1830. All were raised in New England. Sixty-seven of the 200 were sons of farmers and another 19 were sons of farmers who had some other identifiable occupation. It should be added that the sample is biased toward short dependency, since, by definition, all the subjects left the homestead. Of the 67, 40 left between the ages of 17 and 21; of the remainder, only three left after their twenty-second birthday. Sons of farmers with some other identifiable occupation were more likely to leave home to enter an apprenticeship or a factory at an earlier period. Nine of the 19 left before the age of 17.

The second survey derives from a festival held in Boston in 1849 by the "Sons of New Hampshire," a fraternal organization; see *Festival of the Sons of New Hampshire, . . . Nov. 7, 1849* (Boston, 1850). Appended to the speeches is a list of some 1,500 New Hampshire boys who came to Massachusetts before 1849. The majority came between 1830 and 1849. The list gives, besides names and occupations, places of birth and the years in which the subjects came to Massachusetts. Working with local histories and death records I have ascertained the year of birth of 150 of the sons. The data indicates that those who left home were most likely to do so after their seventeenth and before their twenty-second birthday.

15. William W. Woodward, ed., *Surprising Accounts of the Revival of Religion in the United States of America, . . .* (n.p., 1803), 12, 44, 231; Joshua Bradley, *Accounts of Religious Revivals in Many Parts of the United States from 1815 to 1818* (Albany, N.Y., 1819); Daniel W. Fisher, *A Human Life: An Autobiography with Excursions* (New York, 1909), 58.

16. Reuben Smith, *Truth Without Controversy: A Series of Doctrinal Lectures, Intended Principally for Young Professors of Religion* (Saratoga Springs, N.Y., 1824), Lecture IX. The doctrine of regeneration originated in the Great Awakening.

17. Orestes A. Brownson, *The Convert: or, Leaves from My Experience* (New York, 1857), 9.

18. *A Brief History of Joseph Smith, The Prophet, by Himself* (Salt Lake City, 1910), 6–8.

19. John Demos, A Little Commonwealth: *Family Life in Plymouth Colony* (New York, 1970), Chap. 10; Philip J. Greven, Jr., *Four Generations: Population, Land, and Family in Colonial Andover, Massachusetts* (Ithaca, 1970), 126, *passim*.

20. The appearance of a number of advice books aimed at youth after 1830 indicated the growing popular awareness of the critical nature of youth. See Demos and Demos, "Adolescence in Historical Perspective," 634.

21. John Albee, *Confessions of Boyhood* (Boston, 1910); B. M. Hall, *The Life of Rev. John Clark* (New York, 1856), 21.

STEPHAN THERNSTROM/PETER R. KNIGHTS

Men in Motion: Some Data and Speculations about Urban Population Mobility in Nineteenth-Century America

Americans have long been a restless, migratory people, a fact which has left a deep impression on our national folklore if not yet on the writing of American history. Though it had earlier antecedents, the faith in spatial mobility as the key to virtue and success came into full flower in the nineteenth century. With an open continent beckoning, it was natural that mobility and opportunity were linked in the popular mind with the West and the frontier. But the supply of virgin land, though vast, was not limitless. As early as 1852, brooding about the future, the Superintendent of the U.S. Census saw trouble ahead:

> The roving tendency of our people is incident to the peculiar condition of their country, and each succeeding Census will prove that it is diminishing. When the fertile plains of the West shall have been filled up, and men of scanty means cannot by a mere change of location acquire a homestead, the inhabitants of each State will become comparatively stationary. . . .[1]

Cities, many feared, were serpents in Eden, ensnaring, enfeebling, and corrupting their inhabitants. They pinned a man down and drained him of the vital energies that he needed to pull up stakes and

This essay is adapted from *Journal of Interdisciplinary History*, I, No. 1 (1970), by permission of the M.I.T. Press. Although publication in the *Journal* precedes this volume, the essay was originally written for this volume.

move on to the greener pastures that lay ahead. Well after urbanization and industrialization had transformed agrarian America, a residue
of these suspicions remained. To many the city seemed a closed, confining, static environment. Certain areas of the city—"slums," "ghettos"—were especially confining. Poor people were permanently
trapped there, unable to escape from a degrading environment. An
observer of New York's appalling Hell's Kitchen on the eve of World
War I summed it up in a vivid metaphor. The district, he declared,
was a giant "spider's web": "of those who come to it, very few . . .
ever leave." [2]

At the level of popular thought, migration was understood to be
a major determinant of the shape of the American social order, and
urbanization was viewed as problematical because it seemed to restrict
the spatial mobility of city-dwellers, or at least of poor city-dwellers.
This is surely an issue worth exploring, but few historians have seen fit
to do so. How volatile was the population of the United States in the
nineteenth century? Were city-dwellers notably less migratory than
farmers, poor people less than rich, immigrants less than natives? How
was movement through space related to economic opportunity? Were
the slums and ghettos of the era indeed giant spider webs which en-
trapped the unfortunate?

Until quite recently, the only available systematic studies of
population mobility in nineteenth-century America dealt with frontier
communities.[3] It is clear that the population of such communities was
extraordinarily restless and footloose. A number of scholarly efforts to
test Frederick Jackson Turner's frontier thesis have yielded similar conclusions on this point.[4] Barely a quarter of the farm operators found
in 1860 in the five Kansas townships examined by James C. Malin
in his pioneering 1935 inquiry could be located there a mere ten years
later. In Trempealeau County, Wisconsin, the comparable figure for all
employed males was nearly identical—25 per cent for 1860–1870, and
29 per cent for 1870–1880. Likewise, a mere 30 per cent of the male
labor force enumerated by the census taker in Wapello County, Iowa,
in 1850 was there to greet his successor a decade later. Over a slightly
longer interval—from 1880 to 1895—only 22 per cent of the households in five townships of Grant County, Wisconsin, remained. Clearly
the agricultural communities of the West in the latter half of the century were not, in the simple demographic sense, stable "island com-

munities" with a large core of permanent residents.[5] They were more like busy railroad stations, into which many travelers poured but in which few stopped for long.

But what of the cities of the era? Critics of the Turner thesis long ago challenged the identification of mobility with the frontier, and demonstrated that, important as the westward movement was in our national history, a far larger migratory stream moved eastward and cityward. It was the burgeoning cities which provided the safety valve for the surplus rural population, and for the bulk of the European immigrants who came in such large numbers starting in the late 1840's.[6]

That general point, effectively argued by Turner's critics, was soon widely accepted. But, perhaps because these critics failed to advance a compelling general theory of the American city that could stimulate and guide empirical research in the way that the frontier thesis did, or perhaps because of professional reluctance to tackle a subject which demanded the mastery of masses of quantitative data, the matter was left there.[7] The capacity of the emerging cities to draw in new migrants was recognized, but there was no effort to trace migratory currents beyond the initial point of entry into the city. The result of this failure was a partial and distorted view of the process of migration and of the dynamics of urban growth. The first step in a complex process—the initial move from country to city—was taken for the whole, and the fluidity of urban population was grossly underestimated. Cities were thought to grow like brickpiles. Throw fifty bricks on the pile and it grows correspondingly larger; if 50,000 migrants enter Chicago in a given decade, the Chicago population would increase by 50,000. Net population changes from census to census were thus taken to be an adequate measure of the volume of in-migration. But this assumes that migration was a one-way, one-step process, and that all 50,000 of the newcomers *stayed* in Chicago. This was far from the case. Migration *out of* nineteenth-century cities took place on a massive scale. Most American communities of the era grew rapidly, but net population changes from census to census, though often dramatic, become insignificant in comparison with the actual gross volume of in and out movement. A number of recent investigations, which we shall review here, indicate that the composition of the urban population was far more fluid than has been suspected. Understanding this

crucial fact will give us new insights into the nature of the urbanization process, and will dispel some common misconceptions concerning immigrant and working class "ghettos" in the nineteenth-century
city.

GEOGRAPHIC MOBILITY IN
SEVERAL NINETEENTH-CENTURY CITIES

One of the authors first gained some hint of the remarkable
fluidity of the nineteenth-century urban population in the course
of an effort to plot the career patterns of common laborers living in
Newburyport, Massachusetts, between 1850 and 1880.[8] Newburyport,
it soon became clear, was no more a permanent resting place for these
men than Trempealeau County and other frontier communities had
been for their inhabitants. Nor was the volatility of the city's population confined to the largely Irish unskilled workers; less than a fifth
of all the families listed in the local city directory of 1849 were to be
found in the community 30 years later. Rochester, New York, had an
even less stable population in this period; only 20 per cent of its 1849
residents could be traced in the city ten years later.[9]

But this evidence was far from decisive. Newburyport, after all,
was a way station in the orbit of a major metropolis, and Rochester
was a steppingstone to the West. These might have been special cases.
There were grounds for wondering if major cities were not notably
more stable in population than smaller places, for it was the Bostons,
Philadelphias, and New Yorks of America that were the sites of the
classic big city ghettos. There one might still expect to find a settled
population, trapped in misery, huddled together in some kind of
"culture of poverty."

Recent work, however, makes it appear that these doubts are un-
founded, and indicates that the urban as well as the rural population
was extraordinarily volatile in nineteenth-century America. Newburyport and Rochester were not atypical of smaller cities in the period as
a result of the former's proximity to a major metropolis and the
latter's location along a well-worn path to the West. Poughkeepsie,
New York, fits neither category, and yet only 30 per cent of its 1850
residents were still living there ten years later.[10] Although North-

ampton, Massachusetts, had a rather more stable population, little more than half (53 per cent) of its inhabitants at midcentury were present to be counted by the time of the Census of 1860.[11] Atlanta, Georgia, a city of 22,000 in 1870, ranked between Poughkeepsie and Northampton in stability; 43 per cent of its white residents remained in the community from 1870 to 1880.[12] There was some variation from city to city, but in even the most stable small or medium size community which has as yet been examined, approximately half of the population was transient within a relatively brief span of years.

What of the really big cities of the era, the cities which we might naturally assume were the end of the road for the drifters who passed through smaller places like Newburyport, Northampton, and Poughkeepsie? Only one—Boston—has as yet been studied systematically, but if it was at all typical, then the great metropolitan centers were not notably more stable in population composition. One would expect to find somewhat higher persistence rates and lower out-migration rates in a sprawling metropolis, simply because it is possible to move farther—both physically and socially—and still remain within its boundaries. All other things being equal, the probability of out-migration decreases as the area of the unit examined increases.[13] Large cities should display higher persistence rates than smaller cities, and the rate for any one community should increase as the city grows.

POPULATION TURNOVER IN NINETEENTH-CENTURY BOSTON

With this caveat in mind, the Boston figures indicate that the city's population was remarkably volatile. The city's total population grew from 61,000 in 1830 to 178,000 in 1860; the decade persistence rates for heads of households in this period were 44 per cent for 1830–1840, 49 per cent for 1840–1850, and 39 per cent for 1850–1860.[14] If unmarried males had been included in the samples, the figures would doubtless be even lower. Again we have a community in which a distinct minority of men remained in the city long enough to be counted by two successive census takers.

By 1880 the Boston population had climbed to 363,000, by 1890 to 448,000, and the physical boundaries of the city had been much enlarged through the annexation in the 1860's and 1870's of such towns as Roxbury, Dorchester, and Charlestown. Much of the short-distance movement which previously would have been classified as out-migration now was intracity movement, and the persistence rate rose accordingly. But it was still only 64 per cent for all adult males for 1880–1890, 45 per cent for unmarried men, and 53 per cent for blue collar workers aged 20 to 29 in 1880.[15]

A different measure of persistence and turnover yields a more dramatic indication of the volatility of the Boston population. Instead of asking what fraction of the residents present at the start of a decade were still there at its end, we may ask about movement from year to year. Here the decennial census is of no value, and we must turn to another source—the annual city directory. Virtually all nineteenth-century American cities had regularly published directories by the time they had reached a population of 30,000. Printed by private firms and sold largely to businessmen, they were prepared from a careful canvass of each house in the community and supplied a relatively accurate listing of the population.[16] The Boston directories provided a convenient, if crude, measure of annual population turnover for the city, in the form of tables noting the number of names expunged from the preceding year's directory in making up the current one.[17] One of the first of these tables appeared in the directory for 1836, and it disclosed that fully 24 per cent of the individuals and business firms listed in the directory for 1835 could no longer be located by the canvasser. Lest it be thought that 1835–1836 was an exceptional year, illustrative figures for selected years in the rest of the century are given in Table 1. As this makes clear, the rate of annual out-migration from Boston, at least by this crude index, was remarkably high, and surprisingly uniform.

TABLE 1   *Percentage of Listings in Preceding Year's Boston City Directory Dropped in Preparation of Current Directory*

1840—19%	1865[a]—24%	1885—20%
1845—25	1870 —24	1890—21
1850—25	1875 —25	1895—19
1855—26	1880 —18	1900—21

[a] This information was not provided in the directories for 1859–1863.

The measure is imperfect in a number of ways, however, and it seemed worthwhile to refine these calculations for at least one decade, that of the 1880's. There are two principal flaws in using the number of listings dropped from the directory as a measure of migration out of the city. First, some names were dropped from the directories because of death. Second, the directories listed not only individual household heads but other employed adults not heads of families, and also business firms; with the rate of business mortality notoriously high for small marginal enterprises, there is the possibility that the estimated out-migration rate would be seriously exaggerated. These two distorting influences have been reduced or eliminated by the procedure followed in Table 2. From the U.S. Censuses of 1880 and 1890 and the

TABLE 2   *Annual Out-Migration Rates*
for Boston Families, 1880, 1885, 1890

	1880	1885	1890
1. Number of households, by census count	72,763	80,207	89,716
2. Number of listings dropped from directory	27,938	32,507	39,885
3. Ratio of directory listings to households	1.967	2.088	2.175
4. Estimated families dropped (2 ÷ 3)	14,201	15,570	18,336
5. Deaths of household heads[a]	2,527	3,050	3,363
6. Families migrating from Boston (4 − 5)	11,674	12,520	14,973
7. Per cent of families disappearing because of death (5 ÷ 1)	3.5	3.8	3.8
8. Per cent of families migrating from the city (6 ÷ 1)	16.0	15.6	16.7

[a] This figure is the total of adult male deaths in the city, as given in the reports of the City Registrar, plus one-sixth of the adult female deaths, to allow for female-headed households.

Massachusetts State Census of 1885 we discovered the total number of families living in the city at those dates. Dividing the number of households by the number of listings in the directories of 1880, 1885, and 1890 supplied the ratio of households to total listings, a figure fluctuating from 1.967 to 2.175. Because many households contained more than one employed adult, and because some individuals were in business for themselves and hence double-counted, once at their residence and once at their place of business, there were roughly twice as many listings as households in the city. It is necessary, therefore, to divide the number of listings dropped by the ratio of total directory listings to total households, to arrive at an estimate of the number of families actually dropped from the directories. (This assumes roughly similar turnover rates for household heads, employed persons who were not heads of households, and business firms—a source of possible error, but not, we believe, of a magnitude to call into question our chief findings.) To find out how many of the families disappeared because of death is simple, and we are left with an estimate of how many actually left the city for other destinations. In each of the three years something under 4 per cent of the households in Boston were deleted from the city directories due to death; in each a high and a similar proportion—16.0 per cent, 15.6 per cent, and 16.7 per cent—moved away from the city altogether. This is a somewhat lower estimate than the 18 per cent, 20 per cent, and 21 per cent figures yielded by the cruder method of dividing listings dropped by total listings, but it still indicates that one Bostonian in seven moved out of the city over as short a period as 365 days.

(Some readers may find it difficult to reconcile this estimated annual out-migration rate of 16 per cent with our earlier report that 64 per cent of the adult males in Boston in 1880 were still in the city in 1890. If 16 per cent of the population left the city each year, it would seem, the ten-year out-migration rate would be 160 per cent. But one cannot extrapolate annual migration rates in this fashion. Sixteen per cent of the 1880 residents of Boston had left the city by the time a year had elapsed; about 16 per cent of the 1881 residents of Boston probably had likewise left the city by 1882. It does not follow that 32 per cent of the 1880 group had disappeared by 1882, for many of those in the departing 16 per cent of the 1881 group had not been living in Boston in 1880. It would be possible, indeed, for a community to have a 16 per cent annual out-migration rate and a 16 per cent decadal out-migration rate as well, with all out-migration after the first year being migration by recent newcomers. A stable population core of 84 per cent, that is to say, could exist alongside a highly volatile migratory segment which turned over completely each year.[18] Fortunately, we have measures both of annual and of longer-term population flows through the city, for there is no accurate way of translating the one into the other.)

With annual departure rates at this high level, how did the population of Boston grow at all, as it did by 24 per cent between 1880 and 1890? Partly through natural increase—the excess of births over deaths —but largely through continuing in-migration at an even higher level. It is tempting to assume that if a city's population increases by 85,638 in a decade, as Boston's did in that interval, subtracting the gain attributable to natural increase—approximately 20,500 in this instance— will yield a residual which is a valid estimate of the number of migrants who came to the city during the decade. It appears that in the 1880's 65,179 newcomers entered Boston, swelling its population to 448,000 by 1890. The new migrants, therefore, comprised a mere 14.5 per cent of the 1890 total (65,179 ÷ 448,000), suggesting that Boston was a city with an overwhelming preponderance of relatively settled long-term residents.

In fact, however, the vital statistics or residual method employed in this calculation is highly misleading. It is a poor measure even of the population change attributable to *net* migration,[19] and, in any event, it is not net migration but gross migration which is relevant to the question of how settled a city's population actually was. Analysis of the volume of in-migration and out-migration on an *annual* basis provides a far different, and far more revealing, estimate of the composition of the Boston population. It indicates that the proportion of the city's 1890 residents who had moved into Boston in the preceding decade was not 14.5 per cent but fully one-third, and that the stream of in-migration into the community during the decade was more than *12 times* as large as the net in-migration estimate would suggest. nearly 800,000 people moved into Boston between 1880 and 1890 to produce the net migration increase of 65,179.

These startling, indeed hardly credible, conclusions may be substantiated as follows. The Boston population grew from 363,000 to 448,000 between 1880 and 1890; the number of listings in the Boston city directories increased from 143,140 to 195,149. (There were fewer listings than persons, of course, because the directories excluded dependent women and children.) The "listings added" and "listings dropped" totals given in the annual directories allow us to determine, with the aid of some further data, how large a volume of gross population movement into and out of the city was required to produce the net increase of about 50,000 listings. As Table 3 indicates, the net increase

TABLE 3   *Total In- and Out-migration and*
            Population Turnover in Boston, 1880–1890

	1881–1885	1886–1890	DECADE TOTAL
1. Listings added	187,946	211,049	398,995
2. Listings dropped	161,755	189,774	351,529
3. Listings/household ratio[a]	2.029	2.131	
4. Families added	92,698	99,015	191,713
5. Families dropped	79,780	89,033	164,813
6. Males reaching 21	16,388	17,509	33,897
7. Deaths of household heads	14,126	16,115	30,241
8. Families in-migrating (4 − 6)	76,310	81,506	157,816
9. Families out-migrating (5 − 7)	65,654	72,918	138,572
10. Population turnover (families)[b] (8 + 9)	141,964	154,424	296,388
11. Population turnover (individuals)[b]	709,820	772,120	1,481,940

[a] These ratios differ slightly from those for 1880, 1885, and 1890 given in Table 2. The ratio used here for 1880–1885 is the mean of the 1880 and 1885 figures, and that for 1885–1890 is the mean of the 1885 and 1890 figures.
[b] Population turnover is the sum of in- and out-migration. To estimate total turnover of individuals we multiplied the family turnover figures by five, since mean family size in Boston was 4.99 in 1880 and 5.00 in 1890. It is possible, of course, that migratory households were typically smaller than the mean, and indeed probable, since many were unmarried males. The staggering total individual turnover of 1,481,940, therefore, may be inflated. But the 296,338 family total is accurate, we believe, and we are certain from our analysis of persistence rates for married men with children that much of this turnover involved entire families, so that total individual turnover was at a minimum far above 296,338 for the decade, though possibly well below the 1,481,940 estimate.

of 50,000 occurred because no less than 398,995 listings were added to the directories in the decade, and just over 350,000 listings were dropped.

These raw figures must be adjusted, however, to provide true estimates of the migration flows to and from Boston. First we must attempt to eliminate the disturbing influence of business turnover by applying the ratio of directory listings to total households in the city to the listings added and listings dropped figures, to yield estimates of the number of families added and dropped. Applying these ratios, we learn that some 191,713 families were newly listed in the directories at some point in the 1880's, and that 168,813 were dropped.

The families added and families dropped estimates need two further corrections to become valid measures of migration into and out of the city. Some of the new listings were caused not by the arrival of newcomers from outside the city but by young residents of the city reaching the age of 21, at which time they were eligible for listing. Likewise, some of the names dropped disappeared from the directories because of death. The magnitude of these two influences can be estimated with data from the Censuses and the City Registrar's reports and their effect removed, and we are left with the final in- and out-migration estimates in Table 3.

During the 1880's, 157,816 families moved into Boston, more than twice the total number of families living there as of 1880. If the in-migrating households were of the same average size as those already in the city—namely, five persons—this would mean that nearly 800,000 (157,816 × 5 = 789,080) individuals moved into Boston in this short period. But the net increase in the city's population over the decade that was attributable to migration was only *one-twelfth* of the total volume of in-migration (789,080 ÷ 65,179), for tremendous numbers of people were also moving out of Boston in those years, 138,572 households or approximately 690,000 (138,572 × 5 = 692,860) individuals. Enormous though the stream of new arrivals was, it exceeded the total of individuals departing by only 14 per cent. The turnover of the Boston population in the decade, the total of families moving either in or out, was 296,388, a stunning *4.07 times* the total number of households in the city in 1880.

The simple residual method of estimating net migration employed earlier indicated that less than 15 per cent of Boston's 1890 population was comprised of recent migrants to the community. In this respect, too, the net figures greatly underestimate the volatility of the Boston population. Two different and more satisfactory estimates reveal that the true proportion of recent newcomers in the population was more than twice that.

The first of these derives from an effort to trace in the 1890 city directory a sample of adult male Bostonians drawn from the 1880 U.S. Census, which disclosed that 64 per cent of them were still in the city in 1890; applying this persistence rate to the entire population would yield 232,217 people for 1890. In addition, there were children born in the city during the decade who were present to swell the population total in 1890. Through a calculation which utilized the total number of births in Boston during the decade, the number of deaths of children under ten, and an estimated out-migration rate for young children, we estimated that 47,059 of the 115,974 infants born in Boston in the 1880's were there to be counted by the census taker in 1890.[20] Adding these children to the 232,217 persisters, we find that 279,276 of the 448,477 residents of Boston in 1890 had either been living in the city since 1880 or had been born there during the decade; the residual, 169,201, were migrants who had arrived in the 1880's and remained. That would mean that 37.7 per cent of the 1890 population of Boston was comprised of recent migrants.

Long after this estimate was first developed we stumbled upon some support for our argument from another quarter. To our surprise, we learned that the Massachusetts State Census of 1895 had inquired into length of residence in the state, though not in particular cities within it. These data were tabulated for Boston separately, and they indicated that 24.4 per cent of the city's population aged ten or more in 1895 had moved into the state since 1885.[21] What we want to know, however, is how many had moved into *Boston* during that interval, since residence in the state is not equivalent to residence in the city; a good many newcomers to Boston, after all, came from other parts of Massachusetts. To the 24.4 per cent of migrants from outside the state we would have to add some allowance for such intrastate migrants. No solid basis for an estimate of this migratory stream exists, but some clue may be gained from the fact that 8 per cent of the 1895 population of the city had been born in Massachusetts but outside of Boston. This figure is for the entire population, including young children; the proportion of intrastate migrants in the Boston population aged ten or more was doubtless significantly higher. There must, in addition, have been migrants born in other states or abroad who had moved into Massachusetts by 1885, but had only come to the city itself between 1886 and 1895. On the other hand, the 8 per cent figure pertains to individuals who moved to Boston at any time after their birth, and many must have done so more than ten years earlier. It is hard to believe that this last consideration was as potent as the influences biasing the estimate in the other direction, however, so that we would judge from this source that an absolute minimum of 32.4 per cent (24.4 per cent plus 8 per cent) and probably 35 to 40 per cent of the 1895 residents of Boston had moved into the community during the preceding decade, which fits nicely with the estimate for 1880–1890. Some guesswork could not be avoided in adjusting the figures from the 1895 State Census, but this second independent estimate increases our confidence in the first. A more precise figure cannot be obtained, but it seems indisputable that about a third, and probably a little more, of the people living in Boston in 1890 had migrated into the community during the preceding decade.

Boston experienced only a modest population increase of 24 per cent between 1880 and 1890, and the commonly used vital statistics or residual method of estimating net migration makes it seem that the volume of migration to the community was similarly modest. Approximately 65,000 newcomers came into the city, and they comprised less than 15 per cent of its population at the end of the decade. But these undramatic conclusions are utterly erroneous. At least a third of the 1890 residents of Boston had come to the city within the past few years, and the total number of migrants who had entered the community at some point in the decade was not 65,000 but nearly 800,000, more than twice the total population of the city in 1880. Net population change in the city between 1880 and 1890 was on a modest scale, but only because two very powerful migratory currents flowing through the community nearly canceled each other out, leaving only the small rivulet registered by the net figures.

Similar analyses of the changing Boston population from 1830 to 1890 reveal that the 1880's were by no means peculiar or deviant in this respect. The city grew from 61,000 to 448,000 over this 60-year period, a net increase of 387,000. But the number of migrants entering Boston in those years was an amazing 3,325,000, eight and a half times the net population increase. It would take further spade work in other cities to be sure, but we strongly suspect that adding gross in-migration figures for New York, Philadelphia, Chicago, and hundreds of smaller cities would give a total far exceeding the total urban population of the United States, suggesting that the typical urban migrant went not to one city but to three or four (or perhaps a dozen) in the course of his wanderings.

Yet another revealing measure of the stability of the urban population may be gleaned from the city directories, for directory compilers normally indicated not only how many listings had been deleted in making up each new edition, but also how many house-holds were still listed, but at a new address within the city. Adding the proportion of names dropped and of listings with a change of address enables us to determine how many families were residentially stable in the sense that they lived at the same address for at least a year. Approximately 80 per cent of American families today remain in the same dwelling from one year to the next;[22] in Boston in the 1880's, Table 4 makes clear, hardly half did so. The annual residential

TABLE 4   *Percentage of Listings Dropped, Changes of Address,*
and Unchanged Listings in Boston, 1881–1890

YEAR	LISTINGS DROPPED FROM PRECEDING CITY DIRECTORY	LISTINGS WITH NEW BOSTON ADDRESS	LISTINGS RESIDENTIALLY STABLE
1881	20%	31%	49%
1882	21	39	40
1883	20	29	51
1884	21	29	50
1885	20	29	51
1886	20	30	50
1887	20	33	47
1888	20	34	46
1889	20	27	53
1890	20	29	51

stability rate ranged from a low of 40 per cent in 1882 to a high of 53 per cent in 1889, with 49 per cent the mean. Returning to the same dwelling after the passage of only 365 days, the city directory canvasser had a less than even chance of finding its former inhabitants living there. Not even in contemporary Los Angeles, supposedly the ultimate in residential instability, do people change their dwellings so frequently; only about a third of the population there moves annually.[23]

It should be evident from all this that if Boston was at all typical of nineteenth-century American cities—and one would imagine that if it was a deviant case, it was deviant in having a *less* fluid and volatile population than more rapidly growing cities like New York or Chicago—we must think about the process of past urban growth in quite a different way, with a heightened sense of the incredible fluidity of the urban as well as the rural population.

POPULATION MOBILITY
IN BLACK AND IMMIGRANT GHETTOS

The typical city dweller of nineteenth-century America had not been born in the city in which he resided, nor was he likely to live out his entire life there. But if city dwellers in general were a mobile breed, some city dwellers were more mobile than others.

It is widely believed that immigrants and poor people were commonly clustered in ghettos in the nineteenth-century city, forming a permanent proletariat of sorts. An abundance of impressionistic evidence in support of this view may be gleaned from the literature of the era. Thus the testimony of Francis A. Walker in 1876:

> If we consider the population of the more squalid sections of any city, we can only conclude that . . . the more miserable men are, the less . . . likely they are to seek and find a better place in society and industry. Their poverty, their ignorance, their superstitious fears and, perhaps more than all, the apathy that comes with a broken spirit, bind them in their place and to their fate. *Such populations do not migrate; they abide in their lot; sinking lower in helplessness, hopelessness and squalor* [italics added]. . . .[24]

Immigrants were thought especially vulnerable to entrapment:

> . . . with no small proportion of our vast foreign element, occupation is determined by a location that is accidental . . . these people are doing what they are doing because they are where they are. . . . There is a tendency at every harbor which lies at the debouche of a river, to the formation of a bar composed of mud and sand brought down by the current which yet has not the force to scour its channel clear out to deep water. And in much the same way, there is a tendency at every port of immigration to the accumulation, from the failure of the immigrating force, of large deposits of more or less helpless labor. . . .[25]

That there were neighborhoods of the nineteenth-century city which at various points in time had large concentrations of particular ethnic and occupational groups cannot be denied (though their prevalence may have been exaggerated).[26] But computation of indices of residential concentration from aggregate data provides no valid basis for inferences about the experiences of individuals over time. Were the Irish of Boston in 1850 trapped in their ghettos? Plotting measures of residential concentration for the Irish in the city two or three decades later provides no answer, for we do not know that many of the individuals who comprised "the Irish of Boston in 1850" were in fact present to be counted as "the Irish of Boston in 1870." Direct tracing of individuals is necessary to deal with the question of how confining the ethnic or class ghettos of the city actually were.

Much more work needs to be done on these issues before we can speak with great assurance, but two tentative conclusions may be drawn from the evidence now available. One is that men on the lower rungs of the class ladder were less rooted, not more rooted, than their betters. Persistence rates for blue collar workers were generally well below those for white collar workers, with unskilled and semiskilled laborers the least stable of all. Second, there seems to be little evidence of ethnic subcultures which exerted a sufficient hold over their members to yield unusually high persistence rates for the group. Indeed, there is some indication that ethnic minorities were more transient than WASPs of comparable economic status.

In support of the former proposition we might cite the following evidence. Seventy-six per cent of the upper white collar workers (professionals and proprietors or managers of large enterprises) in Boston in 1880 remained in the city in 1890, as opposed to 68 per cent of the lower white collar employees, 63 per cent of the skilled workers, and 59 per cent of the unskilled or semiskilled. Of a sample of migrants to Boston from rural New England taken from the 1870 Census, 62 per cent of the upper white collar, 50 per cent of the lower white collar, 34 per cent of the skilled, and 32 per cent of the unskilled and semiskilled workers persisted through the decade.[27] For second generation Irish youths in Boston in the same years, the figures were 63 per cent for lower white collar workers (there were no upper white collar workers among them), 48 per cent for skilled, and 39 per cent for unskilled and semiskilled employees. Comparable data for the white males of Atlanta between 1870 and 1880 show a persistence rate of 50 per cent for those in white collar positions, but only 39 per cent for the skilled and 30 per cent for the unskilled or semi-skilled.[28] A full report on persistence by the broad occupational class in Poughkeepsie is not yet available, but the data for selected occupations look fully consistent with this pattern. Fifty-six per cent of the doctors in the city in 1850 were still there in 1860, 43 per cent of the lawyers, and 59 per cent of the merchants, as opposed to 25 per cent of the day laborers, 26 per cent of the gardeners, 17 per cent of the bakers, 35 per cent of the blacksmiths, 36 per cent of the painters, and 36 per cent of the carpenters. Comparable figures for 1870–1880 are 59 per cent for doctors, 58 per cent for lawyers, and 45 per cent for merchants, as opposed to 30 per cent for laborers, 34 per cent for gardeners, 34 per cent for bakers, 40 per cent for black-smiths, 41 per cent for painters, and 40 per cent for carpenters.[29]

As for the matter of ethnic ghettos, we have yet to find a city in which most members of any minority group remained for long in the community at all, much less within the confines of their particular neighborhood or neighborhoods. Close examination of the Fifth Ward of Providence, Rhode Island, the Irish ghetto of the city, reveals that only a quarter of its 1850 residents were still to be found in Providence in 1860, and the 1860–1870 persistence rate was little higher—31 per cent.[30] Only 21 per cent of the Irish in Poughkeepsie at midcentury survived for ten years in the community, 24 per cent of the English and Scottish immigrants, and 29 per cent of the Germans, as compared to 34 per cent of the native-born Americans.[31] The Irish laborers of New-buryport had lower persistence rates than their Yankee counterparts both for 1850–1860 and 1860–1870.[32] Some 40 per cent of the foreign-born residents of Atlanta in 1870 remained in the city in 1880, as op-posed to 45 per cent of the native-born; by 1896, 18 per cent of the immigrants were still traceable, and 23 per cent of the natives.[33] In Boston earlier, from 1830 to 1860, native-born persons stayed in the city, on an average, two to three times as long as did foreign-born persons.

It would be going too far to conclude, as these figures would suggest, that immigrants were notably *more* transient than natives in the nineteenth-century city. That seems to have been true around midcentury, when the first heavy migratory waves were breaking on

American shores, but after a decade or two there seems to have been a settling-in process. The Irish laborers of Newburyport had a slightly higher persistence rate than the native-born in the 1870's.[34] Both the Irish and the Germans of Poughkeepsie were a little more rooted than the natives in that decade, though the English and Scottish remained more volatile.[35] In Boston in the 1880's there were no consistent ethnic differences in persistence once occupational level was held constant; first and second generation immigrants were somewhat more transient than old-stock Americans, but only because they were more heavily concentrated in lower status occupations which had generally higher transiency rates. Still, the overriding fact to emphasize is that immigrants and their children were at least as transient as, and at some points more transient than, the American norm, which is to say that they were very transient indeed. Therefore, the familiar image of the closed ghetto, sealed off from the rest of society, must be considerably revised.[36]

DESTINATIONS OF OUT-MIGRANTS

If the flow of migration *out of* the nineteenth-century American city was of such massive proportions—with a city of 363,000 inhabitants dispatching from it more than 690,000 out-migrants in the course of a decade—obviously it is important to inquire what happened to the typical transient after he left the city in which he was first observed. As far as we know, this question has never been explored systematically. This is hardly surprising, for there are no historical records which conveniently draw the necessary information together in one place.[37] Instead, the patient sifting of an awesome mass of materials is required to obtain even a few clues about where the out-migrants went and what they did in their new places of residence.

A pilot effort in this direction, carried out by the junior author, utilized four principal sources to locate migrants who left Boston in the 1830–1860 period. After 1850, city directories began listing commuters' suburban residences, and cemetery records provided some information. More important was the state registration system for vital statistics established in 1841, which listed alphabetically all persons who died in the Commonwealth of Massachusetts. Finally, there were the manuscript schedules of the U.S. Census for 1850 and 1860; the schedules for 128 suburban cities and towns in the state were searched for sample members who disappeared from Boston in the ante-bellum years.

Three samples, totaling 1,155 individuals, were drawn from the Boston census schedules for 1830, 1840, and 1850. From 14 to 17 per cent of them died in the decade following the census, and 38 to 48 per cent were still to be found in Boston after ten years. Between 5 and 9 per cent were positively identified as having settled in other Massachusetts communities. From 31 to 38 per cent of each sample, therefore, was left unaccounted for at the decade's end and must be presumed to have left the state altogether.[38] (Some of those who left the state would, of course, have died by the decade's end; if their mortality rate was like that of sample members who stayed in Boston, about 30 per cent of each sample was alive and residing in another state by then.) That the great preponderance of migrants from Boston moved at a minimum more than 40 miles (the distance to the nearest state boundary) is startling in light of contemporary demographic studies which suggest that the bulk of migration today is in short-distance movement. This hints at the interesting possibility that migratory patterns in the mid-nineteenth century were fundamentally different from those later, that once people then had pulled up stakes at all—which, as we have already seen, was far more likely than is the case today—they were also more likely to travel long distances to their new destinations, leap-frogging over all of the intervening territory. Possibly the lure of the West was involved here, a conjecture which finds some support in aggregated census data showing that migrants from several eastern, densely populated states, including Massachusetts, were more likely to move to noncontiguous states in 1870 than they were later in the century.[39] We do not know with any certainty whether men who disappeared from Boston went to other cities or to rural areas—there were cities in the West, and there were rural areas even in heavily industrialized contiguous states—but it seems likely that the shift indicates that ever larger numbers of them moved to other cities as the century wore on.

Which types of people were most likely to leave ante-bellum Boston? There was a distinct tendency for migration to be economically selective. Well-to-do proprietors and professionals tended to be underrepresented in the out-migration stream for most of the period, and unskilled and menial workers overrepresented. Possession of property in the city discouraged migration from it, as Table 5 in-

TABLE 5 *Property Holdings of Persisting and Out-Migrating Bostonians, 1830–1860, in Per Cent*

SAMPLE AND CHARACTERISTIC	N	NOT ASSESSED MALE	NOT ASSESSED FEMALE	UNDER $200	$200–$1,000	$1,001–$10,000	OVER $10,000
1830							
Persisting	163	9	15	30	20	19	8
Out-migrating	156	22	19	33	14	10	2
1840							
Persisting	183	5	8	31	21	27	9
Out-migrating	148	24	16	33	16	9	1
1850							
Persisting	145	17	7	44	12	8	12
Out-migrating	180	35	12	33	7	9	3

dicates. Men who were not assessed were from two to five more times as likely to leave Boston as to stay there; those who had a little property (under $200) were about as likely to stay as to leave up to 1850, and somewhat more likely to remain after that. Persons with holdings in the $200 to $1,000 range were from one-and-a-half to two times as apt to remain in Boston as to leave, and those with $1,000 to $10,000 in property were twice as likely to remain as to go in the 1830's, three times in the 1840's, but only four-fifths in the 1850's—a remarkable turnabout testifying to the strong middle class movement to Boston's suburbs that began in the late 1840's. The wealthy, with over $10,000 in property, were from four to six times as likely to remain in Boston as to move away.

We may now ask where out-migrants from Boston went, and how they fared in their new destinations. Only 22 per cent of the sample members who disappeared from the city could later be identified as residents of other Massachusetts communities; nearly four-fifths of them, therefore, apparently left the state altogether. Migrants who could be traced elsewhere in Massachusetts were not a random slice of the entire migratory pool; they tended to be of higher occupational rank than transients moving out of the state, they were more likely to own property, and few of them were foreign-born. These traceable migrants moved relatively short distances within the state, with half of them in the 1830 sample and three-quarters of those in the 1840 and 1850 samples relocating within ten miles of downtown Boston.

The most interesting and important question is whether migrants from the city found greater opportunities for personal advancement elsewhere, as popular folklore about Americans on the move and on the make would suggest. Our answer is severely limited because the four-fifths of the migrants from Boston who could not be traced included disproportionate numbers of laborers, immigrants, and men without property. It would be foolish to assume that their postmigration experience was necessarily like that of the select group of traceable migrants; there are good grounds for suspecting that it was not, and that many of these men continued to drift about as part of a floating proletariat. But it is noteworthy that the special group of migrants who could be located elsewhere in Massachusetts seem to have fared somewhat better than their counterparts who remained behind in Boston. Of the members of the 1850 sample who were still in Boston in 1860, one in five significantly increased his property holdings during the decade, about two-thirds remained at the same level, and about one-ninth suffered some loss. But of the out-migrants from the 1850 sample who were found in other communities, twice as many (or two-fifths) had accumulated additional property by 1860. Of the sample members who owned no property at all in 1850, 22 per cent of those who stayed in Boston, but 44 per cent of those who departed from the city, obtained a property stake during the decade. Although the migration stream from the city was on the whole selective of the least successful (Table 5), that portion of the stream which flowed into other nearby Massachusetts communities contained disproportionate numbers of men who had talent, ambition, ruthlessness, and whatever other traits brought economic success in midnineteenth-century America. We emphasize again that this group of traceable migrants was a rather small minority of all of the men who passed through Boston in the ante-bellum years, but for them at least American folklore about geographical mobility and success had some validity.

SOME TENTATIVE CONCLUSIONS

A number of tentative conclusions about urban population mobility in nineteenth-century America may be advanced on the basis of the evidence surveyed in this paper:

1. Very high rates of population mobility prevailed not only on the western frontier but on the urban frontier as well. Comparable studies for other countries will be needed to establish whether or not rates of spatial mobility in the United States were uniquely high, as American legend would have it, but the absolute figures are certainly striking.[40]

2. The largest cities of the period seemingly had a somewhat more stable population than smaller communities in general, but only because it was possible to move a great deal and still remain within their boundaries. It is doubtful that persistence rates within smaller units that comprised the metropolis—South Boston, for example—were much higher than in cities of comparable area.

3. To estimate the fluidity of a city's population from *net* population changes is like assuming that the fraction of an iceberg projecting above the surface is the whole. Net figures register not the total flow of individuals into and out of the city, but only the magnitude of the difference between the two migratory streams.

4. While the United States might in many respects have been "a nation of loosely connected islands" as late as the 1870's, as Robert Wiebe argues, small islands in which face-to-face relationships predominated, there was a dizzying rate of population turnover well before that time in any community which has as yet been carefully studied. Possibly this movement was largely island-hopping, as it were, in which newcomers were attracted to communities and neighborhoods very much like those they left behind, but in any event it suggests that "interaction among these islands" in a simple demographic sense was far more common than Wiebe's otherwise persuasive synthesis indicates.

5. The concept of the closed ethnic or class ghetto clearly needs reexamination and empirical testing. Poor people, poor immigrants especially, may have been hopelessly entangled in the spider's web of poverty in many instances, but it is doubtful that many were per-

manently trapped in particular slum areas. A majority do not even seem to have remained within the confines of any one city for as long as ten years.

6. Long-distance or leapfrogging mobility seems to have been more common than short-distance movement in the ante-bellum period. There is some indication that in the late nineteenth century the pattern was shifting toward shorter moves, probably to nearby cities.

7. While migration out of contemporary cities is largely in response to the stimulus of superior economic opportunities elsewhere, with relatively well-educated and affluent individuals somewhat over-represented in the migratory stream, the incessant and massive movement of people out of the nineteenth-century city may have been largely of a different character. Certainly there were migrants from Boston who sought—and found—greater opportunity in their new destinations. But the men we were able to trace from ante-bellum Boston to their later residences held better jobs before they left, owned more property, and were more often of native American stock than the typical migrant. It is possible—though by no means certain—that the large majority of out-migrants who disappeared from our view altogether had a radically different experience, that they formed a class of permanent transients who continued to be buffeted about by the vicissitudes of the casual labor market. The likely political consequences of this state of affairs have been sketched elsewhere;[41] suffice it to say here that high rates of transiency for blue collar workers presumably left them alienated but invisible and politically impotent, and minimized the likelihood of effective organized efforts to reshape capitalist society.

Any or all of these conclusions might, of course, be overturned or significantly modified by future research. The spectrum of cities which have been examined from a demographic perspective is still very narrow. Too much of the work done so far deals with eastern, indeed with New England, communities; the West and Midwest are conspicuously absent from the list, and the South is represented only by Atlanta. Smaller cities have attracted more attention than major metropolitan centers, because they are more easily studied, but convenience is no gauge of importance.[42] The knotty, but in principle not insoluble, question of what happened to out-migrants after they left the city cries out for further systematic study. Much of the work that has been done is technically rather primitive, aimed at developing simple decadal persistence rates. Finer-grained analyses of population movements on an annual basis, using some of the methods we have employed in our discussion of Boston in the 1880's, may suggest that differences between cities were more significant than appears at present.[43]

There is, however, unfinished business more important than further data gathering in other cities, or the development of more refined methods of estimating demographic parameters, important though we believe those tasks to be. Quantitative studies of grass-roots social phenomena can help us to grasp basic social processes which left little imprint in conventional historical sources—newspapers, diaries, legislative debates, and so on—thus freeing us, to some extent, from our customary dependence upon materials reflecting the beliefs of the articulate classes who controlled the media of the era. But to trace out the implications of the startling demographic facts disclosed here we must fit our findings into the broad social context to which they pertain, and relate them to less readily measurable features of nineteenth-century urban life. Statistical analysis of historical data may be useful not so much for settling old questions as for posing new ones. If American city-dwellers were as restless and footloose as our evidence suggests, how was any cultural continuity—or even the appearance of it—maintained? A historian describing the Knights of Labor in its heyday, the 1880's, remarks that "so rapidly did its membership change" that "what appeared to be an organization . . . was in fact more like a procession."[44] Likewise, it might be said, American society in the period considered here was more like a procession than a stable social order. How did this social order cohere at all?

This is not the place to attempt an answer to that formidable question. We will content ourselves with two observations. One is that certain aspects of this seemingly unsettling, chaotic social process which kept so many Americans ever on the move were in fact stabilizing. For some—like the traceable out-migrants from ante-bellum Boston—migration brought economic success, and promoted confidence that the society rewarded men on the basis of merit. Others may not have been so fortunate, but the floating urban proletariat we believe to have existed was so transient as to prevent the growth of feelings of collective solidarity.[45] Poor people moved about so rapidly, indeed, that substantial numbers of them must have been legally disenfranchised by the electoral laws of many states, which required a year's residence in the state and six months in the city before voting.

A second observation is that, as Berthoff has suggested, many features of nineteenth-century American society are best understood as efforts to overcome or offset the "excessive" mobility of the era.[46] We are not sure that population mobility was "excessive," and are distressed that Berthoff made no effort to measure mobility systematically, but his speculations about the social consequences of mobility are provocative. Doubtless it is significant that it was precisely during the period which we have analyzed here that Americans became frantic joiners of voluntary associations, lacking as they did traditional ties to particular communities. It was an era in which loyalty to political party and interest in national elections (as indicated by voter turnout rates) were at a high point. Party may have been a substitute for community as a source of personal identity. Even the desperate assertions of communal loyalty of the period, like the Iowa picnics of contemporary California, testify not to the strength of surviving communal loyalties but to the felt lack of community.

Research of the kind reported here deepens our understanding of some key facets of nineteenth-century social history, and dispels some common misconceptions that derive from uncritical acceptance of literary evidence, but it cannot by itself resolve the larger issues which it raises. To do that will require both a sure grasp of the demographic facts and an ample measure of the knowledge that comes from a mastery of traditional historical sources.

FOOTNOTES

1. U.S. Census Office, 7th Census (1850), *Report of the Superintendent of the Census for December 1, 1852* (Washington, 1853), 15.

2. Russell Sage Foundation, *West Side Studies* (New York, 1914), I, 8.

3. The conspicuous exception to this claim is Adna F. Weber's classic volume on *The Growth of Cities in the Nineteenth Century* (New York, 1899; Cornell University Press reprint, 1963), a bold pioneering venture which regrettably fell upon barren ground and was little known until the resurgence of interest in urban studies and quantitative historical analysis that has taken place in the past few years.

4. James C. Malin, "The Turnover of Farm Population in Kansas," *Kansas Historical Quarterly*, IV (1935), 339–372; Merle Curti *et al.*, *The Making of an*

American Community: A Case Study of Democracy in a Frontier County (Stanford, 1959), 68; Mildred Throne, "A Population Study of an Iowa County in 1850," *Iowa Journal of History*, LVII (1959), 305–330; Peter J. Coleman, "Restless Grant County: Americans on the Move," *Wisconsin Magazine of History*, XLVI (Autumn 1962), 16–20. Unless otherwise specified, all persistence figures given in the present paper are for employed adult males. It should be noted that persistence estimates cannot be directly translated into true out-migration rates. A 25 per cent persistence rate for a decade does not necessarily mean that 75 per cent of the population moved out of the community in the interval; some individuals disappeared because of death. Taking death into account, however, does not drastically alter the figures for a population with a normal age distribution, as will be evident from the detailed discussion below of out-migration from Boston in the 1880's, based on calculations which separate deaths from true out-migration.

5. Robert Wiebe, *The Search for Order, 1877–1920* (New York, 1967).

6. Fred A. Shannon, "A Post Mortem on the Labor-Safety-Valve Theory," *Agricultural History*, XIX (1945), 31–37.

7. The most influential effort to advance an "urban" interpretation of American history comparable to the frontier theory, Arthur Schlesinger, Sr.'s "The City in American History," *Mississippi Valley Historical Review*, XXVII (1940), 43–46, was considerably less rich in provocative, testable propositions. Its inadequacies were exposed in William Diamond's thoughtful essay, "On the Dangers of an Urban Interpretation of History," in Eric F. Goldman (ed.), *Historiography and Urbanization* (Baltimore, 1941), 67–108. It was already clear from census state-of-birth data, analyzed in Weber's *The Growth of Cities*, Harvey S. Perloff *et al.*, *Regions, Resources and Economic Growth* (Baltimore, 1960), and Simon Kuznets, Dorothy S. Thomas, Everett S. Lee *et al.*, *Population Redistribution and Economic Growth: United States, 1870–1950* (Philadelphia, 1957, 1960, 1964), 3v., that substantial numbers of Americans moved from state to state and region to region in the course of their lives, but this evidence gave little hint of what would be disclosed by microscopic examination of population movements in particular cities.

8. Stephan Thernstrom, *Poverty and Progress: Social Mobility in a 19th Century City* (Cambridge, Mass., 1964), 96, 168.

9. Blake McKelvey, *Rochester, The Flower City, 1855–1890* (Cambridge, Mass., 1949), 3.

10. Computed from data in Clyde Griffen, "Workers Divided: Social Mobility in Poughkeepsie, 1850–1880," in Stephan Thernstrom and Richard Sennett (eds.), *Nineteenth-Century Cities: Essays in the New Urban History* (New Haven, 1969), 49–97.

11. Robert Doherty, "Industrialization and Social Change: Northampton, Massachusetts, 1800–1860" (unpub. paper for the Yale Conference on 19th Century Cities, November 1968).

12. Computed from data in Richard J. Hopkins, "Occupational and Geographic Mobility in Atlanta, 1870–1890," *Journal of Southern History*, XXXIV (1968), 200–213.

13. Otis Dudley Duncan *et al.*, *Statistical Geography* (Glencoe, 1961), 34.

14. Peter R. Knights, "Population Turnover, Persistence, and Residential Mobility in Boston, 1830–1860," in Thernstrom and Sennett, *Nineteenth-Century Cities*, 272.

15. All Boston data, unless otherwise indicated, were gathered by the authors in the course of research for forthcoming studies. The junior author is preparing a demographic and social study of the city in the ante-bellum period, based on samples

of 385 heads of households from each of the four censuses, 1830–1860. Sample members were traced through city directories, 1830–1860, city assessor's books, 1830, 1840, 1850, and 1860, and the state registration system, 1841–1910. The senior author is completing an analysis of migration and social mobility in Boston, 1880–1968. The figures drawn from this research pertain to 1,982 adult males randomly selected from the manuscript schedules of the U.S. Census of 1880. Sample members were traced in the city directories and assessor's valuation books for 1890. One peculiarity of the sampling procedure could have biased the persistence figures for 1880–1890, but apparently did not. By 1890 Boston was a large city that contained a good many people with extremely common names; there were 122 John Smiths living there, and no less than 235 John Murphys. It would have been quite impossible to determine if a particular John Murphy from the 1880 sample was still living in the community ten years later. Accordingly, men with common names were excluded from the samples. Comparison of the characteristics of the sample with those of the entire population of the city revealed that this produced some underrepresentation of men with Irish names, most of whom were blue collar workers. But the overall occupational distribution of the sample was representative of the city, and Irish workers were no more volatile than other workers, so their underrepresentation did not distort the estimates. A full discussion and defense of the sampling procedure will appear in the senior author's forthcoming book.

16. For a discussion of the usefulness of city directories in urban studies, and some consideration of their reliability, see Peter R. Knights, "City Directories as Aids to Ante-Bellum Urban Studies: A Research Note," *Historical Methods Newsletter,* II (September 1969), 1–10. The directories did not provide a perfectly accurate enumeration of the population. Perfection has not been attained in even the U.S. Census of our own day; see the critical papers by Jacob S. Siegel, "Completeness of Coverage of the Nonwhite Population in the 1960 Census and Current Estimates, and Some Implications," in David M. Heer (ed.), *Social Statistics and the City* (Cambridge, Mass., 1968), 13–54; Leon Pritzker and N. D. Rothwell, "Procedural Difficulties in Taking Past Censuses in Predominantly Negro, Puerto Rican, and Mexican Areas," *ibid.,* 55–79; Jacob S. Siegel and Melvin Zelnik, "An Evaluation of Coverage in the 1960 Census of Population by Techniques of Demographic Analysis and by Composite Methods," *ibid.,* 132–173. The directory canvassing procedure in Boston, however, compared favorably with that employed in the census of the period. The greatest weakness of the city directories was not that they were biased against low status residents *per se,* as has often been assumed, but rather that they were biased against very recent migrants, tending not to include them until they had passed some time in the city and seemed relatively settled. After careful comparisons of directory listings with other sources, the junior author has concluded that the operating rule in the ante-bellum period was to include individuals only after they had lived in the city for two years. To the extent that this bias prevailed, however, it strengthens rather than weakens the argument of this paper. A fully accurate enumeration of every individual living in the community, including casual laborers just passing through, would disclose an even more volatile population. In addition, it should be noted that even a perfectly accurate and comprehensive set of city directories would underestimate the actual volatility of the population, for a canvas in May 1880 and in May 1881 would miss individuals who migrated into the city in June 1880 and left before the May 1881 canvas. A not inconsiderable fraction of the population may have fallen into this category. All in all, it seems likely that the estimates given here err in the conservative direction.

17. The Boston directories also tabulated the total number of names newly

added to each annual directory down to 1922. These computations of listings added and dropped from year to year made possible the analysis offered in this section of our paper. We believe that our results are interesting enough to justify testing for other cities, but are distressed to report that the job may prove more difficult elsewhere, because the practice of tabulating total listings added and dropped was apparently not a common one. We have examined 1850 and 1860 directories for 21 cities, including Albany, Baltimore, Buffalo, Chicago, Cincinnati, Detroit, New Orleans, New York, Philadelphia, and San Francisco, and have not found similar information in summary form. Perhaps the practice was followed later in some of these cities, or in other communities, but it may be that considerably more arduous sampling and tracing procedures will have to be followed by other investigators.

18. For evidence that recent migrants into communities are also those most likely to depart from it in the near future, and hence of the inappropriateness of extrapolating annual out-migration rates over a longer period, see Sidney Goldstein, *Patterns of Mobility, 1910–1950: The Norristown Study* (Philadelphia, 1958), 270ff.

19. The method yields estimates of net migration which are much too low, because it credits all of the vital events occurring during the interval in question to the population resident there at the start of the interval. That is, all of the births and deaths taking place in Boston in the 1880's are removed from the 1890 population total, and only the remaining surplus is attributed to net migration. This ignores the fact that some of these births and deaths were the result of in-migration during the decade. Families who entered the city after the Census of 1880 produced children: in-migration also brought in persons who died before 1890. But these two influences were not of the same magnitude, for newcomers were disproportionately concentrated in the procreative age brackets, in which death rates were low. Via complex estimating procedures unnecessary to describe here, we calculate that a minimum of 27.7 per cent of the births in Boston between 1880 and 1890 were attributable to new migrants, but only 6.7 per cent of the deaths, which means that the true net migration figure was at least 26,000 higher than the residual method would indicate.

20. The 1890 population of Boston may be divided into three components: persons who had been living in the city since 1880 or earlier; individuals born in Boston since 1880 and still residing there in 1890; and migrants who had entered the community from elsewhere during the decade and remained there (the net total of in-migrants). The first of these components was estimated, through a persistence trace of 1880 residents, as 64 per cent of the 1880 population. The third could be gauged accurately if the second were known (1890 population minus the sum of 1880 persisters and surviving newborn children = net in-migration). Much depends, therefore, upon obtaining a valid estimate of the number of children born in Boston during the 1880's and remaining there in 1890; they are the key to a reasonably accurate estimate of net decadal in-migration to the city.

The unwary might conclude that the total number of births in Boston in the 1880's—115,974—would be a satisfactory approximation of the size of this component of the population in 1890, but the true figure—47,059—was a mere 40 per cent of that. Many of the newborn died before 1890; many others moved away along with their parents. To estimate the magnitude of these two influences we made several assumptions. One was that the City Registrar's annual reports of births and deaths were accurate enough for our uses. Second, we assumed that 50 per cent of all deaths of children designated as "U.S.-born" were of children born in Boston. The State Censuses of 1885 and 1895 show that, of all U.S.-born persons residing in Boston, between 50 and 60 per cent were born in Boston. We have used the lower figure as a conservative estimate of the corresponding proportion of children's deaths to assign to the category "born in Boston." Last, from our earlier analysis of changes in the city directory listings, we deduced an annual out-migration rate for 1880, 1885, and 1890 of about 16 per cent for Boston's families. For want of a better figure, we have applied this rate to children's cohorts in our estimate.

The method of producing the estimates was simple but tedious. For children born in Boston in 1880, we know the number of deaths of U.S.-born aged one year and under. For the years 1881–1884, we know the number of deaths of U.S.-born children aged one to five, and for the years 1885–1889 we have the analogous figures for children aged five to ten. The mortality among the 1880 cohort through the decade would then be the sum of all deaths of Boston-born children (equal to half the native-born) in the following groups: for 1880, all aged under one; for 1881, one-fifth of those aged one to five; for 1882, one-fifth of those aged one to five, etc., until 1885, when we shift to taking one-fifth of the deaths of children aged five to ten years, continuing through to and including 1889. This produces for each year of the decade an estimate of the number of deaths of children born in Boston in 1880. The initial size of the cohort born in 1880 was 10,654; we then subtract the estimated deaths of Boston-born children in that year, 333, and 1,776, the estimated out-migration of one-sixth of the children. This leaves 8,545 as the size of the 1880 cohort at the start of 1881. Continuing the estimation process through to 1890 produces a residual for the 1880 cohort of 1,571. The procedure is then carried out for the 1881 cohort, starting with 1881 and going to 1890. When the residuals of all ten cohorts, 1880–1889, are summed, the total is 47,059.

21. Massachusetts Bureau of Labor Statistics, *Census of the Commonwealth of Massachusetts, 1895. Volume II: Population and Social Statistics* (Boston, 1897), 333, 672, 790–791.

22. Donald J. Bogue, *The Population of the United States* (New York, 1959), 384.

23. U.S. Bureau of the Census, *Eighteenth Census of the United States: 1960, General Social and Economic Characteristics* (Washington, 1961), Vol. I, Part 6, California.

24. Francis A. Walker, *The Wages Question: A Treatise on Wages and the Wage Class* (New York, 1876), 188.

25. *Ibid.*, 181–183.

26. The leading study, though scanty on the nineteenth century, is Stanley Lieberson, *Ethnic Patterns in American Cities* (Glencoe, 1963). Cf. the excellent critique of the ghetto hypothesis by Sam B. Warner and Colin B. Burke, "Cultural Change and the Ghetto," *Journal of Contemporary History*, IV (1969), 173–187.

27. Lester Lenoff, "Occupational Mobility Among Yankee Immigrants to Boston, 1870–1880" (unpub. seminar paper, Brandeis University, 1969).

28. Computed from Hopkins, "Occupational and Geographic Mobility."

29. Griffen, "Workers Divided."

30. Robert Wheeler, "The Fifth-Ward Irish: Mobility at Mid-Century" (unpub. seminar paper, Brown University, 1967).

31. Griffen, "Workers Divided."

32. Data developed for, but not included in, Thernstrom, *Poverty and Progress.*

33. Computed from data in Hopkins, "Occupational and Geographic Mobility."

34. Unpublished data gathered in research for Thernstrom, *Poverty and Progress.*

35. Griffen, "Workers Divided."

36. The closest thing to an exception to this proposition which has yet been discovered is the Negro community of Atlanta in the 1870's. Hopkins found blacks persisting more frequently than native whites or immigrants, notably more so when their disproportionate concentration in low status occupations with generally low persistence rates was taken into account. Of the Negro unskilled or semiskilled workers in Atlanta in 1870, 46 per cent were still present ten years later, but only 25 per cent of the natives and 36 per cent of the immigrants; for skilled craftsmen the black figure was 77 per cent, as opposed to 38 per cent for natives and 40 per cent for immigrants. Still, less than half of the Negroes in the city remained there a decade, so that even this ghetto was far from closed. It is likely that the black population of Northern cities in this period was exceptionally volatile. Research in progress by Herbert G. Gutman and Laurence Glasco reveals that only 12 per cent of the Negroes living in Buffalo, New York, at the time of the state census of 1855 were still there in 1875. Of the adult Negro males recorded in Boston by the 1880 Census, little more than half (56 per cent) were to be found at the end of *one year;* Elizabeth H. Pleck, "The Black Family in Boston: 1880" (unpub. seminar paper, Brandeis University, 1969).

37. A partial exception, as yet unexploited by researchers, is found in the manuscript schedules of the U.S. Census for the State of Wisconsin in the 1850–1880 period, which apparently were indexed by W.P.A. workers in the 1930's. This should make it relatively easy to track down migrants from Wisconsin communities who moved elsewhere in the state. It is possible that similar indexes were prepared in other states as well, a question on which we seek further enlightenment. Another source which could be utilized to trace down out-migrants is the manuscript school censuses of the state of Michigan; Sam B. Warner informs us that these indicate the projected destination of families moving out of each school district. Again there may be comparable materials for other states, now moldering in obscurity. The junior author plans extensive further research on patterns of migration.

38. Some of these missing individuals may simply have been missed by the tracing process. This is particularly likely with out-migrants of Irish descent, since the Michael Murphys, John Rileys, etc., were nearly impossible to distinguish from each other in the sources. This difficulty was not of a magnitude, however, to throw into doubt the main conclusions of the analysis.

39. Kuznets *et al., Population Redistribution,* I, 249–298, presents a series of Census data for the states of residence, 1870–1950, of native whites born in each of the states and in the District of Columbia. They provide totals not only for those born in each state and still living in that state, but also for those residing in contiguous states and in all states other than that of birth. If the distances to which persons tended to move from their homes decreased as the nineteenth century went on, as we hypothesize, then we would expect a rise in the proportion of out-migrating individuals who had moved to contiguous states as opposed to states farther from their state of birth. When we calculate the proportion of persons born in a given state and residing in a contiguous state to persons born in that state and residing in all other states, for all states, 1870–1900, we find that the proportion rose consistently in 16 states and fell consistently in nine. The states for which our conjecture was borne out were Arizona, Connecticut, Delaware, Maryland, Massachusetts, Montana, New Hampshire, New Jersey, New York, North Carolina, Oklahoma, Rhode Island, South Carolina, Texas, Vermont, and Wyoming. The nine states exhibiting a regular drop in the proportion were Alabama, Florida, Kentucky, Mississippi, Nebraska, New Mexico, Tennessee, Virginia, and Washington.

It is interesting to note the number of eastern, relatively densely populated states in the first group and the preponderance of southern and more sparsely populated states in the second.

Figures for analogous data for 1850 and 1860 are not available in tabulated form except for state-by-state totals. Accordingly, considerable manipulation of the 1850 and 1860 Census results will be required before we shall be able to determine whether any of these trends were under way before 1870, and whether they remain consistent back that far. These calculations will be prosecuted, and the results reported in time.

40. There are fragments of valuable comparative evidence in Weber's *The Growth of Cities*, especially in Chapter IV, which Weber employed to attack the parochial notion that Americans were the only migratory people in the world. Probably he went too far in denying American uniqueness, as some of his own evidence suggests (see, for example, 259, 264, and 274). It is to be hoped that the research along these lines now going on in Europe will soon permit further exploration of this issue. For a taste of some promising work in progress in England, see E. A. Wrigley (ed.), *An Introduction to English Historical Demography* (London, 1966); D. V. Glass and D. E. C. Eversley, *Population in History: Essays in Historical Demography* (London, 1965); H. J. Dyos (ed.), *The Study of Urban History* (London, 1968). The paucity of information currently available, however, forced us to confine ourselves to the American scene in the present paper.

41. Thernstrom, "Working Class Social Mobility in Industrial America," in Melvin Richter (ed.), *Essays in Theory and History* (Cambridge, Mass., 1970).

42. Richard Sennett's *Families Against the City* (Cambridge, Mass., 1970), a study of a Chicago middle class neighborhood in the late nineteenth century, is a significant exception. Some of the main findings are summarized in Sennett's essay, "Middle Class Families and Urban Violence," in Thernstrom and Sennett, *Nineteenth-Century Cities*.

43. Work in this vein is beginning in Los Angeles; for a preliminary report see Thernstrom, "The Growth of Los Angeles in Historical Perspective: Myth and Reality," Institute of Government and Public Affairs Report, University of California, Los Angeles, 1970 (mimeo). There is a valuable study of "Residential Mobility in Omaha, 1880–1920," by Howard Chudacoff (unpub. Ph.D. Thesis, University of Chicago, 1970).

44. George W. Coleman, "Labor and the Labor Movement, 1860–1930," in A. B. Hart (ed.), *The Commonwealth History of Massachusetts* (Boston, 1933), Vol. V, 433.

45. For further discussion, see Thernstrom, "Working Class Social Mobility," and the works cited there.

46. Rowland Berthoff, "The American Social Order: A Conservative Hypothesis," *American Historical Review*, LXV (1960), 495–514. For further suggestive discussion of the consequences of population mobility, see George W. Pierson, "The Moving American," *Yale Review*, XLIV (1954), 99–112, though this paper too is marred by unsubstantiated, and in some cases mistaken, assumptions about the demographic facts.

MARTYN J. BOWDEN

The Great American Desert and the American Frontier, 1800–1882: Popular Images of the Plains

꠵꠵

> Throughout the history of geography erroneous notions have exerted a powerful fascination over men's minds and mistaken concepts have been hardly less influential than those found finally to be correct.[1]

Since the early 1920's there has been widespread agreement among historians that "in the first half of the nineteenth century, and in some quarters until after the Civil War, there existed in the public mind a Great American Desert situated to the east of the Rocky Mountains. . . . It was a reality in the minds of the people of that time. To them the region was actually a desert, wholly uninhabitable. . . ."[2] This desert image of the western interior is widely assumed to have acted as a psychological barrier to westward migration, effectively halting the frontier at the bend of the Missouri for 30 years or more.[3] To historical geographer Ralph Brown, the Great American Desert idea of the first half of the nineteenth century was "the classic example" of the "effectiveness of beliefs as distinct from actual knowledge in the occupancy and settlement of regions,"[4] while to Ray Billington "The Great Plains country . . . had been so often branded a 'Great American Desert' by explorers that the pioneers had lost interest."[5]

But did all Americans, particularly the frontiersmen, imagine that a desert existed west of the Missouri? As early as 1924, Frederick

L. Paxson maintained that the trappers did not believe in the desert,[6] and in 1930 E. Douglass Branch expressed doubt that fur traders, soldiers on the frontier, and Missourians were affected in any way by the "legend of the Great American Desert." [7] Bernard De Voto in 1947 went further, maintaining that the trappers and those who had read their newspapers, or who had talked to the mountain men, did not believe in the desert's existence.[8] By 1952 James C. Malin had joined the dissenters. While admitting the existence of a desert image of the western interior, he cautioned against acceptance of "another legend that the myth of the Great American Desert was held universally. . . . At no time," he maintained, "were either the literature or the maps in general agreement on the existence of a great desert or of its extent." [9]

G. Malcolm Lewis has recently documented Malin's contention. He concludes that the desert concept was the most popular American view of the western interior between 1810 and 1860, but that it was rivaled increasingly throughout this period by the concept of the "Great Western Prairies"—a potential pastoral region.[10] In the late 1850's a third concept—the Great Plains—began to rival those of the Great Western Prairies and the Great American Desert, and by the early 1870's this idea had become the dominant image of the western interior.[11] Thanks to Lewis's diligent research we know more about the changing geographical knowledge—historical geosophy—of the western interior than about any other region of North America. Unfortunately for our purposes, however, Lewis was more concerned with the effect of westward migration upon images of the western interior than vice versa. Furthermore, he was interested primarily in conceptions of the region found in cartographic, literary, and scientific sources, and only once suggested that the frontiersmen and potential migrants may not have shared the western conceptions of the well-educated.[12]

This paper concerns itself with historians' assumptions that between 1825 and 1870, the average American conceived of the western interior as a desert, and that a perceived Great American Desert curbed migration across the Missouri River before the Civil War. It is an attempt to reconstruct the various conceptions of the western interior held by the American public; to relate changing images of the western interior to phases of migration; to discern who believed in the Great

American Desert, in which regions the idea was strong, when, and
among which elements of the population; and to ascertain whether a
popular image of a western desert was responsible for a 30 year halt
of the frontier.

TEXTBOOK IMAGES
OF THE WESTERN INTERIOR

To ascertain whether the average literate American believed in
the existence of a desert, recourse can be made to at least five sources:
the letters and diaries of western travelers, newspapers, atlases, gazet-
teers, and geographies and school textbooks. It is to the last that I
turned initially, to some extent because of the close association revealed in the accounts of Western travelers between the Great American Desert idea and the school geographies, but primarily because
historians and others have taken the presence of the desert in geographies and school textbooks to signify that the idea was in the public
mind.[13] Paxson, for instance, wrote: "Schoolboys of the thirties, forties,
and fifties were told that from the bend of the Missouri to the Stony
Mountains stretched an American desert. The makers of their geography books drew the desert upon their maps, coloring it brown with
the speckled aspect that connotes Sahara or Arabia, with camels, oases,
and sand dunes." [14] Robert Reigel maintained that, "until after the
Civil War the great majority of American citizens were satisfied that
the plains of the Far West comprised the Great American Desert, and
it was so marked in school geographies. . . . Here, in the words of
the average school geography, was the Great American Desert." [15]
The discovery of three school textbooks, 1840–1850, and three atlases,
1835–1849, carrying the desert idea seems to have been Webb's major
evidence for concluding that the Great American Desert was a reality
in the mind of the American public.[16]

I have examined more than 500 different printings of geographies
and school textbooks published in the United States between 1800 and
1882. Of these, books which had more than 120 words describing the
geography of the western interior were selected for further analysis.[17]
Data were collected on the place and date of publication, and, where
possible, on the outlets for each text. The accounts were scanned for

references to any part of the western interior as "desert" or for acceptable surrogates for "desert," such as "elevated barren waste," "arid
plains or plateaux," "sterile plains," "elevated barren plains," "barren
and sandy plains," and "unproductive wastes." If such references were
found in the body of the text or in an accompanying map or atlas,
the work was considered to be projecting a desert image and was removed from further analysis, even though the greater part of the
description may have conveyed a nondesert image, as was frequently
the case.[18] Other works were classified according to their main characterization of the western interior, e.g., fertile land, prairies, plains
(Table 1).

It is clear from the analysis of these textbooks (Table 1) that the
expedition of Stephen Long, 1819–1820, rather than that of Zebulon
Pike, fixed the desert image in the advanced schoolbooks. Pike's ac-

TABLE 1   *Descriptions of the Western Interior in Textbooks
and Geographies Published in the United States,
1800–1882*

| | | | NONDESERT DESCRIPTIONS | | | | | |
DATES OF PRINTING	TOTAL DES-ERT	TOTAL NON-DESERT	FER-TILE	FERTILE WITH LARGE PRAIRIES	PRAIR-IES	PRAIR-IES AND PLAINS	PLAINS	UNCERTAIN APPRAISAL (NEUTRAL TO UN-FAVORABLE)
1800–1804	0	9	9	0	0	0	0	0
1805–1809	0	17	7	7	0	0	0	3
1810–1814	1	19	2	10	0	0	0	7
1815–1819	0[a]	17	4	1	3	0	1	8
1820–1824	4	13	1	0	2	0	2	8
1825–1829	7	8	0	0	0	2	3	3
1830–1834	10	8	2	0	1	0	5	0
1835–1839	10	4	0	0	2	0	2	0
1840–1844	16	2	0	0	2	0	0	0
1845–1849	5	7	0	0	3	4	0	0
1850–1854	6	4	0	0	0	4	0	0
1855–1859	4	4	0	0	0	3	1	0
1860–1864	5	5	1	0	0	2	2	0
1865–1869	6	5	1	0	0	2	2	0
1870–1874	6	5	0	0	1	2	1	1
1875–1882	1	7	0	0	0	1	6	0
Total	81	134	27	18	14	20	25	30

SOURCES: Libraries of Clark University, American Antiquarian Society, and Old Sturbridge Village.
[a] See footnote 33. The word *desert* appears in a footnote but not in the text.

count (1810)[19] affected only one book (out of 38 consulted) between 1811 and 1820: the last edition of Elijah Parish's *A New System of Modern Geography*.[20] It was almost a decade[21] before the desert concept reappeared in the geographies (1822–1824), after Long and his chronicler Edwin James[22] had presented their findings in the early 1820's. Thereafter the desert idea began to achieve much greater prominence in the textbooks (Table 1) and in atlases and maps.[23]

Early descriptions of desert conditions in the western interior from the seventeenth century onward, documented by Lewis and mentioned by Webb,[24] had no effect on the American view of the area as indicated in the geographies of the early nineteenth century.[25] On the contrary, geographies in the early years of the nineteenth century considered the region to be extremely fertile and productive agricultural land.[26] For example, in 1807 Parish wrote of Louisiana, state and territory, that: "Grass is higher than the tallest man; from the lofty cotton trees the Indians make canoes 100 feet in length; cedars, the finest in the world, enrich the forests; extensive fields are ready for the plow; beans grow without culture, and Indian corn yields 3 or 4 crops in a year. A fine country, if we credit those who have described it." [27]

This favorable view of the plains area was derived primarily from LePage Du Pratz, Louis Hennepin,[28] and, above all, from Thomas Jefferson's description of Upper Louisiana in the "Official Account of Louisiana": "The land yields an abundance of all the necessaries of life, and almost spontaneously. . . . That part of upper Louisiana which borders on North Mexico is one immense *prairie*. It produces nothing but grass . . . that land is represented as too rich for the growth of forest trees." [29] This was the view that Lewis and Clark took to the Trans-Missouri West, and they did not qualify it until their arrival at the Musselshell River.[30]

Between 1805 and 1810, presumably as more information came in, the Garden of the World concept gave way to one of the western interior as a fertile land interspersed with large prairies (Table 1), exemplified in Jedidiah Morse's popular work, *Geography Made Easy*. "The soil of Louisiana in many parts is rich and fertile beyond description," [31] Morse wrote. "In its natural state it is covered with mulberry, locust, sasafras, walnut, hickory, dog-wood, oak, ash, &c with grape vines running up almost every tree. The face of the country is interspersed with large prairies, producing grass, flowering plants, and strawberries; and with cane swamps of a hundred, and some of a thousand acres." [32] All but one of the editions of Nathaniel Dwight's geography text (between 1805 and 1814) introduced qualifications to the Garden of the World view of the western interior presented in the earlier editions.[33]

By 1815 Dwight's characterization had become a minority view of the western interior, for between 1810 and 1820 uncertainty of appraisal became more common, as it was realized that Jefferson's description of Louisiana applied primarily to the state rather than to the recently acquired territory as a whole.[34] Established works withdrew statements on the productiveness and fertility of the soil and salubrity of the climate, while new texts simply described the region without making judgments on the quality of the environment.[35] This ended with the return of the Long expedition, and the appearance of the desert idea in works by John Melish[36] and Joseph Worcester[37] in 1822, and in those of Worcester[38] and William Woodbridge[39] in 1824.

THREE IMAGES OF
THE WESTERN INTERIOR, 1825–1874

At first the desert was not bounded, and was thought by some to constitute a small fraction of the western interior. But in 1822 a sizable "Great Desert" was mapped and delineated in an atlas of wide appeal, which "appeared in three editions within five years." This desert was larger than the "Great Desert" shown on Long and Swift's manuscript map (probably drawn in 1821), and approximately the same size as the first "Great American Desert" which appeared in the atlas volume of James' official account of the Long expedition.[40] These three maps gave the desert a name and bounds that were soon adopted and extended by Woodbridge and Worcester to include most of the western interior. After 1824, the entire region west of the ninety-eighth meridian was being projected by the advanced geographies, with a few notable exceptions, as either a desert or a prairie-plains region of variable, generally low, fertility (Table 1).[41]

There is some suggestion in Table 1 that the desert image, after becoming the major conception conveyed in the texts in the late 1830's

and early 1840's, began to wane rapidly in the late 1840's and early
1850's. Thereafter it appears to have revived again in the mid-1850's,
and was maintained up to the mid-1870's. This is apparently counter
to the views of Lewis, Riegel, and Hollon,[42] who contend that the
desert image faded rapidly after the mid-1840's, and to Webb's view
that it was strongest in the 1850's.[43] In reality, we are dealing with
two quite different deserts. One, a vast desert covering most of the
western interior, was more than 300 miles wide and generally considered to be between 400 and 600 miles long. The other was a smaller
desert set in the central or western sections of a larger prairie-plains
region, a desert that was less than 300 miles wide, and sometimes
thought to be as narrow as 100 miles.

The former—the region as a desert in its entirety—was the more
common desert image between 1822 and 1856 (Table 2). The latter—
the desert set in a prairie-plains region—had originated in the textbooks in the 1820's, and became a strong minority view between 1835
and 1845. But both desert conceptions, particularly that of the small
desert, faded somewhat after 1845, and for almost a decade the prairie-
plains image was more common than either of them (Table 1).

After 1856 the small desert in the western section of the prairie-
plains country became the exclusive desert image. For two decades, this
view was as frequently presented in the advanced texts as was the
conception of the western interior as a prairie-plains region in its
entirety (Table 1). It should be emphasized that in all texts after 1856
the prairie-plains image was the dominant conception of the region;
the desert, when mentioned, was merely a western adjunct. In 1875 the
small desert finally disappeared, and the area between the Missouri
and the Rockies was projected as a land of prairies and plains.[44]

The revived desert of 1856–1874 was neither vast nor a true sandy
desert, as that of 1822–1855 had been. After the 1850's the word "desert"
was used reluctantly by textbook writers to describe the dry region
east of the Rockies. For the first time since the early twenties, desert
surrogates, such as "elevated barren plain," "arid, sterile plains," or
"unproductive wastes," were used more commonly than the word
"desert" to describe the semiarid region (Table 2). By the late fifties
the name "Great American Desert" had fallen from favor after a brief
period of acceptance in the 1840's (Table 2). This is to be compared
with the situation after 1830, when an increasing number of geo-

TABLE 2   *Name, Description, and Extent of the Desert of the Western Interior Found in Geography Texts, 1800–1882*

DATES OF PRINTING	DESERT NAMED GREAT CENTRAL, OR GREAT AMERICAN	DESCRIPTIVE ITEM "DESERT" USED	DESERT SURROGATE USED BUT NOT THE WORD DESERT	DESERT DESCRIBED — APPROXIMATE BREADTH OF THE DESERT, EAST OF THE ROCKIES (IN MILES)—IN MANY CASES ESTIMATED FROM THE ACCOUNT					AUTHORS OF "DESERT" TEXTS
				>500	499–400	399–300	299–200	199–100	
1810–1814	0	1	0	0	1	0	0	0	Parish
1820–1824	1	2	2	2	1	0	1	0	Worcester (2), Woodbridge, Melish
1825–1829	1	5	2	2	3	1	1	0	Worcester (2), Flint, Woodbridge, Cummings, Butler, Boimare
1830–1834	1	8	2	3	5	0	2	0	Woodbridge (2), Flint, S. G. Goodrich (2), Huntington, Olney, Mitchell, Anonymous (2)
1835–1839	1	6	4	0	6	0	4	0	Mitchell (3), Smiley, S. G. Goodrich (2), Murray-R. C. Smith (2), Bradford, Balbi-Bradford
1840–1844	10[a]	13	2	5	5	1	5	0	S. G. Goodrich (5), S. E. Morse, Olney (2), Dezauche, Woodbridge, R. C. Smith (2), Worcester (2), Murray-Bradford (2)
1845–1849	5	5	0	2	0	2	1	0	Woodbridge (2), S. G. Goodrich, Anonymous, R. C. Smith
1850–1854	4	6	0	3	1	1	1	0	Olney, Mitchell, Anonymous, S. G. Goodrich (3)
1855–1859	1	4	0	1	1	0	1	1	Warren (2), S. G. Goodrich (2)
1860–1864	2[a]	2	2	0	0	0	3	2	Warren (2), Morgan-Colton, McNally, Shaw and Fordyce
1865–1869	2	2	4	0	0	0	3	3	Guyot, Cornell (3), Warren (2)
1870–1874	2	2	4	0	0	0	4	2	Guyot, Cornell (3), Warren (2)
1875–1882	0	1	0	0	0	0	1	0	Warren
Total	30	57	22	18	23	5	27	8	81

SOURCES: Geographies in the Libraries of Clark University, American Antiquarian Society, Old Sturbridge Village.
[a] There were two accounts which named the region but which failed to describe the land either as a desert or in terms of the desert surrogates.

55

graphical writers showed little reluctance to describe the dry western interior as a "desert," likening it to the true sandy deserts of Arabia and the Sahara, and in the 1840's proudly accepting its existence as the "Great American Desert" (Table 2).

It may come as a surprise to find that the Great American Desert as a name and unifying image was strong in the textbooks only in the 1840's and early 1850's. Even in the heyday of the Great American Desert idea—the 1840's—the name appeared in but half of the textbooks (Table 2). Until this general name was adopted by William Woodbridge and gradually accepted by others, geographers who thought the western interior to be a true sandy desert compared it to Old World analogues—the African and Arabian deserts—while those who thought of it as a semidesert or grassy plains likened it to the Steppes of Tartary and Central Asia.[45] This practice stopped abruptly in 1841, presumably as the name Great American Desert became associated with the notion of a true sandy desert in the western interior.

Most surprising, perhaps, is that before 1835 the name Great American Desert appeared in only three geographies, all published and, for the most part, distributed in New England and upstate New York. New York City, the main publishing center in the United States after 1815 and the city with the largest hinterland, published and distributed between 1830 and 1859 only four texts (out of the 19 I have examined) carrying the name Great American Desert.

The publication record suggests, therefore, that the conception of the Great American Desert east of the Rockies was available to those who read advanced geographies in New England and upstate New York in the 1840's and early 1850's. During the same period, the Great American Desert idea was presented to a sizable minority of the well-educated in the seaboard sections of the Northeast, and to a small minority of the educated elite outside the Northeast. After 1856 few advanced texts carried the name to the high school, academy, or secondary educated anywhere in the United States.

If a desert image of the western interior (as distinct from the Great American Desert) had begun to emerge among literate Americans before 1820, it did so only in certain parts of New England through Parish's work (1814).[46] After 1824 the desert idea, insofar as textbooks fashioned an image of the western interior, may be assumed to have spread to those educated in the "higher classes" [47] of schools in New England. But even by 1830 this image may have been restricted almost entirely to New England and upstate New York, for of the 11 English-language geographies[48] published in the United States between 1810 and 1829 which described the western interior as desert, nine were published in New England [49] and distributed in that region and its immediate environs.[50]

More effective cooperation among printers began to occur in the 1830's,[51] and this ensured a wider distribution of New England works carrying the desert image, as witnessed by the example of Woodbridge's work.[52] Furthermore, wider diffusion of the desert idea in the 1830's was ensured by the fact that New York City, Baltimore, and Philadelphia all published their first schoolbooks containing the desert idea between 1832 and 1834.[53] But New England remained the center of dissemination of the desert idea until the middle 1850's, and throughout the period 1830–1859 more than half of the geographies published in New England projected a desert image of at least part of the western interior.

For shorter periods, more than half of the advanced geographies published in New York City and Philadephia were also proclaiming the existence of a desert in the western interior: Philadelphia, 1835–1839,[54] and New York, 1840–1850. These geographies were presumably being read in a majority of the high schools in the regional hinterlands of both cities during these periods and in many of the high schools in their extended hinterlands, which stretched west of the Appalachians and into the Southeast.[55] But it seems unlikely that a majority of high schools in any large part of the trans-Appalachian West would be using a "desert" text until such an image was being conveyed in most of the texts published in New York City, the major supply center of the Middle West.[56] This situation did not exist until the early 1840's, and had ceased to exist by the middle 1850's.

Even if desert texts were present in ever-increasing numbers west of the Appalachians and in the South after 1839, it seems unlikely that advanced geographies projecting a desert image were ever numerous in the frontier states of Illinois, Wisconsin, and Iowa between 1840 and 1850, both because of book transport costs and a presumed limited demand in the pioneer schools.[57] Assuming that information in geographies was assimilated and accepted by all readers, an admittedly doubtful proposition, then the desert image of the western interior was shared by perhaps a majority of the well-educated in the Northeast during the 1840's and 1850's, a large minority of the same group in the eastern Middle West and the Southeast by the 1850's, and a small minority of the better educated in the old northwest after 1850.[58]

But was the desert image of the western interior transmitted to the folk[59]—the farmers and frontiersmen of the interior, who were the region's potential migrants? A preliminary analysis of elementary and intermediate geographies published between 1820 and 1865 reveals that very few carried the desert image.[60] Since few of the folk of the interior had more than an intermediate, or even elementary, education, it is suggested that DeVoto was correct in implying that the common man of the interior, who read his newspapers, did not share the desert image with the well-educated, who had culled the image from the geographies.[61]

IMAGES OF THE WESTERN INTERIOR PROJECTED IN NEWSPAPERS, 1849–1859

The newspapers provide one test of DeVoto's hypothesis. He claimed that the "geographers did not read the newspapers . . . the little home-town weeklies." Had they done so they would have gained a more accurate knowledge of the western interior, a knowledge made available to the common man in the letters and diaries of trappers and plains travelers.[62] A difference between the image of the western interior presented by the newspapers and that presented in the geographies would tend to support the view that the folk and educated elite[63] conceptions of the region did differ substantially.

In the late 1840's and early 1850's people were leaving central Vermont in large numbers for the West.[64] How did the newspapers in this region, remote from the frontier and in the area where the educated elite notion of the desert was strongest, describe the western interior? I have examined 134 issues of newspapers printed in this area, 1849–1851.[65] The words "desert" and "arid plains" were used five times to describe portions of the West, in each case in reference to the Great Basin Country of the Far West.[66] No issue described or named any part of the western interior as a desert. References to the western interior were far fewer than in the papers of St. Louis, for instance, yet "The Plains" was used frequently.[67] No other names or terms descriptive of the western interior were discovered. Numerous newspaper accounts of the overland migration made it clear to Vermonters that those traversing the plains with an estimated 30,000 animals in 1849 had no "apprehensions of serious consequences from a dearth of forage" east to the Rockies, but only on "that part of the route which lies in the mountain passes and the Great Basin." [68] The western interior was portrayed in these accounts as a "grazing field" and reports were soon published of the "grass as fine." [69] To the folk of the Northeast who read their small-town weeklies between 1849 and 1851, the region between the Missouri River and the Rockies was known as "the plains," and it was a grazing region of good grassland; this is what the descriptive term "plains" apparently meant to them.[70]

Missouri probably provided more of the folk crossing and later settling the western interior in the 1840's and 1850's than any other state.[71] The St. Louis newspapers printed many letters from travelers on the plains, reports of military explorers, railroad surveyors, and senators, and they were concerned to provide their readers with information about the western interior. The region was called "The Plains" between 1850 and 1853 in the 51 St. Louis and St. Joseph newspapers I have examined, and no other name was used. In the same papers the countryside was described exclusively as "plains," and it was implied that this descriptive term meant rich, yet short, grasslands.[72] In the newspapers of 1858 and 1859 the region was labeled "The Plains" less frequently than in the early 1850's, yet in these issues descriptive terms were more common, and it was clear that "The Plains" region[73] of the western interior consisted of two types of countryside—tall grass "prairies" in the east,[74] and short or bunch grass "plains" which were primarily characteristic of lands west of Fort Kearny, Nebraska, and the great bend of the Arkansas.[75] In my examination of 83 Missouri newspapers issued in 1850–1859, the word "desert" was never used in reference to the western interior. It was used solely, as in the Vermont papers, to describe the lands west of Salt Lake City, especially the Humboldt Desert.[76]

Graphic confirmation of the conclusion in the folk and western images of the Gold Rush period that there was no desert west of the Missouri and east of the Rockies is afforded in a poster proclaiming

Figure 1. Advertisement for an Exhibition, St. Louis, 1850. (Reprinted by permission of the Missouri Historical Society.)

an exhibition of an "Immense Moving Mirror of the Land Route to California" (Fig. 1).[77] The advertisement extracts the maximum sensationalism from the countryside, yet the western interior is called "The Plains"; there is no recognition of "The Great American Desert," or even a desertlike region. Neither artist, advertiser, nor audience knew of, nor expected, a desert east of the Rockies. The only desert mentioned is "The Sandy Desert" east of the Sierra Nevada.

IMAGES PROJECTED IN LETTERS AND MANUSCRIPT DIARIES, 1843–1854

If the newspaper was the major agent of diffusion of the western image of the plains country, the main sources of newspaper imagery were the letters and abstracted diaries of the plains traveler. In the 1840's, when national attention was on the overland migration to Oregon, and then on the Gold Rush, the volume of these letters from plains travelers increased markedly. By 1849 it had become an established tradition to write letters from "The Plains" with the expectation of their publication locally, and sometimes nationally.

An examination of the letters and manuscript diaries of plains travelers, 1843–1854, in the Missouri Historical Society revealed 37 letters and four diaries that described the western interior.[78] At least half of these appeared in newspapers, mainly in Missouri, and there is every reason to believe that the conceptions of the western interior they conveyed were both representative and shared by their readers. In the 1840's the region was named "The Plains," and described equally as "plains" and as "prairies." Use of "prairies" increased markedly in the late 1840's, particularly in descriptions of the area around and east of Fort Kearny on the Platte.[79] In the 1850's "The Plains" was still the exclusive regional name. But by contrast with the 1840's, the term "plains" was used infrequently to describe the land, on all occasions west of the one hundredth meridian, whereas "prairies" was used very frequently, on all but two occasions describing land east of the one hundredth meridian. In no letter or diary in this manuscript collection, 1825–1869, was the word "desert" used as a descriptive term or name in the plains country east of Fort Laramie and Santa Fe, whereas descriptions of grass and grasslands were too numerous to count.

These facts simply add precision and detail to the findings derived from the St. Louis newspapers, and confirm their wider application in the western states: "The Plains" region was conceived as grassland suitable for grazing up to the early 1840's,[80] but by the middle 1840's large parts of "The Plains" were being described as "prairies." Gold Rush travelers confirmed that prairies extended to at least the one hundredth meridian (and sometimes beyond); in the early 1850's at the latest these prairies were being described as good agricultural land. These images were clear in Missouri, less clear and somewhat delayed in formation in Vermont. In neither state is there evidence of a desert east of the Rockies in the popular image of the plains country in the 1840's and 1850's.

IMAGES OF THE WESTERN INTERIOR PROJECTED IN ACCOUNTS OF TRAVELERS AND EXPLORERS

The accounts of travelers and explorers in the western interior present additional proof of this assertion and confirm that the desert image was primarily an elite notion of the higher school and college educated in the Northeast. If a notion of a Great American Desert east of the Rockies existed in the minds of the American public, we should expect travelers and explorers to be looking for signs of it when they moved across the ninety-eighth meridian, if only to affirm or refute the desert's existence. If people believed in a desert they should certainly have been prepared to use that word in describing the country, for there were long sandy stretches on both the Santa Fe and Oregon trails.

An analysis of the accounts of 104 individuals who crossed, or traveled in, the western interior, 1821–1870, reveals that only nine out of 104 mention "The Great American Desert." [81] Those who used the name were well-educated, and all but two—John Beadle and Josiah Gregg[82]—were born, bred, and educated in New England or upstate New York. Thomas Farnham, J. Henry Carleton, and Francis Parkman[83] were in their twenties and thirties when they traveled in the western interior between 1839 and 1846.[84] Albert Richardson, Horace Greeley, and Samuel Bowles[85] were all prominent newspapermen in their thirties and forties when they described the region as the Great American Desert after 1859.[86] All but Gregg had had their schooling when the desert idea was being presented in the advanced geographies of New England and New York.

Of the 18 individuals who wrote of a desert, 17 were well-educated: 12 from the Northeast, two each from Europe and the West, and one from the South[87] (Table 3). The other desert description was

TABLE 3   *Proportion of Accounts by Plains Travelers Describing the Western Interior as Desert, 1821–1870 (by region of traveler's origin and education)*

PLACE OF BIRTH AND EDUCATION	YEAR OF TRAVEL IN THE WESTERN INTERIOR			
	1821–1830	1840–1855	1856–1870	1821–1870
New England	2– 5	3– 5	4– 4	9– 14
New York, New Jersey, Pennsylvania	1– 2	0– 4	2– 3	3– 9
Europe	0– 2	0– 4	2– 3	2– 9
South	0– 0	1– 8	0– 0	1– 8
West	1– 7	1–13	0– 1	2– 21
Transplanted West[a]	0– 5	0– 3	0– 1	0– 9
Unknown Origin	0– 3	1–17	0–14	1– 34
Total	4–24	6–54	7–26	18–104

[a] Persons resident in the West more than ten years but born and educated in the early years in the South or the Northeast.

made by one of 34 individuals whose places of birth and education were unknown. The majority of these were Gold Rush travelers, apparently without higher school education, and mainly westerners. In sum, of 73 plains travelers probably from the South and West, only four (1 in 18) described any part of the western interior as desert. Out of approximately 70 accounts of individuals who were higher school or college educated, 17 (1 in 4) described or named a desert, but only 1 in 30 of the others did so.[88]

An equally low incidence of desert references in the diaries of well-educated plains travelers has been detected by others. Jackson has examined more than 160 diaries of Mormons who crossed the Plains between 1846 and 1855.[89] The Mormon elders mentioned no desert east of the Rockies either in their deliberations about the gathering to the Great Basin or in their journals. None of the rank and file Mormons mentioned a Great American Desert, and only three used the word desert to describe a section of the land east of the Rockies. Merlin Lawson has examined 31 diaries of travelers on the Oregon and Santa Fe trails in 1849.[90] Two mentioned the Great American Desert as a proper name for a region they passed but never entered; no others mentioned the word desert.

In his diaries and letters, the common man of the Mississippi Valley traveling to Oregon and California expressed no surprise in finding the western interior a grassland region of plains and prairies. In the succinct letters sent back to the East from the Missouri ports, Fort Childs (Kearny), and Fort Laramie, the western interior as a whole was characterized as "Plains," occasionally as "Prairies," never as "The Desert." Yet in the detailed daily descriptions of the diaries, references to "prairies" are more than twice as numerous as references to "plains," and at least a hundred times as numerous as references to "deserts." Some used the terms "prairies" and "plains" to describe the same landscape (particularly up to the mid-1840's), implying that a plain was level land, a prairie was grassland, and the western interior as a whole was a prairie-plains region. But most travelers (particularly after 1845) used "prairie" primarily to describe the first 200–250 miles of their journey, before reaching Fort Kearny on the Oregon Trail and the Arkansas River on the Santa Fe Trail. To these people, plains became much more frequent west of the one hundredth meridian, and the term "plains" meant short grass country without trees, as well as level land, in apparent contrast to the rolling tall grass country with wooded bottomland which was "prairie."

In sum, by the early 1850's the western interior was seen as different regions by the well-educated and the elite in the Northeast and by the well-educated in the West and the common man everywhere. The sterile wastes of the former's desert east of the Rockies were short grass plains to the latter; the eastern short grass plains, fit at most for grazing in the eyes of the elite, were rolling tall grass prairies with wooded water courses to the men of the western frontier and to the folk throughout the country. Did the prairie image of the eastern section of "The Plains" among the folk of the Mississippi Valley between 1840 and 1870 act as a psychological barrier in the same way that the desert image was assumed to have done? The answer obviously lies in the changing evaluation and utilization of prairies by the settlers and farmers of the upper Mississippi Valley, particularly in Illinois, Missouri, and Iowa. If the upland prairies were regarded as infertile and uncultivable throughout this period, then the incentive to migrate westward must have been negligible.

Douglas McManis in Illinois and Brown in Ohio[91] have found no contemporary evidence that prairies were regarded by the frontiersman of the period 1800–1840 as infertile and uncultivable because of their treelessness. This notion, accepted by some students of the frontier,[92] seems to have been derived from latter-day reminiscences glorifying the achievements of the pioneers.[93] In the 1830's and 1840's the Illinois prairies were regarded by many contemporaries as less fertile than the wooded bottomlands,[94] but this notion, and the delay in their utilization, stemmed primarily from practical problems of sodbreaking and the absence of water and timber.[95] McManis and others have implied that there were fives stages in the utilization of the prairies in Illinois, each representing slight changes in the practical appraisal of the prairie environment for farming by the region that would provide the migrants for the western interior: (1) avoidance of the prairie habitat, before 1815 throughout Illinois, and appreciably later in the North;[96] (2) initial utilization of the prairie for grazing by farmers settled in the wooded bottomland, after 1815, particularly in the Southeast;[97] (3) marginal settlement with land in woodland and prairie, and cultivation of both; (4) settlement on the open upland prairie, yet fractional wood and water holdings in the wooded bottomlands; (5) straightforward settlement and farming of the upland prairie. Stage three began in some areas of southern Illinois by 1820 and was widespread by the late 1820's and early 1830's, particularly among the Yankees and foreign pioneers in the eastern and central prairies; it spread appreciably later to northern Illinois.[98] By the early 1830's, therefore, the cultivability and fertility of the prairies were widely acknowledged among the pioneers in the upper Mississippi Valley. Stage four was common in the late 1830's and 1840's, and revealed a positive appraisal of the prairie for farming purposes, qualified only by practical considerations of the lack of capital for sodbreaking, well-

drilling, windmills, and wood for fence materials and fuel.[99] The fifth
stage of utilization got underway in the 1840's and was in full sway by
the mid-1850's throughout Illinois, signifying agreement among a majority of the Illinois farmers of the prime value of prairie for general
farming and a growing realization that upland prairie was suitable
for all types of grain farming.[100]

As the eastern "plains" were conceived as prairies in the Mississippi Valley by the mid-1840's, as we have shown, the phases in the
appraisal of their value for farming must have closely paralleled the
changing evaluation of the upland prairies of Illinois. If this parallel
is correct, any barrier to migration west of the Missouri presented by
a prairie image of the western interior was breaking down in the
1840's, and had practically disappeared by the late 1850's.

EVALUATION OF THE EASTERN PLAINS
BY THE ORIGINAL LAND SURVEYORS,
1855–1857

Some support for the contention that the trans-Missouri prairies
were regarded by many as good agricultural land in the early 1850's
has been found in newspapers, letters of plains travelers, and diaries,[101] but this evidence is occasional and at best equivocal. However,
comprehensive and unequivocal evidence of the perceived cultivability
and farming potential of the prairies of the eastern "Plains" in the
1850's is provided in the field notes of the surveyors of the Original
Land Survey. Following the passage of the Kansas-Nebraska Act, the
U.S. Land Office let out survey contracts to a large number of crews
drawn from the interior. Each surveyor provided descriptions of the
land, and most appraised it. Their assessment of the value of prairies
and bottomlands reflected their experience further east, and may be
assumed to have corresponded closely to current popular evaluations
in the interior.

A representative area is Jefferson County, Nebraska, which lies
on the Kansas-Nebraska border and is located 80 miles west of the
Missouri River. Seven different surveyors appraised the area between
1855 and 1857, each making separate reports.[102] All seven agreed in
describing the area as hilly to rolling prairie with wooded bottomland

(the popular frontier image of the eastern plains). The majority view of the surveyors was that these eastern plains were cultivable and suited to general farming, although some surveyors were still skeptical.[103] It should be emphasized that in only one township were the field notes of a surveyor highly positive about the farming potential of the land.[104] All other favorable appraisals were qualified: "Good second rate farming land," "only useful as a medium agricultural district," "general farming purposes," "good farming lands," "half of the township is good for agricultural or graising [sic]." [105]

The rolling prairies of Jefferson County and the eastern plains were not yet regarded as suited to "the growing of grains and fruits of all kinds" as they were by the early 1870's.[106] But the image of the prairies of the eastern plains as cultivable and suited to general farming was certainly no barrier to most pioneers in the 1850's, for this was the conception of Iowa held by the settlers who flooded into that territory from Illinois and points east during the 1840's and early 1850's.

CONCLUSION

In the nineteenth century the dominant image of the West was as the Garden of the World.[107] As the frontier pressed inexorably westward, crossing the Mississippi River, however, "the myth of the garden had to confront and overcome another myth of exactly opposed meaning, although of inferior strength—the myth of the Great American Desert." "The pressures for expansion . . . were certain to give rise eventually to an effort to occupy the plains," wrote Henry Nash Smith. "Such an undertaking would demand a revision of the forbidding image of an American Sahara." [108] No such revision was necessary among the folk of the frontier east of the Missouri, for they had never conceived of the western interior as an American Sahara, a Great American Desert, or even as a desert. When the frontiersmen moved across the Missouri in the 1860's they found what they had expected for more than a decade: cultivable prairies.

Some revision of the desert image among some of the educated elite, particularly in the east, may still have been necessary in the 1860's, but it is erroneous to assume, as Smith and others do, that it was the act of settlement in the valleys of the Platte and Kansas rivers that destroyed the myth of the desert.[109] Insofar as it existed in the minds of the educated elite, the desert had retreated far to the west of the frontier by the middle 1850's, as a consequence of both the positive redefinition of the West in the light of eastern needs which had taken place in the fifties,[110] and of the vast number of accounts of the area east of the Platte forks made available since 1848. The last vestiges of this elite desert were destroyed in the middle 1870's by western "scientists" and the railroad propaganda they fueled.

As a corollary of the destruction of the last remnants of the "elite desert," if such still existed, there was born the legend of the Great American Desert as the popular American image of the western interior before the Civil War. The promoters of the 1870's needed a Great American Desert west of the Missouri, 1830–1870, for they could then show that the dauntless settlers who had pushed 250 miles west of the Missouri had either proven the desert to be a misconception by the very success of their farms, or had changed the climate and transformed the desert by simply plowing the land, planting trees, and heeding the will of the Beneficent Creator.[111] In this manner an ex post facto folk desert was created, possibly unconsciously.[112]

In this reinterpretation of the history of the desert myth, Smith's popular Great American Desert that confronts the Garden myth becomes a "straw" desert, written into the history of the folk encounter with the plains environment. By the 1890's popular works on the American West, such as that "graphically and truthfully described by William M. Thayer," [113] were reconstructing the extent of a vast Great American Desert that had been conquered by the settlers. Reminiscing pioneers were soon recalling that the lands beyond the Missouri were part of the Great American Desert,[114] neglecting to mention that this "fact" had been learned quite recently. The legend was becoming history, and became so with Paxson, Morris, and, above all, Webb.

It has been stated that politicians in the early nineteenth century saw cultivation of the desert image of the western interior as a means of discouraging rapid extension of the frontier.[115] Others have assumed that this purpose was effected by the popular image of the western interior as a desert, whether or not this image had been cultivated by the government.[116] No such negative image of the trans-Missouri West, however, was transmitted to the folk who were the region's potential settlers. Before 1850, only in New England and New York might the negative image of the elite have spread to the folk level, and that seems unlikely. Otherwise the desert image was restricted, before 1850, to the well-educated, perhaps a majority in the Northeast, and a declining minority farther to the west. After the 1850's an image of the western part of the western interior as a desert may have lingered for a decade or so among some of the well-educated. But this desert was less than 300 miles wide and began west of the forks of the Platte in far western Nebraska, much too far west of the frontier to have been a psychological barrier to westward movement.

The pause in the westward movement in the midnineteenth century was not the effect of a western desert, for the legend of the Great American Desert as either the frontier or the popular American image of the western interior before the Civil War is itself a myth.

FOOTNOTES

1. John Kirtland Wright, "Where History and Geography Meet," *Proceedings of the Eighth American Scientific Congress*, XI (1943), 20, reprinted in Wright, *Human Nature in Geography* (Cambridge, 1966), 28.

2. Walter Prescott Webb, *The Great Plains* (Boston, 1931), 152. Others who shared this opinion were Frederic L. Paxson, *The Last American Frontier* (New York, 1922), 11–12; Ralph C. Morris, "The Notion of a Great American Desert East of the Rockies," *Mississippi Valley Historical Review*, XIII (1926–27), 190–200; James C. Malin, *The Grassland of North America* (Lawrence, Kansas, 1947), 173–176; Robert E. Riegel, *America Moves West* (3rd ed.; New York, 1956), 304–305; LeRoy R. Hafen, W. Eugene Hollon, and Carl Coke Rister, *Western America* (3rd ed.; New York, 1970), 138; Ray Allen Billington, *Westward Expansion* (2nd ed.; New York, 1960), 413, 470; Henry Nash Smith, *Virgin Land: The American West as Symbol and Myth* (New York, 1950), 202–205; Richard H. Dillon, "Stephen Long's Great American Desert," *Proceedings of the American Philosophical Society*, CXI (1967), 93 f; John A. Hawgood, *America's Western Frontiers* (New York, 1967), 90; W. Eugene Hollon, *The Southwest: Old and New* (New York, 1961), 315–316; Mary Wilma M. Hargreaves, *Dry Farming in the Northern Great Plains, 1900–1925* (Cambridge, 1957), 25–26; Addison E. Sheldon, *Land Systems and Land Policies in Nebraska* (Lincoln, 1936), 169; Joe B. Frantz and Julian E. Choate, Jr., *The American Cowboy: The Myth and The Reality* (Norman, 1955), 17–18.

3. Paxson, *Last Frontier*, 11–12, 119, 137; Billington, *Westward Expansion*, 453, 471, 481; Ray Allen Billington, *The Far Western Frontier, 1830–1860* (New York, 1956), 22; Hawgood, *America's Western Frontier*, 90, 310, 340; Reigel, *America Moves West*, 304; Hollon, *Southwest*, 102, 316; W. Eugene Hollon, *The Great American Desert* (New York, 1966), 131; Hargreaves, *Dry Farming*, 26–30; Frantz and Choate, *American Cowboy*, 10; Henry Cowles Hart, *The Dark Missouri* (Madison, 1957), 31; Walter Prescott Webb, "The Great Plains and the Industrial Revolu-

tion," in James F. Willard and Colin B. Goodykoontz (eds.), *The Trans-Mississippi West* (Boulder, 1930), 313–314.

4. Ralph Hall Brown, *Historical Geography of the United States* (New York, 1948), iii, 370–372.

5. Billington, *The Far Western Frontier, 1830–1860*, 22.

6. Frederic L. Paxson, *History of the American Frontier, 1763–1893* (Boston, 1924), 332.

7. E. Douglas Branch, *Westward: The Romance of the American Frontier* (New York, 1930), 309.

8. Bernard DeVoto, *Across the Wide Missouri* (Boston, 1947), 3–5.

9. James C. Malin, "Soil, Animal and Plant Relations of the Grassland, Historically Reconsidered," *Scientific Monthly*, LXXVI (April 1953), 210, reprinted in Malin, *The Grassland of North America . . . With Addenda* (Lawrence, 1956), 442–443.

10. G. Malcolm Lewis, "Regional Ideas and Reality in the Cis-Rocky Mountain West," *Transactions, Institute of British Geographers*, XXXVIII (1966), 135–150; "Changing Emphases in the Description of the American Great Plains Area," *Transactions, Institute of British Geographers*, XXX (1962), 75–80.

11. G. Malcolm Lewis, "William Gilpin and the Concept of the Great Plains Region," *Annals, Association of American Geographers*, LVI (1966), 33–51; Lewis, "Changing Emphases," 76–80; "The Great Plains Region and its Image of Flatness," *Journal of the West*, VI (1967), 14–21.

12. Lewis, "Changing Emphases," 77.

13. Richard Irving Dodge, *The Hunting Grounds of the Great West* (London, 1877), 3; Randall Henry Hewitt, *Across the Plains and Over the Divide* (New York, 1906), 101; Lieut. J. Henry Carleton, *The Prairie Logbooks 1844–5*, L. Pelzer (ed.) (Chicago, 1943), 181. Carleton's is the only contemporary account of the association, and the passage suggests skepticism: "The progress of the company of emigrants across what the geographies denominate as 'The Great American Desert' is one of exceeding interest."

14. Paxson, *Last American Frontier*, 11.

15. Riegel, *America Moves West*, 304, 564; see also Hafen, Hollon, and Rister, *Western America*, 138; Hargreaves, *Dry Farming*, 26; Frantz and Choate, *American Cowboy*, 18; Hollon, *The Southwest*, 315–316; Billington, *Westward Expansion*, 413; Randall Parrish, *The Great Plains* (Chicago, 1907), 296, 299.

16. Webb, *Great Plains*, 152–160.

17. I found as a general rule that few texts with less than 120 words describing the western interior ever mentioned a desert, and that a total of 100 words seemed to be the absolute threshold for the presence of the desert idea. "Western interior" was assumed to include the present-day Dakotas, Kansas, Nebraska, Oklahoma, western Texas, and those sections of New Mexico, Colorado, Wyoming, and Montana east of the Rockies.

18. Frederick Butler, *The Elements of Geography and History Combined* (Wethersfield, Conn., 1825), 130–132.

19. Zebulon Pike, *The Expeditions of Zebulon Montgomery Pike*, Elliot Coues (ed.), 3 vol. (New York, 1895).

20. The first four printings of Parish's text included no reference to a desert, but the fifth printing under the heading "Desert" records that "Between the great rivers, Missouri and Rio Bravo, vast sandy deserts present a dismal prospect; not a tree, nor shrub relieves the eye; the salt in the soil forbids vegetation, as in the Tehama of Arabia, and renders the wilds of Louisiana, as cheerless and forlorn,

as the deserts of Tartary or Africa." In a footnote Parish attributes this description to Captain Pike. Elijah Parish, *A New System of Modern Geography* (Newburyport, Mass., 1814), 133. Parish's book has endorsements from Dummer Academy; Newburyport; Williams College; Dartmouth College; Bowdoin College; Salem; Phillips Exeter Academy, New Hampshire; Middlebury College, Vermont. The named bookstores in which the geography was sold were in Boston and Newburyport, Massachusetts, and Portland, Maine. Its distribution was apparently limited to the elite of central New England. It had no apparent successors.

21. The text of the seventh edition of Jedidiah Morse, *The American Universal Geography* (Charlestown, Mass., 1819), 648–649, alludes to conditions in Missouri Territory approaching those of a desert, but does not use the word "desert" or a desert surrogate. The citation is to Brackenridge, not Pike. Morse was a close friend of Parish, and shared Parish's anti-Jefferson, antiexpansionist sentiments (information supplied by Dr. W. A. Koelsch, Clark University, June 1969). Both Parish and Morse would have been extremely receptive to the discovery of a desert in Louisiana Territory.

22. Edwin James, *Account of an Expedition from Pittsburgh to the Rocky Mountains Performed in the Years 1819 and 1820* (Philadelphia, 1823).

23. Of the maps published 1804–1869 and reprinted in Carl I. Wheat, *Mapping the Trans-Mississippi West*, Vol. 2–5 (San Francisco, 1958–1963), 132 present large parts, or all, of the western interior. By my count, four mention the word desert—Long (1823), Steele (1849), Magnus (1851), and a British Railroad Survey (1868). Between 1830 and 1855, two maps showed a desert, 71 did not; and between 1856 and 1869, one map showed a desert, 41 did not. In C.O. Paullin's *Atlas of the Historical Geography of the United States*, John K. Wright (ed.) (New York, 1932), "ten maps were selected to illustrate the development of cartography of the western United States bearing dates from 1804 to 1867. Only two of these used the 'Desert' label" (Malin, *Soil, Animal, and Plant Relations*, 210). The maps were those of Chapin (1839) and Smith (1843).

24. G. Malcolm Lewis, "Three Centuries of Desert Concepts in the Cis-Rocky Mountain West," *Journal of the West*, IV (1965), 457–468; Webb, *Great Plains*, 153.

25. The desert image of the Western Interior was a minority view among all the groups—Spanish, French, British, American—who had approached the region before 1800. John Logan Allen, *Geographical Conceptions of the Trans-Missouri West 1673–1806: An Historical Geosophy* (unpub. Ph.D. Dissertation, Clark University, 1969), 21–217; Dorothy Ann Dondore, *The Prairie and the Making of Middle America: Four Centuries of Description* (Cedar Rapids, Iowa, 1926), 37–40.

26. The favorable American view of the western interior conveyed in the texts is clear in other sources also; see Allen, *Geographical Conceptions*, 229–256.

27. Elijah Parish, *A New System of Modern Geography* (Newburyport, Mass., 1807).

28. LePage du Pratz, *Histoire de la Louisiane* (Paris, 1758; first English ed., London, 1763); Louis Hennepin, *Description de la Louisiane* (Paris, 1683), and *Nouvelle Découverte d'un très Grand Pays situé dans l'Amerique* (Utrecht, 1697). These authors were cited most frequently in the geographies of the time. Others who may have had some influence were Lahontan, Carver, Rogers, Mackenzie, Coxe, Bossu and Charlevoix; see Allen, *Geographical Conceptions*, 30, 43, 66, 70, 92, 114–117, 129.

29. Thomas Jefferson, "Official Account of Louisiana," *American State Papers*, XX ("Miscellaneous," I, Doc. 164, 8th Congress, 1st Session), 346–347. Jefferson's Account was based on many sources (Allen, *Geographical Conceptions*, 285–361).

30. Allen, *Geographical Conceptions,* 463–597, particularly 596–597 and 671–672.

31. John K. Wright, "Some British 'Grandfathers' of American Geography," in R. Miller and J. W. Watson (eds.), *Geographical Essays in Memory of Alan G. Ogilvie* (London, 1959), 146, has pointed out that the later editions of Morse's *The American Universal Geography* (after 1805), of which *Geography Made Easy* was an abridged version for high school children, were due more largely to Morse's sons and other collaborators than to Morse himself. The new abridgement was made in the thirteenth edition of *Geography Made Easy* in 1809.

32. Jedidiah Morse, *Geography Made Easy* (Boston, 1814), 216. This qualified favorable view of the western interior was represented between 1809 and 1820, but was replaced in the twenty-second ed. (1820 or 1821) by a view much less favorable, yet rather vague.

33. Nathaniel Dwight, *A Short But Comprehensive System of the Geography of the World . . . ,* (2nd Northampton ed.; Northampton, Mass., 1805), 193. Compare this view with the sixth Massachusetts ed., Boston, 1801, 194.

34. There were probably other reasons for the uncertainty of appraisal after 1810, notably the publication of a number of works of Plains travelers. For example, Henry M. Brackenridge, *Journal of a Journey up the River Missouri Performed in 1811* (Baltimore, 1816); Pike, *Expeditions;* Nicholas Biddle (ed.), *History of the Expedition Under the Command of Captains Lewis and Clark* (Philadelphia, 1814).

35. See, for example, two works that ran to many editions—Daniel Adams, *Geography: Or a Description of the World* (Boston, 1814), and Jacob Abbott Cummings, *An Introduction to Ancient and Modern Geography* (Boston, 1813).

36. John Melish, *Geographical Description of the United States* (Philadelphia, 1822), 413. Melish's book, which was not a school text, cited "Major Long" as the authority for the statement that "The central part of the district [Missouri Territory] is a great desert, frequented by roving bands of Indians, who have no fixed place of residence."

37. Joseph Emerson Worcester, *Elements of Geography, Ancient and Modern,* 2nd ed. (Boston, 1822), 88 (first published 1818). Worcester does not use the word desert, but the desert idea is conveyed in a description of Missouri Territory.

38. Worcester, *Elements of Geography* (Boston, 1824), 81. "The central and western parts" of Missouri Territory are "for the most part destitute of timber and of vegetation." The word desert did not appear in Worcester's texts which I have examined until 1829 (2nd ed.). Worcester, *Elements of Geography* (Boston, 1829), 77.

39. William Channing Woodbridge, *A System of Universal Geography* (Hartford, 1824), 25–28, 77–79, 266. "At a distance of from 50 to 100 miles, west of the Mississippi, a region of plains and prairies commences, which extends with little interruption, to the foot of the Rocky, or Chippewan Mountains," Woodbridge writes at one point (p. 25). But this statement is contradicted on p. 27, revealing his revision of the image of the western interior: "In North America, between the Platte River, and the head waters of the Colorado and Sabine River, there is an extensive desert tract, which has been called the Great American Desert; stretching from the Ozark Mountains to the Chippewan . . . with an average width of 500 or 600 miles."

40. G. Malcolm Lewis, "Early American Explorations and the Cis-Rocky Mountain Desert, 1803–1823," *Great Plains Journal,* V (1965), 1–11. The atlas of wide appeal was Henry C. Carey and Isaac Lea, *A Complete Historical, Chronologi-*

cal and Geographical American Atlas (Philadelphia, 1822); Wheat, *Mapping the Transmississippi West,* Vol. 2, 80–81.

41. In the texts of J. Olney, R. C. Smith, S. G. Goodrich, J. E. Worcester, W. C. Woodbridge, N. Huntington, and Hugh Murray, the desert image was dominant between 1824 and 1855. The prairie-plains image was dominant in those of S. A. Mitchell, C. A. Goodrich, N. Hale, C. Clute, R. Phillips, and J. L. Blake. Blake's text was one of the notable exceptions to the view of the prairies and plains as of low fertility. John Lauris Blake, *American Universal Geography for Schools and Academies* (Baltimore, 1831), 63–65.

42. Lewis, "Regional Ideas," 135–138; Reigel, *America Moves West,* 305; Hollon, *Great American Desert,* 69; and Paxson, *Last American Frontier,* 119.

43. Webb, *The Great Plains,* 159; Brown, *Historical Geography,* 307; Dillon, "Stephen Long's Great American Desert," 101–107.

44. The one exception to this generalization that I have encountered is D. M. Warren, *The Common-School Geography* (New England ed.; Philadelphia, 1880), 46, which describes the area east of the Rockies as a "desert plateau." Few changes were made in this text between 1850 and 1880.

45. The analogy to the steppes of Tartary had dropped out of the texts by 1839, but the Steppes of Central Asia remained as an analogue into the middle 1840's.

46. Parish, *A New System of Modern Geography.*

47. Woodbridge's *System of Universal Geography* was "for the use of Higher Classes in Schools" and Worcester's *Elements of Geography* was for "respectable schools, academies, and seminaries."

48. I have discovered four French-language geographies, published in New Orleans in 1828, 1841, 1845, and 1850. All carried the desert image and were for use in "Collège et Écoles de la Louisiane."

49. Neither of the geographies published outside New England were school books. Both were specialized works on the United States: Melish, *Geographical Description of the United States,* and Timothy Flint, *A Condensed Geography and History of the Western States or the Mississippi Valley* (Cincinnati, 1828). Flint was a transplanted New Englander who attributes his desert conception to S. H. Long.

50. Nietz has made it clear that easy mailing and shipping facilities for textbooks were not available in the early nineteenth century. In most cases textbook publishers had to await "the more common use of steamboats and the railroads for mailing and shipping the books." Until this time book sales "apparently were still largely local or regional." A few printers began to form partnerships to publish books after 1800, their object being to extend the sales to a wider market, but there were only a few publishing companies serving a large part of the country before 1850. John A. Nietz, *The Evolution of American Secondary School Textbooks* (Rutland, Vt., 1966), 7–8. Confirmation of this is found in the lists of authorized booksellers appended to many of the works published between 1820 and 1835. For example, Woodbridge's *Universal Geography* of 1824, which carried the desert idea and was published in Hartford, Conn., had 16 outlets in seven states: 12 in New England and New York, two in Pennsylvania, and two outside the Northeast.

51. Nietz, *American Secondary School Textbooks.*

52. William C. Woodbridge, *A System of Universal Geography* (5th ed.; Hartford, 1833). This work ("for higher classes in schools and private libraries") had 29 outlets in 14 states. Two-thirds of these were in New England and New

York, and there were two each in Philadelphia and Baltimore, but there were now three outlets in the Southeast (Richmond, Charleston, and Augusta), and three in the trans-Appalachian West (Pittsburgh, Louisville, and Cincinnati).

53. See Table 2 in Martyn J. Bowden, "The Perception of the Western Interior of the United States, 1800–1870, A Problem in Historical Geosophy," *Proceedings, Association of American Geographers,* I (1969), 20.

54. The emergence of Philadelphia as a center for the dissemination of the desert image results from the adoption of the desert image in certain of Samuel A. Mitchell's books, and in the American editions of Hugh Murray's *The Encyclopedia of Geography.* The latter was published by Carey, Lea, and Blanchard, who had published Edwin James' *Account* (1823) and the first atlas bearing the name "The Great Desert." The desert references were in sections of the text written by Americans—Thomas G. Bradford and "Professor Rogers of the University of Pennsylvania."

55. British texts, sometimes reprinted in the United States (usually in Philadelphia), appear to have had a wide circulation in the South, at least in the years during which booksellers' names were appended to geographies (i.e., 1800–1835): William Guthrie, *A Universal Geography* (Philadelphia, 1820); Sir Richard Phillips, *An Easy Grammar of Geography* (Philadelphia, 1820); and John Pinkerton, *Modern Geography* (Philadelphia, 1804), all had more named booksellers in the South than in the North and West. None of these projected a desert image.

56. According to Nietz, *American Secondary School Textbooks,* New York City gradually became the leading printing center "after about 1815," and had become so by 1850. New York City's hinterland was the most national of all cities on the eastern seaboard after 1825.

57. Ray Allen Billington, *America's Frontier Heritage* (New York, 1966), 88–89, produced impressive evidence of low levels of school attendance in frontier states in 1840—one-twenty-third in Missouri, compared with one-sixth in Massachusetts, New York, and Pennsylvania.

58. There is no doubt that there were well-educated persons in frontier areas, and that these people had impressive libraries, but they were a very small minority: Billington, *America's Frontier Heritage,* 75–94; John Francis McDermott, "Frontier Re-examined," in J. F. McDermott (ed.), *The Frontier Re-Examined* (Urbana, 1967), 1–11.

59. The folk are assumed to be the rank and file frontiersmen, settlers, and farmers (particularly the small-to-medium propertied) of the interior. Among this group a "higher school" education was probably rare, and the main sources of information were oral and the newspaper.

60. Analysis of 194 of the geography textbooks that failed to meet the 120 word standard (note 17) shows that five carried the desert image.

61. DeVoto, *Across the Wide Missouri,* 3–5.

62. *Ibid.*

63. The educated elite are assumed to be highly literate persons educated in academies, high schools, and colleges, and who may be in important educational or political decision-making positions. They rely primarily on books for information.

64. Harold Fisher Wilson, *The Hill Country of Northern New England: Its Social and Economic History 1790–1930* (New York, 1936), 48–66, particularly the maps on p. 49 showing population trends by township 1830–1870. Central Vermont reached a peak of emigration 1840–1860, interior New Hampshire a little earlier.

65. The 134 issues consisted of: *Vermont Chronicle* (Windsor), 51 (1849); 25 (1850); 25 (1851); *Vermont Watchman and State Journal* (Montpelier), 27 (1849); and *Burlington Free Press*, 6 (1851).

66. *Vermont Chronicle* (Windsor), May 16, 1849, 2; August 22, 1849, 4; October 24, 1849, 3.

67. "The Plains" was used ten times as the name of the region, and the land was described as "the plains" five times and "ocean plains" once. Two papers reprinted an article drawn from the *Lexington [Missouri] Express*, May 1, 1849, which twice describes the western interior as "the plains" (*Vermont Chronicle*, June 6, 1849, 3, and *Vermont Watchman and State Journal*, May 24, 1849, 2). Similarly, a letter from St. Joseph, Missouri (dated May 18), naming the western interior "The Plains" was found in two newspapers: *Vermont Chronicle*, June 27, 1849, and *Vermont Watchman and State Journal*, June 14, 1849, 3. These examples alone serve to explain why the folk image of the western interior was a shared image, primarily of western origin, which was diffused via newspaper articles and letters first printed close to the western frontier. By contrast, the desert image, transmitted via advanced school texts and school atlases, diffused slowly and was found only in some regions.

68. *Vermont Chronicle*, May 16, 1849, 3.

69. *Vermont Chronicle*, June 27, 1849, 3; May 16, 1849, 3; *Vermont Watchman and State Journal*, May 24, 1849, 2.

70. It is possible that large portions of the western interior were thought of as rich agricultural land even in Vermont in 1849. An article in the *Vermont Chronicle*, April 18, 1849, 1, includes this passage: "That Minesota [sic] and Nebraska must in half a century be populous and powerful states no man doubts." Wilson cites much evidence for a favorable agricultural image of the "Midwest, and later the trans-Missouri territory" in the Vermont newspapers of 1849 and the early 1850's (Wilson, *Hill Country*, 56–64).

71. For confirmation of this conclusion see *Vermont Chronicle*, May 7, 1850, 2; *St. Louis Weekly Missouri Republican*, December 24, 1852, 3; February 11, 1853, 2; *List of Emigrants to Oregon, 1843*, in Oregon Envelope, ms., Missouri Historical Society; also Billington, *Westward Expansion*, 466–469, 474–476.

72. *St. Louis Daily Missouri Republican*, January 1, 1850, 2; February 6, 1850, 2; *St. Louis Weekly Missouri Republican*, February 11, 1853, 2; June 6, 1853, 3.

73. A letter from Nebraska Territory dated August 22, 1858, and printed in the *St. Louis Daily Missouri Republican*, September 1, 1858, 1, found that "The Plains are alive with men, teams, and business," and went on to describe the land as very fertile, with abundant timber. The letter pointed that fair crops of corn were being harvested on the Platte. A similar point had been made earlier concerning "the fine agricultural country back of Kansas" in a long and well-balanced letter (to which an editorial drew the readers' attention) in the *St. Louis Weekly Missouri Republican*, February 11, 1853, 2. For similarly favorable statements concerning rich lands in the eastern "Plains," see also the *St. Louis Central Christian Advocate*, July 14, 1858, 1; and *St. Louis Weekly Missouri Republican*, September 2, 1853, 1. Hart, *Dark Missouri*, 36, among others, has shown that to the people of the West, "Plains seemed to include prairies."

74. A long article entitled "A Trip to Nebraska" (*St. Louis Daily Missouri Republican*, November 11, 1858, 1) describes southeastern Nebraska as a land of "broad prairies," "high prairie land," with "prairie bottoms" having grass six to eight feet high. In the same year another correspondent described the "Plains"

west of the Cross Timbers as "fine undulating prairies covered with rich prairie and bunch grass . . . very good grazing" (*St. Louis Daily Missouri Republican*, September 11, 1858, 2). Other issues that describe "prairies" within "The Plains" region can be found in the *St. Louis Daily Missouri Republican*, April 19, 1859, 2; September 12, 1859, 1; and September 1, 1858, 1.

75. The association between "plains" and short grass for grazing is illustrated in two articles that imply that the plains areas on the South Platte, on the Central Platte, and in the area west of Council Grove on the Santa Fe Trail, are poor to moderate grazing lands (*St. Louis Daily Missouri Republican*, September 1, 1858, 1; September 8, 1858, 2).

76. For references to deserts in the Far West, see *St. Louis Sunday Missouri Republican*, January 6, 1850, 2; November 17, 1850, 2; *St. Louis Weekly Missouri Republican*, February 11, 1853, 2.

77. *Immense Moving Mirror of the Land Route to California by the South Pass of the Rocky Mountains*, ms., Missouri Historical Society. Reprinted by permission of the Society's archivist, Mrs. Ernst Stadler. This is probably the panorama of Mr. Wilken, artist, advertised in the *St. Louis Missouri Republican*, October 6, 1850. The Moving Mirror was exhibited at the Odd Fellows Hall, St. Louis, on October 14, 1850. Mr. Wilken was fully aware of the accounts of Fremont (cited twice) and Edwin Bryant, neither of whom mention the Great American Desert.

78. Most of these letters and diaries are in the Oregon and California Envelope in the Manuscript Collection of the Missouri Historical Society, St. Louis.

79. See, for example, the Diary of Col. James Tate, Overland to California, April 5 to October 7, 1849; and the Diary of Lydia A. Rudd, May 6 to October 27, 1852, in the Manuscript Collection of the Missouri Historical Society.

80. This was the view of the plains conveyed in Josiah Gregg, *Commerce of the Prairies* (New York, 1845), an image based on Gregg's travels in the western interior in the 1830's. Confirmation of the notion that the eastern plains were generally thought in the middle 1840's to be rich prairies is found in Francis Parkman, *The Oregon Trail* (Boston, 1872), 31.

81. Eight of these, all desert accounts, were discovered by Morris, "The Notion of a Great American Desert East of the Rockies," *The Mississippi Valley Historical Review*, XIII (1926–1927), 190–198. I have examined another 96 accounts, of which ten used the word desert to denominate or describe some part of the western interior.

82. Gregg uses the word desert rarely, compared to his use of the term prairies, and the western interior is "The Great Western Prairies." His only use of the term Great American Desert may not apply to the western interior exclusively. He calls the "wilder Indians—the *unconquered Sabaeans* of the Great American Deserts." Josiah Gregg, *Commerce of the Prairies*, Max L. Moorhead (ed.) (Norman, 1954), 330. The inconsistency in usage suggests that this flourish may have been added by Gregg's editor, John Bigelow, at the time a New York lawyer. See Max Moorhead's "Introduction" to Gregg, *Commerce of the Prairies*, xxix–xxxviii. I have not been able to glean detailed biographical material on John H. Beadle, author of *The Undeveloped West* (Philadelphia, 1873).

83. Carleton, *Prairie Logbooks*, traveled in 1845, described parts of the western interior as desert, and had gleaned the name Great American Desert from geography texts; Thomas J. Farnham's *Travels in the Great Western Prairies* (London, 1843) is reprinted as Vols. XXVIII and XXIX in Reuben Gold Thwaites (ed.), *Early Western Travels, 1748–1846* (Cleveland, 1904–1907). Farnham traveled in

1839 and owed much in his account to the Long expedition. He notes that the lands 300 miles east of the Rockies are in "arid waste . . . usually called the 'Great American Desert,' " Vol. XXIX, 108; Parkman traveled in 1846 and told his readers, in his sole mention of the name which is set in quotation marks—that "a dreary preliminary, a protracted crossing of the threshold awaits him before he finds himself fairly upon the verge of the 'great American desert.' " Parkman, *Oregon Trail*, 31.

84. Except for Gregg and Richardson, none of those who mentioned the Great American Desert had much experience in the West before traveling in the western interior. Their accounts are examples of what Dondore calls "true travel literature . . . to some extent their opinions are already formulated by the early relations they have read; they exult or criticize sharply as their preconceptions are surpassed or disappointed; in short, reaction to established tradition is exceedingly pronounced." Dondore, *Prairie*, 64–65.

85. Albert D. Richardson, *Beyond the Mississippi* (Hartford, 1867), 135; Samuel Bowles, *Across the Continent* (New York, 1865), 20; Horace Greeley, *An Overland Journey* (New York, 1860), 98–105. Bowles calls it the "Great Central Desert," but concludes that it is "not yet a desert . . . not worthless by any means."

86. Randall Hewitt, *Across the Plains*, the ninth person to write of the Great American Desert, had read much about the West before traveling in 1862, if his Introduction is taken at face value. His family was from Seneca Falls, New York.

87. The 17 well-educated individuals were Carleton, Parkman, Farnham, Richardson, Greeley, Gregg, Beadle, Hewitt, Bowles, Randolph B. Marcy, J. K. Townsend, J. B. Wyeth, G. K. Warren, M. O'C. Morris, R. F. Burton, Overton Johnson, and J. J. Abert.

88. An indication of the lower level of education of these diarists is, of course, the misspelling and grammar in the accounts. However, it is very probable that these diarists were more literate than the average plains traveler.

89. Richard Jackson, *Myth and Reality: Environmental Perception of the Mormons, 1840–1865, An Historical Geosophy* (unpub. Ph.D. Dissertation, Clark University, 1970), 142–149.

90. Merlin Lawson, *The Climate of the Great American Desert* (Ph.D. Dissertation, Clark University, in progress).

91. Douglas R. McManis, *The Initial Evaluation and Utilization of the Illinois Prairies, 1815–1840* (Chicago, 1964), 50; Brown, *Historical Geography*, 204.

92. The following have regarded the pioneer notion of infertile prairies as a major factor in the settlement history of the Middle West: V. E. Shelford, "Deciduous Forest Man and the Grassland Fauna," *Science*, C (1944), 135–140, 160–162; Carl O. Sauer, *Geography of the Upper Illinois Valley and History of Development*, Vol. XXVII of *Bulletin of the Illinois State Geological Survey* (Urbana, 1916), 154–155; Paul W. Gates, *The Illinois Central Railroad and its Colonization Work* (Cambridge, 1934), 11; W. V. Pooley, *The Settlement of Illinois from 1830 to 1850* (Madison, 1908), 540. One recent study notes that "if the American pioneers had once believed that the prairies were infertile because trees did not grow there, they were rejecting this misconception by the 1820's." Allan G. Bogue, "Farming in the Prairie Peninsula, 1830–1890," in Harry N. Scheiber (ed.), *The Old Northwest: Studies in Regional History, 1787–1910* (Lincoln, 1969), 171.

93. I have never encountered contemporary records of the notion that treeless prairies were infertile, and have not encountered any cited by others. The references to this myth are restrospective. Martyn J. Bowden, *Changes in Land Use in Jefferson County, Nebraska, 1857–1957* (unpub. M.A. Thesis, University of Ne-

braska, 1959), 79–80. McManis has found the same, yet concludes that "the belief was widely held" (McManis, *Initial Evaluation*, 50; see also Bogue, "Farming"). I am inclined to believe that this myth may result from self-glorification and exaggeration of achievements common in pioneer reminiscences and nineteenth century county histories.

94. McManis, *Initial Evaluation*, 53–58; Bogue, "Farming"; Allan G. Bogue, *From Prairie to Corn Belt: Farming on the Illinois and Iowa Prairies in the Nineteenth Century* (Chicago, 1963), 47–48.

95. McManis, *Initial Evaluation*, 44–53, 93–94; Bogue, *From Prairie to Corn Belt*, 70.

96. Pooley, *Settlement*, 324; Bogue, *From Prairie to Corn Belt*, 47; McManis, *Initial Evaluation*, 62–88.

97. Pooley, *Settlement*, 324–325; Bogue, *From Prairie to Corn Belt*, 92–94; McManis, *Initial Evaluation*, 58–59, 92; Brown, *Historical Geography*, 209.

98. McManis, *Initial Evaluation*, 72–79, 86, 90–92; Bogue, *From Prairie to Corn Belt*, 70.

99. Bogue, "Farming," 172, 191; Bogue, *From Prairie to Corn Belt*, 48, 50, 70, 169; McManis, *Initial Evaluation*, 86–87; Leslie Hewes, "Some Features of Early Woodland and Prairie Settlement in a Central Iowa County," *Annals, Association of American Geographers*, XL (1950), 40–54.

100. Stanley D. Dodge, "Bureau and the Princeton Community," *Annals of the Association of American Geographers*, XXII (1932), 159–200; Pooley, *Settlement*, 418, 440, 558–562; Bogue, "Farming," 174–175; Bogue, *From Prairie to Corn Belt*, 8, 72.

101. See notes 73, 79.

102. The following volumes of the Original Land Survey of Nebraska contain some survey information on Jefferson county: 1—Base Line; 6—Sixth Principal Meridian; 8—First Standard Parallel North; 14—Township Lines; Subdivision Lines; 29—Range one east; 37—Range two east; 45—Range three east; 53—Range four east; 132 (1873)—Otoe Indian lands.

103. McManis found the surveyors in Illinois in 1834–1835 "most often marked rolling prairie as 'fit for cultivation' regardless of the class of the soil" (McManis, *Initial Evaluation*, 54). This was true of eastern Nebraska 20 years later.

104. T1N R3E, Jefferson County, Vol. 45 (October 1856), 53.

105. These particular descriptions will be found in Vol. 14, 50–152; Vol. 45, 106; Vol. 53, 24.

106. T2N R4E and T1N R4E, Jefferson County. Indian sections, Vol. 132 (July 1873), 112, 168.

107. Smith, *Virgin Land*; Leo Marx, *The Machine in the Garden* (New York, 1964), 142.

108. Smith, *Virgin Land*, 202, 207.

109. *Ibid.*, 208; Dillon, "Stephen Long's Great American Desert," 104–108; Lewis, *Regional Ideas*, 137–139.

110. Rush Welter, "The Frontier West as Image of American Society: Conservative Attitudes before the Civil War," *The Mississippi Valley Historical Review*, XLVI (1960), 613.

111. *Report of the Commissioner of General Land Office to the Secretary of the Interior for the Year 1869* (Washington, 1870), 139, 141, 290. See Walter F. Kollmorgen, "The Woodsman's Assaults on the Domain of the Cattleman," *Annals, Association of American Geographers*, LIX (1969), 215–239; Smith, *Virgin Land*, 208–214; Henry Nash Smith, "Rain Follows the Plow: The Notion of Increased

Rainfall for the Great Plains," *Huntington Library Quarterly*, X (1947), 169–193.

112. A similar rewriting of history occurred among the Mormons. While few described a desert while crossing the plains, the region became a desert in retrospect, and while the Wasatch oasis was viewed very favorably by the Mormon settlers, it was quickly made into a transformed desert by the Mormon elders. Jackson, *Myth and Reality*, 194–196.

113. William M. Thayer, *Marvels of the New West: A Vivid Portrayal of the Unparalleled Marvels in the Vast Wonderland West of the Missouri River* (Norwich, Conn., 1892), 220–222, 535. Thayer shows a vast Great American Desert on a map entitled, "The New West as it Was" (p. 220). This map is reproduced above the caption "The West in 1820" in Hafen, Hollon, and Rister, *Western America*, 3rd ed., p. 150, to show that "the Great American Desert [that] . . . persisted in the minds of the people for half a century" (p. 138). This Great American Desert stretches as far east as the 96th meridian; it had not been named by 1820.

114. For example, Alexander Majors, *Seventy Years on the Frontier* (Minneapolis, 1965), 150–152, 172–173, 187 (orig. pub. Chicago, 1893). Majors is inconsistent in the use of the name Great American Desert, applying it to at least two quite discrete regions, one of which was the western interior. The process of transforming the past is revealed, for example, in the *Fairbury Gazette* (Jefferson County, Nebraska), June 20, 1872, which prints an article from the *St. Joseph Standard* (Missouri) telling readers that the grain area of eastern Nebraska was "The Great American Desert" of "school-days."

115. Lewis, "Changing Emphases," 79; Lewis, "Regional Ideas," 137; Lewis, "William Gilpin," 36; Hart, *Dark Missouri*, 36–38. It is clear that both Pike and Long saw the desert they described as a welcome barrier to the westward expansion of the American people. See Goetzmann, *Exploration and Empire*, 51–53, 62–64.

116. See note 3.

DAVID GRIMSTED

Melodrama as Echo
of the Historically Voiceless

Night after night thousands of Americans laughed, chatted, greeted
friends, listened to or drowned out the music, as they awaited the beginning of a dramatic evening. A miscellaneous lot—blacks, sailors,
and apprentices in the balcony, prostitutes in the third tier, ladies and
gentlemen in the boxes, the "middling sort" or "a mixed multitude
of the lower orders of all sorts, sizes, ages, and deportments" in the
pit[1]—they enjoyed the social pleasures of the theater before the cur-
tain rose on that art form which catered most consciously and democratically to their tastes and dreams. Some three hours later, with
echoes of the illusory world they had experienced jarring and jibing
with those of the "real world" to which they returned, they would
leave the candle- or gaslit auditorium and disappear down darkened
streets. The historian loses sight of them, too, because like most of
mankind they left few personal clues about what they actually were
or dreamed; he wonders if by listening to what they heard and responded to he can sound something of the quality of those vanished
lives. Can one understand them better by recapturing what Walt Whitman remembered as "The whole crowded auditorium and what seeth'd
in it, and flush'd from its faces and eyes, to me as much a part of the
show as any . . ."?[2]

Trying to hear the historically voiceless by listening to things
which supposedly echo their attitudes has been the solution of tradi-

tional history to this problem. Implicitly it is done in almost all works that move through an age's or a nation's artifacts to its general character; explicitly it is done in monographs which purport to define "public opinion" by examining public proclamations or press reportage. More recently historians have begun working with popular culture as a means of glimpsing the experiential echoes of a mass society, because here are often intimations of what amounts to the least common denominator of a people's belief: the concerns and convictions of an age in the simplest possible form suggesting their emotive and intellectual context.[3] The nineteenth-century vernacular term "notions" is perhaps suitable to the level of perception implied here, which is simple in its intellectual structure but extraordinarily complex in its nuances, largely because its premises are so little rationalized and so distant from full consciousness.[4]

THE APPEAL OF MELODRAMA

George Steiner has written that "drama is the most social of literary forms," which means "that one cannot separate the condition of drama from that of the audience or, in a larger yet strict sense, from that of the social and political community."[5] In the early nineteenth century the theater was certainly the most democratic institution of public entertainment, dependent for success on the response of people drawn from all parts of the community, and drama was the most social of art forms, in which the will of the audience was immediately influential. The audience, all critics agreed, ruled the kingdom of drama, which survived only by its acute responsiveness to their desires. In explaining the course of drama in the period, critics resorted to nothing more than Samuel Johnson's famous couplet:

> *The Drama's laws the Drama's patrons give*
> *For they that live to please, must please—to live.*[6]

Managers and actors pleased audiences largely by presenting a new type of play, the melodrama, which meshed so exactly with public taste that no amount of critical abuse affected its popularity. Even those playwrights who deplored the form ended up adopting it. Perhaps never before has an artistic formula so flourished in the face of almost total critical and intellectual scorn for "the blue-blazes and bloody-ruin school of drama," and "the childish geegaws of yclap'd Melo-dramas." [7] The easiest explanation of its success was to point to the more democratic audience; the masses had come into their own, and proceeded to massacre theatrical wit, subtlety, and honesty in favor of relentless action, simplicity, and vulgarity. The melodrama got its name and set conventions during the French Revolution, which supported the notion that its strength lay in triumphant democracy and intellectual plebeianism.[8] Yet there is little evidence that, in the United States at least, melodrama appealed any more to the lower classes than to the upper ones, or that these audiences were notably tasteless: year after year Shakespeare was the dramatist most frequently performed, and he seemingly was as popular with lower class as with upper class patrons.[9] Even if one accepts the explanation of democratic vulgarity, the intriguing question remains: why was this particular bundle of simplistic conventions so prominent? If it were democratic drama, it should speak particularly well for that country and its people where democracy flourished with least serious challenge.

Popular culture is seldom a vehicle of realism, but rather reflects preeminently the dreams and fears of its audiences in the context of story and characters to which they readily respond. Accordingly, the melodrama was basically what H. D. F. Kitto labels "religious drama," wherein surface detail, psychological or social, was firmly subordinated to a world view.[10] One looks in it primarily for clues to popular aspirations and uneasiness clothed in their notions of a natural order and in highly selected aspects of social existence. Everyday truth was kept firmly subordinate to universal truth. Nineteenth-century theater-goers, Herman Melville argued, wanted, "at bottom even more reality than real life itself can show. . . . Thus, though they want novelty, they want nature, too; but nature unfettered, exhilarated, in effect transformed. . . . It is . . . as with religion: it should present another world, and yet one to which we feel the tie." [11]

Democratic society insisted that its popular literature uphold the promise of human life within its structure much in the way "Socialist realism" is expected to do in the Soviet Union. Alexander Solzhenitsyn has his spokesman for official culture make dogma of what American audiences implicitly demanded:

to tell the people the truth doesn't mean to tell the bad, to poke into shortcomings. You can speak fearlessly about the good, so that it will become even better. Where do these false demands come from for the so-called "harsh truth"? And why should truth be harsh, all of a sudden? Why shouldn't it be the shining truth, attractive and optimistic? . . . It is much easier to describe things as they are than to describe what does not yet exist but what you know will come about. What we see with our bare eyes today is not necessarily the real truth. Truth is what *ought* to be, what will come about tomorrow.[12]

For both societies, based as they were on premises of human progress through social organization, the "real" truth had to be that which affirmed the optimism of tomorrow over the frequent bleakness of today.

The religious reality of the melodrama revolved around a clear moral order in which reward depended on the righteousness of one's conduct: if one obeyed the code, happiness lay ahead; if one violated it, destruction must follow. The oddity of melodramatic endings—the last minute rescues, the surprising reunions of long separated families and lovers, the foiling of the villains' plots—were in their context metaphysical necessities. Without such conclusions there would be "no impartial distribution of divine justice, no instructive lecture of a particular providence, no imitation of the divine dispensation." [13] The melodrama was bound by its audiences' faith in a universe ruled by moral laws as clear and encompassing as those of Newton's solar system. Characters defined their moral status by their explanations of the melodrama's concluding events, which demonstrated that "the reign of vice though successful, is short, and virtue, though long oppressed, will in the end assuredly receive its bright reward":

HERO: Blessed Heaven!
VILLAIN: Curst Chance!
HEROINE: The hand of providence! [14]

Happy endings for the perfectly good were necessary, the melodrama properly argued, unless one posited a world governed by imperfect justice, chance, or, worse still, mere power or amoral cleverness.

Melodrama insisted upon this ideal universe in part because so much seemed to threaten it. The tension in these plays grew from the often ominous and difficult existence of their good characters inside the fence of universal justice. In the melodramatic world, the hand of providence insured the triumph of the good eventually, but it moved slowly and deviously enough so that the good were sorely tried first. Why this should be was difficult to explain in a world where man was presumably good, nature and God were benevolent, and society, especially American society, was the best possible. Playwrights solved their dilemma by developing the villain as incarnation of evil and demonic disturber of man's natural paradise. Such personification of life's evil crudely distorted the human problem, but nonetheless allowed the reality of life's grimness on stage even while keeping intact society's moral faith.

As the century progressed, domestic and everyday settings for the plays became more common than exotic ones, and social ills were often touched on. In dramas aimed at reforming gamblers and drunkards, for example, evil became a matter of the weakness of the good as well as the machinations of the bad.[15] Plays dealt more and more with realistic causes of difficulty—the hard lot of the poor, the corrupt practices of the rich, the social threat of rapid urbanization, the evil of slavery, the injury of bad family upbringing[16]—but the moralistic framework remained. It was profoundly distorting to suggest, as the melodrama did, that the ills of poverty ended when a villain's oppression ceased, but it was the same distortion that allowed Jacksonians to see the abuses of laissez-faire disappearing when the monster bank was slain, or radicals to argue that mankind would achieve its destined happiness if only a certain reform triumphed to restore a good natural order.[17] In all cases, the solution was a way of handling evil within a framework where evil properly shouldn't exist because of the basic goodness of providence, man, and society. The worst clichés of melodrama in the later nineteenth century—the heroine tied to the railroad tracks or the family about to be tossed into the snow for lack of mortgage money—were telling symbols for the latent fears in a society characterized by rapid technological change and widespread home ownership on time payments. The melodrama gave catharsis to such fear in a structure that soothed with the assurance that if one were good there was finally nothing at all to fear.

THE HEROINE AND THE HOME

The most pervasive fear in the melodrama, the core of its plot structure, was loss of female chastity. The heroine stood in the center of these plays, the fair object of the villain's evil thrusts. If her chastity survived, the play would end happily; in "tragical" melodramas where she fell, only her death or at best many years of repentance could remove the blot. The point of the melodrama, both moral and sexual, was that "virtue can hold no intercourse with vice." [18] Female chastity was the nexus of these plots in large part because of what the woman represented. The heroine's outer loveliness stood symbol for the inner spiritual qualities which rendered her "an object too dazzling bright for man to look upon with aught but mental adoration." [19] These qualities of spirit—gentleness and sensibility, religious and moral strength, and a capacity for wholly unselfish love —made her "man's first and last, his surest, truest friend" and a "chaste-eyed angel, bringing peace and barring out all shape of wrong and discord" for men necessarily caught up in the struggle and bustling competitiveness of the outer world.[20] And she shed her luminous qualities through the institution she represented, the home. The melodrama concentrated on that thin slice of sexual adventure and danger when the heroine ventured into the outer world, sandwiched between the protective domesticity of childhood and the Eden of the happy home restored by marriage.

The Edenic imagery surrounding the home and the heroine who dwelt therein—"one serpent brought ruin upon Eden, but myriads crawl up on the earth, and the daughters of Eve are condemned to dwell among them, and are expected to escape the primeval fall"— mirrored their religious and utopian function in popular culture.[21] In a democratic and bourgeois society where institutions such as class, community, preordained authority, established church, and historic family were weakened to allow the individual competitive mobility, the home came to represent a "mansion of peace," a locus of permanence and order amidst the chaos of social, financial, geographic, and spiritual movement.[22] John Fiske was working in a long American (and melodramatic) tradition after the Civil War when he posed the family as great human buffer against a brutal and threatening Darwinian struggle for existence.[23]

The home, with its cornerstone of feminine purity, was only the most forward symbol of good that the melodrama held out against the maelstrom of surrounding change. Contrast between the city and the country, or more exactly the small farm, served the same purpose. In the country dwelt virtue, associated with noncompetitive repose; the city represented bustle, diversity, change, man's triumphing over nature rather than cooperating with it—"God made the country, man made the town"—and hence evil and danger.[24] The fascination of the city could be admitted in the melodrama, but not explained. The heroine of *Rosina Meadows, The Village Maiden,* leaves a small town 15 miles from Boston to go to the big city and her moral destruction, but the play, in its befuddled honesty, can give no real reason for her leaving the happy village still "enjoying its primitive simplicity." [25] Americans constantly gave up the old home for the new territory, the town for the country, enough for the chance at a little more, but they did so with sense of guilt as well as considerable zest. Perhaps those who succeeded as well as those who failed accepted and regretted that, when they shook off the dust of an Edenic home, they deserved the purgatory of uncertainty and chance that awaited them.[26]

The melodrama also used time to appease its fears of moral loss in the face of change. In melodramas with contemporary settings, virtue was almost invariably associated with an earlier generation, when change was slower, harmony rather than competition prevailed, and men were concerned with doing right rather than getting ahead: the fashionable, newfangled, and overtly contemporary were bad.[27] The melodrama, like Marvin Meyers' Jacksonians or William R. Taylor's northern developers of the cavalier ideal, created a myth of particular goodness in another setting or earlier time, which assuaged fears about a society to which men were too much committed to attack directly.[28] Meyers' description of the Jacksonians as both "the judging and the judged" in their response to economic change is pertinent here, though such a dilemma was hardly limited to supporters of Old Hickory. Those who preferred Old Tippecanoe, Old Rough and Ready, or Old Kentucky also pined for a remembered lost republic, even while they participated in its transformation.

The preeminence of the home as symbol of moral permanence in a world of flux perhaps grew from its reality compared to the other images. Americans continued to leave the farm for the city; they had no real desire to set up the aristocratically ordered society of the cavalier myth; the golden age of some preceding generation was obviously not to be recaptured. But the home was there as potential refuge. However sentimental the picture of "Home Sweet Home" as "abode of universal felicity" or "domestic Eden," it did offer more sphere for unchanging ties and affectional selflessness than did any other part of democratic society.[29]

The American melodrama had no intention of attacking the society about which it showed covert uneasiness. Nationalism, along with domesticity, was among its cardinal virtues, and tributes to the superiority of America and its system of government were constant. Even in plays set in distant times and countries, the heroes were fighting for things like democracy or liberty or the general welfare presumed to be part of the American way of life. Indeed, these plays even prophesied the wonders to come in the United States: Romulus died with a vision of a juster and "a greater Rome in regions yet unborn," and Joan of Arc at the stake foresaw a reign of "universal justice" to be begun by "English colonists." [30] Nationalism, with all the trappings of song, platitude, and pageantry, glittered in the frequent melodramatic celebration of American military victories or military heroes.[31] Faith in the goodness of the United States, its government, and its destiny was modulated only by association with principles of liberty, justice, and equality which were assumed to be the birthright of all men. Vague, malleable, and even dangerous as such principles were, they prevented melodramatic nationalism from becoming pure chauvinism. The emphasis was not on my country right or wrong but on my country because it is based on ideals that belong to all men; as D. H. Lawrence has argued, America was an "ideal home-land" rather than a "blood-home-land." The nation's melodrama flaunted Lawrence's version of American nationalism: "Transcend this home-land business, exalt the idea of these States till you have made it a universal idea, says the true American. The oversoul is world-soul, not a local thing." [32] There was in this vision both nobility and seeds of such abysses as Vietnam.

The nation on a social level and the home on a personal one were particularly democratic ideals because they were readily available to all, and because they gave a sense of belonging to men for whom intervening social groupings became increasingly fluctuating or volitional. By stressing such loyalties and emphasizing characteristics most men shared, the melodrama proclaimed its commitment to its democratic audience, to puting Everyman at its center. Particularly in the early years, melodramatic settings were often exotic and the leading characters of the nobility, but such were used to give a veneer of excitement and dignity to situations, sentiments, and people that were in their nature ordinary rather than extraordinary. Feudal trappings also symbolized the false social distinctions which prevented, for a while, the triumph of the natural order; established caste gave the melodrama ample chance to inveigh against the folly of artificial distinctions. If peasant heroes were ennobled before they married the princess and poor but honest American lads were rendered rich before they wed the heiress, such stratagems simply let democratic man hate such distinctions and, at the same time, have them, too.

A DEMOCRACY OF FEELING

The great equalizer of men in the melodrama was its epistemology. The melodrama taught that knowledge and virtue came from the intuitive impulses that Nature vouchsafed the uncorrupted heart. Feeling was the certain guide to truth, and the simplest man had access to it as readily as the greatest; indeed, simple people had an advantage because they were less burdened with artificial knowledge and distinctions which might disrupt one's reception of Nature's dictates. The simply pure could "judge of true affections by the pulsation of the heart," with full confidence they could "never be deceived when thus it throbs in confirmation of the truth." [33]

The doctrine of feeling could have antisocial implications, as some European romanticists made clear, but the popular romanticism of the melodrama was made perfectly safe by a simple corollary: feeling, if truly interpreted, led one to do only the good, which was defined in terms of moral conventionality. It might lead one to reject the artificialities of society, but not the wisdom of its basic moral maxims. If people acted against these, they were villains who responded not to feeling but to its opposite, passion, which, by melodramatic definition, meant amoral and antisocial feelings. Like the "common sense" philosophy of the universities or Emerson's transcendentalism, feeling protected social standards by making them self-evident truths to every person of untainted heart.

This epistomology of feeling was potent democratic dogma, not only because it equalized men, but because it assured Everyman that, if his heart were pure, his understanding was as good as a sage's, his judgment as much to be respected as any ruler's. If this were true, the average man need not defer to the natural aristocrat whom Thomas Jefferson had expected democratic process to bring to power; Everyman was nature's nobleman. From this idea sprouted Jacksonian America's assertive democracy, its belligerent self-righteousness, and its deep suspicions about the motives of anyone who seriously disagreed. Historians have demonstrated that the Jacksonian period led to no great increase in procedural democracy,[34] but there is still psychological truth in seeing in the age "the rise of the common man" or the "coming of age of American democracy." The melodrama reflected and supported what is perhaps the key element in democratic psychology: the sense which individual men have of their ability to decide, and hence of their right to participate vitally in the wielding of power.

The doctrine of natural impulses guiding the feeling heart left no room for moral ambiguity, nor did the melodrama's categorical imperative that good and bad must be vigorously segregated to make clear the workings of just Providence. As moral dichotomy, these plays posed not good versus bad, but vice against virtue and evil against innocence, with their suggestion of permanency and completeness of moral quality. Heroines always, heroes usually, were exemplars of perfectly disinterested virtue; villains were completely evil "serpents," "vultures," or "wolves" without saving—or even modifying—moral trait. The good world was one of total selflessness, where even the possibility of tainted motivation might temporarily keep true love from running its proper course: the best heroes and heroines, if the playwright allowed the subject to arise, could not bring themselves to make a match in whose promotion interest too obviously seconded affection. The peculiarly dehumanized quality of the melodrama—its status as morality play—arose from the wholly pure motives of its good characters and the totally vicious drives of its villains.

This melodramatic morality play forged the hopes of a competi-

tive society to the traditional virtues of Christian content and generosity. The good were rewarded with modest increases in wealth or
social position at the ends of the plays, but this was never the goal of
the people involved. Indeed, reward came because the good so dili-
gently refused to seek money, place, or sex; only villains were hard
working and calculating toward such ends. American popular culture
of the nineteenth century carefully eschewed "rugged individualism"
or "the gospel of wealth" as social ideals.[35] Melodramatic people who
did well might work hard, but their success was always related to
moral qualities quite opposed to winning out over others: unconcern
for social advancement, total probity, spontaneous affection and generosity, or lack of calculation. The contrasting "friends" in Anna Cora
Mowatt's *Fashion* personify melodramatic values: Mr. Tiffany has
come to the city, striven and schemed for wealth and position, and
become corrupt, bankrupt, and miserable; in the meantime, Adam
Truman has remained pure and spontaneous in heart and principle—
and incidentally fairly rich—back on the farm.[36] The melodrama offered the rewards of a competitive society in modest degree—good
people were assured of "enough," which was usually a little more status
or money than they had—and at the same time insisted that such reward providentially resulted from wholly noncompetitive virtues and
interests.

REALISTIC LAUGHTER

Exclusion of all tainted motives from good people in the center
of melodrama left a human vacuum that was partially filled by the
characters in comic portions of the plays. Usually servants in plays
with European setting and ethnic, racial, or regional stereotypes in
those that occurred in America, these comic characters could, basic
goodness unimpinged, make light of many of the clichés upheld in the
serious part of the melodrama; they shrewdly realized that home life
was as likely to be "squally" as Edenic, that money was a pleasant and
important thing to have, and that one might enjoy sex without becoming vicious. Low comedy stereotypes never scorned the goodness
of the characters in the serious parts of these plays, but indirectly they
did modify their values. Without casting doubt on the truth of the

moral universe at its center, the melodrama suggested there were competing truths as well.

Because of their popularity, low comedy stereotypes took up an increasing proportion of American melodramas in the early nineteenth century, until they were siphoned off into specifically low comedy theaters, beginning with minstrel houses in about 1840.[37] The stereotypes were of many kinds, but the Yankee was the most important until the 1830's, when he increasingly shared the stage with the Irishman, the Negro, and finally, in the late 1840's, the fireboy as representative of the American urban proletariat. All of these characters were treated in much the same way: with some condescension but with even more enthusiastic affection. They were all naïve and uneducated, but endowed with a kind of canniness and goodness that allowed them to take care of themselves, and often of the more elevated characters, who were frequently in need of common sense practicality. Their traits represented qualities rampant in American society, but so dangerous to the melodrama's moral world that they could be dramatically recognized only in humorous guise.[38] The Yankee's acquisitiveness, the Irishman's drinking and sexual escapades, the black's fondness for badges of rank, the fireboy's mistrust of all but his clique, and the brawling aggressiveness of all save the Negro were not condemned, but enjoyed and empathized within this safely comic form.

Those groups which were stereotyped seemingly responded most enthusiastically to the caricature. The Yankee was especially popular in rural New England; urban toughs made a hero of Mose, the fireboy; and, reportedly, conspicuously more Irish went to see the Irish portrayed and more blacks to watch T. D. Rice "jump Jim Crow" than regularly attended the theater. Certainly poorer immigrant groups gave success to theaters of ethnic comedy, such as Harrigan and Hart's in the late nineteenth century.[39] Whatever the long-range effects of such stereotypes, their immediate impact was to suggest the superiority of the simply pure, and to impart a sense of belonging and ability to cope to poor or minority groups facing the amorphous American democratic life. The stereotypes testified to these people's canniness and good hearts, while presenting characters to whom the simplest in the audience could feel comfortably superior.

The language of the melodrama furthered this dichotomy. In the serious portions, a language of great artificiality and elevation connected the action there with transcendent rather than everyday truth; in comic portions, the language was that of exaggerated dialect to tie it to ordinary life, but ordinary life made funny, largely to keep it noncompetitive with the melodrama's serious truth. This division of the world into spheres—the serious versus the comic, the female versus the male, the elevated versus the ordinary—was largely an attempt to hold firm to absolute moral standards and to cling to confidence in a just and all-encompassing natural order, while sub rosa admitting those aspects of human and social conduct that seemed to contradict the ideal. It reflected the core of the genteel faith of the nineteenth century: what ought to be, what must be if there be good men and a just providence, is at least as real as what is, and more to be talked about.

> *Tell me not, in mournful numbers*
> *Life is but an empty dream!—*
> *For the soul is dead that slumbers,*
> *And things are not what they seem.*[40]

wrote America's most popular poet, Henry Wadsworth Longfellow in his "Psalm of Life." This distinction between the "seeming," the morally perplexing surface of life, and the "being," the moral reality that must exist beneath it, is the core of the nineteenth-century "hypocrisy" which early twentieth-century thinkers have taught us to scorn. Yet it was generally a noble hypocrisy, both in its motivation and effect, for it attempted to mediate, and to insist on the simultaneous truth of, an ideal of a humane natural and moral order and the messy business of actually living.

The melodrama night after night assured its audience of the democratic hope that men need but trust their own hearts to find truth, while making clear that the truths found would correspond to basic social maxims—the kind of voluntary uniformity of opinion Alexis de Tocqueville saw as characteristic of democratic society. It spoke of a good nation where a good natural or providential order operated to insure the happiness of good men, and whispered under this assurance of uneasiness about a rapidly changing society where qualities and concerns other than moral integrity seemed to matter most. It promised rewards available to all and said that these need not be won through competitive struggle; it hadn't been that way in an earlier generation, it wasn't that way back in a remembered rural

America, and it wouldn't be like that in the Eden of the happy home. It gave expression to those traits most emphasized by a democratically mobile society—aggressiveness, acquisitiveness, social climbing—and at the same time pretended they weren't fully serious, and hence weren't really dangerous to the desired moral and psychological Utopia.

MELODRAMA AS
A SOURCE OF SOCIAL EXPERIENCE

Ralph Waldo Emerson suggested to "The American Scholar" some 130 years ago those principles which give life to cultural history:

> What would we really know the meaning of? The meal in the fir-
> kin; the milk in the pan; the ballad in the street; the news of the
> boat; the glance of the eye; the form and the gait of the body;—
> show me the ultimate reason of these matters . . . lurking, as it
> always does lurk, in these suburbs and extremities of nature . . . ;
> and the world lies no longer a dull miscellany and lumber-room,
> but has form and order.[41]

The weakness of cultural history has always been that, when so much is rife with broad implications, it's hard to know what to look at and how to be sure that what one sees accords with reality. The popularity of the melodrama, the immediacy of its appeal to a broad audience, is presumptive evidence of its importance; the form bound to it even those who consciously despised it, and seemingly made fable of both what people wanted to believe and the obstacles they sensed in keeping the faith. Of course, the most obscure historical data, sensitively touched, may reveal as much; the clarity of melodrama's appeal simply gives supportive reason for paying it particular heed.

The uncertainties in exploring melodrama, or other aspects of cultural history, grow from the kind of questions that fall within its realm, problems of man's intellectual and emotive handling of surrounding reality. There is less concern in cultural history with what people did than in most other historical fields, and more with why they so acted or what they thought. This dichotomy is, of course, too simple; the most factual of histories succeeds only if it suggests much about questions of why and so what, and much cultural history is

enervated by nonchalance about the general and specific setting of
the ideas and myths investigated, things which always motivate and
modify, and often make clear, ideas. The most careful compilation of
data cannot of itself provide answers. If we knew that 85.3 per cent of
all Americans worth over $100,000 voted Whig in 1840, questions of
significance would remain rampant: Was this because Whiggery was
the party of the "monied aristocracy," or did the wealthy simply see
most clearly the gross mistakes of Jacksonian monetary policy, or were
they driven into opposition by a calculated demagogic attack on
them? On the other hand, any intellectual interpretation of an age
gains substance and significance from the closeness it maintains between data and idea. The frustration and fascination of history is that
it is always partial, and limited of necessity by the approach taken and
material used. Any historical tactic is "heuristic" if happily used, and
the happiest use does as much to deepen as to clarify both the meaning and mystery of human reality.

The level of truth one can explore through a popular art form
is often that which least interests historians. The controversies of an
age which engaged its citizens' conscious concern understandably draw
the attention of later interpreters. Yet if there are certain common
assumptions that bind together a particular society in a given age—
what Alfred North Whitehead calls "first principles almost too obvious to need expression, and almost too general to be capable of expression" [42]—perhaps nothing is more revealing of them than the most
popular of cultural forms. And this single and deep level of truth is
presumably where the historically noisy and voiceless join minds.

Henry Adams' *History of the United States of America During
the Administrations of Thomas Jefferson and James Madison* made
perhaps the classic case for the need of a new history in democratic
society.[43] In democratic nations, Adams concluded, the new history
would have to be social instead of traditional, the history of the people who work the real changes beneath the surface of political, military, and economic leadership, which was the discipline's proper subject matter in an aristocracy.[44] With his sharp eye for the telling detail, Adams mentioned in his last volume that Benjamin Latrobe had
discovered near the Potomac River "a conglomerate rock, containing
rounded pebbles of various sizes and colors, and capable of being
worked in large masses" for the columns of the House of Representa-

tives.[45] Such was Adams' symbol of the conglomerate society in which the new nation's strength rested. Thus the need for a new history "capable of being worked in large masses" was sensed long before Ruth Miller Elson called for historical understanding of the "a-verbal" or Jesse Lemisch pled for treatment of the "inarticulate." [46]

The historical problem laid out by Adams and others is essentially one of sources, or rather the nonexistence of sources. History is always coherence imposed on pieces of the past, pieces selected partly by the historian, but with even more fatality by time and chance. The most available information comes from official sources or from individuals who, because of their writing and its preservation are, if for no other reason, atypical. The vast majority of men die historically voiceless. In a democratic society where this now silent majority presumably ruled, the need to know them better is great.

One cannot be sure how well the melodrama echoed the notions of the historically voiceless, or that we today can accurately catch the cultural reverberations. It is always hard to identify whose voice one hears when listening to echoes, or to be perfectly sure of what is being said. However, because there is no obviously better approach to this level of truth, the historian is justified in assuming that the audience speaks to us tellingly, if tentatively, of its times, ideals, hopes, and fears through the sentiments, situations, and stereotypes it demanded and applauded in its theatrical alter-life.

FOOTNOTES

1. *American Athenaeum*, I (November 17, 1825), 307; *Ladies' Port-Folio*, I (February 5, 1820), 46. For a description of audience composition and behavior see my *Melodrama Unveiled: American Theatre and Culture, 1800–1850* (Chicago, 1968), 46–75, or Ben Graf Henneke, "The Playgoer in America (1752–1952)" (unpub. Ph.D. Dissertation, University of Illinois, 1956).

2. Walt Whitman, "The Old Bowery," in *Complete Prose Works* (New York, 1914), 429.

3. John Bach McMaster touched almost all the sources and concerns that later historians have used in his pioneering attempt to write a "history of the people," in contrast to a history of their leaders, in his eight volume *A History of the People of the United States from the Revolution to the Civil War*, I (New York, 1883), 1. Constance Rourke, *American Humor: A Study of the National Character* (New York, 1931) opened the way to the systemic use of folklore and popular culture for intellectually understanding an age, and many writers such as Mark Sulli-

van in *Our Times*, 6 vols. (New York, 1926–1935) and Frederick Lewis Allen in *Only Yesterday: An Informal History of the 1920's* (New York, 1931) showed how much insight could be gained from mass culture even when treated with much intellectual casualness. Recently, the most important work in this field has been done in the American studies tradition fostered by the *American Quarterly* and Henry Nash Smith's influential *Virgin Land: The American West as Symbol and Myth* (Cambridge, Mass., 1950).

4. For a highly suggestive exploration of the premises of such history, see Alfred North Whitehead, *Adventures in Ideas* (New York, 1933), 3–31.

5. George Steiner, *The Death of Tragedy* (New York, 1963), 113.

6. *Mirror of Taste*, IV (July 1811), 55–56; *American Quarterly Review*, VI (September 1829), 26–28; *Boston Weekly Magazine*, I (June 7, 1817), 139.

7. Robert Ewing, *Theatrical Contributions of "Jacques" to the "United States Gazette"* (Philadelphia, 1826), 9; *Yankee*, VI (August 1829), 58.

8. Paul Ginity, *Le melodrame* (Paris, 1910); E. Jauffret, *Le théâtre révolutionnaire (1788–1799)* (Paris, 1869); George B. Daniel, *The Development of Tragedie Nationale in France from 1552–1800* (Chapel Hill, 1964).

9. The *Daily Picayune* of New Orleans, March 14, 1844, reported that "the colored portion of our population feel more interest in, and go in greater numbers to see, the plays of Shakespeare than any other." Quoted in Joseph Roppolo, "Hamlet in New Orleans," *Tulane Studies in English*, VI (1956), 74.

10. H. D. F. Kitto, *Form and Meaning in Drama: A Study of Six Greek Plays and of Hamlet* (London, 1956), 231–245.

11. Herman Melville, *The Confidence-Man: His Masquerade*, ed. Elizabeth S. Foster (New York, 1954), 206–207.

12. *The Cancer Ward* (New York, 1968), pp. 335–337.

13. *Emerald*, II (March 21, 1807), 137.

14. Joseph Hutton, *The Orphan of Prague* (Philadelphia, 1808), 23; John Howard Payne, *Trial Without Jury; or, The Maid and the Magpie* (1815) in Barrett Clark (ed.), *America's Lost Plays* (Princeton, 1940–1941), V, 53.

15. See, for example, William Dunlap, *Thirty Years; or, The Life of a Gamester*, 1828, in *America's Lost Plays*, II; John Peirpont and W. H. Smith, *The Drunkard; or, The Fallen Saved* (Boston, 1847).

16. Joseph S. Jones, *The People's Lawyer*, 1839 (New York, n.d.); Silas S. Steele, *The Crock of Gold; or, The Toiler's Trials*, 1845, in *America's Lost Plays*, XIV; Lucas Hirst, *Grub Mudge and Co.* (Philadelphia, 1853); H. P. Grattan, *The Mysteries and Miseries of New York Life*, 1848; George Aiken, *Uncle Tom's Cabin; or, Life Among the Lowly*, 1852 (New York, n.d.); J. T. Trowbridge, *Neighbor Jackwood* (Boston, 1857).

17. Marvin Meyers, *The Jacksonian Persuasion: Politics and Belief* (New York, 1960), 32; Edward Pessen, *Most Uncommon Jacksonians: The Radical Leaders of the Early Labor Movement* (Albany, N.Y., 1967), 103–111, 173–203.

18. John Howard Payne, *Clari; or, The Maid of Milan*, 1823 (Boston, 1856), 33.

19. George Watterston, *The Child of Feeling* (Georgetown, 1809), 57.

20. Louisa Medina, *Nick of the Woods* (Boston, n.d.), 28; Elizabeth Oakes Smith, *Old New York* (New York, 1853), 20.

21. Richard Penn Smith, "The Venetian," Harvard Theatre Collection mss., Act IV.

22. William Dunlap, *Ribbemont; or, The Feudal Baron* (New York, 1803), 68.

23. John Fiske, *Outlines of Cosmic Philosophy*, ed. Josiah Royce (Boston, 1902), IV, 119–162.

24. Charles Saunders, *Rosina Meadows, The Village Maiden; or, Temptations Unveiled* (Boston, 1855), 15.

25. *Ibid.*, 11–19.

26. Augustus Longstreet's "The Dance," with its lament for simpler and purer life that one gave up for no good reason and which indeed perhaps never existed, is the classic portrait of American nostalgia for the old that one willingly left behind. *Georgia Scenes* (New York, 1957), 4–13.

27. James Nelson Barker, *Tears and Smiles* (Philadelphia, 1808); Joseph Hutton, *Fashionable Follies*, 1809 (Philadelphia, 1815); H. J. Conway, "The Banker; or, Fashion and Failure," 1844, Harvard Theatre Collection mss.; William I. Paulding, *The Noble Exile*, in *American Comedies* (Philadelphia, 1847); Mrs. Sidney F. Bateman, *Self* (New York, 1856).

28. Meyers, *The Jacksonian Persuasion*, 3–56; William R. Taylor, *Cavalier and Yankee: The Old South and American National Character* (New York, 1961), 72–119.

29. William Charles White, *The Clergyman's Daughter* (Boston, 1810), 80.

30. John Howard Payne, *Romulus* (1839), in *America's Lost Plays*, VI, 244; John Daly Burk, *Female Patriotism; or, The Death of Joan of Arc* (New York, 1789), 39.

31. John Daly Burk, *Bunker Hill; or, The Death of General Warren* (New York, 1797); C. E. Grice, *The Battle of New Orleans, or, Glory, Love, and Loyalty* (Baltimore, 1815); Nathaniel H. Bannister, *Putnam, the Iron Son of 76* (Boston, 1859); John P. Adams, "The Battle of Buena Vista; or, The Heroic Death of Captain Lincoln," 1847, Brown University mss.

32. D. H. Lawrence, *Studies in Classic American Literature* (New York, n.d.), 122–123.

33. "A mechanic," *Knights of the Orange Grove*, in *Rejected Plays* (New York, 1828), 96; Samuel H. Chapman, *The Red Rover* (Philadelphia, 1828), 51.

34. Chilton Williamson, *American Suffrage from Property to Democracy, 1760–1860* (Princeton, 1960); Richard P. McCormick, *The Second American Party System: Party Formation in the Jacksonian Era* (Chapel Hill, 1966), and "New Perspectives on Jacksonian Politics," *American Historical Review*, LXV (January 1960), 288–301.

35. John G. Cawelti's careful look at the Horatio Alger stories show how gross has been the misinterpretation of this "myth" by historians above reading the tales they interpret. Alger's heroes, like those of the melodrama, never seek wealth, but rather gain a respectable competence largely as just reward for their morality, particularly their generosity and loyalty to others. *Apostles of the Self-Made Man* (Chicago, 1965), 101–123.

36. Anna Cora Mowatt, *Fashion; or, Life in New York*, 1845 (London, 1850).

37. Carl Wittke, *Tambo and Bones: A History of the American Minstrel Stage* (Durham, N.C., 1930).

38. The "humorous" Yankee and frontiersman in American jokes and prose fiction served the same function of representing real traits in society which moral faith prevented from being given "serious" sanction.

39. John Bernard, *Retrospections of America*, ed. Mrs. Bayle Bernard (New York, 1807); Walter L. Leman, *Memories of an Old Actor* (San Francisco, 1886); Benjamin Baker, in George O. Seilhamer, *An Interviewer's Album* (New York, 1801); Ely J. Kahn, *The Merry Partners: The Age and Stage of Harrigan and Hart* (New York, 1955); Albert F. McLean, Jr., *American Vaudeville as Ritual* (Louisville, Ky., 1965).

40. Henry Wadsworth Longfellow, *Complete Poetical Works* (Boston, 1893), p. 4.

41. Ralph Waldo Emerson, "The American Scholar," 1837, in *Selected Writings,* ed. William H. Gilman (New York, 1965), 238.

42. Whitehead, *Adventures in Ideas,* 14.

43. Henry Adams, *History of the United States of America During the Administrations of Thomas Jefferson and James Madison* (New York, 1891–1896), IX, 222–227.

44. *Ibid.,* 142–143.

45. *Ibid.*

46. Ruth Miller Elson, "American Schoolbooks and 'Culture' in the Nineteenth Century," *Mississippi Valley Historical Review,* XLVI (December 1959), 411; *Guardians of Tradition: American Schoolbooks in the Nineteenth Century* (Lincoln, Neb., 1964), vii–ix; Jesse Lemisch, "The American Revolution Seen from the Bottom Up," in Barton Bernstein (ed.), *Towards a New Past: Dissenting Views in American History* (New York, 1968), 29; "Jack Tar in the Streets: Merchant Seaman in the Politics of Revolutionary America," *William and Mary Quarterly,* XXV (July 1968), 371–407.

LAWRENCE W. LEVINE

Slave Songs and Slave Consciousness: An Exploration in Neglected Sources

Negroes in the United States, both during and after slavery, were anything but inarticulate. They sang songs, told stories, played verbal games, listened and responded to sermons, and expressed their aspirations, fears, and values through the medium of an oral tradition that had characterized the West African cultures from which their ancestors had come. By largely ignoring this tradition, much of which has been preserved, historians have rendered an articulate people historically inarticulate, and have allowed the record of their consciousness to go unexplored.

Having worked my way carefully through thousands of Negro songs, folktales, jokes, and games, I am painfully aware of the problems inherent in the use of such materials. They are difficult, often impossible, to date with any precision. Their geographical distribution is usually unclear. They were collected belatedly, most frequently by men and women who had little understanding of the culture from which they sprang, and little scruple about altering or suppressing

An earlier version of this essay was presented as a paper at the American Historical Association meetings on December 28, 1969. I am indebted to the two commentators on that occasion, Professors J. Saunders Redding and Mike Thelwell, and to my colleagues Nathan I. Huggins, Robert Middlekauff, and Kenneth M. Stampp for their penetrating criticisms and suggestions.

them. Such major collectors as John Lomax, Howard Odum, and Newman White all admitted openly that many of the songs they collected were "unprintable" by the moral standards which guided them and presumably their readers. But historians have overcome imperfect records before. They have learned how to deal with altered documents, with consciously or unconsciously biased firsthand accounts, with manuscript collections that were deposited in archives only after being filtered through the overprotective hands of fearful relatives, and with the comparative lack of contemporary sources and the need to use their materials retrospectively. The challenge presented by the materials of folk and popular culture is neither totally unique nor insurmountable.

In this essay I want to illustrate the possible use of materials of this kind by discussing the contribution that an understanding of Negro songs can make to the recent debate over slave personality. In the process I will discuss several aspects of the literature and problems related to the use of slave songs.

The subject of Negro music in slavery has produced a large and varied literature, little of which has been devoted to questions of meaning and function. The one major exception is Miles Mark Fisher's 1953 study, *Negro Slave Songs in the United States,* which attempts to get at the essence of slave life through an analysis of slave songs. Unfortunately, Fisher's rich insights are too often marred by his rather loose scholarly standards, and despite its continuing value his study is in many respects an example of how *not* to use Negro songs. Asserting, correctly, that the words of slave songs "show both accidental and intentional errors of transmission," Fisher changes the words almost at will to fit his own image of their pristine form. Arguing persuasively that "transplanted Negroes continued to promote their own culture by music," Fisher makes their songs part of an "African cult" which he simply wills into existence. Maintaining (again, I think, correctly), that "slave songs preserved in joyful strains the adjustment which Negroes made to their living conditions within the United States," Fisher traces the major patterns of that adjustment by arbitrarily dating these songs, apparently unperturbed by the almost total lack of evidence pertaining to the origin and introduction of individual slave songs.[1]

Fisher aside, most other major studies of slave music have focused almost entirely upon musical structure and origin. This latter question especially has given rise to a long and heated debate.[2] The earliest collectors and students of slave music were impressed by how different that music was from anything familiar to them. Following a visit to the Sea Islands in 1862, Lucy McKim despaired of being able "to express the entire character of these negro ballads by mere musical notes and signs. The odd turns made in the throat; and that curious rhythmic effect produced by single voices chiming in at different irregular intervals, seem almost as impossible to place on score, as the singing of birds, or the tones of an Aeolian Harp."[3] Although some of these early collectors maintained, as did W. F. Allen in 1865, that much of the slave's music "might no doubt be traced to tunes which they have heard from the whites, and transformed to their own use, . . . their music . . . is rather European than African in its character,"[4] they more often stressed the distinctiveness of the Negro's music and attributed it to racial characteristics, African origins, and indigenous developments resulting from the slave's unique experience in the New World.

This tradition, which has had many influential twentieth-century adherents,[5] was increasingly challenged in the early decades of this century. Such scholars as Newman White, Guy Johnson, and George Pullen Jackson argued that the earlier school lacked a comparative grounding in Anglo-American folk song. Comparing Negro spirituals with Methodist and Baptist evangelical religious music of the late eighteenth and early nineteenth centuries, White, Johnson, and Jackson found similarities in words, subject matter, tunes, and musical structure.[6] Although they tended to exaggerate both qualitatively and quantitively the degrees of similarity, their comparisons were often a persuasive and important corrective to the work of their predecessors. But their studies were inevitably weakened by their ethnocentric assumption that similarities alone settled the argument over origins. Never could they contemplate the possibility that the direction of cultural diffusion might have been from black to white as well as the other way. In fact, insofar as white evangelical music departed from traditional Protestant hymnology and embodied or approached the complex rhythmic structure, the percussive qualities, the polymeter, the syncopation, the emphasis on overlapping call and response patterns that characterized Negro music both in West Africa and the New World, the possibility that it was influenced by slaves who attended and joined in the singing at religious meetings is quite high.

These scholars tended to use the similarities between black and white religious music to deny the significance of slave songs in still another way. Newman White, for example, argued that since white evangelical hymns also used such expressions as "freedom," the "Promised Land," and the "Egyptian Bondage," "without thought of other than spiritual meaning," these images when they occurred in Negro spirituals could not have been symbolic "of the Negro's longing for physical freedom." [7] The familiar process by which different cultural groups can derive varied meanings from identical images is enough to cast doubt on the logic of White's argument.[8] In the case of white and black religious music, however, the problem may be much less complex, since it is quite possible that the similar images in the songs of both groups in fact served similar purposes. Many of those whites who flocked to the camp meetings of the Methodists and Baptists were themselves on the social and economic margins of their society, and had psychic and emotional needs which, qualitatively, may not have been vastly different from those of black slaves. Interestingly, George Pullen Jackson, in his attempt to prove the white origin of Negro spirituals, makes exactly this point: "I may mention in closing the chief remaining argument of the die-hards for the Negro source of the Negro spirituals. . . . How could any, the argument runs, but a natively musical and sorely oppressed race create such beautiful things as 'Swing Low,' 'Steal Away,' and 'Deep River'? . . . But were not the whites of the mountains and the hard-scrabble hill country also 'musical and oppressed'? . . . Yes, these whites were musical, and oppressed too. If their condition was any more tolerable than that of the Negroes, one certainly does not get that impression from any of their songs of release and escape." [9] If this is true, the presence of similar images in white music would merely heighten rather than detract from the significance of these images in Negro songs. Clearly, the function and meaning of white religious music during the late eighteenth and early nineteenth centuries demands far more attention than it has received. In the interim, we must be wary of allowing the mere fact of similarities to deter us from attempting to comprehend the cultural dynamics of slave music.

Contemporary scholars, tending to transcend the more simplistic lines of the old debate, have focused upon the process of syncretism to explain the development of Negro music in the United States. The rich West African musical tradition common to almost all of the specific cultures from which Negro slaves came, the comparative cultural isolation in which large numbers of slaves lived, the tolerance and even encouragement which their white masters accorded to their musical activities, and the fact that, for all its differences, nothing in the European musical tradition with which they came into contact in America was totally alien to their own traditions—all these were conducive to a situation which allowed the slaves to retain a good deal of the integrity of their own musical heritage while fusing to it compatible elements of Anglo-American music. Slaves often took over entire white hymns and folk songs, as White and Jackson maintained, but altered them significantly in terms of words, musical structure, and especially performance before making them their own. The result was a hybrid with a strong African base.[10]

One of the more interesting aspects of this debate over origins is that no one engaged in it, not even advocates of the white derivation theory, denied that the slaves possessed their own distinctive music. Newman White took particular pains to point out again and again that the notion that Negro song is purely an imitation of the white man's music "is fully as unjust and inaccurate, in the final analysis, as the Negro's assumption that his folk-song is entirely original." He observed that in the slaves' separate religious meetings they were free to do as they would with the music they first learned from the whites, with the result that their spirituals became "the greatest single outlet for the expression of the Negro folk-mind." [11] Similarly, George Pullen Jackson, after admitting that he could find no white parallels for over two-thirds of the existing Negro spirituals, reasoned that these were produced by Negro singers in true folk fashion "by endless singing of heard tunes and by endless, inevitable and concomitant singing differentiation." Going even further, Jackson asserted that the lack of deep roots in Anglo-American culture left the black man "even freer than the white man to make songs over unconsciously as he sang . . . the free play has resulted in the very large number of songs which, though formed primarily in the white man's moulds, have lost all recognizable relationship to known individual white-sung melodic entities." [12] This debate over origins indicates clearly that a belief in the direct continuity of African musical traditions or in the process of syncretism is not a necessary prerequisite to the conclusion that the Negro slaves' music was their own, regardless of where they received the components out of which it was fashioned; a conclusion which is crucial to any attempt to utilize these songs as an aid in reconstructing the slaves' consciousness.

Equally important is the process by which slave songs were created and transmitted. When James McKim asked a freedman on the Sea Islands during the Civil War where the slaves got their songs, the answer was eloquently simple: "Dey make em, sah." [13] Precisely *how* they made them worried and fascinated Thomas Wentworth Higginson, who became familiar with slave music through the singing of the black Union soldiers in his Civil War regiment. Were their songs, he wondered, a "conscious and definite" product of "some leading mind," or did they grow "by gradual accretion, in an almost unconscious way"? A freedman rowing Higginson and some of his troops between the Sea Islands helped to resolve the problem when he described a spiritual which he had a hand in creating:

> Once we boys went for some rice and de nigger-driver he keep a-callin' on us; and I say, "O de ole nigger-driver!" Den anudder said, "Fust ting my mammy tole me was, notin' so bad as nigger-driver." Den I made a sing, just puttin' a word, and den anudder word.

He then began to sing his song:

> *O, de ole nigger-driver!*
> *   O, gwine away!*
> *Fust ting my mammy tell me,*
> *   O, gwine away!*
>
> *Tell me 'bout de nigger-driver,*
> *   O, gwine away!*
> *Nigger-driver second devil,*
> *   O, gwine away!*

Higginson's black soldiers, after a moment's hesitation, joined in the singing of a song they had never heard before as if they had long been familiar with it. "I saw," Higginson concluded, "how easily a new 'sing' took root among them." [14]

This spontaneity, this sense of almost instantaneous community which so impressed Higginson, constitutes a central element in every account of slave singing. The English musician Henry Russell, who lived in the United States in the 1830's, was forcibly struck by the ease with which a slave congregation in Vicksburg, Mississippi, took a "fine old psalm tune" and, by suddenly and spontaneously accelerating the tempo, transformed it "into a kind of negro melody." [15] "Us old heads," an ex-slave told Jeanette Robinson Murphy, "use ter make 'em up on de spurn of de moment. Notes is good enough for you people, but us likes a mixtery." Her account of the creation of a spiritual is typical and important:

> We'd all be at the "prayer house" de Lord's day, and de white preacher he'd splain de word and read whar Esekial done say—
>
> *Dry bones gwine ter lib ergin.*
>
> And, honey, de Lord would come a-shinin' thoo dem pages and revive dis ole nigger's heart, and I'd jump up dar and den and holler and shout and sing and pat, and dey would all cotch de words and I'd sing it to some ole shout song I'd heard 'em sing from Africa, and dey'd all take it up and keep at it, and keep a-addin' to it, and den it would be a spiritual.[16]

This "internal" account has been verified again and again by the descriptions of observers, many of whom were witnessing not slave services but religious meetings of rural southern Negroes long after emancipation. The essential continuity of the Negro folk process in the more isolated sections of the rural South through the early decades of the twentieth century makes these accounts relevant for the slave period as well. Natalie Curtis Burlin, whose collection of spirituals is musically the most accurate one we have, and who had a long and close acquaintance with Negro music, never lost her sense of awe at the process by which these songs were molded. On a hot July Sunday in rural Virginia, she sat in a Negro meeting house listening to the preacher deliver his prayer, interrupted now and then by an "O Lord!" or "Amen, Amen" from the congregation.

> Minutes passed, long minutes of strange intensity. The mutterings, the ejaculations, grew louder, more dramatic, till suddenly I felt the creative thrill dart through the people like an electric vibration, that same half-audible hum arose,—emotion was gathering atmospherically as clouds gather—and then, up from the depths of some "sinner's" remorse and imploring came a pitiful little plea, a real "moan," sobbed in musical cadence. From somewhere in that bowed gathering another voice improvised a response: the plea sounded again, louder this time and more impassioned; then other voices joined in the answer, shaping it into a musical phrase; and so, before our ears, as one might say, from this molten metal of music a new song was smithied out, composed then and there by no one in particular and by everyone in general.[17]

Clifton Furness has given us an even more graphic description. During a visit to an isolated South Carolina plantation in 1926, he attended a prayer meeting held in the old slave cabins. The preacher began his reading of the Scriptures slowly, then increased his tempo and emotional fervor, assuring his flock that "Gawd's lightnin' gwine strike! Gawd's thunder swaller de ert!"

> Gradually moaning became audible in the shadowy corners where the women sat. Some patted their bundled babies in time to the flow of the words, and began swaying backward and forward. Several men moved their feet alternately, in strange syncopation. A rhythm was born, almost without reference to the words that were being spoken by the preacher. It seemed to take shape almost visibly, and grow. I was gripped with the feeling of a mass-intelligence, a self-conscious entity, gradually informing the crowd and taking possession of every mind there, including my own.

In the midst of this increasing intensity, a black man sitting directly in front of Furness, his head bowed, his body swaying, his feet patting up and down, suddenly cried out: "Git right—sodger! Git right— sodger! Git right—wit Gawd!"

Instantly the crowd took it up, moulding a melody out of half-formed familiar phrases based upon a spiritual tune, hummed here and there among the crowd. A distinct melodic outline became more and more prominent, shaping itself around the central theme of the words, "Git right, sodger!"

Scraps of other words and tunes were flung into the medley of sound by individual singers from time to time, but the general trend was carried on by a deep undercurrent, which appeared to be stronger than the mind of any individual present, for it bore the mass of improvised harmony and rhythms into the most effective climax of incremental repetition that I have ever heard. I felt as if some conscious plan or purpose were carrying us along, call it mob-mind, communal composition, or what you will.[18]

Shortly after the Civil War, Elizabeth Kilham witnessed a similar scene among the freedmen, and described it in terms almost identical to those used by observers many years later. "A fog seemed to fill the church," she wrote, ". . . an invisible power seemed to hold us in its iron grasp; . . . A few moments more, and I think we should have shrieked in unison with the crowd." [19]

These accounts and others like them make it clear that spirituals both during and after slavery were the product of an improvisational communal consciousness. They were not, as some observers thought, totally new creations, but were forged out of many preexisting bits of old songs mixed together with snatches of new tunes and lyrics and fit into a fairly traditional but never wholly static metrical pattern. They were, to answer Higginson's question, *simultaneously* the result of individual and mass creativity. They were products of that folk process which has been called "communal re-creation," through which older songs are constantly recreated into essentially new entities.[20] Anyone who has read through large numbers of Negro songs is familiar with this process. Identical or slightly varied stanzas appear in song after song; identical tunes are made to accommodate completely different sets of lyrics; the same song appears in different collections in widely varied forms. In 1845 a traveler observed that the only permanent elements in Negro song were the music and the chorus. "The blacks themselves leave out old stanzas, and introduce new ones at pleasure. Travelling through the South, you may, in passing from Virginia to Louisiana, hear the same tune a hundred times, but seldom the same words accompanying it." [21] Another observer noted in 1870 that during a single religious meeting the freedmen would often sing the words of one spiritual to several different tunes, and then take a tune that particularly pleased them and fit the words of several different songs to it.[22] Slave songs, then, were never static; at no time did Negroes create a "final" version of any spiritual. Always the community felt free to alter and recreate them.

The two facts that I have attempted to establish thus far—that slave music, regardless of its origins, was a distinctive cultural form, and that it was created or constantly recreated through a communal process—are essential if one is to justify the use of these songs as keys to slave consciousness. But these facts in themselves say a good deal about the nature and quality of slave life and personality. That black slaves could create and continually recreate songs marked by the poetic beauty, the emotional intensity, the rich imagery which characterized the spirituals—songs which even one of the most devout proponents of the white man's origins school admits are "the most impressive religious folk songs in our language" [23]—should be enough to make us seriously question recent theories which conceive of slavery as a closed system which destroyed the vitality of the Negro and left him a dependent child. For all of its horrors, slavery was never so complete a system of psychic assault that it prevented the slaves from carving out independent cultural forms. It never pervaded all of the interstices of their minds and their culture, and in those gaps they were able to create an independent art form and a distinctive voice. If North American slavery eroded the African's linguistic and institutional life, if it prevented him from preserving and developing his rich heritage of graphic and plastic art, it nevertheless allowed him to continue and to develop the patterns of verbal art which were so central to his past culture. Historians have not yet come to terms with what the continuance of the oral tradition meant to blacks in slavery.

In Africa, songs, tales, proverbs, and verbal games served the dual function of not only preserving communal values and solidarity, but also of providing occasions for the individual to transcend, at least symbolically, the inevitable restrictions of his environment and his society by permitting him to express deeply held feelings which he ordinarily was not allowed to verbalize. Among the Ashanti and the Dahomeans, for example, periods were set aside when the inhabitants were encouraged to gather together and, through the medium of song, dance, and tales, to openly express their feelings about each other. The psychological release this afforded seems to have been well understood. "You know that everyone has a *sunsum* (soul) that may get hurt or knocked about or become sick, and so make the body ill," an Ashanti high priest explained to the English anthropologist R. S. Rattray:

> Very often . . . ill health is caused by the evil and the hate that another has in his head against you. Again, you too may have hatred in your head against another, because of something that person has done to you, and that, too, causes your *sunsum* to fret and become sick. Our forbears knew this to be the case, and so they ordained a time, once every year, when every man and woman, free man and slave, should have freedom to speak out just what was in their head, to tell their neighbours just what they thought of them, and of their actions, and not only their neighbours, but also the king or chief. When a man has spoken freely thus, he will feel his *sunsum* cool and quieted, and the *sunsum* of the other person against whom he has now openly spoken will be quieted also.

Utilization of verbal art for this purpose was widespread throughout Africa, and was not confined to those ceremonial occasions when one could directly state one's feelings. Through innuendo, metaphor, and circumlocution, Africans could utilize their songs as outlets for individual release without disturbing communal solidarity.[24]

There is abundant internal evidence that the verbal art of the slaves in the United States served many of these traditional functions. Just as the process by which the spirituals were created allowed for simultaneous individual and communal creativity, so their very structure provided simultaneous outlets for individual and communal expression. The overriding antiphonal structure of the spirituals—the call and response pattern which Negroes brought with them from Africa and which was reinforced by the relatively similar white practice of "lining out" hymns—placed the individual in continual dialogue with his community, allowing him at one and the same time to preserve his voice as a distinct entity and to blend it with those of his fellows. Here again slave music confronts us with evidence which indicates that however seriously the slave system may have diminished the strong sense of community that had bound Africans together, it never totally destroyed it or left the individual atomized and emotionally and psychically defenseless before his white masters. In fact, the form and structure of slave music presented the slave with a potential outlet for his individual feelings even while it continually drew him back into the communal presence and permitted him the comfort of basking in the warmth of the shared assumptions of those around him.

Those "shared assumptions" can be further examined by an analysis of the content of slave songs. Our preoccupation in recent years with the degree to which the slaves actually resembled the "Sambo" image held by their white masters has obscured the fact that the slaves developed images of their own which must be consulted and studied before any discussion of slave personality can be meaningful. The image of the trickster, who through cunning and unscrupulousness prevails over his more powerful antagonists, pervades slave tales. The trickster figure is rarely encountered in the slave's religious songs, though its presence is sometimes felt in the slave's many allusions to his narrow escapes from the devil.

> *The Devil's mad and I'm glad,*
> *He lost the soul he thought he had.*[25]

> *Ole Satan toss a ball at me.*
> *O me no weary yet . . .*

> *Him tink de ball would hit my soul.*
> *O me no weary yet . . .*

> *De ball for hell and I for heaven.*
> *O me no weary yet . . .*[26]

> *Ole Satan thought he had a mighty aim;*
> *He missed my soul and caught my sins.*
> *Cry Amen, cry Amen, cry Amen to God!*

> *He took my sins upon his back;*
> *Went muttering and grumbling down to hell.*
> *Cry Amen, cry Amen, cry Amen to God!* [27]

The single most persistent image the slave songs contain, how-ever, is that of the chosen people. The vast majority of the spirituals identify the singers as "de people dat is born of God," "We are the people of God," "we are de people of de Lord," "I really do believe I'm a child of God," "I'm a child ob God, wid my soul sot free," "I'm born of God, I know I am." Nor is there ever any doubt that "To the promised land I'm bound to go," "I walk de heavenly road," "Heav'n shall-a be my home," "I gwine to meet my Saviour," "I seek my Lord and I find Him," "I'll hear the trumpet sound/In that morn-ing." [28]

The force of this image cannot be diminished by the observation that similar images were present in the religious singing of white evangelical churches during the first half of the nineteenth century. White Americans could be expected to sing of triumph and salvation, given their long-standing heritage of the idea of a chosen people which was reinforced in this era by the belief in inevitable progress and manifest destiny, the spread-eagle oratory, the bombastic folklore, and, paradoxically, the deep insecurities concomitant with the tasks of taming a continent and developing an identity. But for this same mes-sage to be expressed by Negro slaves who were told endlessly that they were members of the lowliest of races *is* significant. It offers an insight into the kinds of barriers the slaves had available to them against the internalization of the stereotyped images their masters held and at-tempted consciously and unconsciously to foist upon them.

The question of the chosen people image leads directly into the larger problem of what role religion played in the songs of the slave. Writing in 1862, James McKim noted that the songs of the Sea Island freedmen "are all religious, barcaroles and all. I speak without excep-tion. So far as I heard or was told of their singing, it was all religious." Others who worked with recently emancipated slaves recorded the same experience, and Colonel Higginson reported that he rarely heard his troops sing a profane or vulgar song. With a few exceptions, "all had a religious motive." [29] In spite of this testimony, there can be little doubt that the slaves sang nonreligious songs. In 1774, an Eng-lish visitor to the United States, after his first encounter with slave music, wrote in his journal: "In their songs they generally relate the usage they have received from their Masters or Mistresses in a very satirical stile and manner." [30] Songs fitting this description can be found in the nineteenth-century narratives of fugitive slaves. Harriet Jacobs recorded that during the Christmas season the slaves would ridicule stingy whites by singing:

> *Poor Massa, so dey say;*
> *Down in de heel, so dey say;*
> *Got no money, so dey say;*
> *God A'mighty bress you, so dey say.*[31]

"Once in a while among a mass of nonsense and wild frolic," Frederick Douglass noted, "a sharp hit was given to the meanness of slaveholders."

> *We raise de wheat,*
> *Dey gib us de corn;*
> *We bake de bread,*
> *Dey gib us de crust;*
> *We sif de meal,*
> *Dey gib us de huss;*
> *We peal de meat,*
> *Dey gib us de skin;*
> *And dat's de way*
> *Dey take us in;*
> *We skim de pot,*
> *Dey gib us de liquor,*
> *And say dat's good enough for nigger.*[32]

Both of these songs are in the African tradition of utilizing song to bypass both internal and external censors and give vent to feelings which could be expressed in no other form. Nonreligious songs were not limited to the slave's relations with his masters, however, as these rowing songs, collected by contemporary white observers, indicate:

> *We are going down to Georgia, boys,*
> *Aye, aye.*
> *To see the pretty girls, boys,*
> *Yoe, yoe.*
> *We'll give 'em a pint of brandy, boys,*
> *Aye, aye.*
> *And a hearty kiss, besides, boys,*
> *Yoe, yoe.*[33]

> *Jenny shake her toe at me,*
> *Jenny gone away;*
> *Jenny shake her toe at me,*
> *Jenny gone away.*
> *Hurrah! Miss Susy, oh!*
> *Jenny gone away;*
> *Hurrah! Miss Susy, oh!*
> *Jenny gone away.*[34]

The variety of nonreligious songs in the slave's repertory was wide. There were songs of in-group and out-group satire, songs of nostalgia, nonsense songs, songs of play and work and love. Nevertheless, our total stock of these songs is very small. It is possible to add to these by incorporating such post-bellum secular songs which have an authentic slavery ring to them as "De Blue-Tail Fly," with its ill-concealed satisfaction at the death of a master, or the ubiquitous

> *My ole Mistiss promise me,*
> *W'en she died, she'd set me free,*
> *She lived so long dat 'er head got bal',*
> *An' she give out'n de notion a dyin' at all.*[35]

The number can be further expanded by following Constance Rourke's suggestion that we attempt to disentangle elements of Negro origin from those of white creation in the "Ethiopian melodies" of the white minstrel shows, many of which were similar to the songs I have just quoted.[36] Either of these possibilities, however, forces the historian to work with sources far more potentially spurious than those with which he normally is comfortable.

Spirituals, on the other hand, for all the problems associated with their being filtered through white hands before they were published, and despite the many errors in transcription that inevitably occurred, constitute a much more satisfactory source. They were collected by the hundreds directly from slaves and freedmen during the Civil War and the decades immediately following, and although they came from widely different geographical areas they share a common structure and content, which seems to have been characteristic of Negro music wherever slavery existed in the United States. It is possible that we have a greater number of religious than nonreligious songs because slaves were more willing to sing these ostensibly innocent songs to white collectors who in turn were more anxious to record them, since they fit easily with their positive and negative images of the Negro. But I would argue that the vast preponderance of spirituals over any other sort of slave music, rather than being merely the result of accident or error, is instead an accurate reflection of slave culture during the ante-bellum period. Whatever songs the slaves may have sung before their whole-sale conversion to Christianity in the late eighteenth and early nine-teenth centuries, by the latter century spirituals were quantitatively and qualitatively their most significant musical creation. In this form of expression slaves found a medium which resembled in many im-portant ways the world view they had brought with them from Africa, and afforded them the possibility of both adapting to and transcend-ing their situation.

It is significant that the most common form of slave music we know of is sacred song. I use the term "sacred" not in its present usage as something antithetical to the secular world; neither the slaves nor their African forebears ever drew modernity's clear line between the sacred and the secular. The uses to which spirituals were put are an unmistakable indication of this. They were not sung solely or even pri-marily in churches or praise houses, but were used as rowing songs, field songs, work songs, and social songs. On the Sea Islands during the Civil War, Lucy McKim heard the spiritual "Poor Rosy" sung in a wide variety of contexts and tempos.

> On the water, the oars dip "Poor Rosy" to an even andante; a stout boy and girl at the hominy-mill will make the same "Poor Rosy" fly, to keep up with the whirling stone; and in the evening, after the day's work is done, "Heab'n shall-a be my home" [the final line of each stanza] peals up slowly and mournfully from the distant quarters.[37]

For the slaves, then, songs of God and the mythic heroes of their religion were not confined to any specific time or place, but were ap-propriate to almost every situation. It is in this sense that I use the concept sacred—not to signify a rejection of the present world but to describe the process of incorporating within this world all the elements of the divine. The religious historian Mircea Eliade, whose definition of sacred has shaped my own, has maintained that for men in traditional societies religion is a means of extending the world spatially upward so that communication with the other world becomes ritually possible, and extending it temporally backward so that the paradigmatic acts of the gods and mythical ancestors can be continually re-enacted and indefinitely recoverable. By creating sacred time and space, man can perpetually live in the presence of his gods, can hold on to the certainty that within one's own lifetime "rebirth" is continually possible, and can impose order on the chaos of the universe. "Life," as Eliade puts it, "is lived on a twofold plane; it takes its course as human existence and, at the same time, shares in a trans-human life, that of the cosmos or the gods." [38]

This notion of sacredness gets at the essence of the spirituals, and through them at the essence of the slave's world view. Denied the possibility of achieving an adjustment to the external world of the ante-bellum South which involved meaningful forms of personal integration, attainment of status, and feelings of individual worth that all human beings crave and need, the slaves created a new world by transcending the narrow confines of the one in which they were forced to live. They extended the boundaries of their restrictive universe backward until it fused with the world of the Old Testament, and upward until it became one with the world beyond. The spirituals are the record of a people who found the status, the harmony, the values, the order they needed to survive by internally creating an expanded universe, by literally willing themselves reborn. In this respect I agree with the anthropologist Paul Radin that

> The ante-bellum Negro was not converted to God. He converted God to himself. In the Christian God he found a fixed point and he needed a fixed point, for both within and outside of himself, he could see only vacillation and endless shifting. . . . There was no other safety for people faced on all sides by doubt and the threat of personal disintegration, by the thwarting of instincts and the annihilation of values.[39]

The confinement of much of the slave's new world to dreams and fantasies does not free us from the historical obligation of examining its contours, weighing its implications for the development of the slave's psychic and emotional structure, and eschewing the kind of facile reasoning that leads Professor Elkins to imply that, since the slaves had no alternatives open to them, their fantasy life was "limited to catfish and watermelons." [40] Their spirituals indicate clearly that there *were* alternatives open to them—alternatives which they themselves fashioned out of the fusion of their African heritage and their new religion—and that their fantasy life was so rich and so important to them that it demands understanding if we are even to begin to comprehend their inner world.

The God the slaves sang of was neither remote nor abstract, but as intimate, personal, and immediate as the gods of Africa had been. "O when I talk I talk wid God," "Mass Jesus is my bosom friend," "I'm goin' to walk with [talk with, live with, see] King Jesus by myself, by myself," were refrains that echoed through the spirituals.[41]

> *In de mornin' when I rise,*
> *Tell my Jesus huddy [howdy] oh,*
> *I wash my hands in de mornin' glory,*
> *Tell my Jesus huddy oh.*[42]

> *Gwine to argue wid de Father and chatter wid de son,*
> *The last trumpet shall sound, I'll be there.*
> *Gwine talk 'bout de bright world dey des' come from.*
> *The last trumpet shall sound, I'll be there.*[43]

> *Gwine to write to Massa Jesus,*
> *To send some Valiant soldier*
> *To turn back Pharaoh's army, Hallelu!* [44]

The heroes of the Scriptures—"Sister Mary," "Brudder Jonah," "Brudder Moses," "Brudder Daniel"—were greeted with similar intimacy and immediacy. In the world of the spirituals, it was not the masters and mistresses .but God and Jesus and the entire pantheon of Old Testament figures who set the standards, established the precedents, and defined the values; who, in short, constituted the "significant others." The world described by the slave songs was a black world in which no reference was ever made to any white contem-

poraries. The slave's positive reference group was composed entirely
of his own peers: his mother, father, sister, brother, uncles, aunts,
preacher, fellow "sinners" and "mourners" of whom he sang endlessly,
to whom he sent messages via the dying, and with whom he was reunited joyfully in the next world.

The same sense of sacred time and space which shaped the slave's
portraits of his gods and heroes also made his visions of the past and
future immediate and compelling. Descriptions of the Crucifixion
communicate a sense of the actual presence of the singers: "Dey
pierced Him in the side . . . Dey nail Him to de cross . . . Dey rivet
His feet . . . Dey hanged him high . . . Dey stretch Him wide. . . ."

> *Oh sometimes it causes me to tremble,–tremble,–tremble,*
> *Were you there when they crucified my Lord?* [45]

The Slave's "shout"—that counterclockwise, shuffling dance which
frequently occurred after the religious service and lasted long into
the night—often became a medium through which the ecstatic
dancers were transformed into actual participants in historic actions:
Joshua's army marching around the walls of Jericho, the children of
Israel following Moses out of Egypt.[46]

The thin line between time dimensions is nowhere better illustrated than in the slave's visions of the future, which were, of course,
a direct negation of his present. Among the most striking spirituals are those which pile detail upon detail in describing the Day of
Judgment: "You'll see de world on fire . . . see de element a meltin',
. . . see the stars a fallin' . . . see the moon a bleedin' . . . see the
forked lightning, . . . Hear the rumblin' thunder . . . see the right-
eous marching, . . . see my Jesus coming . . . ," and the world to
come where "Dere's no sun to burn you . . . no hard trials . . . no
whips a crackin' . . . no stormy weather . . . no tribulation . . . no
evil-doers . . . All is gladness in de Kingdom." [47] This vividness was
matched by the slave's certainty that he would partake of the triumph
of judgment and the joys of the new world:

> *Dere's room enough, room enough, room enough in de heaven,*
> *   my Lord*
> *Room enough, room enough, I can't stay behind.*[48]

Continually, the slaves sang of reaching out beyond the world that confined them, of seeing Jesus "in de wilderness," of praying "in de lonesome valley," of breathing in the freedom of the mountain peaks:

> *Did yo' ever*
> *Stan' on mountun,*
> *Wash yo' han's*
> *In a cloud?* [49]

Continually, they held out the possibility of imminent rebirth; "I look at de worl' an' de worl' look new, . . . I look at my hands an' they look so too . . . I looked at my feet, my feet was too." [50]

These possibilities, these certainties were not surprising. The religious revivals which swept large numbers of slaves into the Christian fold in the late eighteenth and early nineteenth centuries were based upon a *practical* (not necessarily theological) Armianism: God would save all who believed in Him; Salvation was there for all to take hold of if they would. The effects of this message upon the slaves who were exposed to and converted by it have been passed over too easily by historians. Those effects are illustrated graphically in the spirituals which were the products of these revivals and which continued to spread the evangelical word long after the revivals had passed into history.

The religious music of the slaves is almost devoid of feelings of depravity or unworthiness, but is rather, as I have tried to show, pervaded by a sense of change, transcendence, ultimate justice, and personal worth. The spirituals have been referred to as "sorrow songs," and in some respects they were. The slaves sang of "rollin' thro' an unfriendly world," of being "a-trouble in de mind," of living in a world which was a "howling wilderness," "a hell to me," of feeling like a "motherless child," "a po' little orphan chile in de worl'," a "home-e-less child," of fearing that "Trouble will bury me down.' " [51]

But these feelings were rarely pervasive or permanent; almost always they were overshadowed by a triumphant note of affirmation. Even so despairing a wail as "Nobody Knows the Trouble I've Had" could suddenly have its mood transformed by lines like: "One morning I was a-walking down, . . . Saw some berries a-hanging down, . . . I pick de berry and I suck de juice, . . . Just as sweet as de honey in de comb." [52] Similarly, amid the deep sorrow of "Sometimes I feel like a Motherless chile," sudden release could come with the lines: "Sometimes I feel like/A eagle in de air. . . . Spread my wings an'/

Fly, fly, fly." [53] Slaves spent little time singing of the horrors of hell or damnation. Their songs of the Devil, quoted earlier, pictured a harsh but almost semicomic figure (often, one suspects, a surrogate for the white man), over whom they triumphed with reassuring regularity. For all their inevitable sadness, slave songs were characterized more by a feeling of confidence than of despair. There was confidence that contemporary power relationships were not immutable: "Did not old Pharaoh get lost, get lost, get lost, . . . get lost in the Red Sea?"; confidence in the possibilities of instantaneous change: "Jesus make de dumb to speak. . . . Jesus make de cripple walk. . . . Jesus give de blind his sight. . . . Jesus do most anything"; confidence in the rewards of persistence: "Keep a' inching along like a poor inch-worm,/ Jesus will come by'nd bye"; confidence that nothing could stand in the way of the justice they would receive: "You kin hender me here, but you can't do it dah," "O no man, no man, no man can hinder me"; confidence in the prospects of the future: "We'll walk de golden streets/Of de New Jerusalem." Religion, the slaves sang, "is good for anything, . . . Religion make you happy, . . . Religion gib me patience . . . O member, get Religion . . . Religion is so sweet." [54]

The slaves often pursued the "sweetness" of their religion in the face of many obstacles. Becky Ilsey, who was 16 when she was emancipated, recalled many years later:

> 'Fo' de war when we'd have a meetin' at night, wuz mos' always 'way in de woods or de bushes some whar so de white folks couldn't hear, an' when dey'd sing a spiritual an' de spirit 'gin to shout some de elders would go 'mongst de folks an' put dey han' over dey mouf an' some times put a clof in dey mouf an' say: "Spirit don talk so loud or de patterol break us up." You know dey had white patterols what went 'roun' at night to see de niggers didn't cut up no devilment, an' den de meetin' would break up an' some would go to one house an' some to er nudder an' dey would groan er w'ile, den go home.[55]

Elizabeth Ross Hite testified that although she and her fellow slaves on a Louisiana plantation were Catholics, "lots didn't like that 'ligion."

> We used to hide behind some bricks and hold church ourselves. You see, the Catholic preachers from France wouldn't let us shout,

and the Lawd done said you gotta shout if you want to be saved.
That's in the Bible.

Sometimes we held church all night long, 'til way in the mornin'.
We burned some grease in a can for the preacher to see the Bible
by. . . .

See, our master didn't like us to have much 'ligion, said
it made us lag in our work. He jest wanted us to be Catholicses
on Sundays and go to mass and not study 'bout nothin' like that
on week days. He didn't want us shoutin' and moanin' all day'-
long, but you gotta shout and you gotta moan if you wants to be
saved.[56]

The slaves clearly craved the affirmation and promise of their religion. It would be a mistake, however, to see this urge as exclusively
otherworldly. When Thomas Wentworth Higginson observed that the
spirituals exhibited "nothing but patience for this life,—nothing but
triumph in the next," he, and later observers who elaborated upon
this judgment, were indulging in hyperbole. Although Jesus was ubiquitous in the spirituals, it was not invariably the Jesus of the New
Testament of whom the slaves sang, but frequently a Jesus transformed into an Old Testament warrior: "Mass' Jesus" who engaged in
personal combat with the Devil; "King Jesus" seated on a milk-white
horse with sword and shield in hand. "Ride on, King Jesus," "Ride on,
conquering King," "The God I serve is a man of war," the slaves
sang.[57] This transformation of Jesus is symptomatic of the slaves'
selectivity in choosing those parts of the Bible which were to serve as
the basis of their religious consciousness. Howard Thurman, a Negro
minister who as a boy had the duty of reading the Bible to his grand-
mother, was perplexed by her refusal to allow him to read from the
Epistles of Paul.

When at length I asked the reason, she told me that during the
days of slavery, the minister (white) on the plantation was always
preaching from the Pauline letters—"Slaves, be obedient to your
masters," etc. "I vowed to myself," she said, "that if freedom ever
came and I learned to read, I would never read that part of the
Bible!" [58]

Nor, apparently, did this part of the Scriptures ever constitute a vital element in slave songs or sermons. The emphasis of the spirituals, as

Higginson himself noted, was upon the Old Testament and the exploits of the Hebrew children.[59] It is important that Daniel and David and Joshua and Jonah and Moses and Noah, all of whom fill the lines of the spirituals, were delivered in *this* world and delivered in ways which struck the imagination of the slaves. Over and over their songs dwelt upon the spectacle of the Red Sea opening to allow the Hebrew slaves past before inundating the mighty armies of the Pharaoh. They lingered delightedly upon the image of little David humbling the great Goliath with a stone—a pretechnological victory which post-bellum Negroes were to expand upon in their songs of John Henry. They retold in endless variation the stories of the blind and humbled Samson bringing down the mansions of his conquerors; of the ridiculed Noah patiently building the ark which would deliver him from the doom of a mocking world; of the timid Jonah attaining freedom from his confinement through faith. The similarity of these tales to the situation of the slave was too clear for him not to see it; too clear for us to believe that the songs had no worldly content for the black man in bondage. "O my Lord delivered Daniel," the slaves observed, and responded logically: "O why not deliver me, too?"

> *He delivered Daniel from de lion's den,*
> *Jonah from de belly ob de whale,*
> *And de Hebrew children from de fiery furnace,*
> *And why not every man?* [60]

These lines state as clearly as anything can the manner in which the sacred world of the slaves was able to fuse the precedents of the past, the conditions of the present, and the promise of the future into one connected reality. In this respect there was always a latent and symbolic element of protest in the slave's religious songs which frequently became overt and explicit. Frederick Douglass asserted that for him and many of his fellow slaves the song, "O Canaan, sweet Canaan,/I am bound for the land of Canaan," symbolized "something more than a hope of reaching heaven. We meant to reach the *North*, and the North was our Canaan," and he wrote that the lines of another spiritual, "Run to Jesus, shun the danger,/I don't expect to stay much longer here," had a double meaning which first suggested to him the thought of escaping from slavery.[61] Similarly, when the black troops in Higginson's regiment sang:

> *We'll soon be free, [three times]*
> *When de Lord will call us home.*

a young drummer boy explained to him, "Dey think *de Lord* mean
for say *de Yankees.*" [62] Nor is there any reason to doubt that slaves
could have used their songs as a means of secret communication. An
ex-slave told Lydia Parrish that when he and his fellow slaves "sus-
picioned" that one of their number was telling tales to the driver,
they would sing lines like the following while working in the field:

> *O Judyas he wuz a 'ceitful man*
> *He went an' betray a mos' innocen' man.*
> *Fo' thirty pieces a silver dat it wuz done*
> *He went in de woods an' e' self he hung.*[63]

And it is possible, as many writers have argued, that such spirituals
as the commonly heard "Steal away, steal away, steal away to Jesus!"
were used as explicit calls to secret meetings.

But it is not necessary to invest the spirituals with a secular function only at the price of divesting them of their religious content, as
Miles Mark Fisher has done.[64] While we may make such clear-cut distinctions, I have tried to show that the slaves did not. For them religion
never constituted a simple escape from this world, because their conception of the world was more expansive than modern man's. Nowhere
is this better illustrated than during the Civil War itself. While the
war gave rise to such new spirituals as "Before I'd be a slave/I'd be
buried in my grave,/And go home to my Lord and be saved!" or the
popular "Many thousand Go," with its jubilant rejection of all the
facets of slave life—"No more peck o' corn for me, . . . No more
driver's lash for me, . . . No more pint o' salt for me, . . . No more
hundred lash for me, . . . No more mistress' call for me" [65]—the
important thing was not that large numbers of slaves now could create
new songs which openly expressed their views of slavery; that was to be
expected. More significant was the ease with which their old songs fit
their new situation. With so much of their inspiration drawn from the
events of the Old Testament and the Book of Revelation, the slaves had
long sung of wars, of battles, of the Army of the Lord, of Soldiers of
the Cross, of trumpets summoning the faithful, of vanquishing the

hosts of evil. These songs especially were, as Higginson put it, "available for camp purposes with very little strain upon their symbolism." "We'll cross de mighty river," his troops sang while marching or rowing,

> *We'll cross de danger water, . . .*
> *O Pharaoh's army drownded!*
> *My army cross over.*

"O blow your trumpet, Gabriel," they sang,

> *Blow your trumpet louder;*
> *And I want dat trumpet to blow me home*
> *To my new Jerusalem.*

But they also found their less overtly militant songs quite as appropriate to warfare. Their most popular and effective marching song was:

> *Jesus call you, Go in de wilderness,*
>   *Go in de wilderness, go in de wilderness,*
> *Jesus call you. Go in de wilderness*
>   *To wait upon de Lord.*[66]

Black Union soldiers found it no more incongruous to accompany their fight for freedom with the sacred songs of their bondage than they had found it inappropriate as slaves to sing their spirituals while picking cotton or shucking corn. Their religious songs, like their religion itself, was of this world as well as the next.

Slave songs by themselves, of course, do not present us with a definitive key to the life and mind of the slave. They have to be seen within the context of the slave's situation and examined alongside such other cultural materials as folk tales. But slave songs do indicate the need to rethink a number of assumptions that have shaped recent interpretations of slavery, such as the assumption that because slavery eroded the linguistic and institutional side of African life it wiped out almost all the more fundamental aspects of African culture. Culture, certainly, is more than merely the sum total of institutions and language. It is also expressed by something less tangible, which the anthropologist Robert Redfield has called "style of life." Peoples as different as the Lapp and the Bedouin, Redfield has argued, with diverse languages, religions, customs, and institutions, may still share an emphasis on certain virtues and ideals, certain manners of independence and hospitality, general ways of looking upon the world, which give them a similar life style.[67] This argument applies to the West African cultures from which the slaves came. Though they varied widely in language, institutions, gods, and familial patterns, they shared a fundamental outlook toward the past, present, and future and common means of cultural expression which could well have constituted the basis of a sense of community and identity capable of surviving the impact of slavery.

Slave songs present us with abundant evidence that in the structure of their music and dance, in the uses to which music was put, in the survival of the oral tradition, in the retention of such practices as spirit possession which often accompanied the creation of spirituals, and in the ways in which the slaves expressed their new religion, important elements of their shared African heritage remained alive not just as quaint cultural vestiges but as vitally creative elements of slave culture. This could never have happened if slavery was, as Professor Elkins maintains, a system which so completely closed in around the slave, so totally penetrated his personality structure as to infantalize him and reduce him to a kind of *tabula rasa* upon which the white man could write what he chose.[68]

Slave songs provide us with the beginnings of a very different kind of hypothesis: that the preliterate, premodern Africans, with their sacred world view, were so imperfectly acculturated into the secular American society into which they were thrust, were so completely denied access to the ideology and dreams which formed the core of the consciousness of other Americans, that they were forced to fall back upon the only cultural frames of reference that made any sense to them and gave them any feeling of security. I use the word "forced" advisedly. Even if the slaves had had the opportunity to enter fully into the life of the larger society, they might still have chosen to retain and perpetuate certain elements of their African heritage. But the point is that they really had no choice. True acculturation was denied to most slaves. The alternatives were either to remain in a state of cultural limbo, divested of the old cultural patterns but not allowed to adopt those of their new homeland—which in the long run is no alternative at all—or to cling to as many as possible of the old ways of thinking and acting. The slaves' oral tradition, their music, and their religious outlook served this latter function and constituted a cultural refuge at least potentially capable of protecting their personalities from some of the worst ravages of the slave system.

The argument of Professors Tannenbaum and Elkins that the Protestant churches in the United States did not act as a buffer between the slave and his master is persuasive enough, but it betrays a modern preoccupation with purely institutional arrangements.[69] Religion is more than an institution, and because Protestant churches failed to protect the slave's inner being from the incursions of the slave system, it does not follow that the spiritual message of Protestantism failed as well. Slave songs are a testament to the ways in which Christianity provided slaves with the precedents, heroes, and future promise that allowed them to transcend the purely temporal bonds of the Peculiar Institution.

Historians have frequently failed to perceive the full importance of this because they have not taken the slave's religiosity seriously enough. A people cannot create a music as forceful and striking as slave music out of a mere uninternalized anodyne. Those who have argued that Negroes did not oppose slavery in any meaningful way are writing from a modern, political context. What they really mean is that the slaves found no *political* means to oppose slavery. But slaves, to borrow Professor Hobsbawm's term, were prepolitical beings in a prepolitical situation.[70] Within their frame of reference there were other—and from the point of view of personality development, not necessarily less effective—means of escape and opposition. If mid-twentieth-century historians have difficulty perceiving the sacred universe created by slaves as a serious alternative to the societal system created by southern slaveholders, the problem may be the historians' and not the slaves'.

Above all, the study of slave songs forces the historian to move out of his own culture, in which music plays a peripheral role, and offers him the opportunity to understand the ways in which black slaves were able to perpetuate much of the centrality and functional importance that music had for their African ancestors. In the con-

cluding lines of his perceptive study of primitive song, C. M. Bowra
has written:

> Primitive song is indispensable to those who practice it. . . . they
> cannot do without song, which both formulates and answers their
> nagging questions, enables them to pursue action with zest and
> confidence, brings them into touch with gods and spirits, and
> makes them feel less strange in the natural world. . . . it gives to
> them a solid centre in what otherwise would be almost chaos, and
> a continuity in their being, which would too easily dissolve before
> the calls of the implacable present . . . through its words men,
> who might otherwise give in to the malice of circumstances, find
> their old powers revived or new powers stirring in them, and
> through these life itself is sustained and renewed and fulfilled.[71]

This, I think, sums up concisely the function of song for the
slave. Without a general understanding of that function, without a
specific understanding of the content and meaning of slave song, there
can be no full comprehension of the effects of slavery upon the slave
or the meaning of the society from which slaves emerged at emancipation.

FOOTNOTES

1. Miles Mark Fisher, *Negro Slave Songs in the United States* (New York,
1963, orig. pub. 1953), 14, 39, 132, and *passim.*
2. The contours of this debate are judiciously outlined in D. K. Wilgus,
Anglo-American Folksong Scholarship Since 1898 (New Brunswick, 1959), App. One,
"The Negro-White Spirituals."
3. Lucy McKim, "Songs of the Port Royal Contrabands," *Dwight's Journal
of Music,* XXII (November 8, 1862), 255.
4. W. F. Allen, "The Negro Dialect," *The Nation,* I (December 14, 1865),
744–745.
5. See, for instance, Henry Edward Krehbiel, *Afro-American Folksongs* (New
York, 1963, orig. pub. 1914); James Wesley Work, *Folk Song of the American Negro*
(Nashville, 1915); James Weldon Johnson, *The Book of American Negro Spirituals*
(New York, 1925), and *The Second Book of Negro Spirituals* (New York, 1926);
Lydia Parrish, *Slave Songs of the Georgia Sea Islands* (Hatboro, Penna., 1965, orig.
pub. 1942); LeRoi Jones, *Blues People* (New York, 1963).
6. Newman I. White, *American Negro Folk-Songs* (Hatboro, Penna., 1965,
orig. pub. 1928); Guy B. Johnson, *Folk Culture on St. Helena Island, South Carolina* (Chapel Hill, 1930); George Pullen Jackson, *White and Negro Spirituals* (New
York, 1943).

7. White, *American Negro Folk-Songs*, 11–13.

8. Professor John William Ward gives an excellent example of this process in his discussion of the different meanings which the newspapers of the United States, France, and India attributed to Charles Lindbergh's flight across the Atlantic in 1927. See "Lindbergh, Dos Passos, and History," in Ward, *Red, White, and Blue* (New York, 1969), 55.

9. George Pullen Jackson, "The Genesis of the Negro Spiritual," *The American Mercury*, XXVI (June 1932), 248.

10. Richard Alan Waterman, "African Influence on the Music of the Americas," in Sol Tax (ed.), *Acculturation in the Americas: Proceedings and Selected Papers of the XXIXth International Congress of Americanists* (Chicago, 1952), 207–218; Wilgus, *Anglo-American Folksong Scholarship Since 1898*, 363–364; Melville H. Herskovits, "Patterns of Negro Music" (pamphlet, no publisher, no date); Gilbert Chase, *America's Music* (New York, 1966), Chap. 12; Alan P. Merriam, "African Music," in William R. Bascom and Melville J. Herskovits (eds.), *Continuity and Change in African Cultures* (Chicago, 1959), 76–80.

11. White, *American Negro Folk-Songs*, 29, 55.

12. Jackson, *White and Negro Spirituals*, 266–267.

13. James Miller McKim, "Negro Songs," *Dwight's Journal of Music*, XXI (August 9, 1862), 149.

14. Thomas Wentworth Higginson, *Army Life in a Black Regiment* (Beacon Press edition, Boston, 1962, orig. pub. 1869), 218–219.

15 Henry Russell, *Cheer! Boys, Cheer!*, 84–85, quoted in Chase, *America's Music*, 235–236.

16. Jeanette Robinson Murphy, "The Survival of African Music in America," *Popular Science Monthly*, 55 (1899), 660–672, reprinted in Bruce Jackson (ed.), *The Negro and His Folklore in Nineteenth-Century Periodicals* (Austin, 1967), 328.

17. Natalie Curtis Burlin, "Negro Music at Birth," *Musical Quarterly*, V (January 1919), 88. For Mrs. Burlin's excellent reproductions of Negro folk songs and spirituals, see her *Negro Folk-Songs* (New York, 1918–1919), Vol. I–IV.

18. Clifton Joseph Furness, "Communal Music Among Arabians and Negroes," *Musical Quarterly*, XVI (January 1930), 49–51.

19. Elizabeth Kilham, "Sketches in Color: IV," *Putnam's Monthly*, XV (March 1870), 304–311, reprinted in Jackson, *The Negro and His Folklore in Nineteenth-Century Periodicals*, 127–128.

20. Bruno Nettl, *Folk and Traditional Music of the Western Continents* (Englewood Cliffs, 1965), 4–5; Chase, *America's Music*, 241–243.

21. J. K., Jr., "Who Are Our National Poets?," *Knickerbocker Magazine*, 26 (October 1845), 336, quoted in Dena J. Epstein, "Slave Music in the United States Before 1860: A Survey of Sources (Part I)," *Music Library Association Notes*, XX (Spring 1963), 208.

22. Elizabeth Kilham, "Sketches in Color: IV," *Putnam's Monthly*, XV (March 1870), 304–311, reprinted in Jackson, *The Negro and His Folklore in Nineteenth-Century Periodicals*, 129.

23. White, *American Negro Folk-Songs*, 57.

24. Alan P. Merriam, "Music and the Dance," in Robert Lystad (ed.), *The African World: A Survey of Social Research* (New York, 1965), 452–468; William Bascom, "Folklore and Literature," in *Ibid.*, 469–488; R. S. Rattray, *Ashanti* (Oxford, 1923), Chap. XV; Melville Herskovits, "Freudian Mechanisms in Primitive Negro Psychology," in E. E. Evans-Pritchard *et al.* (eds.), *Essays Presented to C. G.*

Seligman (London, 1934), 75–84; Alan P. Merriam, "African Music," in Bascom and Herskovits, *Continuity and Change in African Cultures,* 49–86.

25. William Francis Allen, Charles Pickard Ware, and Lucy McKim Garrison, compilers, *Slave Songs of the United States* (New York, 1867, Oak Publications ed., 1965), 164–165.

26. *Ibid.,* 43.

27. Harriet Jacobs, *Incidents in the Life of a Slave Girl* (Boston, 1861), 109.

28. Lines like these could be quoted endlessly. For the specific ones cited, see the songs in the following collections: Higginson, *Army Life in a Black Regiment,* 206, 216–217; Allen *et al., Slave Songs of the United States,* 33–34, 44, 106–108, 131, 160–161; Thomas P. Fenner, compiler, *Religious Folk Songs of the Negro as Sung on the Plantations* (Hampton, Virginia, 1909, orig. pub. 1874), 10–11, 48; J. B. T. Marsh, *The Story of the Jubilee Singers; With Their Songs* (Boston, 1880), 136, 167, 178.

29. McKim, "Negro Songs," 148; H. G. Spaulding, "Under the Palmetto," *Continental Monthly,* IV (1863), 188–203, reprinted in Jackson, *The Negro and His Folklore in Nineteenth-Century Periodicals,* 72; Allen, "The Negro Dialect," 744–745; Higginson, *Army Life in a Black Regiment,* 220–221.

30. *Journal of Nicholas Cresswell, 1774–1777* (New York, 1934), 17–19, quoted in Epstein, *Music Library Association Notes,* XX (Spring 1963), 201.

31. Jacobs, *Incidents in the Life of a Slave Girl,* 180.

32. *Life and Times of Frederick Douglass* (rev. ed., 1892, Collier Books Edition, 1962), 146–147.

33. John Lambert, *Travels Through Canada and the United States of North America in the Years, 1806–1807 and 1808* (London, 1814), II, 253–254, quoted in Dena J. Epstein, "Slave Music in the United States Before 1860: A Survey of Sources (Part 2)," *Music Library Association Notes,* XX (Summer 1963), 377.

34. Frances Anne Kemble, *Journal of a Residence on a Georgian Plantation in 1838–1839* (New York, 1863), 128.

35. For versions of these songs, see Dorothy Scarborough, *On the Trail of Negro Folk-Songs* (Cambridge, 1925), 194, 201–203, 223–225, and Thomas W. Talley, *Negro Folk Rhymes* (New York, 1922), 25–26. Talley claims that the majority of the songs in his large and valuable collection "were sung by Negro fathers and mothers in the dark days of American slavery to their children who listened with eyes as large as saucers and drank them down with mouths wide open," but offers no clue as to why he feels that songs collected for the most part in the twentieth century were slave songs.

36. Constance Rourke, *The Roots of American Culture and Other Essays* (New York, 1942), 262–274. Newman White, on the contrary, has argued that although the earliest minstrel songs were Negro derived, they soon went their own way and that less than ten per cent of them were genuinely Negro. Nevertheless, these white songs "got back to the plantation, largely spurious as they were and were undoubtedly among those which the plantation-owners encouraged the Negroes to sing. They persist to-day in isolated stanzas and lines, among the songs handed down by plantation Negroes . . ." White, *American Negro Folk-Songs,* 7–10 and Appendix IV. There are probably valid elements in both theses. A similarly complex relationship between genuine Negro folk creations and their more commercialized partly white influenced imitations was to take place in the blues of the twentieth century.

37. McKim, "Songs of the Port Royal Contrabands," 255.

38. Mircea Eliade, *The Sacred and the Profane* (New York, 1961), Chaps. 2,

4, and *passim.* For the similarity of Eliade's concept to the world view of West Africa, see W. E. Abraham, *The Mind of Africa* (London, 1962), Chap. 2, and R. S. Rattray, *Religion and Art in Ashanti* (Oxford, 1927).

39. Paul Radin, "Status, Phantasy, and the Christian Dogma," in Social Science Institute, Fisk University, *God Struck Me Dead: Religious Conversion Experiences and Autobiographies of Negro Ex-Slaves* (Nashville, 1945, unpublished typescript).

40. Stanley Elkins, *Slavery* (Chicago, 1959), 136.

41. Allen *et al., Slave Songs of the United States,* 33–34, 105; William E. Barton, *Old Plantation Hymns: A Collection of Hitherto Unpublished Melodies of the Slave and the Freedmen* (Boston, 1899), 30.

42. Allen *et al., Slave Songs of the United States,* 47.

43. Barton, *Old Plantation Hymns,* 19.

44. Marsh, *The Story of the Jubilee Singers,* 132.

45. Fenner, *Religious Folk Songs of the Negro,* 162; E. A. McIlhenny, *Befo' De War Spirituals: Words and Melodies* (Boston, 1933), 39.

46. Barton, *Old Plantation Hymns,* 15; Howard W. Odum and Guy B. Johnson, *The Negro And His Songs* (Hatboro, Penn., 1964, orig. pub. 1925), 33–34; for a vivid description of the "shout" see *The Nation,* May 30, 1867, 432–433; see also Parrish, *Slave Songs of the Georgia Sea Islands,* Chap. III.

47. For examples of songs of this nature, see Fenner, *Religious Folk Songs of the Negro,* 8, 63–65; Marsh, *The Story of the Jubilee Singers,* 240–241; Higginson, *Army Life in a Black Regiment,* 205; Allen *et al., Slave Songs of the United States,* 91, 100; Burlin, *Negro Folk-Songs,* I, 37–42.

48. Allen *et al., Slave Songs of the United States,* 32–33.

49. *Ibid.,* 30–31; Burlin, *Negro Folk-Songs,* II, 8–9; Fenner, *Religious Folk Songs of the Negro,* 12.

50. Allen *et al., Slave Songs of the United States,* 128–129; Fenner, *Religious Folk Songs of the Negro,* 127; Barton, *Old Plantation Hymns,* 26.

51. Allen *et al., Slave Songs of the United States,* 70, 102–103, 147; Barton, *Old Plantation Hymns,* 9, 17–18, 24; Marsh, *The Story of the Jubilee Singers,* 133, 167; Odum and Johnson, *The Negro And His Songs,* 35.

52. Allen *et al., Slave Songs of the United States,* 102–103.

53. Mary Allen Grissom, compiler, *The Negro Sings A New Heaven* (Chapel Hill, 1930), 73.

54. Marsh, *The Story of the Jubilee Singers,* 179, 186; Allen *et al., Slave Songs of the United States,* 40–41, 44, 146; Barton, *Old Plantation Hymns,* 30.

55. McIlhenny, *Befo' De War Spirituals,* 31.

56. *Gumbo Ya-Ya: A Collection of Louisiana Folk Tales,* compiled by Lyle Saxon, Edward Dreyer, and Robert Tallant from materials gathered by workers of the WPA, Louisiana Writer's Project (Boston, 1945), 242.

57. For examples, see Allen *et al., Slave Songs of the United States,* 40–41, 82, 97, 106–108; Marsh, *The Story of the Jubilee Singers,* 168, 203; Burlin, *Negro Folk-Songs,* II, 8–9; Howard Thurman, *Deep River* (New York, 1945), 19–21.

58. Thurman, *Deep River,* 16–17.

59. Higginson, *Army Life in a Black Regiment,* 202–205. Many of those northerners who came to the South to "uplift" the freedmen were deeply disturbed at the Old Testament emphasis of their religion. H. G. Spaulding complained that the ex-slaves needed to be introduced to "the light and warmth of the Gospel," and reported that a Union army officer told him: "Those people had enough of the Old Testament thrown at their heads under slavery. Now give them the glorious utter-

ances and practical teachings of the Great Master." Spaulding, "Under the Palmetto," reprinted in Jackson, *The Negro and His Folklore in Nineteenth-Century Periodicals,* 66.

60. Allen *et al., Slave Songs of the United States,* 148; Fenner, *Religious Folk Songs of the Negro,* 21; Marsh, *The Story of the Jubilee Singers,* 134–135; McIlhenny, *Befo' De War Spirituals,* 248–249.

61. *Life and Times of Frederick Douglass,* 159–160; Marsh, *The Story of the Jubilee Singers,* 188.

62. Higginson, *Army Life in a Black Regiment,* 217.

63. Parrish, *Slave Songs of the Georgia Sea Islands,* 247.

64. "Actually, not one spiritual in its primary form reflected interest in anything other than a full life here and now." Fisher, *Negro Slave Songs in the United States,* 137.

65. Barton, *Old Plantation Hymns,* 25; Allen *et al., Slave Songs of the United States,* 94; McKim, "Negro Songs," 149.

66. Higginson, *Army Life in a Black Regiment,* 201–202, 211–212.

67. Robert Redfield, *The Primitive World and Its Transformations* (Ithaca, 1953), 51–53.

68. Elkins, *Slavery,* Chap. III.

69. *Ibid.,* Chap. II; Frank Tannenbaum, *Slave and Citizen* (New York, 1946).

70. E. J. Hobsbawm, *Primitive Rebels* (New York, 1959), Chap. I.

71. C. M. Bowra, *Primitive Song* (London, 1962), 285–286.

LEON F. LITWACK

Free at Last

𐰀𐰀𐰀𐰀𐰀𐰀𐰀𐰀𐰀𐰀𐰀𐰀𐰀𐰀𐰀𐰀𐰀𐰀𐰀𐰀𐰀𐰀𐰀𐰀𐰀𐰀𐰀𐰀𐰀𐰀𐰀𐰀𐰀𐰀𐰀𐰀𐰀𐰀𐰀

Kingdom Comin'

Say, darkies, hab you seen de massa,
Wid de muffstash on his face.
Go along de road some time dis mornin'.
Like he gwine to leab de place?
He seen a smoke way up de ribber,
Whar de Linkum gunboats lay,
He took his hat, an' lef' berry sudden,
An' I spec' he run away!

Chorus

De massa run! ha, ha!
De darkey stay! ho, ho!
It mus' be now de kingdom comin'
An' de year ob Jubilo!

He six foot one way, two foot tudder,
An' he weigh t'ree hundred pound,
His coat so big, he couldn't pay de tailor,
An' it won't go half way round.
He drill so much, dey call him Cap'an,
An' he get so drefful tanned,

I spec' he try an' fool dem Yankees,
*   For to tink he's contraband.*

De darkeys feel so berry lonsome,
*   Libing in de log house on de lawn,*
Dey move dar tings to massa's parlor.
*   For to keep it while he's gone.*
Dar's wine an' cider in de kitchen,
*   An' de darkeys de'll hab some;*
I spose dey'll all be confiscated,
*   When de Linkum sojers come.*

De oberseer he make us trouble,
*   An' he dribe us round a spell;*
We lock him up in de smoke-house cellar,
*   Wid de key trown in de well.*
De whip is lost, de han'cuff broken,
*   But de massa'll hab his pay,*
He's old enuff, beg enuff, ought to know better
*   Dan to went an' run away.*[1]

On April 12, 1864, George W. Hatton thought there was sufficient cause for celebration. It had been three years since Confederate batteries had opened fire on Fort Sumter, and he could only marvel at the changes that had taken place in his own life as well as in the lives of his people. "Who would not celebrate this day?" he asked. "What has the colored man done for himself in the past three years? Why, sir, he has proved . . . that he is a man." Hatton was a sergeant in Company C, First Regiment, United States Colored Troops, and his unit was encamped near Newbern, North Carolina. The regimental chaplain —apparently the first black man ever so designated—was Henry McNeal Turner, a native of South Carolina, most recently pastor of the Israel Bethel Church in Washington, D.C., who was to remain in the South and play an active role in Georgia Reconstruction politics. At the outset of the Civil War, when black men had come forth to volunteer their services, the federal government had spurned them. But here they were, three years later, uniformed, armed, experienced in combat, and ready to make their way into Virginia for the final onslaught on the Confederacy. It seemed incredible. "Though the Government

openly declared that it did not want the negroes in this conflict,"
Sergeant Hatton reflected, "I look around me and see hundreds of
colored men armed and ready to defend the Government at any moment; and such are my feelings, that I can only say, the fetters have
fallen—our bondage is over." [2]

Less than a month later, the First Regiment was encamped by
the James River, only a few miles from Jamestown. This was the very
place, Sergeant Hatton noted, where some 264 years before "the first
sons of Africa" had been landed on American soil. The area took on
a special meaning for several of the men in the regiment who had only
recently been held as slaves here. Whatever memories they retained
of those days were no doubt revived when several black women
reached the camp, still bearing the marks of a severe whipping. While
out on a foraging expedition the next day, the soldiers captured the
man who had meted out the punishment—"a Mr. Clayton, a noted
reb in this part of the country, and from his appearance, one of the
F.F.V's." Before an apparently appreciative audience, which included
the black women he had only recently whipped, the slave owner was
tied to a tree and stripped of his clothes; one of his former slaves, now
a soldier in the regiment, took up a whip and lashed him some 20
times, "bringing the blood from his loins at every stroke, and not for-
getting to remind the gentleman of days gone by." The whip was then
handed over to the black women who "one after another, came up and
gave him a like number, to remind him that they were no longer his,
but safely housed in Abraham's bosom, and under the protection of
the Star Spangled Banner, and guarded by their own patriotic, though
once down-trodden race." In attempting to describe his impressions of
that day, Sergeant Hatton confessed that he was at a loss for the
proper words. "Oh, that I had the tongue to express my feelings while
standing upon the banks of the James river, on the soil of Virginia,
the mother state of slavery, as a witness of such a sudden reverse! The
day is clear, the fields of grain are beautiful, and the birds are singing
sweet melodious songs, while poor Mr. C. is crying to his servants for
mercy." [3]

It was no longer the white man's war. What had started out as a
war to save the Union had become, for scores of black people at least,
a war of liberation.

2.

With the approach of the Union Army, even the less observant plantation whites might have sensed the restlessness, the apprehension, the suppressed feelings of excitement that pervaded the slave quarters and affected the demeanor of the most trusted household servants. "[H]e won't look at me now," Mary Chesnut wrote of her mother's butler, with whom she had played as a child and had taught to read. "He looks over my head, he scents freedom in the air." On numerous plantations, particularly those lying in the anticipated path of the Union Army, the slaves suddenly seemed less willing to work, some refused to submit to any further punishment, they grumbled more than usual about orders, and a few insisted that they be paid for any future services—and not in worthless Confederate currency. The once clandestine slave meetings were less secretive. The singing in the slave quarters was apt to be more frequent and louder, often lasting late into the night, and the content of their songs was noticeably bolder. Freedom was no longer a furtive dream. It was to be realized here on earth, not in some heavenly kingdom. "Now they gradually threw off the mask," one slave recalled, "and were not afraid to let it be known that the 'freedom' in their songs meant freedom of the body in this world." [4]

For nearly every slave, there was that moment when freedom suddenly became a distinct possibility. Perhaps it was the sight of retreating Confederate soldiers, or the frantic preparations for evacuation of the "big house," or simply that look of despair on the faces of the white folks. To one elderly slave woman, cooking the Sunday dinner on a plantation in eastern Virginia, it was the sound of the Union cannons at nearby Manassas, each blast of which she greeted with a subdued, "ride on Massa Jesus." To the young Sam Mitchell, listening to the Union Navy guns echo through the Sea Islands, it was the reassurance of his mother that "dat ain't no t'under, dat Yankee come to gib you Freedom." To one South Carolina slave on his way to the stake for a whipping, it was the report that Union gunboats were coming up the river. "Yanks coming, Massa!" he shouted, as he took off for the river bank. His master ran in the other direction. To Nellie, a young Mississippi black girl waiting for the bugle to call the slaves out to the fields, it was the sound of Yankee drums down the road. "They knew it was all over then," she recalled.[5]

The knowledge that the Yankees were somewhere within reach could precipitate the rapid depopulation of the slave quarters. When a large Union force passed near A. Franklin Pugh's sugar plantations in Louisiana, he noted "great excitement among the slaves"; the next day, he found them "in a very bad way"; two days later, they were "completely demoralized, some gone and more preparing to go," and before the week was over "a rebellion among the negroes" had broken out on a neighboring plantation.[6] The movement of refugees became so intense in some areas that one Union officer described them as "an army in themselves." They would leave the plantations at night, conceal themselves in the woods or swamps during the day, and proceed to the nearest Yankee camp. Some ran away with the Union raiding parties, or straggled behind the columns of Union troops, or sought out the Federal warships blockading the coast and the gunboats plying the southern rivers. Occasionally they traveled in well-organized and partially armed groups. Elijah Marrs, for example, mobilized 27 blacks in Simpsonville, Kentucky, for an escape to Union-occupied Louisville; they used the black church for a headquarters, elected Marrs their captain, and accumulated an arsenal of "twenty-six war clubs and one old rusty pistol." Reaching Louisville before their owners, the slaves marched to the local recruiting office and enlisted in the Union Army.[7] But most of the escapees apparently traveled alone or in small groups, and invariably the elderly slaves had to be left behind. Even some of these, however, refused to postpone any longer that dream that had eluded them for a lifetime. "Ise eighty-eight year old," one runaway told the Yankees. "Too ole for come? Mas'r joking. Neber too ole for leave de land o' bondage." [8]

To transport themselves to freedom, slaves used crudely built boats (including basket boats made out of swamp reeds), rafts, and canoes, horse-carts and ox-carts, broken-down mules and horses, and occasionally the master's buggy. Some had to walk long distances on swollen and bleeding feet, carrying bundles of clothing or children on their shoulders. Two Louisiana families waded six miles across a swamp, spending two days and nights in mud and water to their waists, their children clinging to their backs, and with nothing to eat.

Many of the refugees fled with nothing but the clothes they were wearing: "Well, massa, we'd thought freedom better than clothes, so we left them." Some, however, managed to carry away their few belongings, usually some old rags, bedding, and furniture which were piled onto carts and wagons. Several of the women attired themselves in their mistress's clothes, and the men occasionally raided the master's wardrobe before departing.[9] By the time they reached the Union Army, the refugees were exhausted, half-starved, frightened, and sick. It was not uncommon for malnutrition and pulmonary disease to claim the lives of three or four blacks every day in the hastily constructed and congested contraband villages. Most of the casualties were children. "The poor Negroes die as fast as ever," a missionary teacher reported. "The children are all emaciated to the last degree and have such violent coughs and dysenteries that few survive. It is frightful to see such suffering among children." [10]

To seek freedom by flight was a difficult and perilous undertaking. There were citizens' patrols and Confederate sentinels that had to be eluded, as well as pursuing bloodhounds (for which the blacks devised some rather ingenious homemade recipes). Many escapees never made it to the Union lines. Of the 25 blacks who set out one night from Richmond to Fortress Monroe, only three were successful; the others were hunted down by bloodhounds and returned to their masters.[11] The punishment that awaited captured runaways was predictably severe. "We'en de Union soldiers wur near us," one slave reported, "some o' de young han's run off to git to de Union folks, an' massa ketch dem an' hang dem to a tree, an' shoot dem; he 'tink no more'n to shoot de culled people right down." [12] If not immediately sold, apprehended runaways were liable to be whipped, chained at night, put to work on Confederate fortifications, or removed for safekeeping to non-threatened areas. (The cook on a Georgia plantation was kept in chains in the kitchen and locked in the cornhouse at night to prevent her from escaping.) Some of these slaves were never even returned to their masters; mounted patrols might run them down with their horses, shoot them on the road, or tie them to the horses and drag them to the nearest jail. An elderly Georgia slave woman who was on her way to the Union lines was stopped by two white men, one of whom shot her while the other broke her ribs and beat her on the head with a stone until she was dead. "She certainly was an old fool," the daughter of a Georgia judge observed, "but I have never heard that folly was a capital offense." What particularly concerned her, however, was how the Yankees would distort the incident. "Father says he would not, for millions, have had such a case as this come under the eyes of the Yankees just at this time, for they will believe everything the negroes say and put the very worst construction on it. Brutal crimes happen in all countries now and then, especially in times of disorder and upheaval such as the South is undergoing. . . ." [13]

Whatever the consequences, the prospect of freedom, and the pride that a slave took in his own liberation, kept the movement alive. They persisted, even in the face of failure. Although frustrated in their first attempt to escape from a plantation near Savannah, a 70-year-old black woman and her husband immediately made plans to try again. While the plantation whites were meting out punishment to her husband, she was collecting their 22 children and grandchildren in a nearby marsh. After drifting some 40 miles down the river in a dilapidated flatboat, the family was finally rescued by a Union gunboat. "My God!" she exclaimed, "are we free?" Her husband subsequently made good on his second escape attempt.[14] The persistence of some black runaways came at the expense of their white pursuers. After overtaking his slave in a swamp, a South Carolina master found himself engaged in a fierce struggle. He managed to shoot the slave in the arm, shattering it badly, but the fugitive grimly fought on, unhorsed his master, and then beat him to death.[15] To make certain that they were not pursued, some slaves bound their master and overseer before leaving the plantation.

How many slaves ran off to the Yankees was never determined precisely, but the number was sufficiently large to alarm Confederate authorities and to cause considerable dismay among Union commanders who found their camps overrun with refugees. It was not uncommon for Union raiding parties to return with more blacks than soldiers; General Sherman's Meridian expedition netted some 8,000 slaves, the Red River expedition yielded 2,500, and the march through Georgia was to attract still more. Vicksburg, Mississippi, became known as "the very gate of heaven" for scores of run-aways, and when black cavalrymen raided Jackson in July, 1864, most of the city's black population reportedly left with them.[16] "History," proclaimed one black newspaper, "furnishes no such intensity of determination, on the part of any race, as that exhibited by these people to be free." But historical comparisons immediately came to mind. This "vast hegira" of blacks, several observers noted, resembled the movement of the Israelites out of Egypt and to the Promised Land. What was lacking was a concerted plan and a Moses.[17] And, they might have added, a Promised Land.

Assumptions about slave contentment, docility, or indifference shared by Northerners and Southerners prepared neither for the extent of this exodus. "Unlettered reason or the mere inarticulate decision of instinct," thought one Union officer, "brought them to us." The refugees themselves were much more explicit. Reflecting upon their flight, exchanging stories across the campfires in the contraband villages, they talked about the oppressiveness of enslavement, the difficulties of carrying out plantation duties while freedom was so close at hand, and the determination to liberate themselves rather than wait for the Yankees. "I run away," one black woman declared, "'cause master too bad; couldn't stay no longer." Some slaves were fearful that they might suddenly be removed or sold elsewhere. One slave made his escape while his master and a slave broker were discussing the terms of the sale. Some slaves had heard rumors that they were about to be conscripted for military service or put to work on Confederate fortifications. "They's jest takin' me, sir, an' I run off." Some were eager to locate their families or join the slaves from their plantation who had already escaped: "All of our friends were ober here." Some slaves fled after their master had warned them that he would rather see them dead than free: "When they git here they gwine find you already free, 'cause I gwine line you up on the bank of Bois d'Arc Creek and free you with my shotgun!" And some slaves insisted that they had not fled at all, but had been evicted; their masters had told them that since the Union Army had come to free the slaves, the Yankees could now feed and clothe them.[18]

The departure of many slaves was hastened by recent whippings, often for trivial reasons or for no ascertainable reason, and with the threat of more to come. The normal frustrations of war, the mounting casualty lists, and the knowledge that slavery was probably doomed made the behavior of slaveholders that much more unpredictable. It was easy to vent one's anger and frustrations on the blacks, particularly when they might be viewed as the essential cause of the war. "They does it to spite us," a slave woman testified, " 'cause you come here. Dey spites us now 'cause de Yankees come." This woman had just escaped with two of her children, apparently leaving behind her eldest son whom the master "had just 'licked' . . . almost to death because he was suspected of wanting to join the Yankees." Similar stories of recent beatings ran through the testimony of the newly arrived refugees. "Master whipped me two or three weeks ago, because I let the cows from the bog road into the yard. Struck me and knocked me down with his fist. Left Monday night, and walked all the way. I am free; come here to be protected; was not safe to stay." [19]

The decision to leave the plantation was not always easy to make. There were not only the difficulties of escape, but some slaves felt a certain attachment to the "home place." Here they had been born, raised families, and sought to make their personal lives as tolerable as was possible. "They all pine for their homes," one reporter wrote, after conversing with some Mississippi refugees. "They long for the old quarters they have lived in; for the old woods they have roamed in, and the old fields they have tilled. . . . They get thinking of their old homes and if they have left their families, or any part of them behind, they long to see them." [20] The wretched conditions which prevailed in the contraband camps, in addition to the unpredictable behavior of their white liberators prompted some slaves to reconsider their hasty departures. This "nostalgia" notwithstanding, many slaves still concluded that flight—whether to or with the Union Army—was the quickest and perhaps the only way to achieve that long sought freedom. Near Milledgeville, Georgia, a staff officer with Sherman's army came upon a scene that could have been enacted almost anywhere the Yankees marched. In a hut he found a slave couple, both of them more than 60 years old. The ensuing conversation suggested in no way that they were displeased with their condition. Suddenly, however, as the Union troops prepared to move on, the woman stood up, and her face assumed an unexpectedly "fierce, almost devilish" expression. "What for you sit dar?" she asked, while contemptuously pointing her finger at the old man crouched in the corner. "[Y]ou s'pose I wait sixty years for nutten? Don't yer see de door open? I'se follow my child; I not stay. Yes, anudder day I goes 'long wid dese people; yes, sar, I walks till I drop in my tracks." The officer thought it the "most terrible sight" he had ever witnessed. Only a Rembrandt, he said, could possibly have done justice to this scene.[21]

3.

The first indication of possible trouble on Louis Manigault's Savannah River rice plantations was when the overseer discovered a cache of stolen "shot and powder." One of the slaves, Ishmael, subsequently confessed that he had accumulated the ammunition with the intention of deserting to the Yankees. It had been some seven months since the outbreak of war, and already there were disconcerting reports of "murmuring" among the Savannah River blacks. "We had no trouble with our own Negroes," Manigault reported, "but from clear indications it was manifest that some of them were preparing to run away, using as a pretext their 'fear of the Yankees.' " The overseer, William Capers, was a man who claimed to know the Negro character. What guided him in the management of black labor was the proven proposition that any man who placed the least confidence in a Negro "was simply a Damned Fool." Manigault had complete confidence in the overseer. When Capers advised him in November, 1861, that "all was not quite correct" upon the plantation, and that certain blacks should be removed to an area "sufficiently remote from all excitement," Manigault readily agreed. Ten slaves—those "we deemed most likely would cause trouble"—were selected. Three of them had to be handcuffed and removed by force; the others went "very willingly."

But trouble persisted on the Manigault plantations. On the night of February 21, 1862, Jack Savage, the carpenter, ran away. "We always considered him a most dangerous character & bad example to the others," and yet for some reason he had not been removed earlier. After his escape, Savage spent almost a year in the nearby swamplands, where he was soon joined by other runaways, including Charles Lucas, a trusted slave who had been placed in charge of the plantation stock. When Savage returned voluntarily to the plantation, "looking half starved and wretched in the extreme," Manigault quickly sold him in Savannah for $1,800. Meanwhile, after considerable personal anguish, Manigault decided to send a slave named Hector to Charleston

for the duration of the war. It was not an easy decision to make. For
nearly 30 years, this slave had been his "favorite Boat Hand" and
"constant companion." He was a competent worker, a trusted slave,
"a Negro We all of us esteemed highly." But it was apparent that the
war had affected Hector. He could no longer be trusted. "Singular to
say this Man 'Hector' was the very first to murmur, and would have
hastened to the embrace of his Northern Brethren, could he have fore-
seen the least prospect of a successful escape." To the discouraged
Manigault, the behavior of Hector was "only One of the numerous
instances of ingratitude evinced in the African character." The house
servants proved untrustworthy, convincing Manigault that constant
contact with the family had "polluted" their minds with "evil
thoughts." Whatever the cause, he was now more convinced than ever
before "that the only suitable occupation for the Negro is to be
a Laborer of the Earth, and to work as a field hand upon a well
disciplined plantation." If the war served no other purpose, it left him
far less deluded as to the real nature of this peculiar species of property. "This war has taught us the perfect impossibility of placing the
least confidence in any Negro. In too numerous instances those we
esteemed the most have been the first to desert us." [22]

In the aftermath of Fort Sumter, the white South had proclaimed
its conviction that the slaves would remain loyal and faithful. Desertion was improbable. Insurrection was unthinkable. "On our farms
and plantations, with hundreds around us," a Southerner wrote in
1861, "we sleep with wooden latched doors, with open windows, and
fear no evil." [23] It was a comforting thought, particularly for the families of those tens of thousands of males who were about to leave the
plantations for service in the Confederate Army. Nor was this confidence entirely misplaced. The faithful slave—that living testimonial
to a system that could emasculate the very spirit and personality of an
individual—was not simply the creation of a vivid postwar Southern
imagination. He existed. And these were the Negroes that the South
would choose to recall—the loyal black "mammies" who hid the silverware from Yankee pillagers, the devoted white-haired "Uncles"
who protected the homestead while the master was away, the field
hands who remained at work, the house servants who stayed in the
kitchens, and the body servants in the Confederate Army whose fidel-

ity stood the test of battle. Who could not recall how certain slaves had comforted the master's family in times of grief and had shared with them the joy of welcome when "massa" had come home. "No one," a Mississippi woman wrote, "showed himself [sic] more happy to see him than 'Mammy' as she fell upon the floor at his feet hugging and kissing him. 'My Massa come.' 'My Massa Come.' " If only, she sighed, some of her deluded Northern friends could have shared with her this moving tribute to the beneficence of slavery.[24] Such faithfulness was to be praised not only by generations of Southern whites but —rather ironically—by black leaders who wanted to allay post-emancipation Southern fears about the Negro violence and retaliation. "We never inaugurated a servile insurrection. We stayed peaceably at our homes, and labored with our usual industry. While you were absent fighting in the field, . . . we knew our power at the same time, and would frequently speak of it. We knew then it was in our power to rise, fire your houses, burn your barns, railroads, and discommode you in a thousand ways. But we prefered then as we do now, to wait on God, and trust to the instincts of your humanity." [25]

To know the black man, and white Southerners professed an intimate knowledge, was to know his propensity for dissembling and saying what the white man wanted to hear. Consequently, it was almost impossible to determine the extent or the authenticity of the black man's outward show of devotion. In a South that never quite trusted its own professions of confidence in the Negro, suspicions could be easily aroused. Whatever the black man did or said, some Southerners were under no illusions. "The tenants act pretty well towards *us*," a Virginian wrote, "but that doesn't prevent our being pretty certain of their intention to stampede when they get a good chance. . . . They are nothing but an ungrateful, discontented lot & I don't care how soon I get rid of mine." [26] In the course of the Civil War, what may have made the faithfulness of certain slaves particularly noteworthy, in the eyes of the white South, were the persistent reports of black disaffection, desertion, and insubordination. "I had taken it too much as a matter of course," Mary Chesnut explained, when contrasting the exemplary behavior of her slaves with the news that some Negro maids had dressed themselves in their mistress's gowns "before their very faces" and had then run off.[27] And that was a relatively minor incident. What about those blacks who told the

Yankees where everything was hidden, the slaves who turned over the house keys to Yankee pillagers, the blacks who ran away as soon as they heard the Union guns or rushed into the "big house" and looted it? How was the white South to explain those Virginia slaves who burned down the overseer's house and deserted their aged, bedridden mistress after stripping the woman of her clothing, or the slave who repeatedly assured his master that he would stay by his side to the bitter end ("I'll nebber leab yer, massa—nebber! I'll stick to my ole massa 'longs I lib!") but who was gone the next morning, along with the master's horse? There was, too, the Confederate lieutenant who had proudly asserted that his slaves "loved their master, and wanted no freedom," only to find himself a prisoner of his own blacks. Not only did his "faithful" slaves unexpectedly turn upon him, but they manifested their delight by improvising some verses as they escorted him to the nearest Union camp."

> *O Massa a rebel, we row him to prison.*
> > *Hallelujah.*
> *We have no massa, now! we free.*
> > *Hallelujah.*
> *We have the Yankees, who no run away.*
> > *Hallelujah.*
> *O! all our old massas run away.*
> > *Hallelujah.*
> *O! massa going to prison now.*
> > *Hallelujah.*[28]

Stories such as these prompted the increasingly gloomy talk about the fragile nature of the black man's affections for his white folks. Little wonder that some Southerners should have thrown up their hands in utter disgust at the black man's behavior. "Oh! deliver me from the 'citizens of African descent,'" a Mississippi woman exclaimed. "I am disgusted forever with the whole race. I have not faith in one single dark individual. They are all alike ungrateful and treacherous—every servant is a spy upon us, & everything we do or say is reported to the Yankees. They know everything." [29]

What compounded the frustrations of white Southerners was their inability to distinguish, as before, between the "good" slaves and the "bad" slaves. "Jonathan, whom we trusted, betrayed us,"

Mary Chesnut wrote. "The plantation house and mills, and Mulberry House were saved by Claiborne, that black rascal who was suspected by all the world!" [30] This was what plagued so many planters—that there was no longer any way one could be absolutely certain about any of his slaves. Even some of the beloved Uncles and Aunties were defecting. "The first news that greeted us this morning before we were out of bed was that Uncle Billy, the servant we trusted most, had gone off to the Yankees." It was "Uncle Billy" who had been entrusted with the house and storeroom keys, who had packed and buried the household silver, and who had been dispatched to inform the Union Army "that we were a household of unprotected ladies." [31] To whom could the South turn, if not to an an "Uncle Billy"? On a number of plantations, the house servants and trusted slave drivers were not simply the first to betray their masters, but actually led the exodus to the Union lines or remained behind to direct the capture and looting of the "big house." It was becoming increasingly obvious that prewar assessments of slaves were no longer dependable, that the old distinctions were not working, that the slaves refused to act along predictable lines. "Lovet disappointed me more than any of them," a planter recalled. "He was about my age and I had always treated him more as a companion than a slave. When I left I put everything in his charge, told him that he was free, but to remain on the place and take care of things. He promised me faithfully that he would, but he was the first one to leave." [32]

When property suddenly assumed a personality, nothing seemed certain any longer. It was downright disconcerting. There was no more plaintive cry among planters than that those in whom they had placed the greatest trust and confidence were the very first to abandon them. To a Louisiana woman, it was the defection of "a colored woman born in the same house with me, always treated as well as me, always till my marriage slept in the same bed with me, and now, she is the first to leave me." To a South Carolina planter, it was the unexpected news that greeted him one morning that his head carpenter and 18 of his "finest, most intelligent and trusted" slaves had escaped to the Yankees—and they had done so in the family boat. To a Tennessee planter, grateful that most of his slaves had remained "pre[t]ty faithful," it was the sudden departure of Tom—"the first to leave me & had thought would have been the last one to go." To the wife of a prominent rice planter, it was the sight of "the man whom they trusted as house-servant" removing the wine and liquor from the house, packing it up and loading it onto a cart, and riding off—never to be seen again. To Eliza Frances Andrews, the daughter of a prominent Georgian, it was the news that Uncle Lewis had deserted. This slave—"an old gray-haired darkey"—had been "petted and coddled and believed in by the whole family." As children, they had always called him "Uncle," because he was considered an honorary member of the family; he had been given a special place at family prayers and was frequently called upon to lead the devotions. "I have often listened to his prayers . . . , and was brought up with as firm a belief in him as in the Bible itself. He was an honored institution of the town." Although there had been some shining examples of black fidelity in the Andrews household, the defection of Uncle Lewis was incomprehensible. It was as though the Civil War had destroyed "all that was most good and beautiful in these simple-hearted folk." Not only had "the pious, the honored, the venerated" Uncle Lewis run off to the Yankees, but he had proclaimed "a pack of lies against his mistress" and had even made a claim to a portion of her lands! [33]

This was the kind of ingratitude that white Southerners found so difficult to accept. What had gone wrong? Some planters argued that the lack of proper discipline had produced pampered and spoiled slaves, and that those who had indulged their Negroes in ante-bellum days were encountering the most difficulty. But this was at best an insufficient explanation, as many whites themselves had to confess. To place the blame on lax discipline was to make the same false assumptions about their blacks. What the war revealed perhaps was simply that they had never really known their Negroes, that far too often they had mistaken the slave's outward demeanor for his inner feelings, and that in some cases they had been deliberately deceived so that they might later be the more easily betrayed. "We had thought there was a strong bond of affection on their side as well as ours!" one planter wrote, after discovering one morning that every servant had departed. "We have ministered to them in sickness, infancy, and age. But poor creatures! they don't know what freedom is, and they are crazy. They think it the opening of the door of Heaven." [34]

It was not simply that many of the "faithful" Negroes had deserted. That was bad enough. But at least they were gone, and the planter could feel relieved at not having to feed them, put up with their insolence, or calculate their next move. Much more troublesome for some planters were those slaves who did not run away, but who remained on the plantations and farms. To measure slave "resistance" during the Civil War is not to count the number of abortive insurrections undertaken; that was never a major problem. Far more significant were the number of rumored uprisings, the reported epidemics of insubordination, the ways in which white communities could be brought to the brink of hysteria, the fears and suspicions that were implanted in the minds of white men and women, the many instances in which the slaves, consciously or otherwise, managed to bring anguish and frustration to their owners. "[T]he black wretches," complained a woman who had been left in charge of the plantation, "[are] trying all they can, it seems to me, to agrivate [sic] me, taking no interest, having no care about the future, neglecting their duty. . . . The negroes care no more for me than if I was an old free darkey and I get so mad sometimes that I think I don't care sometimes if Myers [the overseer] beats the last one of them to death. I can't stay with them another year alone." [35]

No matter how desperately the white Southerner wanted to believe in the black man's faithfulness, there remained an undercurrent of suspicion and fear that could never be successfully repressed, and that surfaced with every report of unmanageable Negroes. Nor were these fears entirely illusory; they could on occasion assume a terrible reality. The war was not even a year old when Mary Chesnut was informed that her cousin had been brutally murdered in bed. The woman had been living alone, knowing "that none of her children would have the patience she had with these people who had been indulged and spoiled by her until they were like spoiled children, simply intolerable." This was a frightening piece of news, and it forced Mary Chestnut to reexamine all of her previous assumptions about what might be expected from the black population. "Hitherto I have never thought of being afraid of Negroes. I had never injured any of them; why should they want to hurt me?" But as of this day, she confessed, "I feel that the ground is cut away from under my feet. Why should they treat me any better than they have done Cousin Betsey Witherspoon?" Unable to sleep because of the murder, Mary Chesnut's sister came into the bedroom, and the two women tried to comfort each other. "The thought of those black hands strangling and smothering Mrs. Witherspoon's grey head under the counterpane haunted her; we sat up and talked the long night through." One month later, although Mary Chesnut expressed confidence in her own slaves, she still found it difficult to sleep at night. "That innocent old lady and her grey hair moved them not a jot. Fancy how we feel. I am sure I will never sleep again without this nightmare of horror haunting me. . . . If they want to kill us, they can do it when they please, they are noiseless as panthers." And yet, Mary Chesnut noted, although "[w]e ought to be grateful that anyone of us is alive, . . . nobody is afraid of their own Negroes." [36]

It was precisely this kind of incident, no matter how isolated, no matter how exceptional within the entire context of slave behavior, that prompted Southerners, while publicly praising the exemplary behavior of their blacks, to reflect upon the combustible and unpredictable nature of a slave society. Most of them might have readily agreed that the faithful slave constituted the vast majority of the black population—and perhaps they were right. But how could anyone be certain that the exception was not on his own plantation or in his own household? That was the essential problem. Many a master was driven to sleepless nights in his attempt to penetrate behind the masks of his blacks, attaching significance to their silence or apparent indifference. The meekest, the most passive, the most submissive slaves could unsettle a household. The very appearance of fidelity was sometimes suspect. "They carry it too far," Mary Chesnut thought. "[P]eople talk before them as if they were chairs and tables, and they make no sign. Are they stolidly stupid, or wiser than we are, silent and strong, biding their time." [37] This particular observation was made on the same day Confederate batteries opened fire on Fort Sumter. What would happen when the issues of the war became clearer to the black man, when their own destiny became involved with the outcome, and when the Union Army drew closer? It was precisely this uncertainty that troubled the white South. In scores of cases, old loyalties and affections suddenly became irrelevant—or perhaps they were finally revealed for what they were.

When the Union Army neared his Savannah River plantations, Louis Manigault fled. That was December, 1864. More than two years later, after having leased out the plantations to a General Harrison, Manigault decided to return and assess the impact of the war. Traveling along the familiar roads between Savannah and his Gowrie and East Hermitage plantations, he noted traces of previous army encampments, the twisted ruins of the Charleston and Savannah Railroad, and the remains of what had once been a magnificent neighboring mansion. Upon entering the Gowrie Settlement, his former slave cooper greeted him enthusiastically, "calling me 'Maussa' as of yore." Standing next to the ruins of his country house, Manigault recalled how he had spent here "the most happy period" of his childhood; he remembered, too, the hurried evacuation as General Sherman's forces drew closer and that "up to the very last moment our Negroes behaved well." All that remained of the house was a tall chimney and some scattered bricks which the slaves had not stolen and sold in Savannah. Except for the "Negro Houses," which he had constructed just before the war, the entire settlement had "a most abandoned and forlorn appearance." As he approached the Negro quarters, some of the blacks came outside. Manigault shook hands with them, called each by his name ("which seemed to please them highly"), and joked with them about his present plight. "Lord! a Massy!," he mocked. "You tink I can lib in de Chimney." At the East Hermitage Settlement, Manigault was greeted by 12 of his former slaves. "They all seemed pleased to see me, calling me 'Maussa' & the Men still showing respect by taking off their caps." There was "Capt'n Hector," his "constant companion" until the war transformed him into "a great Rascal." He was now a foreman on the plantation. Much to Manigault's surprise, Jack Savage had returned. He had been "the greatest Villain on the Plantation, the most notoriously bad character & worst Negro of the place," but at the same time his best carpenter. "He was the only Negro ever in our possession who I considered capable of Murdering me, or burning my dwelling at night, or capable of committing any act." The two men now shook hands and exchanged "a few friendly remarks." To Manigault, it seemed highly ironic that Jack Savage, "the last one I should have dreamt of," greeted him, "whilst sitting idly upon the Negro-House steps dirty & sluggish, I behold young Women to whom I had most frequently presented Earrings, Shoes, Calicos, Kerchiefs &c, &c,—formerly pleased to meet me, but now not even lifting the head as I passed." [38]

Unlike some slaveholders, Louis Manigault had never pretended to understand his blacks. "Our 'Northern Brethren' inform us that we Southerners knew nothing of the Negro Character. This I have always considered *perfectly true,* but they further state that They (the Yankees) have always known the true Character of the Negro which I consider *entirely false* in the extreme. So deceitful is the Negro that as far as my own experience extends I could never in a single instance decipher his character." Conversing with his former slaves, Manigault was suddenly overcome by a strange feeling. His thoughts turned to other countries, and he could almost imagine himself talking with some Chinese, Malays, or even Indians in the interior of the Philippine Islands. It was as though he were on alien turf and had never really known these people. "That former mutual & pleasing feeling of Master towards Slave and vice versa is now as a dream of the past." [39]

Whatever happened in the future, it seemed as though it could never be quite the same again.

4.

The day the Yankees arrived was bound to be memorable. Although apparently anxious for their freedom, some slaves were initially skeptical, particularly after what their masters had told them about the one-eyed, horned Yankee devils. Perhaps, too, the "grapevine" had reported—and with good cause—that slaves often fared badly at the hands of their liberators. Whatever the reason for their apprehension, it was not uncommon for the blacks to run to their quarters and gaze at the soldiers from the windows and doorways until it was deemed safe to greet them. When it became clear that the Yankees were human after all ("Why dey's folks!"), the slaves would run down to the road to welcome them. What some of them had not even dared hope for was suddenly a reality. "I'd always thought about this," exclaimed an old slave woman, shaking her head with disbelief, "and wanted this day to come, and prayed for it, and knew God meant it should be here sometime, but I didn't believe I should ever see it, and it is so great and good a thing, I cannot believe it has come now; and I don't believe I ever shall realize it, but I know it has though, and I bless the Lord for it." [40]

The "delirium of excitement" observed on a Louisiana sugar plantation may not have been true of the entire South, but neither was it exceptional. Until the appearance of the Yankees, the slaves on this plantation had been described as "perfectly quiet"; indeed, "no one would have suspected they were not all of them the faithful or happy beings we see pictured in those fanciful costumes." But the moment the Yankees were sighted down the road "the negroes threw off all disguise" and commenced a celebration that turned into "an ecstacy of joy." By the end of the war, this had become an increasingly familiar scene. Almost everywhere the Yankees marched, their appearance was sufficient to set off an "irruption of negroes." The blacks crowded the roadsides, swarmed around the soldiers, touched them, even hugged them. "Bress de Lord; de day hab come at last—de day hab come at last!" It was observed that when their masters were present, the slaves tended to be more restrained in their celebrations, but "when none were present their delight was boundless." If words or gestures failed to express the proper emotions, the slaves might resort to one of their traditional spirituals or to songs and shouts especially composed for the occasion. "Guess dey made 'em up," one of the slaves recalled, " 'cause purty soon ev'ybody fo' miles around was singin' freedom songs." In Charleston, for example, a 69 year old slave woman greeted the Yankees with a simple, repetitive chant:

> *Ye's long been a-comin',*
> *Ye's long been a-comin',*
> *Ye's long been a-comin',*
> *For to take de land:*

> *And now ye's a-comin',*
> *And now ye's a-comin',*
> *And now ye's a-comin',*
> *For to rule de land.*

On a Virginia plantation, while the blacks danced and shouted around a large fire ("de white folks not darin' to come outside de big house"), they sang an old spiritual that most vividly captured the spirit of the jubilee.

> *I's free, I's free, I's free at las'!*
> *Thank God A'mighty, I's free at las'!*

Once was a moaner, jus' like you
Thank God A'mighty, I's free at las'!

I fasted an' I prayed tell I came thew
Thank God A'mighty, I's free at las'! [41]

Some slaves, bewildered by this sudden change in their condition, felt as though it were necessary to show remorse in the presence of the white folks. "I made out like I was cryin'," one slave recalled, "an' kivered my face wid both hands an' hollered dat I didn't want to leave Missus, but I was gloryin' jus' de same." Where there had been a close relationship between the master and his slaves, the remorse could be quite genuine; such a relationship, on the other hand, might have whetted that much more the slave's appetite for freedom and the opportunity to live like the white folks he had so long and closely observed and envied. Freedom could be downright contagious, affecting the most loyal and degraded of slaves. "When you'all had de power you was good to me," an old Negro informed his master, "and I'll protect you now. If you want anything, call for Sambo." The slave suddenly caught himself. "I mean, call for Mr. Samuel—that's my name now." [42]

The celebration of freedom occasionally took a violent and destructive turn. When the Yankees appeared, a Louisiana planter reported, the blacks suddenly became "crazy." Not only did they refuse to work, but "everything like subordination and restraint was at an end," and those who did not flee with the Union Army "remained at home to do *much worse.*" For nearly a week, he had to stand by while the slaves "had a perfect jubilee." Property was destroyed, livestock slain, the storerooms emptied. The blacks even had the temerity to place a Confederate soldier in stocks and abuse him. "Confound them, they deserve to be half starved and to be worked nearly to death for the way they have acted." What particularly alarmed this planter was that the slave drivers—selected for their dependability and leadership capacity—"everywhere have proved the worst negroes." Only after the Yankees had left the area was this planter able to restore some semblance of order. "I now care nothing for them save for 'their work,' " he declared, and he proposed to get that out of them in any way possible. "Things are just now beginning to work right—the negroes hated awfully to go to work again. Several have been shot and probably more will have to be." [43]

The sacking of Beaufort, South Carolina, when the war was only seven months old, graphically illustrated the potential of the slaves for destructive activity. With the approach of the Union gunboats, most of the planters deserted their houses and outlying plantations, trying desperately—and apparently unsuccessfully—to carry off their slaves with them. When one planter ventured to his home shortly before the Yankees arrived, he found one slave "seated at Phoebe's piano playing away like the very Devil and two damsels upstairs dancing away famously." Meanwhile, field hands from the surrounding countryside were pouring into the town. Over the opposition of a few of the remaining household servants, they left behind a path of devastation that startled even the Union landing party. "We went through spacious houses where only a week ago families were living in luxury, and saw their costly furniture despoiled; books and papers smashed; pianos on the sidewalk, feather beds ripped open, and even the filth of the Negroes left lying in parlors and bedchambers." [44]

To most observers, however, the amount of black destruction was surprisingly minimal. Few towns were sacked with the same thoroughness as Beaufort, and blacks tended to limit their destructive rampages to their own plantations and the property of their masters. Those Southerners who were victimized by such activities found little comfort in the fact that they were exceptional cases. To them, the behavior of their blacks stretched the limits of credulity. "The Negroes as soon as they heard the guns rushed to my house and pillaged it of many things and principally wearing apparel." There was no question in this man's mind but that the entire affair had been "prearranged." [45] To the blacks themselves, the looting of the plantation was not so much a matter of "revenge" as a rare opportunity to supplement their meager diets and improve their way of living. On some plantations, they killed the farm animals, emptied the meat and storerooms, helped themselves to the master's liquors and wines, expropriated the house furniture, and moved from the "big house" whatever was movable. "We looked at the house," one Southerner wrote; "it was a wreck,—the front steps gone, not a door nor shutter left, and not a sash. They had torn out all the mahogany framework around the doors and windows—there were mahogany panels below the windows and above the doors there were panels painted—the mahogany banisters to the staircase going upstairs; everything that could be torn away was gone." Some of these materials were most likely used by the slaves to floor their own cabins and make them more habitable.[46]

Similarly, when the slaves broke into closets, bureaus, trunks, and desks, ripped open the bedding, or scattered the master's private papers, it was invariably in an effort to find money, jewelry, or silverware that might be traded for needed commodities. When the slaves seized the mules, horses, and wagons, it was often with the idea of making their escape from the plantation, taking with them whatever the carts could carry.[47]

What to the white man constituted a clear case of theft was to many slaves simply a long overdue payment for past services. "[T]hey *think it right* to steal from us," wrote one astonished Southerner, "to spoil us, as the Israelites did the Egyptians." [48] When one slave rode into a Union camp, he readily admitted that he had taken the horse from his owner, and had his own notion of the "morality" of such an act.

> "Don't you think you did very wrong, Dick, to take your mistress' horse?"
>
> "Well, I do' know, sah; I didn't take the bes' one. She had three; two of 'em fuss-rate horses, but the one I took is ole, an' not berry fast, an' I offe'd to sell him fo' eight dollars, sah."
>
> "But, Dick, you took at least a thousand dollars from your mistress, besides the horse."
>
> "How, sah?"
>
> "Why, *you* were worth a thousand dollars, and you should have been satisfied with that much, without taking the poor woman's horse," said I, gravely.
>
> The contraband scratched his woolly head, rolled up his eyes at me, and replied with emphasis.
>
> "*I don't look at it jis dat way, massa.* I wo'ked ha'd for' missus mor'n thirty yea's, an' I reckon in dat time I 'bout pay fo' meself. An' dis yea' missus guv me leave to raise a patch o' 'baccy fo' my own. Well, I wo'ked nights, an' Sabbaths, an' spar' times, an' raised a big patch (way prices is, wuff two hun'red dolla's, I reckon) o' 'baccy; an' when I got it tooken car' of dis fall, ole missus took it

'way from me; give some to de neighbors; keep some fo' he' own
use; an' sell some, an' keep de money, an' I reckon dat pay fo' de
ole hoss!"

Failing to find any conscience in the darkey, I gave up the argument.[49]

It was no doubt true that some slaves seemed to gratify themselves in an orgy of "wanton" destruction. "Many of them," one
planter wrote, "I think do all they can to have us destroyed & delight
in seeing the work of destruction done." (Only one year before, this
same planter had thought his slaves to be "Contented & happy." [50]) To
celebrate their liberation, some blacks were apparently intent on ob-
literating anything that reminded them of the old way of life. This
might take the form of plunder, destruction of the cotton gins, ex-
propriation of the land, or even personal violence. Some planters were
assaulted, and a few faced the ultimate humiliation of having their
own slaves whip them. Where the master and his family had fled the
plantation, leaving the overseer in charge, the blacks fastened their
hatred upon this personal symbol of the slave system. Several overseers
were murdered, but more often they were driven off the plantations or
rendered powerless. "Belflowers [the overseer] is cowed by the violence
of the negroes against him," a planter wrote, "and is *afraid* to speak
openly. He is trying to curry favour. His own morals are impaired by
the revolution." Several months earlier, this overseer had confessed
to his employer that he was unable to control the blacks. "I am not allowed to say any[thing] a bout Work . . . [I]t looks Verry hard to
Pull ones hat to a Negro." [51]

Although most Southerners escaped any personal violence at the
hands of their slaves, the scattered reports of murders, rapes, insubordination, and plunder kept alive the threat and the genuine fear that
black freedom might degenerate into insurrectionary violence. It must
have been distressing, for example, to see blacks on a Louisiana plantation erect a gallows intended for their master. That it was never
used was perhaps less important than the vivid impression it made on
the local populace, both black and white.[52] Far more common, in the
aftermath of Union occupation, were reports of armed gangs of blacks
roaming the countryside, raiding the plantations at night for food and
supplies, halting people on the roads and pointing guns at their heads,
breaking into homes and threatening the occupants, or "suddenly sur-

rounding a man on his own plantation attending to his own affairs."
While Union troops remained in the vicinity, 18 South Carolina
planters charged, the blacks had "evinced treachery and vindictive-
ness—illustrated by robbery, plundering, false accusation and insolence." But when the Yankees departed, these planters reported, the
situation had deteriorated even more. The blacks seized a nearby village, patrolled it night and day, and threatened "the lives of men and
the chastity of women." [53]

There was general agreement among Southern whites that many
of these outrages were directly attributable to the presence of black
troops. If the black soldiers were not themselves responsible, the very
sight of armed and uniformed Negroes was sufficient provocation.
"Think of it!" a Georgia woman exclaimed. "Bringing armed negroes
here to threaten and insult us! We were so furious that we shook our
fists and spit at them from behind the window where we were sitting.
It may have been childish, but it relieved our feelings." [54] To many
Southerners, this was, indeed, the most ignominious moment of the
Civil War.

5.

When Union gunboats came up the Combahee River in South
Carolina, the slave laborers on the adjoining plantations soon realized
that this was no ordinary raid. What struck them immediately was
that the soldiers were black. Many of them were, in fact, former slaves;
the commander—Colonel James Montgomery—was a white man who
had fought with John Brown in the Kansas guerilla wars; the "scout"
helping to direct this mission was none other than Harriet Tubman,
the black woman who before the War had made numerous forays into
the South to escort slaves to freedom. When the black soldiers came
ashore, they set fire to the plantation homes and barns. The slaves
looked on in apparent amazement at the sight of black men burning
down the white man's dwellings. "De brack sojer so presumptious,"
one slave kept muttering, his head shaking with admiration at what he
was witnessing. "[D]ey come right ashore, hold up dere head. Fus' ting
I know, dere was a barn, ten tousand bushel rough rice, all in a blaze,
den mas'r's great house, all cracklin' up de roof." It was an imposing

spectacle, every minute of which this slave seemed to relish. "Didn't I keer for see 'em blaze? Lor, mas'r, didn't care notin' at all, *I was gwine to de boat.*" [55]

The black Yankees eagerly accepted the role of liberators. The scenes that greeted them in their march through the South—abandoned plantation homes, slaves lining the streets and roadsides, reunions with members of their family, the sight of their former masters—were bound to make a considerable impression. Perhaps most memorable were those occasions on which they could demonstrate their contempt for the symbols of bondage. "They gutted his mansion of some of the finest furniture in the world," wrote Chaplain Henry M. Turner, in describing a regimental action in North Carolina. Having been told of the cruel reputation of a slaveholder who lived near their encampment, and that only recently this "mean old wretch" had kept a slave woman in irons, the black soldiers resolved to pay him a visit. Before his very eyes they wielded their axes indiscriminately, shattering his piano and most of the furniture and ripping his expensive carpet to pieces. What they did not destroy they distributed among the slaves. When the slaveholder addressed them "rather saucily," he was struck across the mouth and sent reeling to the floor, "his downward tendency being materially accelerated by an application of bootleather to his 'latter end.' " Chaplain Turner, who was present throughout this action, expressed no remorse for what the black soldiers had done. "When the rich owners would use insulting language," he wrote, "we let fire do its work of destruction. A few hours only are necessary to turn what cost years of toil into smoke and ashes." That they should have chosen to camp near the home of this "infamous old rebel" he regarded as Providential. [56]

It was unreal—armed and uniformed black men marching through the South as an occupation army! On streets where slaves and free Negroes had only recently been forbidden to walk after 9 P.M., black soldiers were now drilling and patrolling. "[F]or once in his life," a soldier wrote from New Orleans, "your humble correspondent walked fearlessly and boldly through the streets of a southern city! And he did this without being required to take off his cap at every step, or to give all the side-walks to those lordly princes of the sunny south, the planters' sons!" [57] What an exhilarating and unforgettable moment it must have been for those black soldiers making triumphal entries into Southern cities amidst crowds of cheering slaves who rushed out into the streets to embrace them and clasp their hands. "I was speechless," a soldier wrote from Wilmington, North Carolina, after the tumultuous reception given the Union troops. "I could do nothing but cry to look at the poor creatures so overjoyed." To another soldier, the Wilmington reception was simply a long overdue redemption. "We could then truly see what we had been fighting for, and could almost realize the fruits of our labors." [58] In Charleston, black troops marched into the city singing the John Brown song (with an additional verse promising to hang Jeff Davis on a crab apple tree) and found the streets filled with jubilant Negroes. "The glory and triumph of this hour may be imagined, but can never be described," wrote an officer with one of the black regiments. "It was one of those occasions which happen but once in a lifetime, to be lived over in memory for ever." [59] When the newly commissioned Major Martin R. Delany arrived in Charleston, this veteran black abolitionist could barely restrain himself at the thought of entering that city "which, from earliest childhood and through life, I had learned to contemplate with feelings of the utmost abhorrence. . . . For a moment I paused—then, impelled by the impulse of my mission, I found myself dashing on in unmeasured strides through the city, as if under a forced march to attack the already crushed and fallen enemy." [60]

Wherever the black troops appeared, the native whites generally looked on sullenly and with little apparent emotion. Like those Georgia women, they apparently expressed their anger in the safety of their homes. Perhaps for some it was simply a refusal to believe what they were witnessing. "They are afraid to say anything to us," a black sergeant remarked, "so they take it out in looking. . . . The very people, who, three years ago, crouched at their master's feet, . . . now march in a victorious column of freemen, over the same land. The change seems almost miraculous." Although relatively few attempts were made to provoke the whites, some soldiers found it difficult to repress their feelings. When, for example, several "white ladies and slave oligarchs" came to Henry M. Turner for a permit to draw government rations, he later confessed his immense satisfaction at seeing them "crouching before me, and I a negro." Several weeks later, Turner was with his regiment when they were forced to cross a river near Smithfield, North Carolina. Before wading through the stream, the men stripped off their clothes. The "secesh women" watched the spectacle, Turner wrote, "with the utmost intensity. I suppose they desired to see whether these audacious Yankees were really men, made like other men. . . . So they thronged the windows, porticos and yards, in the finest attire imaginable. Our brave boys would disrobe themselves, hang their garments upon their bayonets and through the water they would come, walk up the street and seem to say to the feminine gazers, 'Yes, though naked, we are your masters.' " [61]

But what had to be the most dramatic moment, if not the climax of the entire war, was that day in April, 1865, when black troops entered Richmond, the capitol of the Confederacy, singing their by now famous refrain:

> De massa run, ha! ha!
> De darkey stay, ho! ho!
> It must be now de kingdom comin',
> An' de yar ob Jubilo.

Within a few hours, a large crowd of soldiers and local blacks had assembled on Broad Street, near "Lumpkin Alley," where the slave jails, auction rooms, and offices of the slave traders were concentrated. "I marched at the head of the column," wrote the black chaplain of the 28th U.S. Colored Troops, "and soon I found myself called upon by the officers and men of my regiment to make a speech. . . . I was aroused amid the shouts of ten thousand voices, and proclaimed for the first time in that city freedom to all mankind." From behind the barred windows of Lumpkin's Jail, the imprisoned slaves began to chant:

> Slavery chain done broke at last!
> Broke at last! Broke at last!
> Slavery chain done broke at last!
> Gonna praise God till I die!

The crowd took up the chant, the slave pens were opened, and the prisoners came pouring out shouting praises for God and Abraham Lincoln. "In this mighty consternation," the chaplain recalled, "I became so overcome with tears, that I could not stand up under the pressure of such fulness of joy in my own heart. I retired to gain strength." Several hours later, this same chaplain, who as a youth had been separated from his family and subsequently escaped to the North, was reunited with his mother. He had not seen her for some 20 years.[62]

What transpired in Richmond that day was an unforgettable Jubilee. In the Hall of Delegates, where the Confederate Congress had once deliberated, black soldiers now took turns swiveling in the Speaker's chair. In the city streets, the blacks wept openly, danced, cheered, embraced the soldiers, and followed them wherever they went. Witnessing this spectacle from her window, a young white woman asked, "Was it to this end we had fought and starved and gone naked and cold?" [63] But for the black soldier, whatever happened to him after the war was over, these memories would not be easily erased. The liberation of the slaves had not been an exclusively white effort, and this was a fact of immense importance. "[S]uppose you had kept your freedom without enlisting in dis army," a black corporal declared, "your chilen might have grown up free and been well cultivated so as to be equal to any business, but it would have been always flung in dere faces—'Your fader never fought for he own freedom'—and what could dey answer? Neber can say that to dis African Race any more." [64]

6.

When the Union Army occupied Augusta, Georgia, Jefferson Thomas assembled his house servants and informed them of their pending freedom. He expressed the desire that they remain and work for wages. The slaves received the news with little apparent emotion, except that they went back to work "very cheerfully"; indeed, Sarah "was realy lively while she was sewing on Franks pants." During the war, the slaves belonging to Jefferson and Gertrude Thomas, both at their Augusta house and on the two plantations, had remained loyal. The only one to defect had been Henry, but that occasioned no surprise since he had been "a runaway from childhood." Yet, within a month after the arrival of the Yankees, nearly every one of their house blacks had deserted them.

There was no Jubilee among the Thomas blacks. They did not suddenly rush out to embrace or celebrate their freedom. When they did leave, the departures were anything but spectacular. There was no insubordination or insolence, the property remained undisturbed, and there were no tearful farewells. The Thomas slaves left in much the same manner as they had received the news that they were free. Daniel, among the most loyal and best liked of the slaves, was the first to depart, and he did so "without saying anything to anyone." Betsy went out to pick up the newspaper, "as she was in the habit of doing every day," and never returned. This loss particularly annoyed Mrs. Thomas. "I felt interested in Betsy, she was a bright quick child and raised in our family would have become a good servant. As it is she will be under her Mothers influence and run wild in the street." Nancy gave no indication of leaving but claimed she was not well enough to work. When the "illness" persisted, Mrs. Thomas asked her: "Nancy, do you expect I can afford to pay you wages in your situation, support your two children and then have you sick as much as you are?" There was no reply. The next day she was gone. Aunt Sarah was noticeably more diligent and cheerful than usual. "Sarah has something on her mind," Mrs. Thomas remarked to her husband. That night she made her departure. So did Willy, thus spurning Mrs. Thomas' offer of clothing and a silver quarter every week. And so it went. Conditions were no better on the Thomas plantations, what with the sudden and unexpected departure of Uncle Sykes, the former slave driver who had been placed in charge of labor after the dismissal of the overseer. Sykes did return, but the Thomases felt he no longer deserved their confidence.[65]

If there was any consolation for the Thomases, it was to know that their neighbors were having similar experiences. For scores of slaves, this was a time to explore the meaning and boundaries of freedom, to begin to act like free men and women, and there was no quicker or more direct way than to desert the master, walk off the plantation, and take to the road. Would it not be "a very sweet thing," one freedwoman thought, "to be able to do as she chose, to sit and do nothing, to work if she desired, or to go out as she liked, and ask nobody's permission." Some freed slaves drifted about trying to locate relatives and friends, some sought to improve their economic position, and some wanted only to satisfy their curiosity about what lay outside the narrow world to which they had been confined. But it made no difference how far the freedman wandered, or even if he remained in the same vicinity; what was important was that feeling of being free. "They were like a bird let out of a cage," one black man explained. "You know how a bird that has been long in a cage will act when the door is opened; he makes a curious fluttering for a little while. It was just so with the colored people. They didn't know at first what to do with themselves." The immediate postwar movement of blacks was actually short-lived, and it involved fewer slaves than the white South imagined. It lasted about as long as some of those dreams and expectations which emancipation had initially encouraged. The ex-slaves ventured out to see what freedom meant, and many of them were to return, deeply disillusioned with their experiences. "De jew and de air hackles we more'n anyting," one migrant declared as she awaited transportation back to her old home. "De rain beats on we, and de sun shines we out. My chil'n so hungry dey can't hole up. De Gov'ment, he han't gib we nottin'. Said dey would put we on board Saturday. Some libs and some dies. If dey libs dey libs, and if dey dies dey dies." [66] To many blacks, the decision to return to the old place was not necessarily a matter of local attachment. It had become a matter of survival.

Viewing the wretched conditions which prevailed among many of the freedmen, the white South was tempted to recall a time when blacks had been guaranteed a certain security. Under slavery, whatever its faults, they had been fed, clothed, and sheltered. Deprived of that "security" and forced to make it on their own, the black man was doomed. Some whites, Southerners, and northern visitors alike made a point of asking the freedmen if they had not been better off under the old system. The response was almost always immediate and unequivocal. The ex-slaves preferred freedom. "Every time I think of slavery and if it done the race any good," a former slave recalled, "I think of the story of the coon and dog who met. The coon said to the dog, 'Why is it you're so fat and I am so poor, and we is both animals?' The dog said: 'I lay round Master's house and let him kick me and he gives me a piece of bread right on.' Said the coon to the dog: 'Better, then, that I stay poor,' Them's my sentiment. I'm like the coon, I don't believe in 'buse." [67]

Although most slaves had welcomed emancipation, and had a rather clear conception of what they wanted from freedom, this was not enough. What was all too often lacking were the necessary means and perhaps even the will to effect a fundamental change in their lives. That many black people in the aftermath of emancipation demonstrated a "new" aggressiveness and independence should not obscure or distort the extent to which life went on very much as it had before the war. This was particularly true of the more remote and secluded regions, often the interior counties, where Union troops seldom set foot and where the news of emancipation had frequently been delayed or deliberately suppressed. "Well, old man, you're free now," a Northern reporter told an old Negro ferryman who for 43 years had conveyed passengers across the Yadkin River in North Carolina. "I dunno, master," he replied. "They say all the colored people's free; they do say it certain; but I'm a-goin on same as I allus has been." Although now a free man, he admitted that he received no wages for his labor. "No, sir; my mistress never said anything to me that I was to have wages, nor yet that I was free; nor I never said anything to her. Ye see I left it to her own honor to talk to me about it, because I was afraid she'd say I was insultin' to her and presumin', so I wouldn't speak first. She ha'n' spoke yet." He was "ashamed" to say anything to the woman but had resolved not to work after Christmas without some compensation. "I want to leave the ferry. I'm a mighty good farmer, and I'll get a piece of ground and a chunk of a hoss, if I can, and work for myself." [68]

Some blacks never permitted themselves any illusions about the nature of freedom. The Civil War had been a struggle among white men ("two dogs fightin ober [a] bone"), the outcome of which left black people essentially as they were. They expected no qualitative change in their day-to-day lives. The gradual return of the ex-slaves to the old routines, plantations, owners, and even the same Negro drivers appeared to confirm this view. The changes were often more symbolic than real. They were no longer slaves but freedmen, the old slave drivers were now called foremen or captains, but the essence of things remained very much the same. It was still the white man who largely determined their fate, and, most immediately and crucially, their food, shelter, and economic livelihood—indeed, the very content of "freedom." Even the Yankees were nothing more than a different set of masters. "The white man do what he pleases with us," a liberated slave told a Yankee officer, "we are yours now, massa." When General Sherman tried to reassure some slaves that the Yankees came as friends, one old black man replied, "I spose dat you'se true; but, massa, you'se'll go way tomorrow, and anudder white man will come." [69] The reply may have been incomprehensible to Sherman, but most blacks knew precisely what the old man was talking about.

When Union troops occupied Norfolk, a local black woman immediately assumed that she was now "Massa Lincoln's slave." What this reaction underscored was the extent to which the slavery heritage —the deeply ingrained feelings of dependency, inferiority, apathy, and indifference—still tended to paralyze the energies of black people. Neither the War nor emancipation could easily dislodge these feelings; indeed, the actions and attitudes of Union soldiers, Freedman's Bureau officials, and well-meaning Northern teachers and missionaries frequently reinforced this dependency relationship. Whether out of fear or from habit, the temptation was for black people not to look to themselves but to the white man for protection and leadership, to shift the dependency in some cases from the old master to the federal government. "We know that you came here to set us free," a Savannah Negro informed a Union officer; "we expect you to tell us what to do, and we shall act in accordance with that." [70]

Early in 1866, a white teacher met an elderly Negro while visiting a fort in the vicinity of Plymouth, North Carolina. "Well, uncle," she asked him, after he had touched his hat and stepped aside to let her pass, "how do you enjoy your freedom?" The man regarded her suspiciously for a moment, and then assumed "a look of stupidity and indifference." "Ah, missus," he replied, "I don' know—don' know as I is free." The teacher expressed astonishment at this response, coming as it did nearly a year after the War, and demanded an explanation. "No, missus," he persisted, "don' know nothin' bout it; nothin' 't all." At that moment an official who had been accompanying the teacher approached. As soon as the black man sighted the federal uniform, "the look of stupidity vanished as if by magic," and with a broad smile across his face, he exclaimed, "Oh! I know you now. You's not secesh; you's friends, an' I know what I is, too. Yes, missus, I's a *free man,* tank God." [71] That the freedom of black people depended upon a military presence hardly augured well for the future. What would happen when the last federal troops were withdrawn? How would they react, some freedmen were asked, if an attempt were made to return them to slavery? " 'Pears to me, if I was forced back into bein' a slave again," one black woman responded, " 'pears to me I should die. I couldn't stand it." Another ex-slave replied that he would "cut his throat"—

that is, his own throat, not the white man's. When a Northern traveler posed this question to a group of freedmen, one young black man insisted that he would fight, several more exclaimed, "We wouldn't let them," but most of them murmured, "The soldiers would stop it." That the federal government would always intervene to rescue them, this traveler concluded, was "the main hope of these submissive, long-enslaved people. They had not reached—not even the oldest of them —the conception of organized effort to protect themselves. 'The soldiers would stop it.' That was all." [72]

Three months after the end of the war, a Mississippi editor insisted that the habit of absolute dependence and the absence of self-reliance still characterized the black population. To a Union officer stationed nearby what depressed him most was the freedman's "natural feeling of timidity and fear when brought into a controversy with white men." [73] Whether these white observers were capable of perceiving black initiative is hardly the point. What they described was real enough, and none realized this fact more fully than did a newly emerging group of black activists who would seek to transform the ex-slave as the first step toward reconstruction of the entire South. They realized that they would have to address themselves at the very outset to this degrading dependence on the white man which had for so long kept the black man down. Emancipation and the enlistment of black soldiers, although welcomed victories, had been dictated largely by military necessities. The basic needs and aspirations of black people remained unfulfilled. It was crucial, these activists believed, that the immense tasks which now confronted the freedmen not be deferred to well-meaning whites. During the war, many slaves had undertaken their own liberation. Now that the war was over, that need was no less acute.

This was precisely the view of Henry M. Turner. While serving in the South as an army chaplain, he had manifested a fierce racial pride which was to characterize him throughout the remainder of his life. Despite the timidity and fearfulness that permeated the freedmen, he claimed for them "superior ability" to the white man and a far greater potential. "I have heard the greatest ministers and statesmen of this country, from Henry Ward Beecher and Charles Sumner down, but I have yet to hear greater eloquence than I have heard from the lips of Austin Allen, a black slave of South Carolina. In short, the ablest historian, the greatest orator, and the most skillful architect and mechanic I have ever seen, were all slaves in the South. Having travelled through all the slave States except Texas, prior to the war, my observations have been extensive: thus I speak what I know, and the fact that one negro is smart argues the possibility of another, and another *ad infinitum.*" To Turner, these outstanding blacks were not, as some whites argued, simply exceptions. What they symbolized was the future greatness of the race—they were, as Turner put it, *"extraordinary projections."* [74]

During his sojourn in the South, Turner was troubled by the apathy and submissiveness that persisted among his people. Although freedom had been proclaimed, far too many ex-slaves were still "afraid to speak above a whisper. That old servile fear still twirls itself around the heart strings, and fills with terror the entire soul at a white man's frown. Just let him say stop, and every fibre is palsied, and this will be the case till they all die." If black people were to achieve real freedom, not this "superficial freedom" and "dreamy idea of 'do as you please,'" they would first have to cast this "white man's foot-kissing party" from their midst. *"As long as negroes will be negroes* (as we are called) *we may be negroes."* Only when black people "unanimously strike" for their rights, Turner concluded, will they achieve freedom. And it was about time. "If we had had one half of the Indian spunk, to-day slavery would have been among the things of the past." [75]

When the war ended, Henry Turner thought he knew where and how he could best serve his people. The white benevolent societies were already active in the field, and they were doing noble work. But millions of slaves, Turner argued, most of them without land, money, or homes, and many of them "insensible" to the "noble purposes of life," had yet to be reached. Except for certain localities, where there was "[n]one of this foolish crouching before white men," he was disgusted with the way in which many freedmen still embraced and even cherished the old slave habits. "Oh, how the foul curse of slavery has blighted the natural greatness of my race!" he wrote in February, 1865, while his regiment was in North Carolina. "It has not only depressed and horror-streaked the should-be glowing countenances of thousands, but it has almost transformed many into inhuman appearance." What was needed were not simply more missionaries and teachers, but *black* missionaries and *black* teachers. "I argue the peculiar fitness of the colored man for that position, because about him the most incredulous would have no doubt." The black man, Turner insisted, would not fall easy prey to "the deceptive flippancy of the oily-tongued slaveocrats, who too often becloud the understanding of the whites. No sumptuous tables, fine chambers, attractive misses, springy buggies, or swinging carriages would filch the time and labor he came to bestow, because he would find his level only among the colored race." Since he would have immediate access to the freedman's homes and social gatherings, "his influence and personal identification with them would go further than the white man's." [76]

When Turner uttered these words, the black Gideonite was already becoming a familiar figure in certain sections of the South, and more were on their way. What many of them envisioned was a new and different kind of Jubilee. It would be celebrated in the halls of Southern state legislatures, where black men would sit with white men to make the laws of a new South. To the mass of freedmen in 1865, this may have seemed like an impossible dream. But to a small committed group of blacks, some only recently slaves, the vision was begining to take hold. The first years of freedom were for them years of organization and preparation. What the white South was about to behold, in the very aftermath of Appomattox, was the spectacle of black people meeting, petitioning, organizing, and expressing themselves openly and frankly. Only a few years ago, that, too, had seemed like an impossible dream.

7.

Shortly after she had been emancipated, a young black girl expressed dismay at the fact that freedom had not turned her white. "You must not be ashamed of the skin God gave you," her white mistress exclaimed. "Your skin is all right." The reassurance made no real impression. "I druther be white," the girl persisted. Reflecting upon this incident, the white woman thought "there was something pathetic in the aspiration." [77] But what this discouraged black girl had suggested, in her own way, was simply the dimensions of the problem. Whatever the results of the Civil War, to be white in American society was to be something, perhaps everything. That was a doctrine more fundamental and far-reaching in its implications than scores of emancipation proclamations, constitutional amendments, and court decisions.

In the afterglow of this War of Liberation, however, some blacks professed to be confident about the future. Surely this nation would recall the black man's services and sacrifices, and reward him for his proven loyalty. Even some of the less optimistic black "spokesmen" were at least certain of one thing: if their people lost out in the impending struggle for equal recognition, they would take down the nation and its pretensions along with them. "Be not deceived," a Philadelphia black minister declared on the day the Emancipation Proclamation went into effect, "the black man under God holds largely the future destiny of this country in his hands. Your destiny as white men, and ours as black men, is one and the same; we are all marching on to the same goal; if you rise, we will rise in the scale of being. If you fall, we will fall, but you will have the worst of it." [78]

FOOTNOTES

1. Sung by black soldiers while marching into Richmond, Virginia, April 3, 1865 (*The Black Republican,* May 20, 1865).

2. *The Christian Recorder* (Philadelphia), April 23, May 28, 1864.

3. *Ibid.*

4. Mary Boykin Chesnut, *A Diary from Dixie* (Boston, 1949), 292; Annette Koch to her husband [Christian D. Koch], June 27, 1863, Christian D. Koch Papers (Louisiana State University Library); Booker T. Washington, *Up From Slavery* (New York, 1965, Laurel-Leaf Library ed.), 26–27.

5. Quoted in Bell Irvin Wiley, *Southern Negroes, 1861–1865* (New Haven, 1938), 19; Willie Lee Rose, *Rehearsal for Reconstruction: The Port Royal Experiment* (Indianapolis, 1964), 12; *The New York Times,* June 19, 1863; B. A. Botkin (ed.), *Lay My Burden Down: A Folk History of Slavery* (Chicago, 1945), 227.

6. A. Franklin Pugh, Plantation Diary (ms.), 1863–64 (Louisiana State University Library).

7. John Eaton, *Grant, Lincoln and the Freedmen: Reminiscences of the Civil War* (New York, 1907), 1–2; James M. McPherson (ed.), *The Negro's Civil War* (New York, 1965), 206–207.

8. Thomas Wentworth Higginson, *Army Life in a Black Regiment* (New York, 1962, Collier Books ed.), 169.

9. Elizabeth Hyde Botume, *First Days Amongst the Contrabands* (Boston, 1893), 178–180; James Edward Glazier to his parents, Glazier Papers (Henry E. Huntington Library, San Marino, Calif.); Myrta Lockett Avary, *Dixie After the War* (New York, 1906), 182–183; Ephraim McDowell Anderson, *Memoirs: Historical and Personal; Including the Campaigns of the First Missouri Confederate Brigade*

(St. Louis, 1868), 364; *The New York Times,* October 27, December 18, 1861; January 14, 19, February 9, 1862; March 9, June 26, July 12, August 8, November 10, 1863; May 7, 1864.

10. Rose, *Rehearsal for Reconstruction,* 322, 332.

11. Higginson, *Army Life in a Black Regiment,* 233–234; Joel Williamson, *After Slavery: The Negro in South Carolina During Reconstruction, 1861–1877* (Chapel Hill, 1965), 6; Benjamin Quarles, *The Negro in the Civil War* (Boston, 1953), 62; *The New York Times,* January 21, February 9, October 19, November 29, 1862; July 3, 1863; July 17, 1864.

12. Botume, *First Days Amongst the Contrabands,* 138–139.

13. Arney R. Childs (ed.), *The Private Journal of Henry William Ravenel, 1859–1887* (Columbia, S.C., 1947), 115–116; Botume, *First Days Amongst the Contrabands,* 140; *The New York Times,* November 23, 1861; June 14, 17, 1863; July 27, 1864; Eliza Frances Andrews, *The War-Time Journal of a Georgia Girl, 1864–1865* (New York, 1908), 341–343.

14. Higginson, *Army Life in a Black Regiment,* 234–235.

15. Ray Allen Billington (ed.), *The Journal of Charlotte L. Forten* (New York, 1953), 160.

16. Wiley, *Southern Negroes,* 9–10, 183–184; Jefferson Davis Bragg, *Louisiana in the Confederacy* (Baton Rouge, 1941), 210–211; Vernon L. Wharton, *The Negro in Mississippi, 1865–1900* (Chapel Hill, N.C., 1947), 26–27; Williamson, *After Slavery,* 4–5; *The New York Times,* June 5, July 20, 1863; November 30, 1862.

17. *The Black Republican* (New Orleans), May 13, 1865; *The New York Times,* November 24, 1862; Eaton, *Grant, Lincoln and the Freedmen,* 2.

18. Eaton, *Grant, Lincoln and the Freedmen,* 2; Botume, *First Days Amongst the Contrabands,* 139; *The New York Times,* June 16, 1861; April 6, December 16, 1862; Botkin, *Lay My Burden Down,* 103–104; Friends' Central Committee for the Relief of the Emancipated Negroes, *Letters from Joseph Simpson* (Manchester, England, 1865), 26–27.

19. Rupert S. Holland (ed.), *Letters and Diary of Laura M. Towne* (Cambridge, 1912), 24; *Letters from Joseph Simpson,* 26.

20. *The New York Times,* November 28, 1863.

21. George W. Nichols, *The Story of the Great March* (New York, 1866), 62.

22. Albert V. House, Jr. (ed.), "Deterioration of a Georgia Rice Plantation During Four Years of Civil War," *The Journal of Southern History,* IX (February 1943), 101–102, 107–108, 111.

23. E. Merton Coulter, *The Confederate States of America, 1861–1865* (Baton Rouge, 1950), 256.

24. Emily Caroline Douglas, Autobiography (ms.), *ca.* 1904 (Louisiana State University Library), 164.

25. *Proceedings of the Freedmen's Convention of Georgia, Assembled at Augusta, January 10th, 1866* (Augusta, 1866), 18.

26. Mrs. Anna Andrews to Mrs. Courtney Jones, April 27, 1862, Andrews Papers (Duke University Library).

27. Chesnut, *Diary From Dixie,* 544.

28. Catherine Barbara Broun, Diary (ms.), entry of May 1, 1864 (Southern Historical Collection, Manuscripts Department, University of North Carolina Library); Botkin, *Lay My Burden Down,* 211; Wiley, *Southern Negroes,* 77; *The New York Times,* June 5, December 12, 1861; July 29, 1863.

29. Louisa T. Lovell to Capt. Joseph Lovell, February 7, 1864, Quitman Papers (University of North Carolina Library).

30. Chesnut, *Diary from Dixie*, 503.

31. Quarles, *Negro in the Civil War*, 57.

32. Robert Philip Howell, Memoirs (ms.), 17–18 (University of North Carolina Library).

33. William Cullen Bryant, II (ed.), "A Yankee Soldier Looks at the Negro," *Civil War History*, VII (June 1961), 145; J. H. Easterby (ed.), *The South Carolina Rice Plantation: As Revealed in the Papers of Robert F. W. Allston* (Chicago, 1945), 190; John Houston Bills, Diary (ms.), IV, 39, entry of May 18, 1863 (University of North Carolina Library); Elizabeth W. Allston Pringle, *Chronicles of Chicora Wood* (New York, 1922), 263; Andrews, *War-Time Journal of a Georgia Girl*, 321–322.

34. Avary, *Dixie After the War*, 190.

35. Mrs. W. H. Neblett to her husband, 1863–1864, quoted in Wiley, *Southern Negroes*, 52 n.

36. Chesnut, *Diary From Dixie*, 139–140, 145–148.

37. *Ibid.*, 38.

38. Louis Manigault, "Visit to 'Gowrie' and 'East Hermitage' Plantations" (ms.), Manigault Plantation Records (University of North Carolina Library).

39. *Ibid.*

40. *The New York Times*, June 14, 1863; Wiley, *Southern Negroes*, 13–14; Henry L. Swint (ed.), *Dear Ones at Home: Letters from Contraband Camps* (Nashville, 1966), 187.

41. *The New York Times*, November 23, December 1, 1862; June 7, 19, 1863; December 23, 1864; April 6, 1865; John Beatty, *The Citizen Soldier; or Memoirs of a Volunteer* (Cincinnati, 1879), 119, 124–125; Bryant, "A Yankee Soldier Looks at the Negro," 138; John William De Forest, *A Volunteer's Adventures: A Union Captain's Record of the Civil War* (New Haven, 1946), 17, 56; George R. Bentley, *A History of the Freedmen's Bureau* (Philadelphia, 1955), 20; John D. Winters, *The Civil War in Louisiana* (Baton Rouge, 1963), 237; *New York Tribune*, March 2, 1865; Work Projects Administration, *The Negro in Virginia* (New York, 1940), 211–212.

42. W.P.A., *Negro in Virginia*, 209; Chesnut, *Diary from Dixie*, 532.

43. G. P. Whittington (ed.), "Concerning the Loyalty of Slaves in North Louisiana in 1863: Letters from John H. Ransdell to Governor Thomas O. Moore, dated 1863," *The Louisiana Historical Quarterly*, 14 (October 1931), 491–493, 494, 500.

44. Rose, *Rehearsal for Reconstruction*, 106–107; *The New York Times*, November 14, 20, 1861.

45. Williamson, *After Slavery*, 5–6.

46. Easterby, *South Carolina Rice Plantation*, 210, 328, 329; Daniel E. Huger Smith *et al.* (eds.), *Mason Smith Family Letters, 1860–1868* (Columbia, S.C., 1950), 187; Williamson, *After Slavery*, 52; Wiley, *Southern Negroes*, 78–79; *The New York Times*, November 20, 1861; Pringle, *Chronicles of Chicora Wood*, 268; Holland, *Letters and Diary of Laura M. Towne*, 34.

47. Pringle, *Chronicles of Chicora Wood*, 269; *The New York Times*, November 16, 20, December 21, 1862; F. W. Smith (ed.), "The Yankees in New Albany: Letter of Elizabeth Jane Beach, July 29, 1864," *The Journal of Mississippi History*, II (January 1940), 46.

48. Easterby, *South Carolina Rice Plantation*, 213.

49. *Christian Recorder*, December 27, 1862.

50. John Houston Bills, Diary (ms.), IV, 13, 115.

51. Easterby, *South Carolina Rice Plantation*, 213, 328–329.

52. Wiley, *Southern Negroes*, 78.

53. Williamson, *After Slavery*, 51–52; Petition of 18 Planters, Pineville, Charleston District, September 1, 1865, Trenholm Papers (University of North Carolina Library).

54. Andrews, *War-Time Journal of a Georgia Girl*, 261–262.

55. Rose, *Rehearsal for Reconstruction*, 244; Sarah Bradford, *Harriet Tubman: The Moses of Her People* (New York, 1961, Corinth Books ed.), 98–102; Higginson, *Army Life in a Black Regiment*, 168.

56. *Christian Recorder*, April 15, 1865.

57. *Ibid.*, May 28, 1864.

58. *Ibid.*, March 25, April 1, 1865.

59. *New York Tribune*, March 2, 1865; *Christian Recorder*, April 15, 1865; McPherson, *Negro's Civil War*, 236–237.

60. Frank A. Rollin, *Life and Public Services of Martin R. Delany* (Boston, 1883), 197–198.

61. *Christian Recorder*, June 25, 1864; May 6, 27, 1865.

62. *New York Tribune*, April 7, 1865; *Christian Recorder*, April 22, 1865; W.P.A., *Negro in Virginia*, 212.

63. Rembert W. Patrick, *The Fall of Richmond* (Baton Rouge, 1960), 68, 115, 117–120.

64. Quoted in the introduction by Howard N. Meyer to Higginson, *Army Life in a Black Regiment*, 20.

65. Ella Gertrude (Clanton) Thomas, Journal (ms.), 1864–1865 (Duke University Library).

66. Grace B. Elmore, Diary (ms.), entry for May 24, 1865 (University of North Carolina Library); J. T. Trowbridge, *The South: A Tour of Its Battle-Fields and Ruined Cities, A Journey Through the Desolated States, and Talks With the People* (Hartford, Conn., 1866), 68, 538.

67. Botkin, *Lay My Burden Down*, 14. The responses of blacks to the question of freedom versus slavery may be found in Whitelaw Reid, *After the War: A Tour of the Southern States, 1865–1866* (New York, 1866), 110, 272–273; Sidney Andrews, *The South Since the War* (Boston, 1866), 352–353; Mary Ames, *From a New England Woman's Diary in Dixie in 1865* (Springfield, Mass., 1906), 45, 118; Swint, *Dear Ones at Home*, 41; Bryant, "A Yankee Soldier Looks at the Negro," 137; Botume, *First Days Amongst the Contrabands*, 86; *The American Freedman*, III (July 1869), 20; Miss Esther W. Douglass to Rev. Samuel Hunt, February 1, 1866 (American Missionary Association Collection, Fisk University Library).

68. John Richard Dennett, *The South As It Is: 1865–1866* (New York, 1965, ed. by Henry M. Christman), 121–122.

69. Wiley, *Southern Negroes*, 84; *The Negroes at Port Royal: Report of E. L. Pierce, Government Agent, to the Hon. Salmon P. Chase, Secretary of the Treasury* (Boston, 1862), 18; *The New York Times*, December 23, 1864.

70. Swint, *Dear Ones at Home*, 61; Nichols, *Story of the Great March*, 103.

71. *New York Tribune*, February 3, 1866, quoted in 39th Congress, 1st Session, *Report of the Joint Committee on Reconstruction* (Washington, D.C., 1866), Part II, 199–200.

72. *American Freedman*, III (July 1869), 20; *Christian Recorder*, January 16, 1864; Reid, *After the War*, 258.

73. Wharton, *Negro in Mississippi*, 50–51.

74. *The Christian Recorder*, August 5, 1865.

75. *The Christian Recorder,* January 31, 1863, August 5, 1865.

76. *The Christian Recorder,* February 25, 1865, August 5, 1865, January 20, 1866.

77. Avary, *Dixie After the War,* 193.

78. *The Christian Recorder,* January 17, 1813. The minister, Jonathan C. Gibbs, migrated to the South after the War, and became the most important black leader in Florida. During Reconstruction, he held the positions of Secretary of State and Superintendent of Public Instruction.

PAUL B. WORTHMAN

Working Class Mobility in Birmingham, Alabama, 1880–1914

The legend that the United States has long been the land of opportunity for the common man has received new attention during the past several years. No longer content to rely on an articulate minority's contemporary impressions about the extent of opportunity and the fluidity of the social order, some historians have recently attempted to assess individual advancement in this country with greater precision by applying the tools and concepts of quantification.[1] Led by the pioneering work of Stephan Thernstrom, they have traced the careers of thousands of people in different communities to determine if the myth of social mobility squared with social reality. By providing some measurements of the distribution and relative frequency of vertical mobility, their findings have enhanced our understanding of the dimensions of economic opportunity and social mobility in the United States during the nineteenth century. Equally important, they furnished tantalizing hypotheses about how the processes of social and geographic mobility might have impeded working class consciousness and functioned as instruments of social order and cohesion in a rapidly industrializing society.[2]

A Yale University Travel Fellowship, a grant from the Huber Foundation of Wellesley College, and a Wellesley College Faculty Research Award made much of the research for this article possible. I am grateful to Stephan Thernstrom for several helpful suggestions regarding the presentation of my data.

Although these studies of individual communities often generalize about the United States, with the exception of one brief study of Atlanta, Georgia, the South has been ignored.[3] As C. Vann Woodward demonstrated almost 20 years ago, the post-Civil War South did not escape the rapid acceleration of industrialization and urban growth, and the accompanying social upheavals and disruptions, experienced by the rest of the United States during the end of the nineteenth century.[4] Profound differences between cities in the South and in the North and West undoubtedly existed, caused in part by the South's heritage of slavery, the nature of the southern economy, and the presence of millions of newly-freed black slaves whose place in the social and industrial order was not yet established. Nevertheless, there were striking parallels between southern industrializing communities and their northern and western counterparts.[5] Hundreds of thousands of blacks and whites, many of them seeking the same opportunities which drew people to northern communities, swarmed into the South's older cities and new industrial towns between the end of the Civil War and the outbreak of World War I. Their encounter with the urban environment is an integral part of the history of the working class in the United States.

This essay summarizes some findings about geographic and economic mobility which are part of a larger study of industrial workers in Birmingham, Alabama, during the end of the nineteenth and beginning of the twentieth century. An examination of the careers of 1,500 workingmen in Birmingham between 1880 and 1914 furnished data with which to compute rates of intragenerational occupational mobility, property acquisition, residential mobility within the city and nearby suburbs, and geographic mobility out of the city. Three stratified samples, each with ten subsets, were drawn on the basis of a random number table from the 1880 manuscript census schedule and from Birmingham city directories for 1890 and 1899.[6] Five occupational groupings—building tradesmen, railroad trainmen, mechanics, service workers, and unskilled, with separate samples for blacks and whites—provided the ten subsets. Information on the occupation and residence of each individual sampled was sought in the first city directory in 1883, and in directories for 1890, 1895, 1899, 1904, 1909, and 1914. Jefferson County tax lists for 1882, 1884, 1890, 1899, and 1909 provided information on property holding.[7]

THE INDUSTRIALIZATION
OF BIRMINGHAM

Birmingham, Alabama, was one of the most rapidly industrializing urban areas in the United States in the half century after the Civil War.[8] Before the war, small farms and scattered villages dominated the region. Although potential ante-bellum entrepreneurs were aware of the large coal and iron ore deposits in the area, shortage of capital, lack of an adequate transportation system, and cultural and political inhibitions of the slave society prevented development of the district. Destruction of the slaveholder's regime, however, brought new efforts to exploit the region's mineral wealth. In 1871 real estate promoters began to sell lots for a new city at the anticipated junction of two railroads in an old cornfield in the heart of the mineral district. Confident that the city they envisioned had a magnificent industrial future, they named the new town Birmingham.

Despite periodic economic setbacks, Birmingham's industrial growth was nothing short of phenomenal. In 1870 only 22 manufacturing establishments, employing 44 people, existed in the county. Industrialists built the first coke ovens in Birmingham in 1876, and by 1880 added several blast furnaces and a rolling mill. By 1900 almost 500 manufacturing establishments in the county, capitalized at over $20 million, employed 14,000 wage-earners. In Birmingham, 282 manufacturing plants employed almost 7,000 workers and made products valued at more than $12 million. The district's coke ovens, many of them in the city or on its outskirts, turned out over two million tons of coke in 1900, and blast furnaces throughout the metropolitan region produced over one million tons of pig iron in that year.[9] Subsidiary industries like iron foundries, machine shops, rolling mills, cast iron pipe factories, and a newly erected steel plant added to the industrial production of the metropolis. Although the city's economy centered around the iron and steel industry, by the beginning of the twentieth century some diversification had been achieved. Eight railroad lines entered the city, and several of them had repair shops located there. The city directory in 1899 listed more than 50 different kinds of manufacturing enterprises in Birmingham, including a dozen clothing manufacturers, three cigar factories, a cotton mill, a broom factory, a soda-water bottling plant, a soap factory, and two breweries.[10]

Birmingham's population growth kept pace with its industrial expansion. Despite the depression of the 1870's and a severe cholera epidemic in 1873, by 1880 the young city had a population of 3,800. Twenty years later Birmingham's population had increased ten times, and by 1910, with further migration and the incorporation of surrounding suburbs, there were over 130,000 people in the city.[11] Some idea of population growth, as well as the demand for labor, can be gathered from Table 1. The number of industrial workers in the designated occupations more than doubled from 1880 to 1883, and tripled again by 1890. Although industrial workers seem to have left the city during the depression of the 1890's, by 1904 there were more than 10,000 workingmen in these occupations in Birmingham.[12]

BLACKS AND IMMIGRANTS
IN THE LABOR FORCE

From its founding Birmingham attracted large numbers of southern blacks. Although there were only 2,500 Afro-Americans in Jefferson County in 1870, by 1910 more than 130,000 black people lived in the county, 52,000 residing within the city limits of Birmingham and making up over 40 per cent of the population.[13] As the economy expanded, moreover, the black worker's role in the industrial labor force expanded with it, as shown in Table 2. In 1880 only 41 per cent of industrial workers listed were black. By 1900, according to figures compiled from the city directory, more than one-half of the city's wage earners were black. Black workers made up 65 per cent of the labor force in the iron and steel industry in 1900, and 75 per cent in 1910.[14] Concentrated in poorly paid, low status jobs, blacks continued to form the base of the southern labor force as they had under slavery.

The burgeoning industrial city attracted not only blacks and southern whites, but also northern white workingmen. Over 2,000 northern-born people lived in Birmingham in 1890, and although the number declined during the depression of the 1890's, by 1910 there were over 7,000 northern-born in the city, constituting perhaps 10 to 15 per cent of the native-born white population.[15] Many of these

TABLE 1 *Number of Workers in Selected Occupations and Per Cent Increase for Selected Years*

OCCUPATION	1880	1883	% INC.	1890	% INC.	1895	% INC.
Building Trades							
Carpenter	110	204	(85%)	841	(312%)	871	(4%)
Brickmason	33	55	(67)	151	(175)	90	(−40)
Plasterer	7	14	(100)	37	(164)	25	(−32)
Plumber, pipefitter	—	10	(—)	39	(290)	35	(−10)
Painter, paperhanger	12	54	(350)	171	(217)	89	(−48)
Electrician	—	—		5	(—)	5	(0)
Total	162	337	(108%)	1244	(269%)	1115	(−10%)
Railroad							
Engineer	33	67	(103%)	291	(334%)	259	(−11%)
Conductor	13	23	(77)	83	(261)	152	(83)
Fireman	2	51	(2450)	252	(394)	267	(6)
Switchman	1	—	(—)	37	(—)	73	(97)
Brakeman	—	35	(—)	74	(111)	183	(147)
Flagman	—	—		12	(—)	74	(517)
Motorman	—	—		31	(—)	40	(29)
Total	49	176	(260%)	780	(343%)	1048	(34%)
Mechanics							
Puddler	1	23	(2300%)	155	(574%)	115	(−26%)
Heater, roller	5	22	(340)	21	(−5)	26	(24)
Molder	31	47	(52)	37	(−21)	53	(43)
Boilermaker	5	39	(680)	47	(21)	77	(64)
Patternmaker	—	12	(—)	23	(92)	14	(−39)
Tinner	2	13	(550)	35	(169)	22	(−37)
Stat. engineer	1	1	(—)	49	(4800)	59	(20)
RR car repairer	4	5	(25)	115	(2200)	269	(134)
Machinist	48	106	(121)	258	(404)	296	(15)
Blacksmith	20	58	(190)	132	(128)	124	(−6)
Printer	3	24	(700)	121	(404)	40	(−67)
Total	120	350	(192%)	993	(183%)	1095	(10%)
Service							
Barber	12	21	(75%)	127	(505%)	93	(−27%)
Shoemaker	3	16	(400)	71	(344)	78	(10)
Tailor	1	7	(600)	43	(514)	28	(−35)
Total	16	44	(175%)	241	(447%)	199	(−17%)
Unskilled							
Avondale Cotton Mill	—	—		—		—	
Other factory worker	—	4	(—)	76	(1900%)	62	(−18%)
Teamster, drayman	8	85	(950%)	335	(299)	335	(0)
Laborer at furnace	n.g.[a]	81	(—)	946	(1068)	718	(−24)
Laborer on railroad	n.g.	30	(—)	316	(1000)	269	(−15)
Laborer at rolling mill	n.g.	25	(—)	445	(1680)	825	(85)
Laborer—n.o.s.	539	1045	(94)	1487	(42)	1546	(4)
Total	547	1270	(133%)	3605	(183%)	3755	(5%)

SOURCE: 1880 U.S. manuscript census schedules; 1883–1909 *Birmingham City Directories*.
[a]Workplace not designated and thus could not be tabulated.

1899	% INC.	1904	% INC.	1909	% INC.
486	(−44%)	731	(50%)	1026	(40%)
89	(−1)	167	(88)	258	(54)
25	(0)	61	(144)	67	(10)
39	(11)	68	(75)	112	(65)
168	(89)	223	(33)	280	(26)
16	(120)	53	(231)	190	(258)
823	(−26%)	1303	(58%)	1933	(48%)
205	(−21%)	289	(41%)	465	(61%)
170	(11)	265	(56)	307	(16)
171	(−36)	134	(−22)	296	(121)
52	(−29)	50	(−4)	133	(166)
154	(−16)	137	(−11)	176	(28)
101	(36)	112	(11)	165	(65)
71	(78)	71	(0)	154	(117)
924	(−12%)	1058	(14%)	1696	(60%)
255	(95%)	33	(−87%)	56	(70%)
3	(−88)	2	(−33)	47	(2250)
64	(21)	143	(123)	266	(86)
84	(9)	106	(26)	164	(55)
21	(50)	27	(29)	59	(119)
29	(32)	30	(3)	64	(113)
59	(0)	80	(36)	227	(184)
250	(−7)	526	(110)	n.g.	
320	(8)	500	(63)	767	(53)
134	(8)	180	(34)	206	(14)
81	(103)	101	(25)	188	(86)
1270	(15%)	1728	(37%)	2044	(19%)
137	(47%)	170	(24%)	310	(82%)
94	(21)	71	(−26)	117	(64)
43	(54)	43	(0)	112	(160)
274	(37%)	284	(3%)	539	(89%)
150	(—)	435	(190%)	214	(−51%)
290	(368%)	852	(308)	907	(6)
249	(−26)	294	(18)	529	(80)
321	(−55)	256	(−43)	n.g.	
215	(−20)	830	(286)	n.g.	
745	(−10)	945	(27)	n.g.	
2571	(36)	3457	(63)	5393	(57)
4481	(19%)	6069	(48%)	7043	(16%)

TABLE 2 *Number and Per Cent of Afro-Americans in Selected Industrial Occupations for Selected Years*[a]

OCCUPATION	1880	% BLACK	1883	% BLACK	1890	% BLACK
Building Trades						
Carpenter	11	(10%)	14	(7%)	77	(9%)
Brickmason	10	(30)	23	(42)	39	(26)
Plasterer	1	(14)	6	(43)	25	(68)
Plumber	—		—		3	(8)
Painter	1	(8)	9	(17)	17	(10)
Electrician	—		—		—	
Total	23	(14%)	52	(15%)	161	(12%)
Railroad						
Engineer	1	(3%)	—		2	(.7%)
Conductor	—		—		—	
Fireman	1	(50)	15	(29)	89	(35)
Switchman	—		—		3	(8)
Brakeman	—		5	(14)	15	(20)
Flagman	—		—		1	(8)
Motorman	—		—		1	(3)
Total	2	(4%)	20	(12%)	110	(15%)
Mechanics						
Puddler	—		—		1	(.8%)
Heater, roller	—		—		2	(9)
Molder	—		1	(2%)	—	
Boilermaker	—		2	(5)	—	
Patternmaker	—		—		—	
Tinner	—		—		—	
Stat. engineer	—		1	(100)	5	(10)
RR car repairer	—		—		9	(8)
Machinist	—		3	(3)	1	(.4)
Blacksmith	5	(25%)	13	(22)	28	(21)
Printer	—		—		5	(4)
Total	5	(4%)	20	(5%)	50	(5%)
Service						
Barber	12	(100%)	21	(100%)	101	(80%)
Shoemaker	1	(33)	6	(38)	21	(30)
Tailor	—		—		1	(2)
Total	13	(81%)	27	(61%)	123	(52%)
Unskilled						
Avondale Cotton Mill	—		—		—	
Other factory worker	—		1	(25%)	59	(43%)
Teamster	5	(63%)	56	(67)	227	(68)
Laborer at furnace	n.g.[b]		75	(93)	830	(88)
Laborer on railroad	n.g.		6	(20)	226	(72)
Laborer at rolling mill	n.g.		—		207	(46)
Laborer—n.o.s.	320	(59)	886	(85)	1207	(81)
Total	325	(59%)	1024	(81%)	2756	(73%)

[a] For a discussion of the changing role of black workers in Birmingham's labor force and in particular occupations, see the author's forthcoming Ph.D. Dissertation on Industrial Workers in Birmingham, Alabama, 1871–1908, Yale University.
[b] Workplace not designated and thus could not be tabulated.

178

1895	% BLACK	1899	% BLACK	1904	% BLACK	1909	% BLACK
57	(7%)	59	(12%)	143	(20%)	152	(15%)
28	(31)	29	(32)	51	(30)	83	(32)
12	(48)	16	(64)	38	(62)	53	(79)
9	(26)	4	(10)	13	(19)	9	(8)
17	(19)	23	(14)	30	(13)	32	(11)
—		—		—		2	(1)
123	(11%)	131	(16%)	275	(21%)	331	(17%)
1	(.3%)	—		—		3	(.3%)
—		—				—	
150	(56)	51	(30%)	96	(72%)	189	(63)
41	(56)	17	(33)	20	(40)	57	(42)
152	(83)	124	(81)	123	(90)	127	(72)
2	(3)	2	(2)	2	(2)	1	(.1)
—		—		—		—	
347	(33%)	194	(21%)	241	(23%)	377	(22%)
—		—		—		11	(19%)
1	(4%)	—·		—		18	(38)
2	(4)	—		1	(.6%)	16	(6)
—		—		6	(6)	11	(6)
—		—		—		1	(1)
4	(7)	5	(8%)	3	(4)	7	(3)
55	(20)	67	(19)	175	(33)	n.g.	
5	(2)	6	(2)	14	(3)	38	(5)
35	(28)	39	(29)	52	(29)	43	(20)
—		4	(5)	1	(1)	5	(2)
103	(9%)	121	(10%)	252	(14%)	150	(8%)
61	(66%)	93	(68%)	113	(66%)	185	(59%)
36	(46)	49	(52)	37	(52)	61	(52)
6	(21)	9	(21)	9	(21)	37	(33)
103	(51%)	151	(55%)	159	(56%)	283	(52%)
—		—		—		—	
46	(74%)	113	(38%)	387	(45%)	53	(49%)
271	(81)	197	(79)	233	(79)	350	(67)
579	(80)	344	(64)	156	(61)	n.g.	
196	(72)	100	(62)	522	(63)	n.g.	
273	(34)	392	(49)	145	(15)	n.g.	
1245	(81)	2048	(81)	2848	(82)	4707	(87)
2601	(69%)	3194	(81%)	4291	(71%)	5110	(72%)

northern-born whites were second generation immigrants. Together with first-generation European immigrants, most of whom also came to Birmingham from northern states, they represented a significant proportion of the white population. Examination of the 1880 manuscript census schedules revealed that almost 30 per cent of the white heads of household in Birmingham that year were first- or second-generation immigrants. A decade later, 28 per cent of the males over 21 in the city were foreign-born or the sons of immigrants. Although the depression of the 1890's slowed the migration of immigrants to the city and intensified the migration of southern whites, in 1900 almost 25 per cent of adult white males in Birmingham were still of immigrant stock.[16]

Like the city's black population, these immigrants were concentrated in industrial activities. In 1880 over one-third of the white workingmen in industrial occupations listed in Table 1 were first- or second-generation immigrants. And as late as 1910 one-quarter of the white wage earners in the city's manufacturing and mechanical industries, and almost one-half of the white iron and steel workers, were first- or second-generation immigrants.[17] In the nineteenth century British iron and steel workers, Irish unskilled laborers and furnacemen, and Germans from Louisville and Cincinnati who worked in the building trades or as tailors or shoemakers made up the bulk of the immigrants. After 1900 the proportion of southern Europeans among the foreign-born increased from 18 per cent in 1890 to 43 per cent in 1910, as industrialists brought Russians, Hungarians, Slavs, and Italians from the North to labor in steel mills and blast furnaces. Since information about the place of birth of workers in 1890 and 1899 was not available, unfortunately no systematic examination of the immigrants' patterns of mobility is presented here. Their presence in the city, however, meant that a distinct proportion of the white workingmen sampled were not native-born southerners.[18]

PERSISTENCE RATES
OF INDUSTRIAL WORKERS

Although the expanding economy continued to attract white and black migrants to Birmingham, the majority of workingmen who came to the city did not settle there permanently. Like workers in other nineteenth-century industrial communities in the United States, most of these migrants worked for a few years, or even months or days, and then left the city to seek employment elsewhere, replaced by other migrants who would repeat this pattern. Some white workingmen who emigrated to Birmingham from northern states in the nineteenth century came as transients, leaving their families behind and returning to the North in the summer or during strikes or slack periods. Special excursion rates on the Louisville and Nashville Railroads facilitated this movement, and Birmingham industrialists urged the railroad to eliminate rate schedules that encouraged and supported the exodus of labor from the city.[19] The periodic recessions that plagued Birmingham's economy also accelerated geographical mobility. Building craftsmen drawn to the city during construction booms departed when a surfeit of building occurred. Recurring shutdowns of the city's blast furnaces and rolling mills drove iron and steel workers from Birmingham. Railroad superintendents complained about the migration of trainmen and trackmen to other branches or to roads in the Southwest. The reopening of industrial plants, the construction or renovation of existing facilities, or the expansion of rail service meant that foremen were forced to go North or to other southern cities to seek skilled workmen or to induce former employees to return. Newspaper editors and industrialists often grumbled about the instability of the labor force and the rapid turnover of black and white workers in the metropolitan region, and, as Table 3 shows, their complaints were not without justification.[20]

The geographic mobility of Birmingham's working class is reflected in the rates of persistence for various occupational categories presented in Table 3. Persistence was defined simply as the reappearance of workers sampled in subsequent city directories studied. These persistence rates almost certainly underestimate the volatility of the population, as Peter Knights has pointed out.[21] People entering and leaving the city between the particular enumerations examined are not included in the population sampled. Moreover, Birmingham directories, like those in other cities, understated the number of recent migrants and low status residents, especially blacks, in the community. On the other hand, almost all renters in Birmingham in the nineteenth century reshuffled their residences every fall, and enumerators therefore probably failed to include in the directories some people still

TABLE 3   Rates of Persistence by Race and Occupational Category[a]

1880 GROUP	NUMBER SAMPLED	1883	1890	1895	1899	1904	1909
White							
Building trades	47	51%	40%	38%	34%	27%	17%
Railroad	23	39	26	22	17	13	4
Mechanics	40	75	45	37	32	32	20
Service	8	25	25	—	—	—	—
Unskilled	60	47	27	10	7	3	3
Total	178	52%	34%	25%	21%	16%	11%
Black							
Building trades	16	63%	44%	13%	6%	6%	6%
Railroad	2	100	100	50	—	—	—
Mechanics	4	100	25	25	—	—	—
Service	11	73	64	55	55	45	36
Unskilled	79	54	28	13	11	8	3
Total	112	60%	40%	18%	14%	11%	6%

1890 GROUP	NUMBER SAMPLED	1895	1899	1904	1909	1914
White						
Building trades	75	43%	33%	28%	13%	9%
Railroad	75	64	44	31	21	20
Mechanics	73	51	38	33	22	11
Service	21	52	38	38	38	29
Unskilled	99	39	30	22	13	8
Total	343	48%	37%	28%	18%	12%
Black						
Building trades	62	42%	26%	23%	13%	10%
Railroad	50	56	28	24	8	—
Mechanics	24	58	58	50	33	25
Service	54	81	78	74	37	30
Unskilled	113	60	47	40	26	12
Total	303	59%	46%	41%	22%	13%

1899 GROUP	NUMBER SAMPLED	1904	1909	1914
White				
Building trades	80	65%	49%	40%
Railroad	70	53	40	30
Mechanics	110	58	44	27
Service	33	64	42	30
Unskilled	133	49	36	24
Total	426	56%	41%	29%
Black				
Building trades	60	53%	33%	17%
Railroad	72	45	30	19
Mechanics	60	64	39	22
Service	34	59	41	32
Unskilled	146	52	34	23
Total	392	53%	32%	20%

[a] Percentages are expressed with the year in which the sample was chosen as the base. Since in certain occupational categories there were few workers, the number sampled was necessarily small, and thus in some instances the resultant changes magnify the percentage changes.

residing in the city. Despite such biases and omissions, however, compilers of the city directories attempted to include all residents in order to validate the Birmingham boosters' assertions of rapid growth. And these directories presumably presented a reasonably accurate compilation of Birmingham's population in the late nineteenth and early twentieth century.

Important racial and occupational distinctions existed in the persistence rates of Birmingham's industrial workers. As Richard Hopkins found in Atlanta, persistence rates for Afro-Americans in Birmingham in the nineteenth century were generally higher than, or in some occupational categories equal to, those for white workingmen.[22] For example, although the numbers sampled in several categories in 1880, are extremely small, in all five occupational categories a higher proportion of blacks could be found three years later in the 1883 city directory. Over a ten year period blacks were less transient than whites in three of the five categories, with only slight differences in the rate for building tradesmen. The same trend held true for the 1890 sample. In three of the five categories, blacks remained in the city at a higher rate than whites over a five year period and over a decade. Transiency among black workers, moreover, did not necessarily increase as occupational status decreased. Among white workers, unskilled laborers had the lowest persistence rate of any occupational category. Black unskilled laborers not only remained in the city at a rate that exceeded whites, but also at a rate higher than several other occupational categories for black workers.

Pooling the samples for 1880 and 1890 gives, perhaps, a better indication of the persistence of Birmingham's workingmen in the nineteenth century. Over a ten-year period, 43 per cent of the black workers and 34 per cent of the white workers remained in the city, which meant that the persistence rate for black workers was 25 per cent greater than that for whites. Among unskilled laborers, 39 per cent of the blacks and only 23 per cent of the whites could be found in the city directories a decade later, and thus the persistence rate of blacks was almost 70 per cent greater than that of whites. As shown in Table 4, however, although a higher proportion of blacks remained in the city for five or ten years, during the second decade examined the persistence rate of whites rose more rapidly than that of blacks as white workingmen who achieved some success settled down in the

TABLE 4   *Rates of Persistence*
for Pooled Samples, 1880 and 1890

OCCUPATIONAL CATEGORY	NUMBER SAMPLED	10 YEARS	15 YEARS	20 YEARS	FROM 10–20 YEARS
White					
Building trades	122	36%	31%	21%	59%
Railroad	98	40	29	20	51
Mechanics	113	41	35	26	63
Service	29	34	27	27	80
Unskilled	159	23	22	11	48
Total	521	34%	28%	19%	57%
Black					
Building trades	78	31%	19%	10%	33%
Railroad	52	33	25	27	22
Mechanics	28	50	43	25	50
Service	65	74	68	42	57
Unskilled	192	39	28	19	51
Total	415	43%	32%	20%	48%

city and its suburbs. One-half to three-quarters of the city's white
workers in the different occupational categories who remained in
Birmingham at least a decade could still be found there ten years later.

One reason for the higher persistence rates for black workers
probably lies in the biases of the directories. Since compilers of
these directories were probably more likely to include recent white
migrants than black ones, Afro-Americans listed in city directories,
especially unskilled workingmen, might have been more "settled"
than their white counterparts. This distinction would be reflected
in the persistence rates.

Biases in directories, however, do not completely explain racial
distinctions in the geographical mobility of Birmingham workingmen.
Black people in Birmingham in the nineteenth century maintained
strong positions as barbers, carpenters, plasterers, teamsters, switch-
men and brakemen, and as laborers in the rolling mill and factories.
Because the occupational and social structure of the black and white
communities differed, these jobs were economically and socially more
important to black workers than to whites, and meant greater success
to a black worker, who might stay in Birmingham rather than gamble

on finding employment elsewhere. Black workers in various occupational categories were also more stable than whites in the nineteenth century partly because they had less knowledge of alternate employment opportunities elsewhere and could not as easily take advantage of opportunities that came to their attention. During times of economic recession in Birmingham, white building tradesmen and mechanics might hope to find jobs in other communities, especially in the North, but proportionately fewer black craftsmen or unskilled laborers knew about such jobs or shared this expectation.

The higher persistence rates for blacks can also be attributed in part to the high transiency of white workingmen. Birmingham's white workers frequently complained about the city's poor working and living conditions, the high cost of living, and the lack of adequate public schooling for their children. That only one-third of white workers sampled in 1880 and in 1890 could be located in Birmingham a decade later reflected their dissatisfaction.[23]

In the twentieth century this situation changed. Economic expansion during the first decade of the century brought a large influx of whites into the metropolitan region. Pressure from these migrants plus an intensification of racial hostility eroded black domination of some trades. At the same time, black workers were becoming increasingly aware of the attractions of northern cities and northern industries as labor agents stepped up recruitment in Birmingham, despite the opposition of Booker T. Washington and the city's industrialists.[24] Persistence rates presented in Table 3 mirror the changed economic and social situation. In the 1880's and 1890's black service workers were one of the most stable groups in the labor force, and white workers in this category among the least stable. Three-quarters of the black workers sampled were still in Birmingham a decade later, although only one-third of the white service workers remained for ten years. After 1900, however, the persistence rate for black service employees declined sharply, while the rate for white workers in this category increased. From 1899 to 1909 persistence rates for black and white service workers was the same. Indeed, for workers sampled in 1899, persistence rates for 10 and 15 years in every category showed that white workers now remained in Birmingham at higher rates than blacks, reversing the situation prevailing in the nineteenth century.

PROPERTY MOBILITY

Differences in the persistence of industrial workingmen in Birmingham can be associated not only with occupation and race, but also with ownership of real estate.[25] In Birmingham, as in Newburyport and Poughkeepsie, proportionately more property owners than propertyless workers remained in the city for a decade, as demonstrated in Table 5. As Stephan Thernstrom pointed out in *Poverty and Progress*, those urban workingmen able to secure steady employment and to acquire property enjoyed an important kind of success in the struggle for existence in nineteenth-century America.[26] In Birmingham

TABLE 5   *Rates of Persistence for Owners and Nonowners*
             of Real Property by Occupational Category
             and Race for Selected Years

OCCUPATIONAL CATEGORY	NO. 1883	NO. AND % PERSIST. 1890	NO. 1890	NO. AND % PERSIST. 1899	NO. 1899	NO. AND % PERSIST. 1909
White skilled and semiskilled						
No property	104	26 (25%)	206	72 (35%)	229	92 (40%)
Property	14	11 (79)	38	22 (58)	64	38 (59)
White unskilled						
No property	57	14 (25%)	91	26 (29%)	117	36 (31%)
Property	3	2 (67)	8	4 (50)	16	12 (75)
All white						
No property	161	40 (25%)	297	98 (33%)	346	128 (37%)
Property	17	13 (76)	46	26 (57)	80	50 (63)
Black skilled and semiskilled						
No property	30	15 (50%)	180	80 (44%)	201	63 (31%)
Property	3	2 (67)	10	6 (60)	25	15 (60)
Black unskilled						
No property	76	21 (28%)	109	49 (44%)	128	35 (27%)
Property	3	1 (33)	4	4 (100)	18	12 (67)
All black						
No property	106	36 (34%)	199	89 (44%)	329	98 (30%)
Property	6	3 (50)	14	10 (71)	43	27 (63)

SOURCE: Jefferson County Tax Collectors' Lists, 1882, 1884; Jefferson County Tax Assessors' Lists, 1890, 1899, Jefferson County Court House, Birmingham, Alabama; *Birmingham City Directory*, 1883, 1890, 1899, 1909.

this was true for both black and white workers, and, as the city grew, workingmen who became settled residents tended to be those who had achieved a modicum of success.

Because Birmingham was not a city of homeowners in the nineteenth century, the extent of propertyholding by workingmen was surprising. In 1890, according to the U.S. census, only 10 per cent of the families in the city owned their homes. Among cities with more than 25,000 people, only New York had a higher percentage of renters. Ten years later, the census reported that only 14 per cent of the city's families owned their homes. As late as 1903, the Birmingham Realty Company, successor to the land company that founded the city 30 years earlier, still owned almost one-third of the land in Birmingham, most of it residential property. Not until 1910 did the proportion of homeowners among the residents of Birmingham reach as high as 30 per cent. At this time, surrounding suburbs with greater numbers of homeowners were incorporated, and the Birmingham Realty Company began to sell house lots throughout the city to the influx of white migrants.[27]

Table 6 indicates the extent of real propertyholding among Birmingham workingmen, and shows that real estate was strikingly available to workers—especially to whites—who remained in the city for any length of time. From one-third to one-half of these white workmen were able to report property after ten years' residence in Birmingham, and one-half to three-quarters of the white workingmen who stayed in the city until 1909 acquired real estate. The extent of propertyholding varied for different occupational categories. For example, less than one-third of the white unskilled workers sampled in 1880 and 1890 who were in Birmingham for ten years held property. While 50 to 60 per cent of the white building tradesmen who remained in Birmingham for ten years accumulated some property, the rate for railroad workers varied from 20 per cent for the decade from 1880 to 1890 to 64 per cent between 1899 and 1909. But in the twentieth century, at least one-half of the white industrial workers in the various groups who had been residing in Birmingham for at least ten years owned some property.

The size of these property holdings was impressive. After ten years, more than one-half of the property owners held at least $500

TABLE 6   *Real Property Holdings of Industrial Workers for Selected Years, by Race*

YEAR	NUMBER WH.	NUMBER BL.	WHITE NO.	WHITE %	BLACK NO.	BLACK %	UNDER $250 WH.	UNDER $250 BL.	$250–$499 WH.	$250–$499 BL.	$500–$999 WH.	$500–$999 BL.	$1000 OR MORE WH.	$1000 OR MORE BL.
1880 group														
1880	not available						not available[a]							
1883	93	67	17	18%	6	9%								
1890	61	26	21	34	5	19	4	—	4	1	2	2	1	2
1899	37	16	21	56	6	37	2	2	5	1	4	1	10	2
1909	19	7	14	73	4	57	—	1	—	1	4	1	10	1
1890 group														
1890	343	303	46	13%	14	5%	13	3	4	3	14	5	15	2
1899	124	139	50	40	28	20	12	17	12	7	18	2	8	2
1909	63	69	37	58	9	12	2	2	3	4	18	2	14	1
1899 group														
1899	436	372	80	18%	43	11%	27	30	13	7	25	5	15	1
1909	177	140	97	54	37	26	9	14	12	8	29	12	47	3

[a] Tax assessors' records for 1882 and 1884 were not found in the Jefferson County Court House, and the tax collectors' records used indicated only the amount of tax paid, not the value of the property owned. Since I have no information on the tax rate, the distribution of real estate could not be computed.

worth of real estate, and a significant proportion of them held more than $1,000 worth. Property ownership was not always the same as home ownership, for many people in Birmingham owned small amounts of real estate in one part of the city and rented in another. But the ownership of land, often only a small house lot, provided a form of savings and security for many of these workingmen, and was often the first important step toward the future acquisition of their own houses.

Although the acquisition of property was not so impressive for the city's black workers, those who were successful enough to remain in Birmingham for any length of time were able to purchase some real estate. Only one of ten or one of twenty black workingmen sampled owned property, but after a decade of residence in Birmingham one-fifth to one-quarter reported some property holdings. One of four black workers remaining in the city until 1909 owned some property (compared with 57 per cent of the white workers). As indicated in Tables 6 and 7, more than one-half the property owned by black workers was assessed at less than $500. Few black workingmen owned $1,000 worth of real estate. Working for lower wages than whites, irregularly employed, and suffering from racial discrimination, black workers had less of a chance than whites to accumulate enough capital to purchase even a small house lot. That almost 25 per cent of the black workers sampled who stayed in Birmingham for 10 or 20 years managed to buy some real estate is a testimony to their perseverance.

Propagandists of the New South and boosters of Birmingham insisted that infinite opportunities existed for individual advancement in the iron and steel capital of the South. "If, with well-directed energy, you will but bend yourselves with patience and perseverance to the tasks set before you," one celebrant of Birmingham instructed prospective immigrants to the city, "you will inevitably succeed, and will be assured as to your reward, plenty, and prosperity." [28] People who seemed to exemplify this Algeresque sentiment regularly walked the streets of Birmingham: Willis Roberts, a printer, came to Birmingham in the 1870's, and by 1890 was the head of one of the state's most successful publishing and printing establishments; William Fulton, a molder, migrated to Birmingham in the early 1880's, and by the beginning of the twentieth century was co-owner of an iron foundry and owned a house lot worth $2,500; James Anderson, also a molder,

TABLE 7 Real Property Holdings of Unskilled Industrial Workers for Selected Years, by Race

| | NUMBER | | PROPERTY OWNERS | | | | DISTRIBUTION OF REAL ESTATE | | | | | | | |
| | | | WHITE | | BLACK | | UNDER $250 | | $250–$499 | | $500–$999 | | $1000 OR MORE | |
YEAR	WH.	BL.	NO.	%	NO.	%	WH.	BL.	WH.	BL.	WH.	BL.	WH.	BL.
1880 group														
1880	60	79	not available				not available							
1883	24	43	2	8%	3	7%								
1890	16	22	2	13	3	14								
1899	4	9	2	50	4	44								
1909	2	2	1	100	2	100								
1890 group														
1890	99	113	8	8%	4	4%	4	—	1	—	1	4	2	—
1899	30	53	9	30	9	17	2	5	4	2	3	1	—	1
1909	13	29	7	54	3	10	1	—	3	2	3	—	—	1
1899 group														
1899	133	146	16	12%	12	8%	7	12	4	3	4	3	1	0
1909	48	49	23	48	12	24	2	5	1	7	8	—	12	—

became owner of a boiler works and a successful real estate dealer; John McLean started his career in Birmingham as a boilermaker and became vice-president of one of the largest stove factories in the South. Nor were these embodiments of diligence confined to white people: Henry Howze, a black coachman, turned to barbering and then became a dentist and proprietor of one of the city's Afro-American newspapers; James Rabb, a former porter and barber, also took up dentistry and by the early twentieth century owned several thousand dollars' worth of real estate.[29] These examples, of course, tell little about the mobility patterns of the rest of the city's working class. Investigation of the careers of thousands of Birmingham workmen uncovered few other industrial workingmen, skilled or unskilled, who rose to positions of wealth and prominence in the city. The absence of such instances, however, should not obscure the more modest opportunities available for occupational mobility among Birmingham's industrial workers.

INDUSTRIAL OCCUPATIONAL MOBILITY

To measure the extent of intragenerational occupational mobility among industrial workingmen in Birmingham, 29 industrial occupations were ranked by wage scales for each occupation in 1887–1888, taken from data in newspapers, union journals, and company records (Table 8). To assure stability in the ranking, a similar ranking was obtained for 1908–1909 and correlated with the earlier order, giving a correlation coefficient of Spearman's $r = .828$, which indicated that the ranking remained stable enough to measure occupational mobility. These occupations were then divided into four categories, with a fifth category of nonmanual employment added as the highest group. Occupational mobility was defined as movement from one category to another. Workers sampled were then checked in the selected city directories to determine the occupations of those people whom the directories continued to list.

This rough classification system, although based upon imprecise wage data gathered from a variety of sources, seemed best suited to an analysis of occupational mobility of urban workingmen. As Stuart Blumin demonstrated, an occupational ranking of the entire labor

TABLE 8   *Rank Order of Occupational Categories
           according to Daily Wage Data for 1887–1888*[a]

OCCUPATION	WAGE RATE REPORTED
1. Nonmanual[a]	
2. Railroad engineer	$ 4.00–$5.00
Puddler	4.00– 5.00
Heater and roller	4.00– 5.00
Molder	3.50– 4.50
3. Stationary engineer	2.50– 4.00
Machinist	3.00– 4.00
Brickmason	3.00– 4.00
Railroad conductor	2.83[b]
Blacksmith	2.50– 3.00
Painter	2.50– 3.00
Plumber	2.50– 3.00
Carpenter	2.50– 3.00
Printer	2.50– 3.00
Shoemaker	2.43
Tailor	2.33
4. Bottler	1.75
Railroad car repair	1.66
Railroad fireman	1.62[b]
Railroad switchman	1.56[b]
Railroad flagman	1.56[b]
Boilermaker	1.50
Street car driver and motorman	1.44
Railroad brakeman	1.20[b]
5. Tramster	$25.00–30.00 per month
Laborer in rolling mill	1.00– 1.50
Laborer in furnace	1.00– 1.65
Railroad laborer	1.00– 1.25
Mine laborer	1.00– 1.35
Day laborer	.75– 1.00

[a] The major shift in occupational status for industrial workers in the nineteenth as in the twentieth century appeared to be the change from manual to nonmanual labor, and I have used this distinction in ranking occupations.
[b] Derived from reports filed with the Alabama Railroad Commission for 1889 in State Department of Archives, Montgomery, Alabama.

force of a city, which reflects the status of nineteenth-century occupations can be derived by computing the mean wealth of each occupation.[30] Sufficient data about the wealth of Birmingham's working-men was not available for this period, however, to utilize this method. Random samples of more than 500 names from tax lists in the 1880's, 1890's, and first decade of the twentieth century turned up only 40 per cent who were listed in city directories for those years, and only 67 people who were industrial workers. But even if sufficient information about wealth were available, working class occupational mobility can probably be better indexed by wage rates for each occupation. Information about the wealth of individuals in different occupations reflects more than the relative status of those occupations. Since some luxury trades are dominated by older workmen, their wealth may reflect their age or their length of residence in the city. Although information about earnings would be preferable to wage rates, since regularity as well as level of wages determined the status of nineteenth-century workingmen's occupations, wage rates do give a broad ranking of working class occupations.[31] As Stephan Thernstrom has noted, moreover, movement into nonmanual employment did define a major shift in occupational status for the industrial proletariat in the nineteenth century, although sufficient data is not available to determine if wages or wealth measure this mobility.

Significant rates of upward occupational mobility did occur for Birmingham's white workingmen, as indicated in Table 9. Most of the mobility occurred within craft lines: a building tradesman became a contractor, a machinist was promoted to foreman or perhaps acquired enough capital to open a small machine shop, a railroad fireman became an engineer, an unskilled rolling mill laborer graduated to a skilled or semiskilled position, a barber purchased his own shop. Although, as noted earlier, some upwardly mobile workmen acquired wealth and prominence, most merely became members of the petite bourgeoisie or labor aristocracy. Among unskilled white workers, movement from the bottom of the industrial pyramid occurred rapidly for those remaining in Birmingham. More than one-half of all three groups of unskilled white workingmen sampled who remained in the city for ten years climbed up the occupational ladder. For other white occupational categories, upward mobility was not so dramatic, although still substantial. Over a five or ten year period, one-quarter to one-third of the workers in most of the groups sampled who continued to work in Birmingham improved their occupational status. After 20 years, almost one-half of the white skilled and semiskilled workmen had experienced upward mobility.

Movement from blue collar to white collar positions was also extensive for Birmingham's white workingmen, as indicated in Table 10. Of workers sampled in 1890, one-quarter of those remaining in

TABLE 9   Upward Occupational Mobility by Race and Occupational Category, 1880–1914[a]

OCCUPATIONAL CATEGORY	5 YEARS[b] WH.	5 YEARS[b] BL.	10 YEARS WH.	10 YEARS BL.	15 YEARS WH.	15 YEARS BL.	20 YEARS WH.	20 YEARS BL.	25 YEARS WH.	25 YEARS BL.
Building Trades										
1880 group	(6) 25%	—	(4) 21%	—	(4) 24%	—	(5) 33%	—	(7) 54%	—
1890 group	(4) 13	(2) 8%	(6) 24	—	(4) 19	—	(4) 40	—	(3) 45	—
1899 group	(13) 25	—	(17) 43	(1) 5%	(14) 41	—				
Railroads										
1880 group	—	—	(1) 20	—	(2) 50	—	(2) 67	—		
1890 group	(9) 19	(4) 14	(9) 27	—	(8) 35	—	(4) 25	—	(5) 33	—
1899 group	(7) 19	(4) 12	(10) 36	(1) 5	(8) 38	(4) 30%				
Mechanics										
1880 group	(3) 10	—	(6) 33	—	(4) 31	—	(5) 38	—	(6) 75	—
1890 group	(8) 23	—	(9) 33	—	(7) 30	—	(12) 75	—	(7) 83	—
1899 group	(11) 17	(17) 32	(20) 41	(1) 5	(10) 33	(1) 9				
Service										
1880 group	not calculated		(5) 63	(6) 37	(5) 63	(6) 39	(6) 75	(8) 50%	(4) 67	(4) 25%
1890 group	(1) 9	(2) 5	(5) 36	(4) 29	(2) 20	(2) 18				
1899 group	(4) 19	(4) 20								
Unskilled										
1880 group	(6) 47	(6) 14	(5) 63	(4) 17	(1) 33	(2) 20	(1) 100	(2) 33	(1) 100	—
1890 group	(11) 28	(6) 9	(15) 50	(10) 19	(12) 55	(13) 29	(8) 62	(9) 31	(4) 50	(4) 31
1899 group	(30) 45	(5) 7	(30) 63	(9) 18	(25) 78	(8) 24				
Total										
1880 group	(15) 19%	(8) 14%	(16) 31%	(4) 13%	(13) 34%	(2) 14%	(16) 48%	(2) 18%	(14) 48%	(6) 18%
1890 group	(48) 29	(16) 9	(41) 33	(10) 8	(33) 34	(13) 13	(21) 34	(10) 16	(17) 39	
1899 group	(65) 23	(30) 14	(72) 40	(15) 17	(59) 43	(15) 18				

[a] Percentages are expressed with *all* workers persisting in Birmingham in a particular year as the base, and are not merely the percentage of those workers persisting whose occupations are given in the city directory. In several occupational categories the percentage of persisting workers for whom no occupation was listed in the city directory was often as high as 25 to 50%, and thus these figures of upward—and in Table 10, downward—mobility undoubtedly understate the extent of occupational mobility.

[b] For the 1880 group, mobility was measured after three years.

TABLE 10 Occupational Mobility for Selected Groups, by Race, 1890–1909

	NO. PERSIST. 1890–1899 N	% CLIMBING TO WHITE COLLAR	NO. PERSIST. 1890–1909 N	% CLIMBING TO WHITE COLLAR	NO. PERSIST. 1899–1909 N	% CLIMBING TO WHITE COLLAR
White						
Building trades	25	20%	10	40%	40	37%
Railroad	33	12	16	25	28	25
Mechanics	28	32	16	63	48	37
Service	8	63	8	75	14	35
Unskilled	30	23	13	62	48	25
Total	124	24%	63	51%	178	31%
Black						
Building trades	16	0	8	0	20	5%
Railroad	14	0	4	0	21	4
Mechanics	14	0	8	0	24	5
Service	42	37%	20	50%	14	21
Unskilled	30	10	13	38	49	4
Total	116	6%	53	18%	128	5%

the city for a decade climbed out of the working class. After 20 years in Birmingham, more than one-half of the persisting workers had risen to nonmanual jobs. For the 1899 group, upward mobility was even more dramatic. By 1909 one-third of the workers remaining in the city were no longer manual laborers or craftsmen. Nonmanual employment for these upwardly mobile workmen generally consisted of employment as clerks, salesmen, policemen, or insurance agents. A number of Birmingham's workers became building contractors or opened grocery stores. Two workmen became music teachers, and one learned dentistry. The most extensive mobility occurred among barbers, tailors, shoemakers, and mechanics. Employees were able to accumulate a small amount of capital to open their own barber, shoe, or tailor shops. Similarly, within a decade, one-third of the mechanics sampled were able to become officials in foundries or boiler factories, or perhaps even owners or partners in one of these manufacturing establishments. Even among unskilled workers, after ten years in Birmingham one-quarter had risen to nonmanual positions, and 62 per cent of those remaining from 1890 to 1909 were no longer manual workmen.

The pattern of occupational mobility was quite different for the city's black workers. While 31 to 40 per cent of Birmingham's white workingmen who remained in the city a decade were upwardly mobile, only 8 to 17 per cent of persisting black workmen were this successful. After 20 years of residence, one in three and one in two white workmen moved up, but only one in six black workingmen. As indicated in Table 9, almost no upward occupational mobility occurred among building tradesmen, railroad employees, and mechanics. A few railroad workers managed to become building tradesmen or proprietors of a grocery or saloon during the 1890's and the first decade of the twentieth century. As a result of a series of railroad strikes in the 1890's, several brakemen and firemen became foremen in railroad yards. The efforts of two Birmingham industrialists to replace whites with black machinists and molders between 1899 and 1904 led to the upgrading of a large number of black mechanics and laborers. By 1909, however, few of the men who had been promoted could be found in Birmingham, and only 5 per cent of the persisting black mechanics had a significantly better position than they had held in 1899. Black barbers and shoemakers, like their white counterparts, frequently secured enough capital to open a small store of their own. As indicated in Table 10, after a decade one-fifth to one-third of the service workers persisting rose to nonmanual employment, and after 20 years one-half of them were no longer manual workers. Upward mobility among black unskilled workmen, while lagging well behind white workers, was nevertheless surprising. Almost 20 per cent of black unskilled sampled who remained in Birmingham a decade rose out of this category, and after 20 years almost 33 per cent of them had succeeded in escaping this category. Between 1890 and 1909, moreover, 38 per cent of the black unskilled workers still in Birmingham in the latter year had even risen to nonmanual employment. Despite these achievements, black upward mobility was significantly poorer than the mobility of white workers. Despite the claims of Booker T. Washington and his Birmingham disciples that hard work and diligence would be rewarded by southern whites, few black people in Birmingham managed to obtain property or to improve their occupational position significantly.

Black workers, in fact, were constantly pushed out of various occupations toward the bottom of the occupational hierarchy. As indicated in Table 11, the longer black workers stayed in Birmingham, the more likely that they would be unable to maintain their precarious position above unskilled labor. The downward mobility of black workingmen contrasted sharply with the slight downward mobility of white people. For the city's black workers, the road to success too often ran in the wrong direction.

RESIDENTIAL MOBILITY

Birmingham's changing residential structure reflected the different racial patterns of economic mobility and the social fragmentation of the city's working class. During the first years of its existence in the 1870's, Birmingham could best be characterized as a "small, insignificant village in America dignified with the title of city; . . . marshes and mud roads everywhere and shallow pine shacks and a box car for a depot." [32] Although slag pavement replaced the mud on most streets and the city's area of settlement grew to about five square miles, at the end of the nineteenth century, railroad tracks and blast furnaces that divided the city continued to dominate the landscape,

TABLE 11   Number and Rate of Downward Occupational Mobility by Race and Occupational Category

OCCUPATIONAL CATEGORY	5 YEARS[a] WH.	BL.	10 YEARS WH.	BL.	15 YEARS WH.	BL.	20 YEARS WH.	BL.	25 YEARS WH.	BL.
Building Trades										
1880 group	2 (8%)	5 (50%)	1 (5%)	3 (43%)	2 (11%)	2 (100%)	2 (13%)	1 (100%)	1 (13%)	1 (100%)
1890 group	2 (6)	16 (62)	2 (10)	8 (29)	—	4 (25)	—	8 (67)	—	8 (67)
1899 group	4 (8)	10 (31)	5 (13)	8 (40)	5 (18)	10 (71)				
Railroad										
1880 group	—	1 (50%)	—	1 (100%)	—	—	—	—	—	—
1890 group	6 (13%)	15 (29)	5 (15%)	14 (100)	2 (9%)	12 (100%)	1 (6%)	4 (100%)	—	—
1899 group	4 (11)	12 (35)	3 (11)	2 (22)	2 (10)	5 (30)				
Mechanics										
1880 group	—	2 (50%)	—	1 (50%)	—	1 (50%)	—	—	—	—
1890 group	5 (14%)	2 (14)	3 (11%)	2 (14)	2 (9%)	4 (33)	2 (13%)	6 (60%)	—	4 (33%)
1899 group	10 (15)	13 (25)	7 (14)	10 (42)	8 (26)	5 (36)				
Service										
1880 group	not calculated									
1890 group	2 (18%)	3 (14%)	—	1 (5%)	—	5 (25%)	—	2 (20%)	—	3 (38%)
1899 group	—	2 (10)	—	2 (15)	—	3 (27)				
Unskilled	no downward mobility									
Total										
1880 group	2 (3%)	8 (44%)	1 (2%)	5 (50%)	2 (6%)	3 (75%)	2 (6%)	1 (50%)	1 (4%)	1 (50%)
1890 group	15 (12)	34 (30)	10 (11)	25 (32)	4 (5)	25 (40)	3 (6)	20 (50)	—	15 (55)
1899 group	18 (10)	37 (27)	15 (12)	22 (28)	15 (15)	23 (43)				

[a] For the 1880 group, mobility was measured after three years.

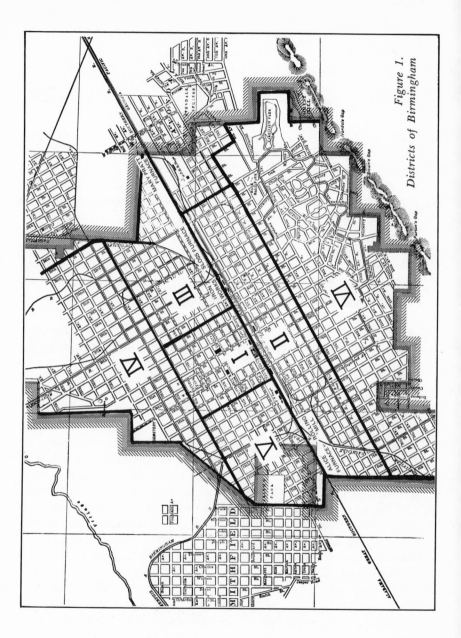

Figure 1.
Districts of Birmingham

and Birmingham retained the atmosphere of a mining boom town.
Most people lived within a ten minute walk of the furnaces whose
stench and smoke permeated the city seven days a week. The city's
commercial and residential life was carried on almost entirely within
a narrow belt 20 blocks long, extending six blocks on each side of the
railroad tracks in the center of Birmingham (see Fig. 1). On the eastern and western boundaries were the region's major blast furnaces,
and within this area of about two square miles were the city's foundries, factories, and most of its residences. Only two miles northwest
of Birmingham, coal mine villages were scattered along the railroad
lines that radiated from downtown. To the south, less than one mile
from the center of the city on top of Red Mountain, iron ore mines
with the rickety company quarters that surrounded them looked down
on Birmingham.[33]

During the nineteenth century identifiable neighborhoods began
to emerge in Birmingham. Iron foundries and other manufacturing
enterprises along First Avenue gave the city a small manufacturing
district by 1890. Office buildings and large stores on North 20th and
North 21st streets were the beginning of a retail–financial center.
Many prominent citizens lived in substantial residences near the
county court house, city hall, and North Side Market, among the
numerous churches built by the 1890's. On the south side, workingmen's homes predominated, and company quarters around the blast
furnaces housed hundreds of laborers employed at each furnace.

Distinctive residential and manufacturing districts appeared
slowly, however, and until the twentieth century the city was composed
largely of heterogeneous neighborhoods.[34] Because Birmingham grew
so rapidly, the housing supply was often unable to keep pace with
demand, and wooden shacks and alley tenements sprang up throughout the city amidst more comfortable four and five room, one-story
houses. Foundries, lumber mills, factories, and breweries mingled
with homes on the city's south side. In 1891, three-quarters of the
boarding houses in Birmingham were still located in the heart of the
downtown business district.[35] Skilled and unskilled workmen lived
on the same blocks, near their work places.[36] On Avenue C and 13th
Street, for example, the residents in 1891 included a shoemaker, two
employees at the rolling mill, a coppersmith at the Louisville & Nashville shops, a black iron worker, and the president of a stove works.

Several blocks away lived a boilermaker, a machinist, a railroad conductor, two barbers, and a downtown merchant. The city tax collector lived on the same block with a railroad flagman, a black gardener, a civil engineer, and a carpenter. On one block on the north side, there were a physician, a newspaper printer, a grocer, a black furnace laborer, a machinist, and a laborer in a railroad repair shop.

Birmingham's black population was concentrated on certain blocks during the nineteenth century, even though racial segregation was not as extensive as it would become in the twentieth century. Some measure of the extent of residential racial segregation was obtained by computing indexes of dissimilarity for race block by block from city directories for 1891, 1899, and 1909.[37] The index of dissimilarity in 1891 was 71.42, and in 1899 it was 75.00. By 1909 the index had risen to 83.73 as racial discrimination and hostility intensified, and 50 years later Karl and Alma Taeuber obtained an index of 92.8 for Birmingham in their study of Negro residential segregation in United States cities.[38]

Racial segregation in Birmingham greatly exceeded the clustering of black homes in other Southern cities during the nineteenth century. The Taeubers report that the index of dissimilarity they computed for Charleston, South Carolina, in 1910 was only 16.8, while in Augusta, Georgia, it was 49.9 in 1899 and 56.1 in 1910.[39] The lower indexes in these cities, especially Charleston, reflect the large number of mixed racial blocks which persisted after the abolition of slavery, as black families continued to live along the alleys and in the backyards of white neighborhoods.[40] Because Birmingham was a totally new city in the post-Civil War period, with no older stock of rundown shacks and Negro quarters along its alleys, a different racial pattern of housing arose. Black workers and their families indeed lived along the city's back alleys in the downtown area, but many more blacks were forced into less desirable outlying areas of the various neighborhoods. Some concentrations of the city's black population occurred at the western fringes near one of the furnaces and the rolling mill, along various blocks on the south side, and near the northern and southern boundaries, isolated from the downtown business–commercial–manufacturing heart of Birmingham. In the twentieth century, these concentrations would increasingly be found near the core of the city, and distinctive large ghettos of black people would gradually emerge.

The values of homes and property in different sections of Birmingham naturally varied a great deal despite heterogeneous neighborhoods and the relative scattering of black homes throughout the city. Computation of the average assessment of residences in different areas of the city based upon a sample taken from tax assessors' records demonstrated the varying quality of neighborhoods.[41] As presented in Table 12, the highest assessments were, not surprisingly, in the down-

TABLE 12   *Average Assessment per Residence*
            for Selected Districts, 1893, 1907

DISTRICT	VALUE OF ALL PROPERTY SAMPLED	# LOTS	AVERAGE VALUE PER LOT
1893			
1	$2,164,550	260	$ 8325.50
2	531,150	158	3361.11
3	304,430	158	1926.12
4	236,700	120	1972.60
5	71,882	47	1711.47
1907			
1	$3,516,100	251	$14,008.92
2	448,470	143	3136.28
3	283,455	133	2131.32
4	392,390	205	1914.20
5	131,620	73	1803.01
6	671,990	206	3262.18

town area. Areas farther away from the center of the city had appreciably lower averages. The same pattern generally prevailed in 1893 and 1907, although by the latter year Birmingham had annexed the formerly independent village of South Highlands on the side of Red Mountain, a wealthy residential area inhabited by some of the most prominent families in the city.[42] South Highlands was only one of many areas on the perimeter of Birmingham that emerged as comfortable neighborhoods after the growth of trolley lines and "dummy" railroads in the early 1890's and the first decade of the twentieth century. As a result of the development of transportation and of large-scale industry, the importance of housing in proximity to urban services declined markedly.[43] Suburban land companies made substantial investments in property outside of Birmingham in the late 1880's and again after the depression of the 1890's. Some of the new communities, like South Highlands, or Highlands or Mountain Brook on the other side of Red Mountain, house the city's elite. Others, such as East Birmingham, North Birmingham, Avondale, Gate City, and Ensley, not only provided inexpensive homes for workingmen, but were also industrial satellites with numerous blast furnaces, coke ovens, railroad repair shops, and other manufacturing establishments. Beyond these new towns were workingmen's residential suburbs like Woodlawn, East Lake, and Powderly.[44]

These new communities transformed the metropolitan region. Birmingham had been a city with an affluent core surrounded by increasingly poorer sections near the periphery. By the early twentieth century, however, a more complex pattern of urban land use developed. The downtown and adjacent manufacturing and residential area on the south side of the city remained the affluent core in 1907, as it had been in 1893. Adjacent to it, however, were both poor neighborhoods to the north and east and wealthy neighborhoods on either side of Red Mountain above the soot and stench of the city's blast furnaces. On the city's outskirts, soon to be incorporated into Birmingham, were industrial satellites with a lower quality of housing than that prevailing within the nicer residential sections of the city. Finally, on the outer ring were workingmen's suburbs with moderately priced housing.

As the heterogeneous neighborhoods broke down, the city's working class became increasingly fragmented in particular areas of the metropolis. By combining the average assessments of residences presented in Table 12 with contemporary descriptions of the Birmingham metropolitan region, four distinct zones, each representing a different level of residential life, were identified. Zone 1 is the central city, comprising districts I, II, and V in Figure 1. Zone 2 consists of residential neighborhoods within Birmingham and includes districts III, IV, and VI. Zone 3 is made up of industrial suburbs like Avondale, Gate City, and North and East Birmingham. The residential suburbs of Woodlawn, East Lake, the West End, and Cleveland form Zone 4 (see Fig. 2). As Table 13 shows, as the city grew and new communities emerged on its outskirts, the racial and occupational mixture of the smaller city of the 1880's began to disappear, replaced by occupational and racial segregation of the city's industrial workingmen. In 1883, 60 to 70 per cent of the white workers were concentrated in the downtown area

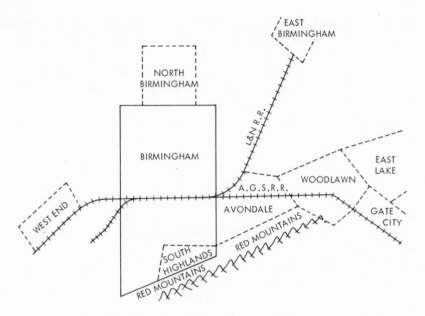

Figure 2. Birmingham and surrounding towns

(Zone 1), while a slightly higher percentage of blacks occupied the poorer outlying area of the city (Zone 2). During the next 25 years, however, as further segregation slowly and steadily developed and the new transportation system transformed the residential patterns of the metropolis, the homes of white workers were no longer concentrated in the region's core. By 1909 only one-third of white workers sampled lived in the downtown area. Almost one-third of the white skilled and semiskilled workingmen sampled now lived in comfortable working class suburbs (Zone 4), while fewer than one in ten workers in any other group lived in these communities. White unskilled workers also found homes outside the central city, but generally not in the same communities as skilled whites.

Less than 10 per cent of the city's unskilled whites sampled in 1909 lived in suburban residential communities, but one-third of the unskilled whites sampled now lived in industrial satellite towns. The city's black workers continued to reside in the worst residential area of the metropolitan region. Unlike the growing residential separation of

TABLE 13   *Percentage of Workers Sampled Living in
Designated Areas of Birmingham and Environs*

| | WHITE SKILLED AND SEMISKILLED | | | | WHITE UNSKILLED | | | |
	1883	1890	1899	1909	1883	1890	1899	1909
Zone 1	61%	48%	38%	32%	71%	46%	45%	36%
Zone 2	30	25	22	21	14	26	14	23
Zone 3	—	18	18	17	—	24	29	33
Zone 4	9	8	22	29	14	4	12	9
Number	54	237	260	283	28	76	73	108

| | BLACK SKILLED AND SEMISKILLED | | | | BLACK UNSKILLED | | | |
	1883	1890	1899	1909	1883	1890	1899	1909
Zone 1	54%	59%	58%	60%	39%	51%	48%	57%
Zone 2	42	32	17	18	56	26	22	17
Zone 3	—	5	12	15	—	20	17	17
Zone 4	4	4	13	7	6	5	13	9
Number	26	73	103	149	36	86	122	112

SOURCE: Compiled from samples taken from *Birmingham City Directories*, 1883, 1890, 1899, and 1909.

white skilled and unskilled workmen, moreover, little difference existed between the residential patterns of black unskilled and other black workingmen. Pushed out of the increasingly desirable Zone 2 residences by whites, yet generally denied housing in the new industrial or residential suburbs outside the central city, black workers in Birmingham by 1909 showed the classic twentieth-century pattern of concentration in poor quality, racially segregated housing in the core city.

This residential segregation within the metropolis also meant that unequal opportunities for residential mobility existed for those workingmen who continued to live in Birmingham for five years or more. Some workers who purchased homes continued to reside in older neighborhoods, but, as shown in Table 14, residential mobility within the metropolitan area reflected the pattern of residential segregation that was evolving in Birmingham. Less than one-third of the white workers sampled lived in the downtown area after ten years residence in Birmingham, while over one-half the Afro-Americans who remained in Birmingham for a decade still made their homes in this area. As the more distant residential areas became increasingly available and attractive, a large number of white skilled and semiskilled

TABLE 14   *Percentage of Workers Persisting in Birmingham*
            Living in Each Zone

| | WHITE SKILLED AND SEMISKILLED | | | | WHITE UNSKILLED | | | |
	5 YEARS	10 YEARS	15 YEARS	20 YEARS[a]	5 YEARS	10 YEARS	15 YEARS	20 YEARS[a]
Zone 1	40%	28%	28%	16%	33%	31%	23%	11%
Zone 2	24	22	21	33	14	21	30	56
Zone 3	17	25	21	10	32	23	28	22
Zone 4	18	22	30	41	21	23	16	11
Number	224	171	156	49	85	60	42	9

| | BLACK SKILLED AND SEMISKILLED | | | | BLACK UNSKILLED | | | |
	5 YEARS	10 YEARS	15 YEARS	20 YEARS[a]	5 YEARS	10 YEARS	15 YEARS	20 YEARS[a]
Zone 1	56%	60%	58%	48%	47%	45%	43%	41%
Zone 2	27	26	30	43	33	28	23	36
Zone 3	9	5	5	5	12	14	21	9
Zone 4	9	8	6	5	7	12	12	14
Number	117	95	62	21	105	64	56	22

SOURCE: Compiled from 1890 and 1899 samples taken from *Birmingham City Directories*, for those workers persisting in city whose addresses are given in the directories.
[a] Computed only from 1890 sample.

workmen moved to these newer communities. After 20 years residence in Birmingham, 40 per cent of these workers lived in the new suburbs, compared to less than 16 per cent of white unskilled or of black workingmen. Longtime black residents, on the other hand, were hardly better off than more recent migrants in acquiring housing in suburban communities. Only about 10 per cent of skilled blacks who continued to live in Birmingham for five years or more found housing outside the city. Some black unskilled workers who lived in company quarters in the industrial satellites or in slums in the back alleys or on the fringes of the residential suburbs managed to move away from the core, but after 10 or 15 years of residence two-thirds to three-quarters of blacks sampled still were confined to the inner city.

The disparate opportunity for individual advancement was also reflected in the different percentage of occupationally mobile workers who were able to move to better neighborhoods as they improved their occupational status. As indicated in Table 15, twice as many whites

TABLE 15   *Percentage of Upward Residential Mobility*
for Workers with Upward Occupational Mobility,
by Race

YEAR SAMPLED	NUMBER UPWARD MOBILITY[a]		NUMBER AND PER CENT UPWARD RESIDENTIAL MOBILITY	
	WHITE	BLACK	WHITE	BLACK
1880	32	9	(18) 56%	(1) 11%
1890	49	27	(22) 44	(7) 26
1899	143	24	(66) 46	(6) 25

[a] Numbers upwardly mobile are only those workers for whom residential changes were given in city directories.

as blacks who moved into substantially better-paying jobs also moved
to better neighborhoods. Almost one-half of these white workingmen,
moreover, ended up in the residential suburbs comprising Zone 4,
while residential mobility for upwardly mobile blacks consisted merely
of moving within Birmingham from the downtown business–manufacturing district to poor residential neighborhoods within the city
(Zone 2).[45]

MOBILITY AND
CLASS CONSCIOUSNESS

The findings about geographic, economic, and residential mobility in Birmingham confirm what students of other rapidly industrializing nineteenth-century cities in the United States have discovered:
high rates of transiency among the urban working class, and (especially for white workingmen) significant opportunities to rise on the
occupational ladder, to accumulate a modest amount of property, and
to move from the inner city to a more pleasant residential neighborhood. Important distinctions existed, of course, in the mobility patterns of different occupational, ethnic, racial, and family groups,
only some of which have been examined here. To understand better
the patterns of social, economic, and geographical mobility, distinctions should be made among different age groups, northern-born,
southern-born, and foreign-born residents of Birmingham, and single
males and heads of households. Some of this work is now in progress.
But evidence presented here seems to indicate that, despite its south-

ern location, Birmingham, like other cities in the United States, provided its workingmen with opportunities for individual advancement.

From evidence of similar mobility patterns in other communities, several historians have drawn conclusions about the failure of American workers to develop class consciousness. As Stephan Thernstrom observed: "The remarkable volatility of the American working class past and present has been an important influence retarding the development and expression of distinctive class loyalties." [46] "The high rate of persistence among the more successful in every occupation and nationality group reduced the likelihood of protest against the status quo," Clyde Griffin concluded after a study of mobility in Poughkeepsie, New York.[47] Improvement in condition, he argued, "held promise enough to prevent . . . rejection of the national faith that success came to the industrious."

A great deal of caution, however, should be exercised in drawing inferences about the presumed failure of working class consciousness and the absence of class conflict in American cities from these patterns of mobility. High rates of transiency need not inhibit class consciousness, and under some historical conditions may have facilitated its growth.[48] Second, no necessary relationship existed between upward occupational mobility or property acquisition and the way that workingmen viewed the world around them. Some militant, class conscious leaders of the American labor movement were skilled workers who progressed through the ranks and achieved a small amount of wealth and security. A study of the careers of American radical labor leaders would shed much light on this point. Third, the concept of the "revolution of rising expectations," which unfortunately has received little systematic examination, should serve as a warning that accumulation of small amounts of property and slight upward occupational mobility may not necessarily produce a conservative outlook.

Any association between mobility and class consciousness that might be discovered in mid-nineteenth-century America, moreover, cannot automatically be applied to the late nineteenth and early twentieth century. Although the process of urbanization and industrialization in the United States began at least a generation before the Civil War, American industrial society reached maturity and dramatically altered every aspect of life in the country in the years after 1880. That American workingmen between 1850 and 1880 may have shown only a dim awareness of class (a point which has not been conclusively demonstrated) would hardly be surprising, since during these years the working class in this country was only in its early formative stages. As Herb Gutman has demonstrated, however, between the late 1870's and the early twentieth century, the new tenets of industrial capitalism clashed with the ideology and perspectives of American workers. Periodic labor violence, the dramatic rise of the Knights of Labor and some early industrial unions like the United Mine Workers of America or the Brewery Workers, emergence of socialist consciousness within these unions, other more radical labor organizations, and even many craft unions, and the tensions produced by the influx of a variety of immigrant and preindustrial cultures into the society were only some manifestations of the worker's resistance and difficult adjustment to the new industrial society.[49]

In another place I have presented evidence that, at the beginning of the twentieth century, during the height of racial discrimination and conflict in Alabama, transient, oppressed, and segregated black workers in Birmingham engaged in militant, sometimes violent, and frequently organized assaults upon the new industrial order. Many white workers who were left behind by other upwardly mobile white workers supported these strikers with words and deeds that indicated awareness of a labor movement that surmounted racial and occupational differences.[50] A full understanding of these workers' actions requires examination of their cultural, social, economic, and political lives, as Edward Thompson has demonstrated in regard to the English working class.[51] Quantitative findings about geographic, social, and economic mobility cannot be isolated from the larger social context.

The techniques of quantification provide excellent insights into some of the social conditions under which people lived in nineteenth- and twentieth-century cities and indicate important clues about the relationships of various groups of people in the society. But identifying the extent of economic and geographic mobility is not enough to tell us the frame of reference with which workers viewed their society. How workers judged their prospects for success, whether they thought in terms of group action or individual advancement, whether they believed that their interests harmonized with the interests of their employer, whether they looked upon a former workingman who now bossed them or sold them groceries as an oppressor or as proof of the soundness of the system depended not simply upon the nature and extent of mobility, but also upon certain traditions within the working class, the strength of the labor movement at the time, and the catalytic presence of an active and articulate socialist leader. Mobility was only one of the historical experiences that shaped workers' outlooks.

FOOTNOTES

1. Stephan Thernstrom, *Poverty and Progress: Social Mobility in a Nineteenth Century City* (Cambridge, Mass., 1964); Richard J. Hopkins, "Occupational and Geographic Mobility in Atlanta, 1870–1896," in *Journal of Southern History,* XXIV (May 1968), 200–213; Clyde Griffin, "Workers Divided: The Effect of Craft and Ethnic Differences in Poughkeepsie, New York, 1850–1880," Herbert G. Gutman, "The Reality of the Rags-to-Riches 'Myth': The Case of the Patterson, New Jersey, Locomotive, Iron, and Machinery Manufacturers, 1830–1880," Stephan Thernstrom, "Immigrants and Wasps: Ethnic Differences in Occupational Mobility in Boston, 1890–1940," and Stuart Blumin, "Mobility and Change in Ante-Bellum Philadelphia," in Stephan Thernstrom and Richard Sennett (eds.), *Nineteenth-Century Cities: Essays in the New Urban History* (New Haven, 1969), 49–208.

2. Thernstrom, *Poverty and Progress,* especially chaps. 6, 7; Griffin, "Workers Divided," 49–97.

3. Hopkins, "Mobility in Atlanta," 200–213.

4. C. Vann Woodward, *Origins of the New South, 1877–1913* (Baton Rouge, La., 1951).

5. Compare Woodward, *Origins of the New South,* 135–138, and Robert David Ward and William Warren Rogers, *Labor Revolt in Alabama: The Great Strike of 1894* (University, Ala., 1965), with Herbert G. Gutman, "The Worker's Search for Power: Labor in the Gilded Age," in H. Wayne Morgan (ed.), *The Gilded Age: A Reappraisal* (Syracuse, N.Y., 1963), 38–68, and Melvin Dubofsky, "The Origins of Western Working Class Radicalism, 1890–1905," in *Labor History,* VII (Spring 1966), 131–155.

6. Unfortunately, United States manuscript census schedules of population are not available after 1880. Birmingham city directories only provided information about an individual's race, residence, and occupation.

7. The city directory for 1899 was used instead of 1900 because it seemed more thorough. The directory for 1909 was used instead of 1910 because it was the last year before Birmingham incorporated a half dozen surrounding suburbs. No tax records were found for 1883, and thus 1882 and 1884 were used to check property holding in the city for 1883. Tax assessors' lists, moreover, were not found for these years, and tax collectors' records which were used only recorded the tax collected and not the value of the property. Since no indication of the tax rate was available, the amount of property held could not be tabulated for 1883.

8. Ethel Armes, *The Story of Coal and Iron in Alabama* (Birmingham, 1910), although anecdotal, is the fullest account of Birmingham's industrial development in the nineteenth century.

9. Armes, *Coal and Iron in Alabama,* 461–472. U.S. Census: *Manufactures:*

Ninth Census, 1870, Vol. III, 392, *Twelfth Census, 1900,* Part II, 8–13, Part IV, 39–78. American Iron and Steel Association, *Statistics of the Foreign and American Iron Trade, 1874– . . . 1900* (Philadelphia, 1874–1900).

10. *Birmingham City Directory, 1900.*

11. U.S. Census: *Population: Twelfth Census, 1900,* Part I, 573.

12. The number of workingmen in selected industrial occupations enumerated in the 1899 city directory was compared with the 1900 Census enumeration of workingmen in specific occupations and industries in Birmingham. Great variation was found in some occupations, and different methods of classification make comparisons of other occupations impossible, but the 1900 Census figures compared with the 1899 data in the following manner: building tradesmen, 25 per cent greater; steam railroad employees, 15 per cent greater; iron and steel workers, 5 per cent less; other mechanics, 10 per cent less; service employees, 7 per cent less; factory operatives, 51 per cent less; and laborers not otherwise specified, 25 per cent less. The total number of industrial workers in Birmingham, according to the 1900 Census, was only .15 per cent greater than the total number calculated a year earlier from the 1899 city directory.

13. U.S. Census: *Population: Ninth Census, 1870,* Vol. I, 11; *Thirteenth Census, 1910,* Part I, 854–855.

14. U.S. Immigration Commission, *Immigrants in Industries: Iron and Steel* (Washington, 1911), IV, 142–161. U.S. Census, *Population: Thirteenth Census, 1910,* Vol. IV, 538–540.

15. Census Bureau statistics for these years only give the total number of native-born from different states residing in Birmingham, and do not distinguish white and black. Since more than 600 northern-born blacks lived in Alabama in 1890 and more than 1,000 in 1910, many of the northern-born Americans living in Birmingham were probably Afro-Americans.

16. U.S. Census, *Tenth Census, 1880,* Manuscript Census Schedules for Jefferson County, Alabama. U.S. Census, *Population: Tenth Census, 1890,* Part I, 451, *Twelfth Census, 1900,* Part I, 573.

17. U.S. Manuscript Census Schedules, Jefferson County, Alabama, 1880. *Immigrants in Industries: Iron and Steel,* IV, 146–160. U.S. Census, *Thirteenth Census: Population,* Vol. IV, 538–540.

18. *Immigrants in Industries: Iron and Steel,* IV, 142–161. Also, accounts about immigrants appeared regularly in Birmingham newspapers during the 1880's and 1890's and first decade of the twentieth century. The careers of only a few immigrants from the 1880 sample could be traced. Since the large influx of immigration into Birmingham occurred after 1880, rates of geographic and economic mobility for most immigrants could not be compared with other white and black workers in the city during the late nineteenth and early twentieth century. Work now in progress, based on an examination of more than 2,000 naturalization records for immigrants in Birmingham, indicates that the immigrants were generally more volatile and experienced less upward mobility than native-born or second generation whites.

19. U.S. Congress, Senate Committee on Education and Labor, *Testimony Before the Committee to Investigate the Relations Between Capital and Labor,* 49, 2 Sess. (1885), III, 304, 308–309, 356–358. *Birmingham Observer,* December 16, 1880, and Birmingham *News,* July 30, 1900, are only two of the many reports in Birmingham newspapers about the influx and exodus of immigrant workmen.

20. Birmingham *News,* July 16, August 5, 1902, *Labor Advocate* (Birmingham), July 27, 1901, and *Birmingham Age,* February 5, 1886, are several examples.

21. For discussion of the conceptual strengths and limitations of city directories as reasonably accurate compilations of nineteenth century cities see Peter R. Knights, "City Directories as Aids, to Ante-Bellum Urban Studies: A Research Note," in *Historical Methods Newsletter*, II (September 1969).

22. Hopkins, "Mobility in Atlanta," 207.

23. Stephan Thernstrom's study of Boston found a persistence rate of 64 per cent for all adult males, 45 per cent for unmarried men, and 53 per cent for blue collar workers aged 20–29 during the decade of the 1880's, while the persistence rates for various occupations in Poughkeepsie during the 1870's varied from 32 per cent to over 50 per cent. Stephan Thernstrom and Peter R. Knights, "Men in Motion: Some Data and Speculations about Urban Population Mobility in Nineteenth-Century America," Paper presented to the Pacific Coast Branch of the American Historical Association, August 28, 1969, 6; Clyde Griffin, "Workers Divided," 76.

24. *Birmingham Age-Herald*, April 1, 1899, May 19, 1906. Birmingham *News*, September 20, 1902. After 1900 Birmingham industrialists prosecuted several labor agents from northern enterprises, who were in Birmingham to recruit workmen, under acts prohibiting any person from enticing away or inducing to leave service any laborer and for failure to pay a $500 license fee for doing business in the city. Birmingham *News*, May 4, 1902, reports one such case.

25. Tax assessors' lists for various years were examined to see if the individuals sampled owned property. Unfortunately, data on personal property could not be used. The records indicated that although assessors were instructed to list both personal and real property, they failed to assess systematically large numbers of people who owned small or even moderate amounts of personal property but who owned no real estate. Records of real estate holdings used are, of course, assessed valuations.

26. Thernstrom, *Poverty and Progress*, 84–90.

27. U.S. Census, *Population: Eleventh Census, 1890: Miscellaneous Statistics*, Part III, 1085, *Twelfth Census, 1900*, Part II, 702, *Thirteenth Census, 1910*, Vol. I, 1355.

28. F. W. Teeple, and A. D. Smith (eds.), *Jefferson County and Birmingham, Alabama, Historical and Biographical, 1887* (Birmingham, 1887), 18.

29. Taken from *Birmingham City Directories*, 1883–1909.

30. See Blumin, "Mobility and Change in Ante-Bellum Philadelphia," 168.

31. See Eric Hobsbawm, "The Labour Aristocracy in Nineteenth-Century Britain," in his *Labouring Men: Studies in the History of Labour* (Garden City, N.Y., 1967), 321–370.

32. Quoted in Armes, *Coal and Iron in Alabama*, 234, 246.

33. Based on street directory in *Birmingham City Directory*, 1891. No street directories were included in prior city directories.

34. Compare Sam Bass Warner, Jr., *The Private City: Philadelphia in Three Periods of its Growth* (Philadelphia, 1968), 49–62, 161–200.

35. *Birmingham City Directory*, 1891.

36. A study of the occupations of residents on almost 100 blocks on the south side of the railroad tracks was made by Linda G. Worthman.

37. The index of dissimilarity was constructed entirely from block data compiled from street directories included in Birmingham city directories. To construct the index, the proportion of black households on each block was calculated. The percentage of black households to white households in the entire city was then calculated. All blocks having proportionately more black homes to white

homes than the proportion in the city were identified, and the number of black homes and white homes on these blocks calculated. The formula which provides the Index of Dissimilarity is $I = 100(N_1/N - W_1/W)$, where N_1 is the number of black households on the designated blocks, W_1 is the white households on those blocks, and N and W are the total number of black and white households in the city. The index which results measures the percentage of blacks who would have to move from each block to bring the percentage of blacks on each block in Birmingham even with the percentage of black households in the city. A full explanation of the Index of Dissimilarity and other methods of measuring racial segregation is in Karl E. and Alma F. Taeuber, *Negroes in Cities: Residential Segregation and Neighborhood Change* (Chicago, 1965), 203–204, 223–238.

38. Taueber, *Negroes in Cities*, 40.

39. *Ibid.*, 45–52.

40. *Ibid.*, 48; Donald O. and Mary S. Cowgill, "An Index of Segregation Based on Block Statistics," *American Sociological Review,* XVI (December 1951), 830; Richard Wade, *Slavery in the Cities: The South, 1820–1860* (London and New York, 1964), 55–79.

41. Ward lines in Birmingham ran north-south and cut across the different neighborhoods that existed. They in no way corresponded to any natural division of the city. From contemporary descriptions of Birmingham, six neighborhoods were identified. From tax assessors' maps for 1893 and 1907, blocks in each neighborhood were sampled at random and the average assessment per residence computed.

42. Birmingham *Weekly Iron Age*, October 4, 1888; Birmingham *News*, July 1, 1904.

43. Blumin, "Mobility and Change in Ante-Bellum Philadelphia," 188. Compare Sam Bass Warner, Jr., *Streetcar Suburbs: The Process of Growth in Boston, 1870–1900* (Cambridge, Mass., 1962), 46–66.

44. Powderly was a small village founded in the 1880's by a group of workingmen belonging to the Knights of Labor who wished to establish a cooperative factory there. By the twentieth century it had been annexed by Birmingham and was known as the West End.

45. Forty-three per cent of the white workingmen who were both occupationally and residentially upwardly mobile moved into the residential suburbs comprising Zone 4. Twenty-eight per cent of the upwardly mobile blacks moved from Zone 1 to Zone 2, twice the proportion of movement from one zone to another of any other group of blacks who were occupationally upwardly mobile.

46. Thernstrom, "Working Class Social Mobility in Industrial America," Paper presented to the Anglo-American Colloquium of the Society for Labour History, London, June 23, 1968, 6.

47. Griffin, "Workers Divided," 92.

48. John C. Leggett, *Class, Race and Labor: Working-Class Consciousness in Detroit* (New York, 1968), 62–75; Melvin Dubofsky, *We Shall Be All: A History of the Industrial Workers of the World* (New York, 1969), *passim.*

49. Herbert G. Gutman, "Protestantism and the American Labor Movement: The Christian Spirit in the Gilded Age," in *American Historical Review,* LXII (October 1966), 74–101.

50. Worthman, "Black Workers and Labor Unions in Birmingham, Alabama, 1897–1904," in *Labor History,* X (Summer 1969), 375–407.

51. Edward P. Thompson, *The Making of the English Working Class* (New York, 1963), *passim.*

TIMOTHY L. SMITH

Lay Initiative in the Religious Life of American Immigrants, 1880–1950

Growing scholarly appreciation of the ways in which the beliefs and practices of Protestants of English backgrounds have reinforced certain democratic tendencies in American society[1] has recently begun to inform reexaminations of the religious history of Catholic, Protestant, and Jewish immigrants whose first large contingents arrived in this country during the middle decades of the nineteenth century.[2] It has as yet awakened little curiosity, however, as to whether commitments to freedom of belief and association, to equality of opportunity, and to the right of individuals to participate in decisions which affect their lives also stemmed from the faith and worship of the groups once called "new immigrants," whose large-scale migration from Central and Southern Europe began about 1880. These include Slavs, Magyars, and Romanians of Roman Catholic, Byzantine Catholic, Eastern Orthodox, or Protestant persuasions; Jews from Romania and from the Russian and Austro-Hungarian empires; Lutherans from what are now Finland, Slovakia, or Transylvania; Italian and Portuguese Roman Catholics; Greeks and Albanians of Byzantine Catholic or Eastern Orthodox faith; and Christian or Moslem Syrians, Turks, Lebanese, and Armenians.

Historical and sociological interpretations of the role of religion among these latter groups continue to perpetuate the prejudices with which the established Protestant, Catholic, and Jewish leadership

214

greeted the arrival of their first representatives.[3] The older Americans assumed, as does Professor Robert Cross in his recent introduction to *The Church and the City*, that the faith of the newcomers stemmed from blind adherence to village or ethnic traditions which were irrelevant in a commercial or industrial society. They believed that Old World bishops and the rabbis and pastors who accompanied the displaced villagers to America used superstition and fear to persuade them to continue their support of institutions and beliefs whose chief function was to perpetuate clerical power. And they considered the alliances, synods, or dioceses which eventually united the congregations of each group in the New World to be sectarian anachronisms which met neither the emotional, intellectual, nor social needs of their membership. To convince the newcomers that they should reject these old traditions seemed to many of their confessional kinsmen among the older American population, whether they were Catholics, Protestants or Jews, an act of religious charity.[4]

A survey of the contemporary evidence available to one who reads only English, French, and German, coupled with several brief forays in company with translators in regional and town archives and village church records in Eastern Slovakia, Transylvania, and Slovenia, have pressed upon me a diametrically opposite framework of interpretation. Village religion in Central and Southern Europe on the eve of the mass migrations to America was by no means a bastion of social or ecclesiastical privilege. On the contrary, laymen often played key roles in both local and regional religious affairs and expected priests, bishops, and rabbis to support lay social and political interests. Moreover, the earliest religious organizations that immigrants from these areas formed in America greatly enlarged the scope and significance of lay responsibility and initiative, making their congregations appear in retrospect as "democratic" as those of the Methodist, Presbyterian, or Hebrew Reformed faith. Finally, the national ethno-religious organizations which eventually emerged to bind together each group's congregations were at least as responsive to popular will as were the governments of their Protestant denominational counterparts. "New" immigrant and Protestant sects differed chiefly in the degree to which transatlantic confessional or ethnic ties broadened the horizon of the former.

Associated with this interpretation is a general hypothesis about urbanization which this essay does not attempt to demonstrate so much as, by illustration, to suggest. The social and cultural changes which occurred among immigrant groups in America seem to have been more a consequence of their urbanization than the result of conflicts with the "host" culture. The myopic concept of "Americanization" distorts an understanding of what really happened. The most bitter conflicts arose among rival groups of the same nationality. The social role of religion among them resembles to a marked degree its role in the lives of native Americans, both white and black, who were moving to some of the same cities at the same time. And it also resembles what I have been able to learn about the role of religious beliefs and institutions among their fellow European villagers who chose to settle in cities of the Old World instead of the New. Moreover, the changes of religious attitude and of institutional structure which urbanization involved began some time before the migrants left their fathers' hearthsides. For that as well as other reasons, the extensive adjustments they made in their new homes seemed to participants to have grown naturally out of their past experiences, rather than to have been imposed upon them by the host society.

VILLAGE RELIGION ON THE EVE OF MIGRATION

The belief that monolithic state churches dominated both religion and culture in the Old World has distorted understanding by American scholars of the situation in Central and Southeastern Europe, particularly in agricultural villages, from whence most emigrants to the United States departed. Even when a region knew only one faith and nationality, as in Roman Catholic Sicily or Slovenia, Orthodox Greece or Lutheran Finland, parishes rooted in peasant societies often reflected the needs and aspirations of the villagers as much as the traditions or prerogatives dear to their ecclesiastical overlords.[5] Such a situation was even more likely when ethnic and religious diversity prevailed, as was the case in the areas from which the overwhelming majority of the immigrants from the Austro-Hungarian Empire came to North America. These included what is now Southeastern Poland and the adjoining portions of the Ukraine, which before World War

II comprised the Austrian provinces of Galicia and The Bukovina; The Subcarpathian Ukraine and Eastern Slovakia, which in the same period were the northeastern counties of the Old Kingdom of Hungary; Transylvania, Vojvodina, the Banat, and the Croatian borderland with Bosnia, now in Romania and Yugoslavia, but then also part of the Old Kingdom; and the Dalmatian coast, which was then under Austrian administration. Previous migrations into these regions which had given them their multiethnic character produced intense political and economic rivalries which found expression in the life of religious congregations. The Magyarization policies which the Kingdom of Hungary put in operation after 1867 compounded these rivalries. Thereafter, lay people of many faiths identified their religious with their ethnic commitments, and the varied economic and political strategies which these inspired. Priests, bishops, or rabbis who would not support those commitments risked alienating many of their followers.[6]

In the Austrian province of Galicia, for example, Rusin Catholics of the Byzantine Rite, ancestors to the great majority of Americans now called Ukrainians, shared with Jews of several traditions and with lesser numbers of Poles, Russians, and German Lutherans the cultural borderland between Roman Catholic Poland and Orthodox Russia. During the latter half of the nineteenth century, while Poland was partitioned among Russia, Germany, and Austria, an ethnic awakening took place among the Rusins in this province. Priests and lay leaders, a growing number of whom called themselves Ukrainians, promoted educational and cultural activities and popularized the new phonetic spelling of their language, in order both to counter the political power of Poles in Galicia and to help Rusins beyond the border eastward resist the efforts of the Orthodox Church of Russia to swallow up the Byzantine Rite.[7] They also established mutual benefit and savings and loan societies so as to lessen their dependence upon Jewish merchants and moneylenders for capital with which to buy land. These societies soon were active in financing short trips to industrial Silesia or longer ones to the United States through which peasants' sons hoped to earn such capital.[8] Galician Jewish congregations had for generations maintained similar associations for mutual aid in cultural and economic matters.[9] Polish Roman Catholics who had remained or planted themselves in areas largely Rusin followed similar strategies, learning rapidly (as did the Poles settled among Germans in Pomerania or

Silesia) to sustain by voluntary action parochial schools, cultural associations, and mutual benefit societies. Priests and rabbis were always mainstays of these congregational efforts at mutual aid.[10]

Farther east, in The Bukovina, a more nearly balanced population of Orthodox Romanians, Greek Catholic and Orthodox Rusins, Lutheran Germans, and Jews enjoyed a remarkably even-handed support from their Austrian rulers, as did the relatively much smaller groups of Poles and Magyars. Congregational action in behalf of lay interests was a principal characteristic of Bukovinian life, as it continued to be in Western Canada, where so many migrants from that region settled.[11]

Similarly pragmatic uses of congregational fellowship prevailed among Rusins, Magyars, Slovaks, Germans, and Jews settled on the southern side of the same mountains, in what is now Eastern Slovakia and sub-Carpathian Ukraine. The Greek Catholic Rusins who had lived there for centuries experienced no national cultural awakening to match that of their ethnic cousins north of the Carpathians, but their competition with other peoples for land, power, and status prompted diverse congregational tactics, tending sometimes toward assimilation, sometimes toward separatism. Many of the Rusin clergymen worked closely with the great Magyar landlords to keep down peasant discontent, and received in turn special privileges for their own sons and daughters. In some cases, such priests and their children persuaded entire congregations to accept Magyarization, thus sacrificing linguistic but not religious identity in return for economic, educational, and political advantages. Contributing to this outcome was the centuries-long custom of the uplanders of leaving their remote mountain villages in the spring and working all summer as laborers for Magyar farmers on the rich Tisza river plains. Inevitably, some stayed each year, eventually forming tiny Greek Catholic communities whose members, overwhelmed by the Magyar influences surrounding them, had in some cases by 1900 all but forgotten their own ethnic past.[12] A contemporaneous movement of Rusins westward to Szepes and Šaros counties, in what is now Eastern Slovakia, planted congregations in or beside Slovak and German villages located near narrow valleys or wooded uplands where the newcomers might acquire unoccupied land. Using faith as an instrument to secure group cohesion and advancement, some of these Greek Catholic congregations held on to their

Rusin identity, while others allowed their pastors or Magyar patrons to make them allies of Hungarian national policy, and still others warmed to their Slovak neighbors, dropping specifically Rusin dialectical forms and increasing their use of words and phrases from the East Slovak dialect. Large numbers of the last group came eventually to identify themselves as Slovak Rusins—that is, Greek Catholics of Rusin ancestry who had adopted Slovak nationality.[13]

Most Rusins in Hungary, however, clung to their remote and ancient villages under the crest of the Carpathians, quite beyond the effective reach of either Slovak or Magyar influence. On the eve of World War I, many of their congregations in larger towns converted to Orthodox faith, hoping to preserve their separateness through another kind of congregational adjustment: identification with the Pan-Slav movement and "Mother" Russia. The transition was not difficult, since the only change necessary was to drop from the Divine Liturgy the prayer for the Roman Pope and substitute the ancient petition their forefathers had chanted for the heirarchs of the Orthodox Church.[14]

The great majority of America's "Hungarian Jews" are descended from the Magyarized Jews whose ancestors had, during the previous centuries, crowded into these same northern counties of the Old Kingdom. The forebears of some of these had come from Germany with the merchants whom Maria Theresa settled in her eastern lands. Far more of them, however, were offspring of migrants from Galicia who spoke either Yiddish or Ashkenazi Hebrew. Their ancestors had moved southward across the mountains by the hundreds in the seventeenth and eighteenth centuries, and by thousands in the nineteenth. In Mukačevo, one of the largest and wealthiest towns of the region, Jewish culture, ranging in variety from the Chassidic to the fully assimilationist Neolog sect, was by the midnineteenth century so predominant that the city was called the "Jewish Rome." [15]

Although most Jews of the sub-Carpathian region were strictly Orthodox, they developed the practice of cultural pluralism into an ethnic art. By 1900, for example, at the ancient Lutheran academy John Amos Comenius had founded in Prešov, the 19 Jewish boys from that town and the 18 others from the surrounding region outnumbered by almost two to one the Slovak Protestants enrolled in the first-year class.[16] In other towns, such as Humenné, Jewish congregations founded for boys and girls both academic and business schools which gentile students often attended. They organized welfare and work relief societies for their own people, and joined interfaith ladies' clubs and cultural associations.[17] Long accustomed to using the German language as a means of advancement in the educational and professional as well as the economic affairs of the Hapsburg realm, rabbis and leading Jewish laymen even in isolated villages accepted Magyar speech and identity after 1867, in return for the favor of government officials, for tavern and brewery licenses, or for educational or professional advantage. As happened later in America, religious loyalty, relatively uncomplicated by linguistic and national aspirations, served to maintain the identity and to promote through educational and economic cooperation the group interests of Hungarian Jews.[18]

Slovaks, Magyars, and Germans residing in these northeasterly counties of the Old Kingdom were in each case divided between a Roman Catholic majority and a Reformed and Lutheran minority, the German Protestants being nearly all Lutherans. In the valleys of the Hornad and the Topolz, around Prešov, Košice, and Michalovce, villages composed wholly of people of one faith and nationality were a rarity. The proportions varied, of course, Magyar predominance at the edge of the plains giving way as one moved northward into the foothills to numerical superiorities of Rusins in the East or of Slovaks in the West. At the eastern base of the High Tatras, German descendants of ancient colonists of the Poprad valley sometimes outnumbered Slovaks.[19]

At Obysovce, for example, a village of 130 homes on the railway between Prešov and Košice, Lutheran and Roman Catholic parishes stood side by side, each with its own elementary school, and each church parent to filial congregations worshiping in their own buildings at the nearby villages of Kyšak and Trebejov. Additional Lutheran congregations standing in filial relationship to the one at Obysovce and served by the same pastor were located at Lemešany, two miles distant, which also had a Roman Catholic congregation; at Drienovska Nova Ves, six miles northward, where another Roman Catholic parish had a filial congregation; and at Sucha Dolina, two miles farther up the valley, where a Rusin Greek Catholic congregation served the rest of the inhabitants. Additional members of the

Obysovce Lutheran parish were scattered through a half dozen other villages, each of which had either a Roman or a Greek Catholic congregation, or both.[20] On his visit to Obysovce in 1883, the Lutheran Bishop noted that Slovak village society was remarkably mobile and diverse. Of the 130 house lots in Obysovce itself, Lutherans owned 60, Roman Catholics 57, and Jews 13. In nearby Trebejov 30 lots had gone over to Jews in the past few years. Fifty-nine of the male members of the Obysovce parish, nearly one-sixth of the total, were already in America, together with 14 of the women, though the first emigrants had departed only three years before.[21] Of 36 marriages between 1895 and 1900, ten united a native of the parish with a partner born outside it, two of the husbands being Roman Catholic and one Greek Catholic. Ten others united partners who lived in different villages of the parish itself, two of the husbands again being Roman Catholic.[22]

Hungarian law recognized the right of each village congregation to maintain an elementary school, though public officials steadily increased their efforts to enforce and expand the scope of the statutes requiring instruction in Magyar language and history. All the religious hierarchies were, moreover, firmly pro-Magyar. The assimilationist pressures emanating from the great Reformed center at Debrecen, from the Lutheran National Synod in Budapest, and from the Roman Catholic Archbishops of Estergom made loyalty to a minority ethnic tradition a congregational rather than a confessional matter, just as happened later in America. Among the minority congregations of all faiths, except possibly the Greek Catholic, lay associations operating both on a local and a regional basis helped to maintain church buildings and support schools, engendered pride in language and culture, and attempted to maintain and extend members' land holdings in the villages or their economic opportunities in cities.[23] German and Slovak Lutherans enjoyed a somewhat stronger tradition of lay prerogative than other Christian groups. The electing of teachers, the maintenance of regional teachers associations, the appointment for each district of a lay "director" to advise the clerical "senior," and participation by members of a congregation in the formulation of the evaluations bishops made on their occasional visitations were all ritualized expressions of the Lutheran doctrine of the priesthood of believers.[24]

The processes of urbanization, though slower in this region than elsewhere in Europe, made each large town a mosaic of ethno-religious groupings. In ancient Bardejov, nestled beneath the Carpathians, Slovak Roman Catholics worshiped in the fourteenth century cathedral recovered from the Protestants during the Catholic Reformation, while Germans and Magyars met together in another church nearby. A large Lutheran population, one part German and Magyar and one part Slovak, maintained two congregations; two or three synagogues served various sects of Jews; Rusins worshiped in a relatively new Byzantine Rite Catholic church; and at least one congregation of Slovak Catholics worshiped in their own church rather than in the cathedral.[25] Prešov's population and church organizations displayed an almost identical variety, its distance from Rusin villages being compensated for by the fact that a Byzantine Rite bishop was seated there, and a seminary for the training of priests stood across the street from his cathedral.[26] Košice, farther south, boasted fine buildings for the same Slovak, German, Rusin, and Jewish contingents, as well as others for the Slovak Reformed, Hungarian Reformed, and Hungarian Roman Catholic groups. Most of these congregations maintained a school. All, save possibly the Greek Catholic Rusins, sponsored cultural and mutual benefit societies of some sort.[27] Both in the complexity and intensity of their religious pluralism, then, Prešov and Košice were in 1910 like South Pittsburgh and East Cleveland: cultural artifacts of the Kingdom of Hungary's ethnic diversity.

So also were the villages and towns of the Banat and the Batchka, from whence many Romanians and some Croats, Serbs, Slovaks, and Catholic Germans emigrated to America. A variegated pattern of ethnic and religious settlement developed there from the eighteenth century onward, as agriculturalists of many nationalities crowded into the rich region to reclaim lands from the Danube swamps. As in Eastern Slovakia, villages of two to five thousand souls often had Protestant, Roman Catholic, Orthodox, and Byzantine Rite Catholic congregations, and occasionally a tiny synagogue of Jews as well. Each congregation was the center of educational and cultural activities aimed to help its laymen seize and hold as large a share as possible of economic and political power. The religious edifices in larger towns, such as Zrenjenen, display to this day a variety similar to what one finds in American industrial cities like Scranton or Passaic. Yet the congregations date back in many cases 200 years or more.[28] In Croatia-Slavonia, and especially along the old military border South of Zagreb from whence so many American Serbs and Croats emigrated, the majority population was Catholic and Croatian, and the only substantial minority were the Orthodox Serbs. The language of the two ethnic groups was the same, but their identities and, therefore, their rivalries, whether for land, political power, or cultural achievement, were defined by their religious differences.[29]

The population of Transylvania was ethnically as diverse as that of the Northern counties, and religion there was even more clearly an instrument of intergroup rivalry for political and economic advantage. German Roman Catholics from Saxony occupied this great plateau in the thirteenth century, whether before or after the first settlements of Romanians and Szekely Magyars none can surely say. Most of the Germans converted to Lutheranism during the Reformation. Enjoying for centuries political autonomy and efficient religious and economic organization, they remained the dominant class until World War II. From the seventeenth century onward, if not earlier, Orthodox Romanians and tiny groups of Jews began crowding in from the Old Kingdom to the South. The Romanians often built their homes beside Saxon villages, taking nearby hilly and unoccupied lands for their farms, which explains the origin of numerous such twin towns as Chirpar-Kirchenberg. Sometimes, however, they established entirely separate villages in rugged valleys or uplands whose forests they cleared away. From the North, meanwhile, a mixed body of Magyars, Rusins, and Jews moved across the Tisza valley to settle the rolling hill country beyond, while Hungarians of Reformed and Catholic persuasions trekked upward from the Tisza plains to fill the valleys opening to the West. An Orthodox-Greek Catholic schism in the eighteenth century split the Romanian population of Transylvania into two groups, but left ethnic commitments largely undivided. On the eve of large-scale emigration to America, then, hundreds of villages displayed only little less than did such larger Transylvania towns as Cluj, Blaj, and Sibiu a pattern of ethnic rivalry to which religious affiliation contributed much. The complex of tensions over language, education, land, and economic opportunity equaled that prevailing in the towns of Galicia, the Northern Counties of Hungary, and the Banat.[30]

Two institutional arrangements, one confessional and the other congregational, helped preserve religious order in the multinational Austro-Hungarian Empire. Each gave laymen of the several faiths important preparation for their future in America. In the early seventeenth century, Lutheran and Reformed Protestants had secured from their Catholic rulers statutes of autonomy which provided for representative government of their religious institutions. Each parish elected a council of elders, to which the pastor and the teacher belonged. These units in turn chose representatives to the first level of a hierarchy of confessional assemblies, at the head of which stood the Reformed "General Conventus" and the Lutheran "National Synod." The monarch's confirmation of the decisions of the annual meetings of these two latter organizations was necessary, but he could not alter them. Somewhat later, the Serbian and the Romanian archbishops were able to secure comparable statutes of autonomy which provided for lay representation in governing bodies at each level of Orthodox church administration. In these cases, however, the crown enjoyed the right to prorogue, dissolve, or veto the calling of a national congress. Jews eventually established similar unifying institutions, but their national organization was not officially recognized in the Kingdom of Hungary until 1896, their chief Rabbi meanwhile sitting in the House of Magnates not by right but as a nominee of the crown.[31]

The second arrangement was the system of parish organization illustrated in the Obysovce case described above. It prevailed among Protestant, Roman Catholic, Byzantine Rite, Eastern Orthodox, and Jewish groups, in all the multiethnic village societies. Since the members were scattered and always poor, rarely could those of the same faith in a single village support a pastor or rabbi. Instead, a parish or congregation usually comprised a parent organization with its filial congregations in villages from a mile to ten or more miles distant and scattered groups in other villages which were too small to justify a chapel or synagogue of their own. One pastor or rabbi served the entire congregation. The people usually maintained only one parochial school, located in the village where their numbers were largest, electing their schoolmaster and paying many expenses by voluntary subscription. A leading layman in each village watched over the property of his segment of the congregation. He forwarded news of need or tragedy to the pastor, priest, or rabbi, led in the observance of sacred days and, in general, symbolized the unity of the faithful who lived in out-of-the-way places. On the most important holy days, members of a congregation often assembled from their several villages at the central house of worship, renewing by rituals both sacred and secular the ties which bound them to one another and to their spiritual leaders.[32]

FOUNDING CONGREGATIONS IN THE NEW WORLD

Little wonder that when laymen of these various backgrounds reached America, they did not wait for the arrival of a pastor or a rabbi to organize a religious congregation, but undertook the task themselves. Social and psychological need as well as the shortage of clergymen—severe in all cases but that of the Slovenes—prompted them to build upon and extend those aspects of their traditions which emphasized lay leadership. Those from multiethnic regions, accustomed to a large degree of initiative, seem to have set the pace. Laymen of all groups, however, retained long after the shortage of pastors ended many of the enlarged prerogatives they had assumed in their earliest years in the New World.

The shortage of clergymen stemmed in part from the voluntary and economic nature of the decision to emigrate and in part from the dispersion and constant movement of laborers among small mining and industrial towns in America. The first local groups to organize in such places as Scranton or Toledo were at the outset too poor to support a minister. The canonical tangle afflicting Eastern Orthodox and Byzantine Catholic administrations in America deterred Romanian, Rusin, and Serbian priests from answering such calls as were made, just as suspicions of Irish and German bishops caused Roman Catholic priests from Sicily, Dalmatia, and Poland to hesitate. Young Lutheran clergymen in Finland and Slovakia and graduates of the Hungarian Reformed seminary in Debrecen realized that, in American pastorates, they would be much more dependent upon the voluntary support of lay people. They often sought ironclad guarantees of salary and housing which the tiny New World congregations were unable to give.[33]

Thus Rusins from south of the Carpathians who began settling

in Minneapolis in the early 1880's worshiped first in the Polish Roman Catholic parish, but soon began meeting separately, reciting from
memory the rituals of the Byzantine Rite. A parish committee made
plans for a church building and requested their Bishop in Prešov to
send them a pastor. Father Alex Toth arrived in due time, only to
find that Roman Catholic Archbishop John Ireland was unwilling to
permit a married priest to administer the sacraments in his diocese.
Shortly thereafter, two laymen returned from a trip to San Francisco,
where they had chanced upon the Russian Orthodox cathedral and
received from the archbishop who resided there an offer to accept
their congregation under his care and to provide a regular subsidy for
the support of a pastor. Father Toth and the entire Minneapolis congregation thereupon decided to forsake the ancient union which had
tied their European parishes to Rome and became the first permanent
Russian Orthodox organization east of the Rocky Mountains.[34] Father
Toth soon left Minneapolis to seek the conversion to Orthodoxy of
Byzantine Catholic Rusins who had settled in the anthracite towns
around Scranton, Pennsylvania. The Minneapolis congregation continued to flourish, despite the strange ways of their Great Russian
pastors. Its parish committee constructed a fine building, modeling it
upon pictures of a provincial church in Russia, which was quite unlike anything in their own homeland. They operated a parochial
school after public school hours weekdays and on Saturdays, and in
1907 the first Orthodox theological seminary in the United States
began classes in the parish hall.[35]

Meanwhile, single men and a few families of Slovak or Hungarian Protestant persuasion, some Lutherans and others Reformed, followed one another from villages in the northern counties of Hungary
to such industrial or mining communities as Raritan and Passaic, New
Jersey, Mount Carmel and Braddock, Pennsylvania, and Streator, Illinois, as well as to the cities of Cleveland, Minneapolis, Pittsburgh,
and Chicago. Long accustomed to relying upon religious associations
to sustain social and cultural goals, they moved at once to organize
congregations and mutual benefit insurance societies, even though
many of their members planned to return home after a few years. A
diverse company established at Pittsburgh in 1890 a congregation
which bore the ecumenical name, "First Hungarian and Slovak Evangelical and Reformed Church of St. Paul." Heirs of the two national

and two confessional traditions worshiped together successfully for almost a year in the Grand Avenue Lutheran Church, Pittsburgh, in services led by a Hungarian layman, Gustav Hamborszky. Each group maintained a separate "religious society" for mutual aid, however, and language and perhaps other differences soon forced the congregation itself to divide. The Lutheran Slovaks built a house of worship on Braddock Street and the Reformed Hungarians erected another on Bates Street.[36]

Existing American denominations helped the Hungarians to resolve their problem of pastoral leadership. Andrew Hornyak, leader of the Pittsburgh congregation, wrote Bishop Bertalan Kun in Hungary, asking for a minister. The Bishop replied in January 1891 that they must be willing to accept a young and unmarried man who had not yet found a "permanent position" in Hungary, and must "first guarantee to such a minister a salary sufficient to enable him to live properly, because the minister cannot expose himself to an insecure future." [37] Hornyak and his fellow laymen had meanwhile contacted the Home Mission Board of the Reformed Church of America, and shortly secured a guarantee of support for two such Hungarian Reformed pastors from the homeland. Both arrived before the year was out, and traveled through towns from New Jersey to Ohio, encouraging the formal organization of congregations whose members had for some years met under the leadership of laymen. Some of these contained for a long time thereafter members who spoke both Magyar and Slovak. At Mount Carmel, Pennsylvania, the group which had been organized on June 9, 1890, had no pastor until one arrived from Hungary in 1895. A layman taught the new domini Slovak and he thereafter conducted each month two services in that language, as well as one in Magyar and one in English.[38]

Among Orthodox Romanians from Transylvania, the first bonds of friendship and association in the New World likewise stemmed from their common origins. The pioneer group in each American town or city usually came from two or three clusters of homeland villages. Newcomers in succeeding years often went directly to the homes of men they had known or were related to in their own or neighboring villages in Transylvania, the Banat, or the Bukovina. Those in Chicago early formed the habit of singing chants and responses together on Sunday, gathering for this purpose at the saloon

which was their social center on weekdays. They soon realized that
among them they were able to reconstruct from memory most of the
Orthodox service. So without waiting for liturgical books to arrive
from Romania they began in a room at the back of the tavern the
rituals of worship which they shared, without benefit of clergy until
sometime after 1908, when the Orthodox Bishop of Sibiu sent them
a priest. Meanwhile, they had organized, as had other Orthodox Romanians in Cleveland and Indiana Harbor, Michigan, a mutual benefit insurance society which paved the way in both sentiment and
practice for the formation of a religious congregation. The Cleveland
society sponsored the formal organization of St. Mary's parish there
in 1904, two years before the first priest arrived. The homeland custom of a single priest ministering to a central church and its daughter
congregations in nearby places was easily transferred to the New
World. Here, however, each one of the clustered congregations was
independently organized and its parish society incorporated, so as to
enable it to purchase property, erect a building, and establish a parish
school.[39]

The Roman Catholic immigrants from the Northern Counties
of Hungary likewise formed mutual benefit societies which doubled
as organizing units for parishes. At McKeesport, Pennsylvania, those
who spoke Magyar united in 1889 with others who spoke Slovak to
establish St. Stephens Roman Catholic Church. Their first pastor, a
Hungarian, resisted for a time what he called the "pan-Slav priests"—
Czechs who took a paternal interest in Slovak settlers. The Slovak
group soon split off from this parish, however, and organized their
own congregation at nearby Braddock.[40] In Cleveland, meanwhile,
Father Stefan Furdek, Slovak pastor of a Czech congregation, promoted the organization of mutual benefit societies as a first step toward the formation of Slovak parishes among laymen in that and
nearby cities who were for the moment worshiping in Czech, German,
or Hungarian congregations.[41]

During the same decades, Italian, Slovenian, Finnish, Polish, and
Greek laymen who had recently arrived from lands which knew only
one faith and nationality established mutual benefit societies and
congregations in a similar pattern.[42]

Although numerous Slovenian priests had followed Frederick

Barraga to America to do missionary work among the Winnebago Indians and were, therefore, on hand to become pastors of the earliest mining town congregations in northern Michigan and Minnesota, the first Slovenian parishes which appeared in industrial towns were the fruit of extensive lay effort. The earliest immigrants arrived at Joliet, Illinois, in the mid-1880's to take jobs in the steel plants. They and those who followed them attended the German Catholic church of St. John the Baptist, soon growing so numerous as to fill half the pews. Realizing they were posing a threat to the Germans, the Slovenes began collecting money and in 1891 requested the Bishop to allow them to form their own parish, St. Joseph's. Permission being granted, they brought a pastor from the old country and erected in rapid succession a fine church, a school, and a parish house. Although the number of women and children in the congregation was relatively small, the group showed great competitive excitement over such "projects" as the purchase of altars, statuary, and bells, and the planning of a cemetery. Local mutual benefit lodges, though initially allied with a Czech society to assure their financial strength, served as centers of ethnic feeling and in every way nurtured the establishment of the congregation, as they sustain its life to this day.[43]

Chicago's South Italians had by 1905 erected a dozen church buildings and had managed to secure for most of them priests of their own nationality. Despite charges by one anticlerical newspaper editor that the Irish bishops were not so much concerned to save Italians as to keep from "losing faithful clients," laymen made great sacrifices to pay for buildings which were, legally, the archbishop's property.[44] Such editors, who like most of the earlier immigrants from Italy styled themselves "Northern Italians" or "Lombards," deplored the fact that parish committees in the dozen or so Chicago neighborhoods where the newcomers had settled insisted upon raising money through crude street processions and outdoor celebrations, just as they had in their native Sicily or Calabria. The faithful would carry a statue of the Virgin Mary in these processions, and members or friends would come out of houses and business establishments to pin money on her clothing. The celebrants would wind up at a public park to enjoy food, drink, gambling, and other diversions. The insistence of Catholic bishops "that the early Italian immigrant should erect and support his own church and parish school, or else do without them" seemed to a later writer an adequate defense of this importation of paraliturgical traditions from the Old World.[45] In any event, the founding of each South Italian parish reflected a decision to establish a formal organization which the members hoped would not only preserve their religious identity but also further their common interests in a non-Italian world.[46]

Victor Greene has recently argued in similar vein that the inner life of Chicago's great Polish community revolved about two vast and competing national parishes. Social, cultural, and economic associations bound laymen to one another and to their Catholic faith. Poles in Chicago were simply too numerous for bishops to restrain their desire for separate national congregations.[47]

In the anthracite towns of Eastern Pennsylvania, however, as in smaller industrial cities elsewhere, bishops could and did heartily resist this desire; the result was a widespread movement of lay protest which resulted in the founding of the first Polish National Catholic congregation at Scranton, Pennsylvania, in 1898. Several years before, Poles in the city had won permission to establish a new parish. They erected a building and were assigned a German pastor, who was at first aided by a Polish curate, Francis Hodur. When the laymen sought through their parish committee a larger role in managing the church property, the priest scorned them publicly. The congregation appealed in vain to the bishop. Finally, one Sunday in October 1896, they refused to allow the pastor to enter the church for mass. The police were called, and after what partisans remembered as a bloody battle involving both men and women, the officers turned the building over to the priest and arrested nine men. A delegation of laymen then sought the counsel of Francis Hodur, who was by then a curate at nearby Nanticoke. The fiery young Pole encouraged them to form and incorporate a new congregation, and to erect their own building on property belonging to the corporation. The task was completed, but the bishop refused either to consecrate the new church or to appoint a priest. The laymen then presented Hodur with a petition bearing 200 names, asking him to be their pastor. He accepted in March 1897.[48]

Hodur sought first to get the new group properly accepted.

Spurned by his bishop, he journeyed to Rome in January and February 1898, bearing a petition from the parish committee which had also been signed by pastors and laymen of neighboring Polish congregations. The petition asked the Holy Father to make the congregation a part of the diocese; to vest title to the property in the local parish organization; to empower the congregation to elect administrative committees without interference from either pastor or bishop; and to give laymen a voice in the selection of their pastor. Told that he was to be sternly refused, Hodur returned home without awaiting audience with the Pope, intending to withdraw from the Roman Church. When leading laymen at St. Stanislaus learned of his decision, they declared they would join him. In an emotional scene resembling that for which Methodist camp meetings were famous, the entire congregation made his decision their own.[49] Some weeks later, as Hodur read to the congregation the decree of his excommunication, the sighing and quiet sobbing of the women gave way slowly, we are told, to spontaneous prayers, songs, and shouts of happiness. Hodur burned the document and directed that its ashes be strewn in the waters of the brook which flowed at the foot of the hill. At that point some became excited enough to jump over the balustrade and press their priest to the altar, crying loudly, "God is with us, Father! He will not leave His children; God is with us!"[50]

Brief reflection upon these patterns of congregation-founding will suggest the tenuousness of the argument that Jews from Central and Eastern Europe were more sophisticated in the use of formal organization or, by reason of the persecution they had suffered, more alert to the advantages of communal solidarity than other immigrants. The hundreds of storefront synagogues which Romanian, Galician, and Hungarian Jews founded in America, and the mutual aid societies which sustained both their congregations and their schools, seem in retrospect to reflect a lay initiative which was both in motive and form closely comparable to that which prevailed among Magyars, Italians, and Slavs. The initiative stemmed from a similar reaction to the prejudice which the older German Jewish community showed toward the newcomers from Central Europe.[51]

When Magyarized Jews from Hungary arrived in Cleveland during the Civil War, they established a "Hungarian Aid Society," and in October 1866 formed the Orthodox "Hungarian Congregation Bene Jeshurun," disdaining the Bohemian and the German synagogues already in existence. Chief among the founders of the new congregation was Herman Sampliner, presumably a native of Zemplin County in Northeastern Hungary. The group first met in his home, renting a large hall for high holidays, then moved to a succession of storefronts and halls. When, at the dedication of a new temple purchased in 1887 from another Jewish congregation, sermons by visiting Reformed rabbis, including Dr. A. Friedman of Cleveland and Isaac M. Wise from Cincinnati, urged the "Hungarians" to lay aside outmoded traditions, the pastor spoke out firmly in opposition, and the congregation continued in its Orthodox way. The story was repeated hundreds of times in cities large and small.[52]

Moreover, the notion that the establishment of immigrant congregations depended upon the action of ecclesiastical leaders either in America or the home countries contradicts not only the evidence of their founding but that of their financing as well. Laymen employed attorneys to help them incorporate congregational organizations under state laws, and in most cases raised every dollar used to purchase lots and build churches, synagogues, and rectories. Peter Roberts reported in 1903 that of the 143 Catholic parishes which worshiped in their own buildings in the anthracite towns, almost half were either Polish, Rusin, Slovak, Lithuanian, or Italian. Their members had paid for their buildings almost entirely by voluntary contributions, while securing and supporting pastors of their own nationality.[53] A few years later, Roberts noted that Poles, Lithuanians, Croats, and Serbs living in Pittsburgh's south side had accumulated, after only 20 years of residence there, church property valued at three-quarters of a million dollars, most of it paid for. The priests kept in close touch with newcomers, taking a census each year, and assisted laymen in promoting mutual benefit societies and building and loan associations. Though women were yet few in their communities, Slavic men often went to confession at six in the morning so as to be ready for mass on the following day. "I have seen in Pittsburgh a congregation of 1,000 men, all in the prime of life," Roberts wrote, "so intent upon the religious exercises that the least movement of the priest at the altar found immediate response in every member of the audience." [54]

THE EMERGENCE OF
NATIONAL RELIGIOUS ORGANIZATIONS

These manifold lay initiatives in local religious association led very early to the establishment under predominantly lay auspices of denominational and quasi-denominational organizations which sustained and united the scattered units of each group. The idea of congregational independence never took root among the "new immigrants." Instead, almost from the moment of the formation of their congregations, lay leaders of mutual benefit societies pressed upon the flocks and their newly arrived pastors the necessity of forming national alliances which, whether uniting congregations or lodges, aimed to bring together all immigrants of the same ethnic and confessional commitments in one American organization. Contributing to this outcome was the great mobility of pastors and of laymen during the early years of settlement. The rapid development of newspapers, almanacs, and other means of communication, including intercity travel among widely separated settlements, also played a part, as did the tradition that a religious congregation must depend upon an authority higher and broader than its own to legitimize and sustain its existence.

The governments of these national organizations depended far more upon lay participation and leadership than the synods and dioceses of the Old World. They were more responsive to popular impulses, in my judgment, than were the governments of mainstream Protestant communions, and their responsibilities were the same: to promote the founding of new congregations and to sustain struggling ones; to keep each local unit abreast of matters of interest to all; to publish newspapers and yearbooks, as well as special magazines for women and children; to provide materials for the education of the young in both religious and secular aspects of their parents' way of life; and to recruit and assign pastors to the congregations which needed them. They often carried out these functions in a manner opposed to the traditions of ecclesiastical government which had prevailed among the parent communions in the Old World.

Immigrant Protestant sects such as the Slovak Evangelical Lutheran Church revealed explicitly the extensions of lay prerogative which were implicit in the organizations which emerged to serve Catholic and Orthodox minorities. The eight or more Slovak Lutheran mutual benefit societies which had helped establish congregations in various cities and towns between 1890 and 1893 coalesced in the latter year in a lay organization called "The Slovak Evangelical Church and Sick Benefit Union of the Augsburg Confession." One of the local units, the Holy Trinity Society organized at Cleveland in 1892, included in one body a congregation and an insurance brotherhood, as did another organized at Raritan, New Jersey, two years later. Members of local brotherhoods which adhered to the Union soon withdrew from the nonsectarian National Slovak Society. By that action they opted for a specifically Lutheran basis of their Slovak identity in the New World, just as Stefan Furdek's followers had chosen a Catholic definition of their identity two years earlier. The few Slovak Lutheran pastors in the country in the 1890's were active members of the Union, but lay leaders long held the initiative in both church and fraternal affairs. The pastoral "seniorate" formed in 1893 reported its business to the annual meeting of the Union. The seniorate died of neglect, partly from differences among the pastors as to whether their congregations should be associated with the Evangelical Lutheran Synod of Missouri. The lay officers of the Union thereupon invited all pastors to attend the convention of 1899 at its expense, and persuaded them to form a "pastoral conference." Under its constitution, the Union's officers were to approve plans for the division of the field in which each pastor was to work, as well as to oversee the adjudication of misunderstandings among pastors and of complaints against those charged with behavior unbecoming a minister.[55]

With continuous prodding from the laymen in charge of the Union, the "Slovak Evangelical Church of the Augsburg Confession" finally came into being in September 1902 at a joint meeting of pastors and lay delegates in Connellsville, Pennsylvania. The synod thereafter decided upon a wide range of questions brought to its attention from congregations, many of them dealing with clarification of the rights and duties of pastors and people. The lay office of "church inspector" was widely introduced, according to the custom then prevailing in Slovakia. The Union meanwhile increased its annual contributions to the support of Slovak Lutheran students of theology, shared the expenses and often the editorship of the synod's publications, and continued for some years to discuss church affairs at its annual meetings as though they were its primary business. Eventually, however, a separation of responsibilities emerged, the professed reasons being the synod's opposition to dancing and other forms of "worldliness" in lodge activities, the insistence of the pastors upon doctrinal and confessional purity, and their sharp opposition to a fraternal ritual containing "non-Christian" funeral prayers. But the pattern of lay prerogative in both church and society was fully established in these early years.[56]

Perhaps the largest of the Protestant movements emanating from Central Europe is the Hungarian Reformed. Its earliest congregations in America united first in what was called a "classis" of the Reformed Church in the United States. Many of the congregations organized later affiliated with the Presbyterian Church, U.S.A. Most also maintained close ties with the Reformed Conventus in Budapest, however, receiving visitations from Magyar church officials, securing their pastors from the theological seminary in Debrecen, and following in their American publications detailed accounts of religious developments in Hungary. In 1904 the lay president of the Conventus visited the American settlements and provoked a crisis among them, resulting in the creation of three separate denominational or quasi-denominational structures. One group associated closely with the Reformed Church in the United States, another with the Presbyterian Church, U.S.A., and a third adhered officially to the Old World communion. In all three, lay leaders and clergymen who were responsive to lay initiatives seem to have exercised a controlling influence. After World War II, the Reformed Church in the United States received into its ranks most of the congregations which had been up to then subject to the Conventus in Budapest, and an independent Free Magyar Reformed Church came into existence to provide a home for the rest.[57]

In roughly similar fashion, denominational order emerged among Slovak Calvinists, although their leaders were more closely identified with American Presbyterian and Reformed communions[58]; among Magyar-speaking Lutherans, most of whom affiliated with the Missouri Synod[59]; among Italian and Romanian Baptists[60]; and among Finnish Lutherans, about whose tripartite denominational structure in the United States I have written elsewhere.[61]

The lay-directed national fraternal societies which provided

Roman Catholic ethnic minorities a measure of religious autonomy indicate with equal clarity the relationship between migration and voluntarism. Such organizations as the Polish Roman Catholic Union, the Croatian Catholic Union, the First Catholic Slovak Union, the Grand Carniolian (Slovenian) Catholic Union, and the first Greek Catholic Union competed directly with non-sectarian, secular, or socialist societies which appealed for membership on a purely ethnic or political basis. These Catholic societies, like the Protestants, Eastern Orthodox, and Jewish ones which I treat in this essay, defined their purposes in specifically religious terms, restricted their membership to practicing communicants, and spent a substantial portion of their money and energies in promoting their faith. Their activities included founding and supporting congregations, recruiting pastors from the Old World and arranging their appointments in the New, publishing Sunday School and other religious periodicals, sponsoring parochial schools, and defending the ethnic version of their faith from attacks within as well as from outside their nationality. The national officers of some of them performed for many years all but the specifically spiritual functions of a bishop, securing when possible canonical approval and support for their actions, and when that was not possible, managing by some means to give the congregations the help they needed. The little-known history of these societies dramatizes the diversity of real power which has long flourished beneath the externally monolithic structure of authority in American Catholicism.

Even when clergymen were the principal founders of such organizations, as was true for Catholic Slovaks and Slovenes, laymen were soon in effective control. The Slovenian congregation in Joliet referred to above was host in 1893 to a meeting of delegates from lay brotherhoods which priests had helped form in the multiethnic mining town parishes of northern Michigan and Minnesota and in Chicago and Cleveland. The Joliet pastor, F. S. Šušteršič, accepted the first presidency of the national body. The leader of a group of immigrant seminarians at St. Paul Theological Seminary, Mat Šavs, was elected secretary. However, laymen soon replaced clergymen in all the national offices, as well as in the editorship of the weekly newspaper which Father Joseph Buh edited at Tower, Minnesota, from 1891 until 1899. Only the office of "Spiritual Advisor" remained an important priestly function. The clergyman who held it sat on the "Supreme

Board" and hence shared in all decision-making, but he rarely exercised anything like a controlling influence.[62]

The proliferation of an elaborate array of officials with high-sounding titles gave to the national boards of such brotherhoods a ritualistic appearance which belied the pragmatic functions the officers served. All were subject to annual reelection by representatively constituted national conventions. The "supreme presidents" and "supreme secretaries" were salaried professionals, charged with promoting not only cultural and religious goals but also the enrollment of members in the mutual benefit insurance program. The treasurers soon became responsible for the administration of very large sums of money held in reserve against future insurance claims. Every society published a newspaper circulated automatically to each member. The editors, also elected annually at the national conventions, filled their columns with news of the home country and of lodges in America, as well as with accounts of the deeds of immigrant pastors and laymen and of the work of lay or religious organizations in establishing parish schools. A Slav or Magyar reader of such a newspaper saw Catholicism or Orthodoxy from the perspective of his own ethnic interests, and America as a land where he should combine traditional ways of acting and thinking with newly-acquired ones. To a Slovenian Catholic immigrant, the most important churchman was neither his local bishop nor an archbishop or cardinal of the American church, but the monsignor of his own nationality who was spiritual advisor to his fraternal order, usually the pastor of either St. Vitus parish, Cleveland, or St. Joseph's in Joliet.[63]

Father Stefan Furdek's career illustrates these points. A native of Slovakia who had answered Cleveland Bishop Richard Gilmour's plea for clergymen from central Europe in 1882, Furdek supervised the formation of numerous Slovak congregations in Ohio and Pennsylvania while serving as pastor of Our Lady of Lourdes parish in Cleveland. His first step in every case was to form a local unit of the First Catholic Slovak Union, the national fraternal benefit society that he founded in 1890, known popularly as *Jednota*. Furdek launched a weekly newspaper for the organization during its second year, and in 1896 published at his own expense the first volume of an annual almanac. He promoted the study of English and filled the columns of his paper with articles and poems expressing love and loyalty to America

as well as to the Roman Catholic Church. During his several visits to
Slovakia in search of priests, he explained to large audiences that their
kinsmen in America loved both their old and their new land, just as
any normal man loved both his mother and his wife.[64]

Many facets of Furdek's leadership reflected the extension of lay
responsibility and prerogative which was central to the religious life
of migrating Slovaks. He was a publicist, recruiting members among
people who had to join voluntarily, if at all. He was a politician, acting steadily to oppose the claims of the rival and somewhat more
secular National Slovak Society. He was a cultural innovator, seeking
to build an identity for his followers which was at once Catholic,
American, and Slovak. And he was a democrat, who must speak the
language of persuasion rather than command. He welcomed laymen
to share the leadership of local parishes and lodges and of the national
organization which sustained and united them. Despite an intense
campaign of opposition from fellow Roman Catholics, Furdek organized a Slovak Catholic Congress which drew 10,000 immigrants to a
convention at Wilkes-Barre, Pennsylvania, on Labor Day, September
3, 1906. Rumors that a movement was afoot to found an independent
Slovak Catholic church did not impress the local Irish bishop. The
latter appeared at the gathering to announce his faith in the loyalty
of Furdek and his associates to the Roman communion and his sympathy with every oppressed nationality, noting that the Irish had
likewise endured a long history of exploitation. The convention contributed much to a renaissance of Slovak national feeling on both
continents, partly through the formation of The Slovak League of
America, a political organization which soon supplanted Peter Rov-
nianek's National Slovak Society.[65]

American Roman Catholics of Polish, Lithuanian, Croatian, and
Hungarian backgrounds fashioned similar national societies, drawing
in many cases upon the example set earlier by Czech and German
Catholics. The histories of two unusual "denominations," the Polish
National Catholic Church and the First Greek Catholic Union, seem
in the light of the foregoing examples unique only in the extent to
which they made explicit the meaning of their religious experimenta-
tion.

Within two years of the founding of the independent St. Stanis-
las Polish Catholic Church in Scranton, Father Hodur answered

appeals from lay groups at nearby Dickson City, Duryea, Wilkes-Barre, and Nanticoke, Pennsylvania, to help them form parish committees and establish sister congregations. He also received into his fellowship a congregation organized at Baltimore, Maryland, in 1898, and two others located at Fall River and Lowell, Massachusetts. In December 1900, Hodur announced that he would celebrate the Christmas Mass at Scranton in the Polish language. Latin thereafter disappeared from Polish National Catholic worship. The first meeting of a formal synod took place in 1904. Sixteen priests and 130 lay delegates from the parishes and ethnic societies supporting the National Church movement gathered at Scranton that year, chose Hodur their bishop, and voted to establish a theological seminary to train young men for the priesthood, all amidst scenes, as a *Scranton Times* reporter put it, in which "people embraced one another, kissed one another, shouted, the church bells pealed," and "the throngs gathered on the street around the Convention Hall" were "carried away with . . . sincere feelings of joy." [66] Soon after Hodur organized the Polish National Union, a fraternal insurance society. It brought lay communicants together in local lodge meetings and in regional and national conventions, and nurtured through its newspaper and other publications, through its evening school in Scranton and through its advocacy of social justice for workers the community of religious conviction which the new denomination required.[67]

Equally illuminating is the story of the "Greek Catholic Union of Rusin Brotherhoods," as it was first called, organized at Wilkes-Barre, Pennsylvania, in February 1892. The founding convention, attended by six priests and lay representatives from 14 local mutual benefit societies scattered from Bridgeport, Connecticut, to Streator, Illinois, declared that the aim of the Greek Catholic Union was to spread love and friendship among the Rusin people in America, to provide insurance against death and accidents, to educate the people in "national and religious requirements," and "to aid churches and schools." The founders began issuing a weekly newspaper and adopted a constitution which provided equal lay and clerical membership on a supervisory commission. The early years of the organization were wracked by controversy, rooted in the fact that Rusins from Galicia resisted identification with those from sub-Carpathian Hungary. The Galicians founded a competing national organization open to persons who were not practicing Greek Catholics, which eventually became the Ukrainian National Union.[68] Meanwhile, local groups of Rusins from both sides of the Carpathians followed Father Alexander Toth into the Russian Orthodox fold. They soon formed two competing national unions of Russian Orthodox brotherhoods, both of which maintained units in some Orthodox congregations.[69]

In the years which followed, the Greek Catholic Union became in all but formalities a separate denomination. Although the membership remained overwhelmingly Rusin, it welcomed to its rolls lodges associated with congregations of Slovak or Hungarian Greek Catholics. Until 1906 the officers of the Union performed all of the functions of a bishop: recruitment of pastors from the Old World and their assignment in the New; adjudication of controversies between lay parish organizations and their pastors; encouragement of parochial schools, and provision of literature for them; sponsorship of affiliate religious societies for women, children, and youth; and the publication of a weekly newspaper which gave to the Carpatho-Rusins their understanding of America, of their own Greek Catholic culture, of affairs in their homeland, and of the Roman Catholic Church of which they were in form but never in feeling a part. Having misunderstood the depth of the ethnic division which separated the Ukrainians from the Carpatho-Rusins, the Roman Curia in 1906 appointed a bishop to serve all Greek Catholics in the United States. The bishop, Stephen Ortinsky, a native of Galicia, strove for ten frustrating years to unite the two groups, but the net result was to increase the insistence of laymen upon the prerogatives which they perceived as their only sure means of protecting their congregations and lodges from aggression by the other side.[70]

Ortinsky died in 1916, amidst rumors that he had himself converted to Eastern Orthodoxy. Certainly he had suffered mounting frustration in his effort to reconcile the sub-Carpathian, the Russophile, and the Ukrainian parties. The Holy See replaced him with two apostolic administrators, one to care for the congregations who called themselves Ukrainians and the other to serve the remaining Greek Catholics from Northern Hungary, including the few whose members spoke Magyar or Slovak. The two administrators became bishops in 1924, one sitting in Pittsburgh and the other in Philadelphia; but the boundaries of their exarchates, as their jurisdictions were called, were defined not by geography at all but by the ethnic commitments of the congregations adhering to each of them.[71] Sectarian rivalry provided an additional outlet for lay independence—the option Rusin congregations often exercised of moving back and forth in moments of crisis or conflict between the Ukrainian and Carpatho-Rusin communions or, when it suited their purposes, into the Russian Orthodox and, after a further division in 1937, the Carpatho-Russian Orthodox folds.[72]

RELIGIOUS ORGANIZATIONS AND URBAN SOCIETY: A HYPOTHESIS

Thus did the local and national religious organizations established by immigrant groups in America after 1880 come to resemble in structure and function as well as in their intergroup relationships those organizations which had for many decades served the native Protestant population. In retrospect, evidence that the newcomers borrowed ideas of lay prerogative or democratic procedure from the host society is less persuasive than that which suggests that new social and psychological conditions prompted them to cultivate and extend traditions of lay participation and initiative which were rooted in their past experience in Central or Southern Europe. Immigrant pastors and laymen sometimes fought sharp battles with entrenched leaders of their own faith and, because newcomers were generally economic underdogs, the lines of conflict often paralleled those which delineated social privilege. Nevertheless, what the innovators fought for was not a new religious order tailored to the demands of the disinherited, but freedom to participate on their own terms in the system of denominational pluralism which already prevailed here.

Viewed thus from its religious underside, the social history of immigrant workingmen in America displays a striking unanimity of preference for what scholars persist in labeling the middle class way. That this preference should have prevailed in that area of their lives which was perhaps least subject to legal or other coercions suggests how broad are the foundations of the social consensus of which the nation's religious institutions are but one facet.

The events I have described also raise the question whether the religious aspects of this consensus stem more from general urban than from specifically American conditioning. The role of ethnic congregations and of ethno-religious denominations has become increasingly important in the cities of the homeland from which the newer immigrant groups hailed. Moreover, tendencies toward voluntarism, lay initiative, and denominational pluralism in religion seem to have grown steadily in all urban societies during the last century, not only on both sides of the North Atlantic but on opposite shores of the South Atlantic, the Pacific, and the Indian Oceans as well—wherever urban expansion has rested upon the decision of large numbers of men to move to cities in search of a new start for themselves and their children. To be sure, the early renunciation in America of the state-church tradition, the comparative freedom allowed minority groups to conduct parochial schools, the specific support which state laws gave congregations engaged in battles with bishops or other central authorities, and the extensive second-stage mobility of immigrants during the years after they had settled in the United States all reinforced the principle of religious voluntarism which the first arrivals of each group had found compelling. The contrasts, however, between the pattern of religious organization which prevails today in, for example, Pittsburgh and those prevailing in Budapest, Beirut, Buenos Aires, Durban, Singapore or El Monte, California, do not seem large enough to substantiate the claim that ethno-religious pluralism, denominationalism, voluntarism, or lay prerogative give to the history of religion in America a special mystique. Events in ancient Hellenistic and in modern Oriental and Israeli cities suggest, moreover, that neither modernity nor a predominantly Christian setting is essential to the emergence of such a pattern.

The mobility and diverse origins of their populations require urban societies to be publicly and officially secular. Religion does not lose its force in such an environment merely because its support and structuring rest upon voluntary choice. Communities of faith may by that circumstance acquire enlarged vitality, developing new modes of winning adherents, sustaining new patterns of association which cut across traditional class lines, and showing in both idea and structure more responsiveness to the needs and wishes of their members than either established or dissenting sects in old commonwealths display. True, many elements of traditional structure persist. Romantics on the inside and social critics on the outside often identify these with conservative interpretations of religious doctrine which seem to sanctify the privileges of urban elites. But to conceive religious organizations in cities either as united fronts for the privileged or as arenas of conflict between the elite and the disinherited is to obscure their main purpose.

The centuries-long experience of urban migration required adherents of America's older faiths to make profound changes in the structures, beliefs, and ethical rules which they had inherited. The process began in colonial Boston, New York, and Philadelphia long before the migrants whom this essay describes arrived in search of the freedom and affluence which America promised. What these new citizens demanded in their religious life, once they had determined to stay here, was the right to do what their predecessors of the three major faiths had done—to fashion religious communities suited to their own needs. They conceived those needs in new as well as in traditional terms, with earthly as well as heavenly ends in view. None should be surprised that once the right was granted or gained, the congregational and denominational organizations they founded resembled those which earlier settlers, enjoying similar freedom and like aspirations, had established for themselves.

FOOTNOTES

1. Sidney Mead's title essay for Jerald C. Brauer *et al.*, *Reinterpretation in American Church History* (Chicago, 1968), 185–192, is a thoughtful restatement of one aspect of this view.

2. Philip Gleason, *The Conservative Reformers: German-American Catholics and the Social Order* (Notre Dame, Indiana, 1968), 76–82, 91–102; Robert D. Cross, *The Emergence of Liberal Catholicism in America* (Cambridge, Mass., 1958); Aaron I. Abell, *American Catholicism and Social Action: A Search for Social Justice, 1865–1950* (Garden City, N.Y., 1960).

3. See, for example, Rudolph J. Vecoli, "Prelates and Peasants: Italian Immigrants and the Catholic Church," *Journal of Social History*, II (Spring 1969), 228–235, 248–251; Fred L. Strodtbeck, "Family Interaction, Values and Achievement," in David C. McClelland *et al.*, *Talent and Society: New Perspectives in the Identification of Talent* (Princeton, N.J., 1958), 149–158.

4. Robert D. Cross (ed.), *The Church and the City, 1865–1910* (New York, 1967), xx–xxi, 115; Henry J. Browne, "The 'Italian Problem' in the Catholic Church of the United States, 1880–1900," *United States Catholic Historical Records and Studies*, XXXV (New York, 1946), 46–72; and Testimony of Mr. Simon Wolf, past

vice-president of B'nai B'rith, in U.S. Industrial Commission, *Reports . . . Volume 15 . . .* (Washington, 1901), 245–249.

5. Theodore Saloutos, *Greeks in the United States* (Cambridge, Mass., 1965), 18–19, 97; Donald Treadgold, "The Peasant and Religion," in Wayne S. Vucenich (ed.), *The Peasant in Nineteenth Century Russia* (Stanford, 1968); Uuras Saarnivaara, *The History of the Laestadian or Apostolic-Lutheran Movement in America* (Ironwood, Mich., 1947), 13–15, summary of a more detailed work in Finnish published the same year.

6. Summaries of religious aspects of the history of minority problems in Hungary up to 1918 in Carlile A. Macartney, *Hungary and Her Successors: The Treaty of Trianon and Its Consequences, 1918–1937* (London, 1937), 83–94, 200–212, 262–275, 356–362, 380–390, agree in this point with the pro-minority views in Robert W. Seton-Watson, *Racial Problems in Hungary* (London, 1908), 224–233, 331–351, 440. Cf. Peter F. Sugar, "The Nature of Non-Germanic Societies under Hapsburg Rule," *Slavic Review*, XX (March 1963), 16–18, 17–24; and Stephen Fischer-Galati, "The Peasantry as a Revolutionary Force in the Balkans," *Journal of Central European Affairs*, XXIII (1963), 20–22.

7. Emily Greene Balch, *Our Slavic Fellow-Citizens* (New York, 1911), 121–131, 141; Ivan L. Rudnytsky, "The Role of the Ukraine in Modern History," *The Slavic Review*, XXII (June 1963), 203–215; Dmytro Doroshenko, *History of the Ukraine* (tr. Hanna C. Keller; Edmonton, Alberta, 1939), 585–594; R. Smol-Stotsky, "Centers of Ukrainian Learning," *Slavic (and East European) Review*, II (March 1924), 556–558; and Henry Baerlein, *Over the Hills of Ruthenia* (London, 1923), 9–10, 21–23, 38, 61, 88–89, 98–109, reveal effects of this awakening.

8. Balch, *Our Slavic Fellow Citizens*, 134–135, 138–140, 144–145.

9. Mark Zborowski and Elizabeth Herzog, *Life is With People: The Jewish Little-Town of Eastern Europe* (New York, 1955).

10. My student and colleague William Galush has examined at the Jagellonian University Library, Krakow, annual and other publications of *Towo Sakoty Ludowej* [The Society for Popular Education] and *Towo Oświatowy Ludowej* [The Society for General Education], both of which organizations were based in Krakow and both of which had local units in Eastern Galicia.

11. Erich Prokopowitsch, *Die Rumanische Nationalbewegung in der Bukowina und der Dako-Romanismus* (*Studien zur Geschichte der Österreichisch-Ungarischen Monarchie*, III, Graz, 1965), 35–110. Vladimir Kaye, *Early Ukrainian Settlements in Canada, 1895–1900. Dr. Josef Oeskow's Role in the Settlement of the Canadian Northwest* (Toronto, 1964), deals chiefly with Galicians from Lvov and its environs.

12. Jean Mousset, *Les Villes de la Russie Subcarpatique (1919–1938)*; *L'Effort Tchecoslovaque* (Paris, Travaux Publies par l'Institut des Études Slaves, XVIII, 1938), 17–26; Macartney, *Hungary and Her Successors*, 202–204, 209; Baerlein, *Over the Hills of Ruthenia*, 194.

13. Macartney, *Hungary and Her Successors*, 205–211. Ladislav A. Potemra, "Ruthenians in Slovakia and the Greek Catholic Diocese of Prešov," *Slovak Studies*, I (Rome, 1961), 200–219, summarizes, by villages, Czechoslovak census statistics for 1930.

14. Macartney, *Hungary and Her Successors*, 231–241; Oscar Jaszi, *The Dissolution of the Habsburg Monarchy* (Chicago, 1929), 391–393.

15. Mousset, *Les Villes de la Russie Subcarpatique*, 21–26, 67–69; Macartney, *Hungary and Her Successors*, 212.

16. A. Tiszai Ag. Hitv. Ev. Egyházkerület Értesítoje Az 1900–1901. Iskolai

Euröl [The Yearbook of the Evangelical College in Prešov, 1900–1901] (Prešov, 1901), 73–74.

17. David Friedmann, *Geschichte der Juden in Humenné vom 13 Jahrhundert bis auf die Gegenwart (Beregsas*, 1933), 48–74; see also Wilhelm Austerlitz, *Leben und Werken von Weiland Rabbi Dr.* [*Mayer*] *Austerlitz* . . . (Prešov, 1928), 8–13, 15–16, on the work of a German Rabbi from Eisenstadt in pluralistic Prešov in the years after 1860, and Nandor Szilagyi, *A. Kassai izraelita elemi iskola ertesiitoje az 1906–1907* [A Yearbook of Jewish Elementary Schools in Košice] (Košice, 1907), *passim.*

18. *Jahresbericht der Eperieser Isr. Kultusgemeinde und der Eperieser "Chewra Kadischa," 1925* (Prešov, 1925), 6–7, 12, 22–23, reflects an urbanized Jewish community's effort to preserve Hebrew culture in a situation of long-standing pluralism.

19. Macartney, *Hungary and Her Successors,* 77.

20. Interviews at Obysovce, August 26, 1968, including oral translations from the church membership records and from editions of Lutheran and Greek Catholic almanacs for Hungary published before World War I.

21. MS. Puspoki egyházlátogatás: Czékus István, 1883, Obos [Record of Bishops' visits: Czekus Istvan, 1883, Obysovce], Tiza Kerulet Mepiskolai Iratok [Archives of the Lutheran Church in Hungary], Budapest, 10, 12. Dr. Joseph Kovacs assisted me in the translation of this and numerous similar documents from the same archive.

22. Obysovce Evangelical [Lutheran] Church, ms. records of burials and of marriages.

23. Fedor Ruppeldt, "The Lutheran Church in Slovakia," in R. W. Seton-Watson (ed.), *Slovakia Then and Now: A Political Survey* (London, 1931), 196–203, 208; A. Hlinka, "The Influence of Religion and Catholicism on States and Individuals," *ibid.,* 168; and M. Emma Hovozdovič, "History and Accomplishments of the Society of St. Adalbert, Trnava, Slovakia," *Slovak Studies,* V (Cleveland, 1965), 207–211, 221–222; *A VI szab. Kir. Varosi ág hitv. evang. esperesség . . . Rendes Evi Közgyullésének Jeg Gyzökönye, 1891* [Report of the Annual Meeting of the Lutheran Seniorat in the Free Royal Cities, 1891] (Budapest, 1891), 4–5; *ibid., 1892* (Budapest, 1892) 9; *ibid., 1893* (Budapest, 1893), 11. *Evangelischer Glaubensboten für die Zips,* August 22, 1909, 145, and September 5, 1909, 153, describe a Lutheran Lyceum and an elementary boarding school for boys and girls at Kesmarok, the former of which enrolled 24 Roman Catholics and 36 Jews among a total of 214 students. The girls' school enrolled 31 Jews in its total of 102. See *ibid.,* October 17, 1909, 176–177, for annual meeting of the "Luther Society."

24. See, for the Lutherans, *Almanach cirkvi evangelickej a.v. na slovensku z rokov, 1919–1928* (Sv. Martine, 1930), 200–203, for elementary schools using the German and Slovak languages in Szepes and Saros counties. On Lutheran teachers' associations see Márton Roth, *Lövy Mór: A szepesi tanitoegyesület natvan éves totonete* [A Sixty-Year History of the Teachers' Association in Szepes] (Iglo, 1896), 7–27, describing an association which down to 1868 was exclusively Lutheran. *Evangelische Glocken. Blätter für Kirche, Schule und Haus* (Bratislava, 1889–1900), a biweekly, served the German Lutherans of the Old Kingdom, while *Evangelikus Egyház és iskola* (Bratislava, 1883–1895) served Lutherans of Magyar speech.

25. I talked with church officers at Bardejov in August 1968, and made photographs of the physical structures.

26. Mark Stolarik's work in Prešov Roman Catholic marriage and death records for the years after 1894, and Oksana Dragan's in those of Byzantine Rite

Rusins, will, when published, show a substantial and continuing migration into this town from both nearby and distant villages. My own cursory examination of marriage and death records of the Prešov Lutheran congregation showed that between 1895 and 1902, 14 of the 43 husbands married there were born outside the parish (which included the town itself and nine neighboring villages), as were 20 of the 38 communicants who died in the year 1896 at age 10 or over.

27. The foregoing is based upon observation and conversations with pastors of several of these congregations. Many of the school buildings, including a large one attached to the town's largest synagogue, are still standing. The enrollment register of the Lutheran *Volkschule* in Košice, in the pastor's office, lists occupations of students' fathers. In the 1880's, merchants and craftsmen were predominant.

28. Again, Macartney, *Hungary and Her Successors*, 383–389, 406–407, 414–416, is a convenient summary. An auto trip through the countryside was for me an enlightening experience.

29. Balch, *Slavic Fellow Citizens*, 156–157, 441, 454; Macartney, *Hungary and Her Successors*, 356–361; Gunther E. Rothenberg, "The Croatian Military Border and the Rise of Yugoslav Nationalism," *Slavonic and East European Review*, XLIII (December 1964), 35–38, 42; Louis P. M. Leger, *La Save, le Danube, et le Balkan, Voyage chez les Slovenes, les Croates, les Serbes et les Bulgares* (Paris, 1884), 62–70.

30. Macartney, *Hungary and Her Successors*, 256–281, is a splendid summary, though prejudiced in seemingly personal ways against the Germans. Josef Barton aided me in scanning constitutions and bylaws of Romanian, Magyar, and German voluntary associations organized after 1867, which lie in police records at the Sibiu state archives: we also visited several multiethnic villages together. Nicholae Iorga, *My American Lectures* (Bucharest, 1932), 36–40, argues forcefully that congregational autonomy has been for centuries a central aspect of Romanian Orthodox culture.

31. C. A. Macartney, *Hungary* (London, 1934), 152–154; cf. *ibid.*, 149–151, on Reformed Protestant identification with Magyar sentiment through the centuries.

32. Almanacs published by the several communions before 1914 are exceedingly informative on all these points, as are the congregational *matriken* (records of baptisms, marriages, and deaths) for špiš County which are in the Slovak State Archives at Levoca.

33. Andrew J. Shipman, "Greek Catholics in America," *The Catholic Encyclopedia* (15 vols.; New York, 1907–1912), VI, 745; Douglas Ollila, "The Formative Period of the Finnish Evangelical Lutheran Church in America, or Suomi Synod" (unpub. Ph.D. Dissertation, Boston University, 1962 [Ann Arbor microfilms]), 166–187.

34. Alex Simerenko, *Pilgrims, Colonists, and Frontiersmen: An Ethnic Community in Transition* (Minneapolis, 1964), 37–52; John Dzubay, *The Light of Orthodoxy, The Sixty-Sixth Anniversary of St. Mary's Russian Orthodox Greek Catholic Church* (Minneapolis, 1953), 1–20; Dimitry Gregorieff, "The Historical Background of Orthodoxy in America," *St. Vladimer's Seminary Quarterly*, V (1961), 9–12.

35. Dzubay, *The Light of Orthodoxy, passim;* Simerenko, *Pilgrims, Colonists and Frontiersmen*, 52–53. The early records of the Minneapolis seminary are on deposit with other Russian Orthodox materials at the Immigrant Archives, The University of Minnesota, but they are not yet open for research.

36. Louis A. Kalassy, "The Educational and Religious History of the Hungarian Reformed Church in the United States" (unpub. Ph.D. Dissertation, The University of Pittsburgh, 1939), 23.

37. *Ibid.*, 24–25.

38. *Ibid.*, 25–54. In a conversation at Ligonier, Pennsylvania, March 15, 1968, Alexander Doroczy confirmed the persistence as late as 1920 of bilingual parishes under Magyar priests.

39. Christine A. Galitzi, *A Study of Assimilation Among the Romanians in the United States* (New York, 1929), 88–89, 94–95; Vasile Hategan, *Fifty Years of the Romanian Orthodox Church in America* (pamphlet; Jackson, Michigan, 1959), 15–16.

40. Kalassy, "Educational and Religious History of Hungarian Reformed Church," 23–26.

41. Of many worshipful accounts, see esp. [Sister] M. Martina Tybor, "Father of American Slovaks," *Slovakia*, XVI, no. 39 (Middletown, Penna., 1966), 28–30.

42. On the South Slavs and the Finns, see Timothy Smith, "Religious Denominations as Ethnic Communities: A Regional Case Study," *Church History*, XXXV (June 1966), 207, 226. Cf. Saloutos, *Greeks in the U.S.*, 123–127, on Greeks; and, for a Polish land speculation which gave rise to a parish, Edward A. Masalewicz, *History of St. Hedwig's Congregation, Thoro, Wisconsin. Commemorating the Diamond Anniversary, 1891–1966* (Thoro, Wisconsin, 1966), 19.

43. F. S. Šušteršič, "History of the Slovenian Community of Joliet, Illinois," *Koledar Amerikanskega Slovenca, 1899* (Joliet, Ill., 1899), 94–100. Cf., on Steelton, Penna., lodges and congregations in 1900, Ivan Molek, MS "Over Hill and Dale; Autobiographical Sketches" (Mary Molek, tr. The Immigrant Archives, The University of Minnesota), 115 ff.; and the diamond jubilee volume, *Saint Vitus Church, Cleveland, Ohio* (Cleveland, 1968), 4–5.

44. *La Tribuna Italia* (Chicago), January 14, 1905, tr. in Chicago Foreign Language Press Survey, microfilm edition, reel 30.

45. John Tollino, "Solving the Italian Problem," *The American Ecclesiastical Review*, XCIX (September 1938), 48–51. On the street processions, see *La Tribuna Italia*, September 21 and August 30, 1907, and *The Chicago Chronicle*, July 24, 1905, tr. in Chicago Foreign Language Press Survey, microfilm edition, reel 30.

46. John Briggs, in a forthcoming dissertation at the University of Minnesota, will substantially revise Rudolph Vecoli, "Prelates and Peasants: Italian Immigrants and the Catholic Church," *Journal of Social History*, II (Spring 1969), 241–242, on these points.

47. Victor R. Greene, "For God and Country: The Origins of Slavic Self-Consciousness in America," *Church History*, XXXV (December 1966), 447–452.

48. Paul Fox, *The Polish National Catholic Church* (Scranton, Penna. [195?]), 22–24.

49. Boleslaw R. Bak, *A Short History of the Life and Struggles of Bishop Francis Hodur* (Scranton, Penna., 1954), 16–25.

50. *Ibid.*, 25–26. Cf. Fox, *The Polish National Catholic Church*, 24–27.

51. Bernard D. Weinrib, "Jewish Immigration and Accommodation to America," in Marshal Sklare (ed.), *The Jews: Social Patterns of an American Group* (Glencoe, Ill., 1958), 17–19. Cf., on the parallel forces at work in Zionism, Jacob Kabakoff, "The Role of Wolf Shur as Hebraist and Zionist," in Jacob R. Marcus (comp.), *Essays in American Jewish History to Commemorate the Tenth Anniversary of the Founding of the American Jewish Archives* (Cincinnati, 1958), 427, 443, 450–453.

52. I am indebted to Yeshayahu Jelinek for photocopies of *The American Israelite*, Vol. 34 (September 26, 1887), 3, and *The Cleveland Plain Dealer*, September 5, 1887, 8, cols. 1–3, which recount the history of the congregation; and of *The*

Jewish Review and Observer, 39, no. 43 (October 17, 1913), 5, and 39, no. 45 (October 31, 1913), 3, and *The Cleveland Plain Dealer*, September 8, 1880, 4, col. 4, on the history of the society. Cf., on Romanian Jewish congregations in Minneapolis, Albert I. Gordon, *Jews in Transition* (Minneapolis, 1949), 13–20.

53. Peter Roberts, *Anthracite Coal Communities: A Study of the Demography, the Social, Educational, and Moral Life of the Anthracite Regions* (New York, 1904), 209–210.

54. Peter Roberts, "The New Pittsburghers: Slavs and Kindred Immigrants in Pittsburgh," *Charities and the Commons*, XXI (January 2, 1909), 550–551. Cf. Peter Roberts, *The New Immigration* (New York, 1913), 200–201.

55. George Dolak, *A History of the Slovak Evangelical Lutheran Church in the United States of America, 1902–1927* (St. Louis, Mo., 1955), 14–15, 24–26, 31, 33–43, 51–53.

56. *Ibid.*, 53, 63–67; cf., on Old World background of lay prerogatives, esp. the office of inspector, Ruppeldt, "The Lutheran Church in Slovakia," 193.

57. Kalassy, "Educational and Religious History of Hungarian Reformed Church," 23–26, 65–72, 132.

58. Theodore F. Abel, *Protestant Home Missions to Catholic Immigrants* (New York, 1933).

59. Records in the office of the Hungarian Lutheran Church, Cleveland, reveal parts of this development.

60. Galitzi, *Assimilation Among Romanians*, 101–102; Antonia Mangano, *Sons of Italy, a Social and Religious Study of the Italians in America* (New York, 1917).

61. Smith, "Religious Denominations as Ethnic Communities," 212–215.

62. See selection of historical documents reprinted in *Glasilo K.S.K.J.* (Chicago) for April 7, 1915; *Amerikanski Slovenec* (Tower, Minnesota), April 20, 1894, 2; Matija Šavs, "Monsignor Fran Josef Buh," *Ave Maria Koedar*, X (1923).

63. The paragraph is based on interviews with a dozen-odd Slovenian pioneer priests and laymen, and with local and national officers of K.S.K.J.

64. Tybor, "Father of American Slovaks," 25–32. For the lay impulse in the early days of Jednota, see *Memoirs of the Golden Jubilee of the St. Cyril and Methodius Society, Branch 3, First Catholic Slovak Union, Minneapolis, Minnesota* (pamphlet, Minneapolis, 1938), 12, 18–21.

65. Tybor, "Father of American Slovaks," 33–38.

66. Bak, *Life and Struggles*, 35–39; the newspaper quotation is on p. 39.

67. *Ibid.*, 44–46. A microfilm edition of the weekly newspaper *Strasz*, organ of the Union, is at the Immigrant Archives, the University of Minnesota.

68. Greek Catholic Union of the U.S.A., *Jubilee Almanac* (Munhall, Penna., 1967), 34–44, quotes extensively from the minute books. Files of the newspaper *Amerkansky Russky Viestnik*, which began publication in 1892, are on microfilm at the University of Pittsburgh Library. Cf. Ukrainian National Association, *Jubilee Book . . . In Commemoration of the Fortieth Anniversary of its Existence* (Jersey City, N.J., 1933), 194–198, and *passim*. Andrew J. Shipman, "Greek Catholics in America," *Catholic Encyclopedia*, VI, 745–749, is based on the almanacs of all parties.

69. Shipman, "Greek Catholics in America," 749; Andrew J. Shipman, "Our Russian Catholics: The Greek Ruthenian Church in America," in *The* [Russian Orthodox] *Messenger*, XLII (November 1912), 664–667.

70. Stephen E. Gulovich, *Windows Westward: Rome, Russia, Reunion* (New York, 1947), 124–135; Walter C. Warzeski, "Religion and National Consciousness in

the History of the Rusins of Carpatho-Ruthenia and the Byzantine Rite Pittsburgh Exarchate" (unpub. Ph.D. Dissertation, The University of Pittsburgh, 1964), 118–139.

71. Shipman, "Greek Catholics in America," *Catholic Encyclopedia*, VI, 748; John A. Duskie, *The Canonical Status of the Orientals in the United States* (Washington, D.C., 1928), 30–42; and Stephen C. Gulovich, "The Rusin Exarchate in the United States," *The Eastern Churches Quarterly*, VI (October–December 1946), 459–486, *passim*.

72. Gregorieff, "Historical Background of Orthodoxy in America," 41; Warzeski, 269–306; *American Carpatho-Russian Youth Annual*, IX (Johnstown, Penna., 1957), *passim*; Michael Lacko, S.J., "The Churches of the Eastern Rite in North America," *Unitas*, XVI (1964), 104–108.

GERALD N. GROB

Mental Illness, Indigency, and Welfare: The Mental Hospital in Nineteenth-Century America

During the first half of the nineteenth century Americans were to face a variety of social problems, a few of which were familiar and many that were novel. Some of these problems were dealt with in terms of past experience; others required entirely new solutions. But whatever the issue, it was clear that many Americans were convinced that no problem was so difficult that it could not be solved; no evil was so extreme as to be ineradicable; no person was so sinful as to be unredeemable; no situation was so far gone as to be beyond control; and no illness was so severe as to be incurable.

Such optimistic views resulted in the appearance of literally dozens of reform movements. Some of these movements—abolitionism in particular—were anti-institutional in that they sought the destruction of an allegedly immoral institution. Other people recognized heretofore unmet needs that had arisen out of neglect or social change and urged the founding of new institutions to deal with these needs. The result was often the creation of structures to further education, to reform criminals, and to provide care for dependent groups of all varieties. Especially notable was the movement to establish a universal system of public mental hospitals that would provide care and treat-

I am greatly indebted to the National Institute of Mental Health, United States Public Health Service, which supported this study by Grant 12743.

ment for all mentally ill persons irrespective of their condition or ability to pay.[1]

To most individuals, a mental hospital hardly merits the attention of a historian interested in understanding the structure and dominant characteristics of nineteenth-century American society. A hospital, after all, is simply a place where sick or injured persons are given medical or surgical care. Thus a mental hospital is presumably an institution treating persons suffering from various forms of mental illness. In this sense there is little difference between a general and a mental hospital; the latter is a specialized version of the former. Similarly, the function of the psychiatrist is precisely that of the general physician or specialist, namely, to diagnose the nature of the illness and to prescribe appropriate remedies.

In reality, of course, a mental hospital is not like any other hospital, nor is mental illness like other illnesses. Consider, for example, some of the questions that have arisen within the corpus of psychiatric knowledge. What is the *nature* of mental illness? At what point do individual differences in behavior become classified as mental illness? Who defines the normative standards that determine whether or not an individual is healthy? The answer to these questions clearly involved far more than medical considerations. Moreover, public mental hospitals performed a variety of roles not always related to illness per se, some of which were thrust on them by a society that lacked effective means of accomplishing certain ends. Mental hospitals were not only entrusted with the function of caring for sick individuals, but often with the custody of the aged and the indigent as well as with people whose behavior was deemed socially disruptive by the community. Care and treatment of the mentally ill was frequently a function of individual and group values not directly related to scientific or medical considerations. Above all, it was inextricably involved with a series of socioeconomic factors, in part because of the high costs of protracted institutionalization, and in part because a significant proportion of patients came from lower-class and minority ethnic backgrounds. Neither American psychiatry nor the mental hospital, then, can be studied solely in medical terms; both developed out of the interaction of complex social, economic, and intellectual forces, and must be viewed within an institutional framework related to the broader problems of welfare, indigency, and especially the behavioral norms of society.

The origins of the mental hospital were rooted not merely in contemporary medical or psychiatric definitions of mental illness, but also in the social, cultural, and economic fabric of society. As early as the eighteenth century, the mental hospital—its forerunner often being a local institution such as a jail, a workhouse, or a poorhouse—had a dual purpose. It was to protect the community against individuals who ostensibly threatened its security and well-being, and it was also entrusted with the responsibility of providing therapeutic care for some patients and humane custodial care for others. In the former case the hospital owed its allegiance to the community, in the latter to the welfare of the individual patient. Such divided allegiance was to give the mental hospital an ambivalent character, for it was by no means unusual to find the two roles in conflict. Indeed, it must be emphasized that one of the major functions of the mental hospital, at least in its beginnings, was the protection of the community and the care of groups unable to provide for themselves because of their illness. It is significant that the mentally ill were originally classified with indigent and dependent groups of all varieties, including vagrants, criminals, unemployed, and aged people lacking resources for survival. While the mental hospital had already taken its modern form by the midnineteenth century, it would never completely outgrow its early character as an undifferentiated welfare institution.[2]

An analysis of the mental hospital within this broader framework offers a unique opportunity to understand the peculiar nature of American institutions in the nineteenth century. Much of the history of these decades has been written from the point of view of the reformers themselves. Consequently, the nature and functions of an institution like the mental hospital have either been ignored or simply viewed as a beneficent creation of socially-minded individuals and groups to meet the needs of the American people. When the mental hospital is perceived from a different angle—especially that of the groups that it served—its function appears in a somewhat new light. When we consider that the majority of patients in public mental hospitals came from impoverished groups, we can begin to grasp more fully the nature of group and class relationships in America as well as the workings of a welfare system.

URBAN ORIGINS
OF THE MENTAL HOSPITAL

The mental hospital fulfilled not only a medical but a welfare role as well, since the overwhelming majority of its patients came from low socioeconomic groups concentrated in urban areas. The origins of the American mental hospital, then, were closely related to the emergence of an urban-industrial society in the nineteenth century. That such institutions appeared initially in an urban rather than a rural setting is not too difficult to understand. Urbanization was responsible for a heightened social sensitivity toward deviant behavior and mental illness; it had also caused informal mechanisms for the care of mentally ill persons to break down. Consequently, there were demands that special provision be made for the mentally ill, not only to protect the general public, but to provide as well for the care and welfare of such persons. Pressure for institutionalization probably came from lower-class immigrant families which were unable to care for their mentally ill members, since it was common for both parents and children to work. (Whether the level of tolerance of abnormal behavior varied by class or ethnic group is difficult to ascertain because of the paucity of source material on this subject.)

Individuals who took the lead in founding mental hospitals in the United States were recruited (as they were abroad) from the ranks of the middle class, and included not only physicians, but clergymen and reformers active in a variety of occupations. The close interconnection between these reformers and Protestantism, particularly middle-class Protestantism, was especially evident. A number of Protestant thinkers had developed a theology based on the doctrines of the free individual and a moral universe, which, when applied to society, resulted in the transformation of Evangelical Protestantism into a radical social force seeking the abolition of restraints that bound the individual and hindered his self-development. All persons, they forcefully argued, were under a moral law that gave them a responsibility for the welfare of their fellow man.[3] As a result of the teachings and agitation of these leaders, virtually dozens of reform movements appeared during the first half of the nineteenth century, including movements to better the condition of the insane, the inebriate, the blind, the deaf, the slave, the convict, and other less fortunate members of society. Some of these reform movements were intended to help those individuals and groups powerless to change their condition; others had broader social and humanitarian goals, including abolition of war, the remaking of society by establishing model utopian communities, and the founding of a free universal system of public education.

Many of the intended beneficiaries of reform, it should be noted, were either from the lower classes or included a disproportionately high percentage of lower-class members. Responsibility for the welfare of these groups was generally entrusted to individuals in more fortunate straits, if only because of the inability of dependent groups to change significantly the conditions under which they lived. The slave, for example, was in no position to effect his own liberation. Nor could mentally ill individuals agitate for the establishment of therapeutic and custodial institutions. Reformers had to have both leisure time and some sort of income base that would permit them to pursue careers as social activists, so reform movements drew much of their inspiration and personnel from the ranks of the middle class and well-to-do. The results of such a situation were not difficult to fathom. The reform movements of this period were imbued with a middle class outlook; reformers, rejecting most radical proposals, worked to eliminate the more glaring defects in a society whose basic framework they accepted without any major reservations.[4]

In many respects mental hospitals—which were among the fruits of early nineteenth-century reform—reflected the values and aspirations of their supporters. So long as they accepted a homogeneous population consisting of native-born patients, their structure and inner workings fulfilled the functions for which they had been established. When, however, patient populations became more heterogeneous in nature and included a large proportion of individuals from immigrant backgrounds, mental hospitals found themselves beset by problems for which there were few precedents and for which their staffs were largely unprepared. Consequently, their growth and development, as we shall see, occurred in ways alien to the ideals of those individuals and groups responsible for their founding.

Between 1800 and 1860, institutions providing care and treatment for the mentally ill began to proliferate rapidly. In 1820 there were fewer than ten mental hospitals in the United States, some of which were private institutions intended largely for patients from relatively affluent circumstances. By the time of the Civil War, on the other hand, virtually every state had one or more public institutions that catered to the various groups.

Oddly enough, the growth of the mental hospital preceded the emergence of psychiatry as both a scientific discipline and a profession. This is a fact of paramount importance, for it meant that psychiatric thought and practice was not the dominant factor in shaping the structure and function of institutions. On the contrary, psychiatry was to a large extent molded and shaped by the institutional setting within which it was born and grew to maturity. Many of the dominant characteristics of psychiatric ideology were simply rationalizations of existing conditions within mental institutions as well as popular attitudes. Since the mental hospital, at least during its formative years, was an institution created by society to cope with abnormal behavior and to provide care and treatment for a variety of dependent groups, the result was that psychiatry, although a scientific and medical discipline, reflected the role assigned to it by society. This is not to imply that psychiatrists *consciously* or *deliberately* attempted to define their discipline within such a context, or to justify institutionalization on other than medical grounds. It is only that psychiatry, perhaps because of the philosophical and scientific complexities posed by the very concept of mental illness and the difficulties of providing adequate definitions, was shaped by external social, psychological, economic, and intellectual influences.

THE PSYCHIATRISTS' MODEL OF MENTAL ILLNESS

Let us first consider some of the dominant currents in early and midnineteenth-century American psychiatric thought.[5] Although assuming that mental illness was a somatic illness—usually involving lesions of the brain (regarded as the organ of the mind)—psychiatrists had much difficulty in providing empirical evidence to prove this assertion. Consequently, they identified mental illness by observing a person's outward behavioral symptoms. Identification in these terms, however, caused some difficulties. In some cases the criteria for diagnosing cases of mental illness seemed clear. Hallucinations, smearing of feces, and dramatic neurological symptoms associated with advanced cases of syphilis, to cite only a few examples, seemed to place the individual clearly within an ill category. Other types of abnormal behavior, however, were less distinct. The normative standard of the psychiatrist at times became of considerable significance, if only because it entered into his relationship with the individual under his care. This normative standard was not only a physical one that involved proper organic functioning; in some respects it was culturally defined and often placed a premium on middle-class, Protestant, and agrarian values. Such values were to play a significant internal role in mental institutions, particularly those which catered to heterogeneous groups coming from quite different social, economic, and cultural backgrounds.

Defining mental illness in terms of outward behavioral manifestations and yet claiming that it was organic in nature created serious theoretical problems. Yet these did not pose insurmountable barriers, nor were these issues neglected or ignored. On the contrary, American psychiatrists, borrowing heavily from European and English intellectual traditions, constructed an imposing theoretical model of mental illness that minimized internal contradictions.

The model of mental illness held by early and midnineteenth-century American psychiatrists was an interesting blend of ideas, including sensationalist and associationist psychology, phrenology, and behaviorism, as well as ideas borrowed from the Scottish Common Sense school of philosophy. Most psychiatrists began with Lockean assumptions; they believed that knowledge came to the mind through sensory organs. If the senses (or the brain) became impaired, false impressions would be conveyed to the mind, leading in turn to faulty thinking and abnormal behavior. Phrenology, which gained a foothold in the United States after being imported from Europe in the 1820's and 1830's, provided a means of connecting mind and matter. The mind, according to phrenological theorists, was not unitary, but was composed of independent and identifiable faculties localized in different regions of the brain. To this theory they added the postulates of a behavioristic psychology and a belief that individuals could deliberately and consciously cultivate different faculties by following the natural laws that governed physical development and human behavior.

From phrenology psychiatrists took the idea that the normal and abnormal functioning of the mind was dependent on the physical condition of the brain.[6]

Such reasoning provided psychiatrists with a medical model of mental illness that still permitted them to account for psychological or environmental factors. This sort of model was by no means unique to psychiatry, for it was widely accepted by a variety of "empirics" enjoying considerable popularity during these decades. Mankind, reasoned many psychiatrists, was governed by certain immutable natural laws that provided a guide to proper living. If an individual followed these laws, a healthy mind and body would result. If these laws were violated, however, the physical organs would not develop or function normally. In other words, mental illness, though somatic in nature, could have psychological as well as physical causes: the abnormal behavior of the individual (who possessed free will) was the primary cause of insanity, leading as it did to impairment of the brain (the organ of the mind). Mental illness, therefore, was in some respects self-inflicted; by ignoring the laws governing human behavior the individual placed himself on the road to disease.

This model of mental illness appeared, at least superficially, to be neutral insofar as socioeconomic factors were concerned. But when psychiatrists took up the problem of etiology, their own values became clear. In hundreds of reports, books, articles, and speeches, they listed what they believed to be the leading causes of disease. These included intemperance, overwork, domestic difficulties, striving after wealth, and, above all, the pressures of an urban, industrial, and commercial civilization (which was not natural to the human organism) upon the individual. Psychiatrists, in other words, saw mental illness as the inevitable consequence of behavior that represented a departure from their own normative model. Like many Americans during the first half of the nineteenth century, they held a romantic and sentimental ideal of mankind which seemed threatened by developments that augured ill for the future. Thus they extolled agrarian virtues and denigrated sharply urban life. "We find," wrote Thomas S. Kirkbride, one of the most influential psychiatrists of his time, "as was always believed, that no life is so generally conducive to health as one that, like agriculture, gives active exercise in the open air, that none is so likely to be troubled with nervous affections, and none so generally to be preferred for those who are constitutionally disposed to this class of infirmities." [7] As Isaac Ray, the most dominant figure in American psychiatry in the midnineteenth century, put it, mental illness was "the price we pay for civilization." [8] In many ways the thought of most midnineteenth-century psychiatrists was not fundamentally dissimilar from other critics of American society whose values were notably hostile to social and economic change and who bitterly resented the newly emerging urban–industrial social order. A substantial part of psychiatric theory, therefore, was but a reflection of a particular social ideology, even though it was presented as an empirical and objective statement of fact.

Before 1850, most psychiatrists did not necessarily draw pessimistic conclusions from their view of the causes of mental illness. Influenced by the faith in progress and optimism that was characteristic of their generation, they believed that mental illness could be conquered. From their theoretical model they drew the conclusion that mental illness was as curable as, if not more curable than, other somatic illnesses. If derangements of the brain and nervous system produced the various types of insanity, the removal of such causal abnormalities should result in the disappearance of the symptoms and, therefore, the disease. The prognosis for insanity was thus quite hopeful (provided that the mentally ill were treated before the disease had entered the chronic stage).

Along with an optimistic view about the prognosis of mental illness went a well-defined and carefully thought-out therapeutical system. In general, the treatment of insanity in mental hospitals during the first half of the nineteenth century fell into two broad categories: medical and moral (i.e., psychological). The former, intended to build up the patient physically, included tonics, laxatives, baths, exercises, and special diets, as well as narcotics to quiet active and violent patients. Medical treatment, however, was but a prelude to what was known in the nineteenth century as moral therapy (corresponding somewhat to contemporary milieu therapy). While susceptible to many interpretations, moral therapy meant kind, individualized care in a small hospital, with occupational therapy, religious exercises, amusements and games, and in large measure a repudiation of all threats of physical violence and an infrequent resort to mechanical restraint. Moral therapy in effect involved reeducating the patient in a proper moral atmosphere. Hospitalization was an indispensable feature of moral treatment, for it separated the patient from his former environment and placed him in an institution controlled by the psychiatrist, who presumably could provide all of the beneficent influences that would promote recovery.[9]

Such—at least in brief—was the theoretical and therapeutic outlook of the young psychiatric profession. These optimistic views about the nature and prognosis of mental illness seemed to be confirmed by the results achieved in a number of mental hospitals. During these years the patient population tended to come from the same background and environment as psychiatrists. Most mental hospitals accepted relatively few lower-class immigrants and members of minority ethnic groups, if only because such groups (as late as 1840) constituted a very small percentage of the total population. The fact that hospital populations, especially in the 1830's and 1840's, remained relatively small also contributed to the maintenance of an internal therapeutic atmosphere. In addition, many of the early figures prominent in American psychiatry had entered the field because of humanitarian and religious convictions about being of service to those less fortunate than themselves. In their eyes a hospital superintendency was a response to the same calling that led some to enter the ministry or others to spend their lives furthering the elimination of institutional evils. Many early superintendents brought to their vocation, therefore, a personality-type that promoted beneficent personal relationships with patients. Consequently, the feelings between physician and patient were often harmonious and trusting. The recovery rates of this period—even by the best of contemporary standards—were imposing. Hospital superintendents claimed that up to 90 per cent of recent cases (defined as cases of less than one year's duration) were curable, given prompt and proper treatment. One follow-up study, which took nearly 20 years to complete and included nearly 1,200 patients, demonstrated that 58 per cent of those discharged as recovered remained well until their death and never again required treatment in a mental hospital. It is therefore possible to infer that the internal environment of many institutions, both public and private, coupled with the kind, humane, and optimistic attitudes of many psychiatrists toward their patients, produced a psychological climate which had a marked therapeutic impact upon inmates.[10]

Between 1830 and 1850, therefore, the character of some mental hospitals seemed to be undergoing a sharp transformation. This is not to imply that social and class factors played no role within mental hospitals, or that such institutions had abandoned completely their custodial and welfare character. The organization of hospitals reflected to some degree the social and class structure of American society. At public mental hospitals it was not uncommon for patients to be classified on the basis of socioeconomic differences and then separated physically, with individuals of a higher status being given more privileges and better care.[11] Indeed, few Americans questioned the practice of providing more affluent individuals with superior care. Moreover, it was the general practice of the majority of public institutions to either exclude or provide separate (but unequal) facilities for black insane persons. Most psychiatrists never seriously entertained the thought of treating blacks and whites as equals. With some exceptions, most hospitals prior to 1860 would not accept black patients, since separate facilities had not been provided for by the state legislatures.[12]

Nevertheless, because class differentials and patterns of deference in the United States were becoming less distinct in the early nineteenth century (as compared with Europe), the mental hospital began to deemphasize its older and more traditional role as a custodial and undifferentiated welfare institution by the middle of the century. Swept up in their enthusiasm to extend the benefits of hospitals to all Americans irrespective of their backgrounds, lay reformers such as Dorothea L. Dix and Horace Mann set to work to convince Americans of the desirability of founding an extensive system of public mental hospitals. In general, their efforts met with considerable success. By the third quarter of the nineteenth century virtually every state had one (and in most cases several) mental hospital supported by public funds and caring for all patients regardless of their ability to pay.

SOCIETAL FACTORS
INFLUENCING MENTAL HOSPITALS

The transformation of the mental hospital that seemed to be taking place was more apparent than real. Within a short time a variety of factors converged to force the mental hospital into its older and more familiar role as an undifferentiated welfare and custodial-type institution. The result was that psychiatry, like innumerable other disciplines, continued to develop after 1850 within an institutional framework that placed a premium on extrascientific and extra-medical factors. In order to understand the social context within which psychiatry developed, it is necessary to sketch the social, economic, and intellectual forces that played major roles in determining the structure and functions of mental hospitals after 1850.

At the same time that the state mental hospital was coming into existence, the United States was undergoing extraordinarily rapid growth. The rise of industry, the quickening pace of urbanization, and, above all, the increase in population, combined to alter the character of American society. Along with these changes went an increase in the number of the mentally ill. Mental illness, as has already been noted, was somewhat less likely to be tolerated in highly populated than in rural areas; the result was a rapid rise in the number of institutionalized individuals. The growth of public mental hospitals was further stimulated by the fact that such institutions often played a variety of roles, including that of a home for aged persons unable to care for themselves or to be cared for by their families, and a haven for unemployed and dependent individuals apparently incapable of surviving the vicissitudes of life without some type of aid. "The feeling is quite too common," complained the head of the New York City Lunatic Asylum in 1861, "that a lunatic asylum is a grand receptacle for all who are troublesome." [13] His feelings were echoed by other superintendents who recognized the ambiguous role that their institutions played, but were unable, because of legal and practical difficulties, to alter a distressing state of affairs. [14]

The increase in patient populations at public mental hospitals usually included a disproportionate number from the lower classes, including minority and immigrant groups. At the New York City Lunatic Asylum, Blackwell's Island, in 1850, 534 patients were immigrants (of whom virtually every one was destitute) and only 121 native-born, despite the fact that the foreign-born constituted slightly less than half of the city's total population. [15] While hospitals in the Northeast generally had the highest proportion of foreign-born patients, virtually all hospitals in the United States had a disproportionate number of lower-class immigrants. [16]

The high proportion of foreign-born (especially the Irish) in public mental hospitals was by no means an isolated or unique phenomenon. At the New York City House of Refuge (an institution that cared for delinquent and neglected children), for example, a disproportionate number of inmates were Irish. Not only did the Irish—to take the most important immigrant group in the three decades prior to the Civil War—provide a far higher percentage of admissions to a variety of welfare institutions, but their death rate during cholera epidemics as well as during normal periods was significantly higher than that of native groups. The reason for this distressing state of affairs is not difficult to understand. The Irish arrived in the United States in a state of almost total destitution; their impoverished situation contributed to the disruption of the family unit. Fathers were often compelled to accept jobs as unskilled laborers away from their families on such projects as canal building, where the mortality rate from what officials called "canal fever" was abnormally high. The marginal economic situation of most Irish families, moreover, encouraged mothers and children to seek employment in order to survive. Some immigrants turned to criminal activities, thereby making the crime rate in Irish slums appreciably higher than in other areas of the city. The result was a vicious cycle of poverty, disease, and delinquency among Irish immigrants, who then entered welfare and penal institutions at a significantly higher rate than their proportion in the general population.[17]

The growing heterogeneity of patients in public mental institutions began to undermine the basis of moral therapy, which assumed a close and trusting relationship between doctor and patient. Most psychiatrists had come from a middle-class background and shared its values. So long as they treated patients with similar values, no conflict ensued. But when these psychiatrists began to deal with patients—especially impoverished immigrants—whose customs, culture, traditions, and values diverged sharply from their own, they were unable to communicate in the easy manner to which they had grown accustomed. Even those psychiatrists who genuinely sympathized with the plight of less fortunate individuals found themselves in a difficult situation, for they recognized their inability to create the type of therapeutic relationship that was essential if the patient was to be helped. "Our want of success in the treatment of their mental diseases," observed Isaac Ray with both chagrin and sympathy,

> is in some degree to be attributed, I imagine, to our inability to approach them in a proper way. . . . Modes of address like those used in our intercourse with our own people, generally fall upon their ears like an unknown tongue, or are comprehended just enough to render the whole misunderstood, and thereby excite feelings very different from such as were intended.[18]

As the patient populations at public institutions began to include a disproportionate number from lower-class groups, the feelings of optimism that mental illness could be conquered began to undergo a subtle transformation. While psychiatrists continued to affirm their belief that mental illness was curable, they also began to argue that lower-class, particularly immigrant lower-class, groups had far less of a chance of recovering than other groups. Edward Jarvis, who undertook a major investigation of the problems of mental illness for the Massachusetts legislature in 1854, drew an equation between poverty, mental illness, and immigrants (especially the Irish). After lengthy study he came to the conclusion that the interests of the Commonwealth could best be served by having separate institutions for native and foreign-born patients, since the latter had a far more dismal prognosis than the former and required custodial as opposed to therapeutic care.[19] Jarvis' sentiments were by no means uncommon. "It is the experience of all, I believe, who have had the care of the insane Irish in this country," wrote the superintendent of the Maine Insane Hospital in 1852, "that they, from some cause or other, seldom recover." [20]

Most psychiatrists and public officials were aware of the complex relationships between lower-class immigrants and mental illness, and the consequent implications for public welfare policy. Some advocated adoption of a policy that would limit the migration of socially undesirable groups; others advocated separate institutions for immigrants that would not drain the public treasury. The solutions advanced made it evident that most individuals holding responsible positions had what could be described as an ambiguous attitude toward impoverished immigrants. Those who saw America as a land of equal opportunity and a haven for the oppressed sympathized with the new-comers and looked forward to the day when the immigrant would share in the benefits of American society. Others saw in such groups a threat to American institutions and a danger to the peculiar genius of the American people. "Never was a sovereign State so grievously burdened," observed the *Boston Medical and Surgical Journal* in speaking about the growing number of foreign paupers in public hospitals in the Bay State. "The people bear the growing evil without a murmur, and it is therefore taken for granted that taxation for the support of the cast-off humanity of Europe is an agreeable exercise of their charity." [21]

Hostility toward lower-class immigrant groups tended to be fairly widespread in the three decades prior to the Civil War, although this hostility was often tempered by a faith that America could somehow assimilate them. Such attitudes often played a part in shaping public welfare policies. Indeed, the twin problems of pauperism and mental illness seemed so serious that a number of state legislatures authorized lengthy investigations in the 1850's and 1860's in order to help them devise policies that would cope with the mounting social problems involved, and also would safeguard the financial interests of their con-stituents.[22]

By the third quarter of the nineteenth century it had become evi-dent that the state mental hospital was an institution that provided relatively inexpensive care for a patient population drawn largely from poor and minority ethnic groups. The fact that a large percentage of patients came from such groups proved a crucial element in shaping public policy toward mental hospitals. Most Americans were ambi-valent in their attitude toward poor and indigent groups. While they held feelings of sympathy and compassion toward less fortunate groups that often resulted in widespread charitable and philanthropic activi-ties, many Americans attributed poverty to improvident and evil behavior on the part of the individual. A person was poor because of his own laziness and character defects, not because of any structural defects in society that prevented self-improvement and upward mobil-ity. Society's obligation toward the poor, therefore, was minimal.[23]

The result of such polar attitudes (often held in conjunction with each other despite their outwardly contradictory nature) was a reinforcement of the image of the state mental hospital as both a medical and a welfare institution. In the former case the function of the hospital was to provide medical care for groups that could not afford treatment of an illness of such long duration. The hospital thus fulfilled the humanitarian obligation of society to care for its sick and needy. In the latter case, the hospital provided care for individuals whose diseased mind was a product of their own shortcomings (a view reflected in psychiatric etiological theories). In this sense, the justification for its existence was the protection it afforded the community against socially disruptive and threatening behavior by lower-class groups. Consequently, public mental hospitals were often classified in the same general category as welfare and penal institutions and tended to receive the same level of funding as these other institutions, thereby undermining their therapeutic and medical roles and reinforcing a custodial function.

A brief analysis of some municipal institutions that served the cities of New York, Boston, and Philadelphia provides convincing evidence of some of these generalizations. By the early nineteenth century New York City had the largest urban population in the United States, including a significant proportion of impoverished immigrant groups. Its citizens were forced to confront a variety of social problems at a relatively early date. Prior to 1839 New York had maintained a "Lunatic Asylum" as part of its almshouse and prison complex. Conditions at that time were so depressing that the Commissioners charged with responsibility for the institution described it in the following words:

> [The Lunatic Asylum] yet remains, a witness of the blind infatuation of prejudice and miscalculation; affording to a class more deserving commiseration than any other among the afflicted catalogue of humanity, a miserable refuge in their trials, undeserving the *name* of an "Asylum," in these enlightened days. These apartments, under the best superintendence, cannot be made to afford proper accommodations for the inmates, much less can they be so, when (as your Commissioners first saw them,) the same neglect and want of cleanliness witnessed in other parts of the building, was visible here; and a portion of the rooms seemed more like those receptacles of *crime,* "to whose foul mouth no healthsome air breathes in," than tenements prepared for the recipients of an awful visitation of Divine Providence, justly considered the worst "of all the ills that flesh is heir to." [24]

In 1839 the Lunatic Asylum was separated from the other municipal welfare and penal institutions and given autonomy as a mental hospital. The change in structure, however, proved more apparent than real. Conditions at the New York City Lunatic Asylum remained an open scandal for the next three or four decades. The number of patients increased from 278 in 1840 to about 1,300 in 1870, even though the physical plant was incapable of caring for anywhere near that number. Convicts at the penitentiary on Blackwell's Island were employed as attendants in order to save money; the diet of patients remained far below even the minimum standard for a hospital; epidemics were not infrequent; and political considerations often dictated hospital policy.[25] In general, the hospital was used as a dumping ground for impoverished, mentally ill immigrants. In 1856, for example, 297 out of 366 patients admitted were foreign-born, and little pretense was made about providing therapy.[26] Conditions at the New York City Lunatic Asylum, Ward's Island (opened 1871) and the Kings County Lunatic Asylum (which grew out of the poorhouse) were scarcely better.[27] Indeed, a committee appointed to investigate abuses at the latter institution reported in 1877 that the Lunatic Asylum was "a reproach and disgrace to Kings County." [28]

Nor was the situation in Philadelphia different from that in New York. Prior to 1859 there was no formal structure within the municipal almshouse specializing in the care of the pauper insane. Such persons were simply kept in the almshouse along with the indigent, the sick, and the aged. After 1859 the Insane Department of the Philadelphia Almshouse came into existence, but conditions did not appreciably improve. The majority of inmates were impoverished immigrants (in 1863, 501 inmates were foreign-born, as contrasted with only 360 native Americans), and by 1874 the department had over 1,000 residents.[29] The distinguished English psychiatrist John C. Bucknill—by no means an unfriendly critic—could find few good things to say about the institution when he visited it during his American tour in 1875.[30]

The municipal mental hospitals in New York City and Philadelphia had grown out of an undifferentiated welfare and penal institution. Boston, on the other hand, established an entirely new and independent hospital to deal with cases of mental illness. The Commonwealth of Massachusetts, undoubtedly the pioneer state in developing a system of public charitable and welfare institutions during the nineteenth century, founded the prototype of the modern mental hospital when the State Lunatic Asylum at Worcester opened in 1833. By 1837, however, the Worcester institution had become so crowded that its officials began to return mentally ill persons to their original place of residence. In order to deal with this problem, the municipal authorities decided to establish their own institution, and in 1839 the Boston Lunatic Hospital received its first patients.[31]

Nevertheless, the history of the Boston institution was essentially the same as that of the New York and Philadelphia hospitals. The hospital rapidly filled up with indigent and immigrant patients, and all pretenses at providing therapy were soon abandoned. In 1846, 90 out of 169 patients were foreign-born, and the hospital had in effect become an institution for lower-class groups whose behavior was deemed socially unacceptable.[32] "Our inmates," complained the superintendent in 1850, "are principally foreigners; and of this class a large majority are from Ireland. . . . [The Irish] are generally found to be uneducated, superstitious, and jealous; and, being unused to the manners and customs of our countrymen, they are very suspicious of us; and therefore it is quite difficult to win their confidence, and of course, to treat them satisfactorily." [33] More than 20 years later the secretary of the Massachusetts Board of State Charities condemned the institution as completely unfit for either therapy or custody.[34] But despite a clear recognition by Boston community leaders as early as the 1850's that drastic action was required, the hospital continued to serve as a custodial institution for lower-class groups.[35]

The transformation of the state mental hospital into a custodial lower-class institution was accompanied by the rise of exclusive private institutions caring for middle- and upper-class patients. Although many of the mental hospitals established prior to 1850 were private institutions, they had always attempted to make at least some provision for poorer and indigent patients. The Friends' Asylum in Pennsylvania, the Bloomingdale Asylum in New York, the Butler Hospital in Rhode Island, McLean Asylum in Massachusetts, and the Hartford Retreat in Connecticut had all accepted indigent cases in their early days. But as various states and municipalities opened public institutions, these private hospitals began to limit their patient body to those groups willing and able to pay high charges for superior care. Such a policy was usually defended on the grounds that individuals were en-

titled to receive the type of care to which they had been accustomed
in their private lives, and also that they should not be forced to mix
with groups with whom they had little in common.[36] As the superintendent of the Hartford Retreat remarked in 1867:

> It is evident that different classes will require different styles of ac-
> commodation. The State should provide for its indigent insane,
> liberally and abundantly, all the needful means of treatment, but
> in a plain and rigidly economical way. Other classes of more abun-
> dant means will require, with an increased expenditure, a corre-
> sponding increase of conveniences and comforts, it may be of lux-
> uries, that use has made essential. This common sense rule is
> adopted in other arrangements of our social life—our hotels, water-
> ing places, private dwellings and various personal expenditures.
>
> In my opinion, it would be a very good general rule which
> should give to every case of insanity, when placed under treat-
> ment, all those essential, and not injurious or excessively costly in-
> dulgences which previous habits, tastes and even prejudices may
> require. Certainly it is evident that the more ignorant, unrefined
> and uncultivated do not require the same surroundings and ap-
> pliances as the intelligent, cultivated and refined.[37]

By the time of the Civil War most of the private mental hospitals
had effectively excluded lower-class patients. This development had an
unforeseen consequence. So long as the mental hospital had not distinguished (at least in theory) between paying and nonpaying patients, the movement to upgrade conditions at public facilities had
remained strong. When public institutions began to serve a predominantly lower-class population, there was a noticeable diminution in
the pressure to improve conditions. The famous midnineteenth-century
reformer, Samuel Gridley Howe, speaking for the trustees of the
Worcester States Lunatic Hospital in 1854, warned of the dangers
of a dual system of private and public hospitals. "The multiplication
of these private establishments," he pointed out, "would be a great
evil. It is one that may be prevented by making public hospitals
unobjectionable residences for patients of any class; but it will be
difficult of cure, if once it obtains footing." [38] Howe's warning went
unheeded, and the state mental hospital became identified more and
more in the public eye as a welfare-type institution caring for lower-
class and minority groups.

The role of the state mental hospital as more of a welfare than a medical institution was given further legitimacy in the 1860's by the growth of administrative structures established by most states and a few larger urban areas as part of a drive to develop a comprehensive public policy on indigency. During the first half of the nineteenth century local and state governments had become increasingly sensitive to the problems arising out of poverty. These problems were exacerbated not only by the general increase in population, but by the arrival in the United States of large numbers of impoverished immigrants, many of whom remained in the major urban areas. The concentration of indigent groups in localized geographical areas limited the possibility of maintaining an informal and voluntary approach to welfare. By the 1860's welfare had grown sufficiently complex to induce a number of states to attempt to formulate a more rational and efficient means of administering their charitable institutions. The search for a new policy was often dominated by a sincere desire to create a situation in which the need for welfare would no longer exist, for few Americans defended public charity as the solution to poverty.

The process of rationalization and centralization of welfare became evident in the larger urban areas, which were often among the first to confront complex social problems. As early as 1849, for example, the governing body of New York City passed an act that placed responsibility for its welfare institutions (including the mental hospital, penitentiary, almshouse, and other similar organizations) in the hands of a Board of Governors. Eleven years later a new body—the Commissioners of Public Charities and Correction—replaced the older one. In both reorganizations it was clear that economy and efficiency were among the dominant motives in establishing a legal agency vested with full authority and responsibility for welfare and indigency. The goal was not the perpetuation of state support of public welfare, but rather its elimination. How this objective would be reached, however, was not clear.[39]

After 1863, when Massachusetts established the first Board of State Charities, a number of states founded central agencies vested with the responsibility of overseeing public welfare institutions and developing uniform policies to promote efficiency. Most of these agencies had loose authority over the operations of state mental hospitals as well as other institutions caring for various indigent groups.

From the very beginning of the movement to rationalize welfare, then, the state mental hospital was considered as much an institution for poor and indigent groups as it was a medical facility. The relationship between pauperism and mental illness was further reinforced by the manner in which most state boards of charities approached the problems of indigency, illness, and welfare. In general, their members (who shared the traditional American ambivalence toward poverty and a feeling that the cure for poverty lay in the inculcation of proper attitudes in the individual) often related crime, indolence, alcoholism, vagrancy, and poverty with mental illness. The latter was not considered to be a consequence of the former, but the general framework established by the words and deeds of state boards was such as to create in the mind of the public a relationship between poverty and mental illness.[40] Since virtually no state or city government was ever able to develop effective policies and institutions to cope with the problems of the poor and indigent, few welfare institutions—including the mental hospital—ever lived up to the optimistic expectations of their supporters.

As the state mental hospital became an institution serving a predominantly lower-class population, its inner structure began to undergo important changes. The role of the psychiatrist, for example, slowly altered. When hospitals were small (fewer than 200 patients in residence) and cared for a relatively homogeneous patient population, psychiatrists found their own ideology sufficiently broad to provide a rationale for treatment. But when they were confronted with large numbers of patients coming from socioeconomic and ethnic backgrounds unfamiliar to them, they found themselves incapable of surmounting the barriers of class and ethnic differences. The result was a sharp decline in the effectiveness of moral therapy, which rested on the assumption that therapist and patient would have a trusting and harmonious relationship. As custodial considerations increased because of the influx of large numbers of lower-class patients, the tendency was for the demands of the mental hospital as a social system to outweigh the needs of therapy. Psychiatrists became hospital managers and administrators; their primary concern was with maintaining order and rationality in a large complex institution owing a greater allegiance to society than to the welfare of the individual patient.[41]

Outside pressures further compounded the difficulties faced by institutional psychiatrists. The hospital, for example, played a dual role, both therapeutic and custodial. As long as it remained small, it was easy for the psychiatrist to combine both of these roles. The gradual growth in size of hospitals, however, made this more difficult. Superintendents were increasingly confronted with the necessity of having to sacrifice one of these goals in order to achieve the other. Given a choice, therapeutic considerations might have been dominant. But the superintendent could not be concerned only with the welfare of the patient; he had to take into account the demands of society for protection against those who ostensibly menaced the community. As more lower-class patients entered hospitals, such pressures increased, and therapeutic considerations consequently receded into the background.[42]

Under these circumstances psychiatry's immersion in administrative problems was hardly surprising. An intricate social institution like a mental hospital required formal mechanisms to ensure order and efficiency; formal mechanisms, in turn, often defeated the aim of moral treatment, which was based on the ability of the physician to manipulate the environment of the individual and group as the need arose. Custodial considerations merely reinforced administrative concerns, for custody required a tight and efficiently run institution governed by rational and clearly defined procedures. In effect, the rise of what may be conveniently designated as administrative psychiatry reflected the dominance of an institution providing custodial care for poor and indigent groups.

SOCIETY IN MICROCOSM

The history of the mental hospital in the nineteenth century offers an illustrative case study of the ironies and ambiguities posed by complex social problems, and the reaction of a society to these problems. Convinced of their moral obligation to help individuals afflicted with mental disease, a group of reformers set to work to found a comprehensive system of public institutions which would provide care and therapy, and therefore help to eliminate or contain once and for all this dreaded malady. While they succeeded in their efforts to found institutions, they were never fully aware that within a brief period of time the care and treatment of the mentally ill would become inextricably intertwined with broader problems of welfare and indigency, as well as conflicting attitudes and values on the part of society, therapists, and patients. The mental hospital in its early years was simply conceived as an institution that would help all groups; it was not intended in any way to provide differential or discriminatory care. Within a short time, however, other factors—most of which could not have been predicted or anticipated—converged to transform the state mental hospital into more of an undifferentiated welfare-type institution. In this sense the mental hospital reflected the broad dimensions of the larger society in which it existed, with all of the strengths—as well as the weaknesses and shortcomings—of that society.

FOOTNOTES

1. A brief word about the terminology used in this essay. I have generally used the word "psychiatrist" even when referring to the early part of the nineteenth century, when the psychiatrist was known either as a hospital superintendent or an alienist. Similarly, I have not attempted to distinguish between an "asylum" and a "hospital," for both usually performed the same functions. By the same token, I have used the terms "insane" and "insanity" interchangeably with "mentally ill" and "mental illness." Although the former two have acquired an odious reputation, they were perfectly good terms in the past. My usage, therefore, is historical and not intended to imply any derogatory connotation. After all, it is quite probable that the term "mental illness" will in the future be looked down upon with the same disfavor as "insanity" is at present.

2. One of the best brief discussions of the origins of the modern hospital is George Rosen's essay, "The Hospital: Historical Sociology of a Community Institution," in *The Hospital in Modern Society*, Eliot Freidson (ed.) (New York, 1963), 1–36. See also W. K. Jordan, *Philanthropy in England 1480–1660: A Study of the Changing Pattern of English Social Aspirations* (London, 1959), and George Rosen, "Social Attitudes to Irrationality and Madness in 17th and 18th Century Europe," *Journal of the History of Medicine and Allied Sciences*, XVIII (July 1963), 220–240. The development of attitudes toward mental illness and the rise of the mental hospital in Europe are explored in a collection of the essays of George Rosen entitled *Madness in Society: Chapters in the Historical Sociology of Mental Illness* (Chicago, 1968), and Michel Foucalt's thought-provoking work, *Madness and Civilization: A History of Insanity in the Age of Reason* (New York, 1965).

3. This theme is especially evident in the careers of the Rev. Louis Dwight, secretary of the Boston Prison Discipline Society (an organization that helped to focus attention on the confinement of deranged individuals in jails and poorhouses), Dorothea L. Dix, who was instrumental in helping to establish several dozen or more state mental hospitals between the 1840's and the 1870's, Samuel B. Woodward, who served as the first president of what is today the American Psychiatric Association, and Samuel Gridley Howe, who was active in a variety of re-

form movements. For Dwight's views see William Jenks, "Memoir of Rev. Louis Dwight," in *Reports of the Boston Prison Discipline Society,* 3 vols. (Boston, 1855), I, 5–41, and the *Annual Reports* of the Society, I–XXIX (1826–1854). Dix's attitudes are revealed in her famous memorials to the legislatures of well over a dozen states. Two typical examples are the *Memorial Soliciting a State Hospital for the Insane, Submitted to the Legislature of Pennsylvania, February 3, 1845* (Harrisburg, 1845), and the *Memorial Soliciting Adequate Appropriations for the Construction of a State Hospital for the Insane, in the State of Mississippi, February, 1850* (Jackson, 1850). For Woodward's career see Gerald N. Grob, "Samuel B. Woodward and the Practice of Psychiatry in Early Nineteenth-Century America," *Bulletin of the History of Medicine,* XXXVI (September–October 1962), 420–443, and the Woodward Papers in the American Antiquarian Society, Worcester, Mass. On Howe see his article "Insanity in Massachusetts," *North American Review,* LVI (January 1843), 171–191. The Howe papers are in Houghton Library, Harvard University, Cambridge, Mass.; there is also an excellent biography by Harold Schwartz entitled *Samuel Gridley Howe: Social Reformer 1801–1876* (Cambridge, 1956).

4. Some recent historians have begun to reinterpret the nature of reform movements in American history by arguing that their basic objective was a form of social control of lower-class and minority groups. Michael Katz, *The Irony of Early School Reform: Educational Innovation in Mid-Nineteenth Century Massachusetts* (Cambridge, 1968), hints at this in his important and insightful study by utilizing the point that reform was very often "imposed" on lower class groups by middle and upper class groups. Also within this newer tradition are Clifford S. Griffin's *Their Brothers' Keepers: Moral Stewardship in the United States, 1800–1865* (New Brunswick, 1960), and Roy Lubove, *The Professional Altruist: The Emergence of Social Work as a Career, 1880–1930* (Cambridge, 1965). Obviously, all institutions perform the function of social control to some extent. That their establishment came about because of a desire to institute controls is less obvious. Moreover, institutions serve a variety of purposes, and to single out one in particular (especially when it is by no means evident that this purpose is of primary significance) and deprecate others is an unjustifiable technique that more often than not arises out of an activistic and moralistic commitment on the part of the historian.

5. Norman Dain's book, *Concepts of Insanity in the United States, 1789–1865* (New Brunswick, 1964), is the most authoritative recent discussion of American psychiatric thought. The classic work on the mentally ill in the United States is Albert Deutsch's *The Mentally Ill in America: A History of Their Care and Treatment from Colonial Times* (New York, 1937), a work that still remains one of the best single surveys on the subject, despite the fact that its perspective is somewhat dated. There is also useful information in J. K. Hall *et al., One Hundred Years of American Psychiatry* (New York, 1944), although this book suffers because most of its contributors were psychiatrists who lacked a sense of history.

6. The best discussions by American psychiatrists on the nature of mental illness are to be found in the annual reports of mental hospitals (the *American Journal of Insanity,* which began publication in 1844, was for many years the only periodical of its kind). For typical examples of concepts of mental illness, see the following: Amariah Brigham, "Insanity and Insane Hospitals," *North American Review,* XLIV (January 1837), 91–121; Worcester State Lunatic Hospital, *Annual Report,* VII (1839), 65–66, X (1842), 64–65 (Samuel B. Woodward); John M. Galt, *The Treatment of Insanity* (New York, 1846); Edward Jarvis, "Causes of Insanity," *Boston Medical and Surgical Journal,* XLV (November 12, 1851), 289–305; New

Jersey State Lunatic Asylum, *Annual Report,* VI (1852), 22–28 (H. A. Buttolph);
Butler Hospital for the Insane, *Annual Report,* 1853, 11–29 (Isaac Ray); Maine
Insane Hospital, *Annual Report,* XIV (1854), 25 (Henry M. Harlow); Northern Ohio
Lunatic Asylum, *Annual Report,* I (1855), 12 (L. Firestone); McLean Asylum for the
Insane, *Annual Report,* XLII (1859), in Massachusetts General Hospital, *Annual
Report,* 1859, 26–31 (John E. Tyler); Alabama Insane Hospital, *Annual Report,* II
(1862), 20–22 (Peter Bryce); Utica State Lunatic Asylum, *Annual Report,* XXI
(1863), 34–40, XXVII (1869), 16–23, XXIX (1871), 62–63, XXXII (1874), 23–24 (John
P. Gray). John D. Davies, *Phrenology: Fad and Science: A 19th-Century American
Crusade* (New Haven, 1955), is an excellent study dealing with the relationship of
phrenology to American society in the ante-bellum decades.

    7. Pennsylvania Hospital for the Insane, *Annual Report,* XXII (1862), 15. For
a similar statement by John S. Butler, superintendent of the Connecticut Retreat
for the Insane, see Connecticut Retreat for the Insane, *Annual Report,* XXIV
(1848), 16–17.

    8. Butler Hospital for the Insane, *Annual Report,* 1852, 19. For similar ex-
pressions of opinion, see the following: Connecticut Retreat for the Insane, *Annual
Report,* XXII (1846), 24 (John S. Butler); Indiana Hospital for the Insane, *Annual
Report,* I (1849), 15 (Richard J. Patterson); Edward Jarvis, "On the Supposed Increase of Insanity," *American Journal of Insanity,* VIII (April 1852), 363–364; South
Carolina Lunatic Asylum, *Annual Report,* 1853, 16 (Daniel H. Trezevant); Virginia
Eastern Asylum, *Report,* 1853–1854/1854–1855, 18–23 (John M. Galt). See also the
discussion of this issue at the sixteenth annual meeting of the Association of Medical Superintendents of American Institutions for the Insane in the *American Journal of Insanity,* XIX (July 1862), 47–81.

    9. For fuller discussions of moral treatment see Dain, *Concepts of Insanity,
passim,* and Gerald N. Grob, *The State and the Mentally Ill: A History of Worcester State Hospital in Massachusetts, 1830–1920* (Chapel Hill, 1966), 43–79.

    10. Worcester Lunatic Hospital, *Annual Report,* XLVII (1879), 14–15, XLIX
(1881), 12–14, L (1882), 13–14, 57, LI (1883), 14, 59, LII (1884), 59, LIII (1885), 63,
LIV (1886), 64, LV (1887), 64, LXI (1893), 70.

    11. As one superintendent remarked: "It is certainly exceedingly unpleasant,
to be almost compelled to associate with those whose education, conduct and moral
habits, are unlike and repugnant to us. Because persons are insane, we must not
conclude that they always lose the power of appreciating suitable associates, or are
insensible to the influence of improper communications. This is by no means true.
It is among our greatest perplexities here, to know how to quiet the complaints of
those whose delicacy is shocked, whose tempers are perturbed, and whose quietude
is annoyed by improper and unwelcome associates." [Eastern] Kentucky Lunatic
Asylum, *Annual Report,* 1845, 24. Such sentiments, which were widespread among
hospital officials, usually led to differential care and therapy based on class and
status. For evidence on this point see the following: Worcester State Lunatic Hospital, *Annual Report,* VII (1839), 89, XII (1844), 88–89, XV (1847), 33, XXVI (1858),
60, XXXVI (1869), 73, 83; South Carolina Lunatic Asylum, *Annual Report,* 1871,
27–29; Taunton State Lunatic Hospital, *Annual Report,* XV (1868), 14–15; Vermont
Asylum for the Insane, *Annual Report,* XXIV (1860), 12; Insane Asylum of Louisiana, *Annual Report,* 1866, 5; Massachusetts Board of State Charities, *Annual Report,* X (1873), 19.

    12. For the policy of some states prior to 1860 regarding the treatment of
black insane persons, see the following: Kentucky Eastern Lunatic Asylum, *Biennial Report,* XXXIII/XXXIV (1856/1857), 24; Maryland Hospital for the Insane,

Annual Report, 1851, 7–8; Mississippi State Lunatic Asylum, *Annual Report*, IV (1858), 11–12, V (1859), 24; South Carolina Lunatic Asylum, *Annual Report*, 1844, 5, 1850, 12, 1851, 8–9, 1858, 12, 1860, 13; Tennessee Hospital for the Insane, *Biennial Report*, I (1852/1853), 21; Virginia Western Lunatic Asylum, *Annual Report*, XVII (1844), 26–27, XVIII (1845), 7–8, 29–30, XXI (1848), 4–5, 32–34; Virginia Eastern Asylum, *Annual Report*, 1848, 23–29, 1849, 5–6; American Freedmen's Inquiry Commission Mss. Collection, Houghton Library, Harvard University, Cambridge, Massachusetts.

The segregation in or exclusion of blacks from mental hospitals was by no means a unique phenomenon. Indeed, a comparative study of mental hospitals with other welfare-type institutions would show much the same pattern. Witness, for example, the following description of conditions among black inmates at the New York City Almshouse in 1837: "In the Building assigned to colored subjects, was an exhibition of squalid misery and its concomitants, never witnessed by your Commissioners in any public receptacle, for even the most abandoned dregs of human society. Here, where the healing art had objects for its highest commiseration, was a scene of neglect, and filth, and putrefaction, and vermin. Of system or subordination, there was none. The same apparel and the same bedding, had been alternately used by the sick, the dying, the convalescent, and those in health, for a long period, as we were informed by inmates. The situation of one room was such, that it would have created contagion as the warm season came on; the air seeming to carry poison with every breath. It was a scene, the recollections of which are too sickening to describe." *Report of the Commissioners of the Alms House, Bridewell and Penitentiary* (1837), New York City Board of Aldermen, *Document No. 32* (1837), 204.

13. New York City Lunatic Asylum, Blackwell's Island, *Annual Report*, 1861, 18.

14. See, for example, New Hampshire Asylum for the Insane, *Annual Report*, XXIII (1864), 16; Longview Asylum, *Annual Report*, XII (1871), 7–8; Insane Asylum of California, *Annual Report*, XI (1863), 29.

15. New York City Lunatic Asylum, Blackwell's Island, *Annual Report*, 1858, 12.

16. At Longview Asylum (Ohio) in 1861, 353 out of 521 patients were foreign-born. At Taunton State Lunatic Hospital (Massachusetts), comparable figures for 1854 were 118 out of 330; at the Wisconsin State Hospital for the Insane the figures for 1872 were 221 out of 365. Longview Asylum, *Annual Report*, II (1861), 13; Taunton State Lunatic Hospital, *Annual Report*, I (1854), 32; Wisconsin State Board of Charities and Reform, *Annual Report*, II (1872), 291. An analysis of several public institutions in Massachusetts in the early 1880's revealed much the same picture. Out of 1,932 patients classified as to parentage, 1,132 were of foreign parentage (including 800 of Irish descent). Massachusetts State Board of Health, Lunacy, and Charity, *Annual Report*, IV (1882), lxix. These figures were representative of the situation throughout the United States.

17. Robert S. Pickett, *House of Refuge: Origins of Juvenile Reform in New York State, 1815–1857* (Syracuse, 1969), 1–20.

18. Butler Hospital for the Insane, *Annual Report*, 1849, 32. George Chandler, superintendent of the Worcester State Lunatic Hospital, had much the same comment. "Most of the foreigners are Irish," he reported in 1847. "The want of forethought in them to save their earnings for the day of sickness, the indulgence of their appetites for stimulating drinks, which are too easily obtained among us, and their strong love for their native land, which is characteristic with them, are the fruitful causes of insanity among them. As a class, we are not so successful in

our treatment of them as with the native population of New England. It is difficult to obtain their confidence, for they seem to be jealous of our motives; and the embarrassment they are under, from not clearly comprehending our language, is another obstacle in the way of their recovery." Worcester State Lunatic Hospital, *Annual Report*, XV (1847), 33.

19. *Report on Insanity and Idiocy in Massachusetts, by the Commission on Lunacy, Under Resolve of the Legislature of 1854.* Massachusetts *House Document No. 144* (1855), *passim.*

20. Maine Insane Hospital, *Annual Report*, XII (1852), 19. For similar expressions of opinion see the following: *American Journal of Insanity*, VII (October 1850), 176, XIV (July 1857), 79–80, XXVII (October 1870), 157–159; Taunton State Lunatic Hospital, *Annual Report*, III (1856), 18, 25–26.

21. *Boston Medical and Surgical Journal*, XLV (January 28, 1852), 537. See also *ibid.*, XLVI (February 25, 1852), 85; *New Orleans Medical and Surgical Journal*, IV (July 1847), 133–135, VI (November 1849), 399–402; and the Conference of Charities, *Proceedings*, III (1876), 162–185.

22. See, for example, the *Report on Insanity and Idiocy in Massachusetts, op. cit.;* Thomas R. Hazard, *Report on the Poor and Insane in Rhode Island; Made to the General Assembly at Its January Session, 1851* (Providence, 1851); *Report of Select Committee Appointed to Visit Charitable Institutions Supported by the State, and all City and County Poor and Work Houses and Jails.* New York *Senate Document No. 8* (January 9, 1857); Sylvester D. Willard, *Report on the Condition of the Insane Poor in the County Poor Houses of New York.* New York *Assembly Document No. 19* (January 13, 1865); *Report of the Commissioner to Visit Almshouses and Asylums, for the Insane Poor, Indigent Persons, or Paupers.* Rhode Island *Public Document No. 20, Appendix* (1865). These are only a few examples of the concern of legislatures with policy issues raised by poverty and mental illness. In other states investigations took a variety of forms, including establishment of central boards to coordinate welfare policies.

23. One of the most perceptive analyses of poverty was made by Thomas R. Hazard in a report to the legislature of Rhode Island concerning the poor and insane in the state. In words that could have easily been written by a contemporary radical, Hazard pointed out that to most Americans poverty was a crime. "I believe," he wrote, "that it was a maxim of some ancient sage or philosopher— *that, that government was the best, which gave equal protection to its citizens, without distinction* of persons.

"If I understand the theory of our own republican institutions, they are sought to be based on this maxim. Our laws are not intended to be framed in reference to persons, but to things. It supposes the administrators of the law, to be deaf and blind to all but the facts relating to the subject before them. Under the same circumstances the same judgment is to be meted to the rich and the poor, the little and the great. It is a maxim of our laws that the *punishment shall not exceed the offence.* The Constitution of our country declares '*that cruel and unusual punishment shall not be inflicted.*'

"Now admitting the extremity of poverty to be a crime—in the name and in behalf of the pauper poor of the State, in all seriousness, I respectfully ask you as conservators of the people of Rhode-Island, to define what the punishment of that crime shall be." Thomas R. Hazard, *Report on the Poor and Insane in Rhode Island, op. cit.*, 92.

24. *Report of the Commissioners of the Alms House* (1837), *op. cit.*, 208.

25. *Report of the Resident Physician of the Alms-House Establishment.* New

York City Board of Aldermen, *Document No. 119* (May 8, 1843), 1403–1409; New York City Lunatic Asylum, Blackwell's Island, *Annual Report*, 1848, in New York City Alms House Commissioner, *Annual Report*, 1848, 119–120; New York City Lunatic Asylum, *Annual Report*, 1851, in New York City Governors of the Alms House, *Annual Report*, III (1851), 98; New York City Lunatic Asylum, Blackwell's Island, *Annual Report*, 1856, 5, 11–12, 1865, 3–15; New York State Commissioner in Lunacy, *Annual Report*, II (1874), 22–24, III (1875), 10–16; James C. Hallock to Dorothea L. Dix, July 21, 1870, Dix Papers, Houghton Library, Harvard University, Cambridge, Mass.

26. New York City Lunatic Asylum, Blackwell's Island, *Annual Report*, 1856, 6, 1870, 6–8.

27. James C. Hallock to Dorothea L. Dix, December 25, 1871, January 22, 1873, Dix Papers; New York Board of State Commissioners of Public Charities, *Annual Report*, VI (1872), 64–71; New York City Asylum for the Insane, Ward's Island, *Annual Report*, III (1874), 13–19, IV (1875), 21–25; New York State Commissioner in Lunacy, *Annual Report*, II (1874), 28–44, III (1875), 25–64.

28. *Report of the Investigation of the Board of Supervisors of Kings County, in the Matter of Alleged Abuses at the Lunatic Asylum, Together with the Evidence Taken by the Committee*. Presented April 19, 1877 (New York, 1877), 6.

29. "The Insane Poor of Philadelphia," *Journal of Prison Discipline and Philanthropy*, II (January 1846), 61–66; N. D. Benedict to Dorothea L. Dix, February 26, 1859, Dix Papers; Insane Department of the Philadelphia Almshouse, *Annual Report*, XIII (1863), 5–6, XIV (1864), 49, XV (1865), 42–44; *American Journal of Insanity*, XXI (January 1865), 419; Pennsylvania Board of Commissioners of Public Charities, *Annual Report*, VI (1875), 379; Charles K. Mills and Roland G. Curtin, "Notes on the History and Organization of the Philadelphia Hospital since 1860," in Charles K. Mills (ed.), *Philadelphia Hospital Reports. Volume I. 1890* (Philadelphia, 1890), 332.

30. John C. Bucknill, *Notes on Asylums for the Insane in America* (London, 1876), 42–43. Bucknill's description of conditions in New York City were in the same vein. He also thought that New York City and Philadelphia had probably the worst asylums in the United States. See *ibid.*, 40–41, 46–53, and John C. Bucknill to Henry I. Bowditch, January 23, 1877, Countway Medical Library, Harvard Medical School, Boston, Mass.

31. For the origins of the Boston Lunatic Hospital see the *Memorial of the Board of Directors for Public Institutions in Relation to the Lunatic Hospital. 1863*. Boston *City Document No. 11* (1863), 21–23.

32. Boston Lunatic Hospital, *Annual Report*, VII (1846), 11. See also *ibid.*, IV (1843), 15–16, VI (1845), 16–17, IX (1848), 3–4.

33. *Ibid.*, XI (1850), 15.

34. Massachusetts Board of State Charities, *Annual Report*, X (1873), 12.

35. *Report of a Committee of the Board of Directors for Public Institutions in Relation to the Condition of the Lunatic Hospital, Made May 23, 1862* (Boston, 1862), 5–6; *Memorial of the Board of Directors for Public Institutions in Relation to the Lunatic Hospital. 1863*, Boston *City Document No. 11* (1863), 23–39. The situation in New York City, Philadelphia, and Boston was not unique. Similar conditions existed in Chicago. See Roswell Park, "The Medical Charities of Cook County, Illinois," Conference of Charities and Correction, *Proceedings*, VII (1880), li.

Massachusetts, in addition to establishing the first comprehensive system of public mental hospitals, also used its state almshouses to care for chronic indigent cases of mental illness. The State Almshouse at Tewksbury by 1874 had over 300 insane inmates, and conditions there were about as substandard as those at any of the other charitable and penal institutions in the state. See Massachusetts State Almshouse at Tewksbury, *Annual Report*, III (1856), 5–6, V (1858), 4–5, VIII (1861), 14, XIII (1866), 6–7, XXI (1874), 9–13, 33–34; Massachusetts Board of State Charities, *Annual Report*, I (1864), 265–266, II (1865), 149–150, III (1866), 150–151, X (1873), liv, XII (1875), lviii–lx.

36. Connecticut Retreat for the Insane, *Annual Report*, XXIX (1853), 23, XXXV (1859), 21–25, XLII (1866), 20–21, XLIV (1868), 22, XLV–XLVI (1869–1870), 5–22, L (1874), 13; Butler Hospital for the Insane, *Annual Report*, XV (1861), 3–6, 1870, 7–9, 11–12; McLean Asylum for the Insane, *Annual Report*, in Massachusetts General Hospital, *Annual Report*, 1833, 2–8, 1839, 10–18, 1841, 20–21, 1844, 12–13, 1846, 19, 1851, 15–22, 1853, 20, 1868, 34–37; Massachusetts Board of State Charities, *Annual Report*, I (1864), 85–86; New York Hospital and Bloomingdale Asylum, *Annual Report*, 1851, 15–16, 1852, 16–17, 1856, 19–20, 1862, 11, 1866, 17–25; Friends' Asylum for the Insane, *Annual Report*, XXIV (1841), 4–5, XXXII (1849), 5–6, XLVIII (1865), 7–8, LI (1868), 4–5.

37. Connecticut Retreat for the Insane, *Annual Report*, XLIII (1867), 33. The superintendent of the Butler Hospital thought that the policy of keeping paupers at public institutions rather than private hospitals was a beneficent one. "I think it will result in increased usefulness and a firmer hold upon the interest and good will of the people." John W. Sawyer to Dorothea L. Dix, September 16, 1870, Dix Papers.

38. Worcester State Lunatic Hospital, *Annual Report*, XXII (1854), 12.

39. See New York City Governors of the Almshouse, *Annual Report*, I (1849), *passim*, and New York City Commissioners of Public Charities and Correction, *Annual Report*, I (1860), *passim*.

40. In the third annual report of the Massachusetts Board of State Charities, to cite only one example, Franklin B. Sanborn (secretary of the Board and one of the most prominent figures in public welfare in the latter half of the nineteenth century) wrote as follows: "The four topics of this last division of this Report are so closely connected as to make any exact separation of them difficult. Pauperism and Crime; Pauperism and Disease; Crime and Disease; Insanity and Crime; Insanity and Pauperism,—how frequent are the permutations and combinations of these evils! Like Sin and Death, in Milton's allegory,—what are they indeed but forms of sin and death?—they breed from each other a mixed and woeful progeny." Massachusetts Board of State Charities, *Annual Report*, III (1866), 204.

For other examples of discussions by boards of charities, see the following: Massachusetts Board of State Charities, *Annual Report*, I (1864), 409–410, II (1865), 213–220, IV (1867), 129–144, V (1868), xix–xl, IX (1872), xvii–l; Rhode Island Board of State Charities and Correction, *Annual Report*, I (1869), 23–34; North Carolina Board of Public Charities, *Annual Report*, II (1870), 2–44; Illinois Board of State Commissioners of Public Charities, *Biennial Report*, IV (1875–1876), 195–209; Pennsylvania Board of Commissioners of Public Charities, *Annual Report*, II (1871), lxxxiv–lxxxviii.

For a contemporary discussion of the need for central supervision of state charities see Franklin B. Sanborn, "The Supervision of Public Charities," *Journal of Social Science*, I (June 1869), 72–87.

41. The dilemma facing a hospital superintendent was well illustrated by the following statement of George Chandler, superintendent of the Worcester State Lunatic Hospital, in the late 1840's: "I confess my inability to do justice to my feel-

ing in its management. I cannot sufficiently keep myself acquainted with the various departments to act understandingly. I cannot know the daily changes in the symptoms of 450 patients—the operations on the farm and in the workshops—the domestic operations—direct the moral treatment—conduct the correspondence with friends—wait upon such visitors as demand my personal attention and various other things which are daily pressing upon the attention of this Superintendent. Many of these matters in large Hospitals must be attended to, if attended to at all, by those who do not and cannot act so faithfully and understandingly as the Superintendent could and would." George Chandler, "On the proper number of patients for an institution. . . ." Undated Mss. (*ca.* late 1840's), Chandler Papers, American Antiquarian Society, Worcester, Massachusetts.

42. For a case study of the evolution of a somewhat typical state mental hospital in the nineteenth century, see Grob, *State and the Mentally Ill, passim.* James Leiby's *Charity and Correction in New Jersey: A History of State Welfare Institutions* (New Brunswick, 1967), is a revealing and informative state study.

RICHARD SENNETT

Middle-Class Families and Urban Violence: The Experience of a Chicago Community in the Nineteenth Century

꘡꘡꘡

Unlike the other writers in this volume, I have sought in this essay to make historical judgments that cannot be proved in a rigorous way. Historians using sociological tools find in quantitative methods and constructs the possibility of achieving great precision in describing the past; for sociologists like myself who turn to the historical frame, a rather opposite possibility exists. For us, the complexities and contradictions found in the "actual time" of human life suggest ways in which abstract concepts can be made more dense and more subtle, and so less precise, in their evocation of men's experience.

This study seeks the hidden connections between two seemingly disparate phenomena in a quiet middle-class neighborhood of Chicago in the late nineteenth century: the family patterns of the people of the community and the peculiar response made by men living there to the eruption of violence in their midst. In imagining how the structure of family life was related to the character of men's reaction to violence, I have tried to recapture some of the subtlety of what it was like to be a middle-class city dweller during this era of rapid urban growth.

Reprinted from Stephan Thernstrom and Richard Sennett, eds., *Nineteenth-Century Cities: Essays in the New Urban History* (New Haven: Yale University Press, 1969), pp. 386–420, by permission of the publisher. Copyright © 1969 by Yale University Press.

In the years 1886 and 1888 an epidemic of violence broke out in this quiet neighborhood of Chicago. The striking feature of this epidemic lay not in the violent events themselves but in the reaction of shopkeepers, store clerks, accountants, and highly skilled laborers to the disorder suddenly rampant among their sedate homes. Their reaction to violence was impassioned to an extent that in retrospect seems unwarranted by events; indeed, it is the contrast between the limited character of the disorder and the sense residents had of being overwhelmingly threatened by anarchy that suggests that the response could have been a product of larger, seemingly unrelated social forces, such as the structure of family life.

THE COMMUNITY SETTING

The scene of the disturbance, which I shall name Union Park, was an area centered on the near West Side of Chicago around a rather large park formally landscaped in the early 1850s. Like most of the middle and lower middle-class neighborhoods of American industrial cities in the later nineteenth century, the area was considered so nondescript that it was never given a special name, as were the richer and poorer sections of Chicago. Its people were the forgotten men of that era, neither poor enough to be rebels nor affluent enough to count in the affairs of the city. For a quarter century, from 1865 to 1890, Union Park epitomized that tawdry respectability of native-born, lower middle-class Americans that Dreiser was to capture in the early sections of *Sister Carrie,* or that Farrell would later rediscover in the bourgeois life of Catholic Chicago.

The beginnings of Union Park, when Chicago was a commercial town rather than a diverse manufacturing city, were much grander. For in the 1830s and 1840s it was a fashionable western suburb on the outskirts of town, separated by open land from the bustle of the business district and the noisome, unhealthy river at the heart of the city. A change in the pattern of commercial land investment, the filling in of a swamp on the edge of Lake Michigan by Potter Palmer, and the growth of a manufacturing district to the south of Union Park in the years after the Civil War led fashionable people to desert the old suburb for newer, more magnificent residences along the lake shore of

Chicago. In their place, in the 1870s, came people of much lesser means, seeking a respectable place to live where rents and land were becoming cheap. Union Park for these new people was a neighborhood where they could enjoy the prestige of a once-fashionable address, and even pretend themselves to be a little grander than they were. "The social Brooklyn of Chicago," Mayor Harrison called it; "a place where modest women became immodest in their pretensions," wrote another contemporary observer of the area. For twenty-five years, the old holdings were gradually divided up into little plots, and native-born Americans—who were the bulk of the migrants to the cities of the Midwest before the 1880s—rented small brick houses or a half floor in one of the converted mansions.

During the middle 1880s, it was in modest, cheerless Union Park that a series of unexpected events broke out. A bloody encounter between laborers and police took place on its borders during the Haymarket Riot of 1886, to be followed eighteen months later by a series of highly expert robberies in the community, a crime wave that culminated in the murder of a leading Union Park resident. Union Park reacted by holding a whole class—the poor, and especially the immigrant poor—responsible for the course of unique and rather narrow events.

THE HAYMARKET BOMBING

Certain people, mostly foreigners of brief residence among us, whose ideas of government were derived from their experience in despotic Germany, sought by means of violence and murder to inaugurate a carnival of crime. *F. H. Head, official orator at the unveiling of the Haymarket Square Statue for policemen slain in the riot, reported in the* Chicago Daily Tribune, *May 31, 1889, p. 5.*

During the 1870s and early 1880s the warehouse district of Chicago grew in a straight line west, across the Chicago River, up to the edge of Union Park. The haymarket constituted the farthest boundary of this district; it was the dividing line between the residences and neighborhood stores of Union Park and the warehouses of Chicago's growing central city. Haymarket Square itself was enclosed by large buildings and the Des Plaines Street Police Station was just off the Square. It was hardly a place to engage in clandestine activity, but, for a peaceful meeting, the Square was an ideal forum, since it could accommodate roughly 20,000 people.[1]

The common notion of what happened on May 4, 1886, is that a group of labor unionists assembled in Haymarket Square to listen to speeches and that, when the police moved in to break up the meeting, someone in the crowd threw a bomb, killing and wounding many policemen and bystanders. This account is true as far as it goes, but explains little of what determined the event's effect on the community and city in the aftermath.

The people who came to the meeting were the elite of the working class, those who belonged to the most skilled crafts;[2] they were hardly the "dregs" of society. The crowd itself was small, although it had been supposed that events in Chicago during the preceding days would have drawn a large gathering. On May 3, demonstrations had been organized in the southwestern part of the city against the McCormick Works, where a lockout of some union members had occurred. The police had responded with brutal force to disperse the crowd. Later that same night, at a number of prescheduled union meetings, it was resolved to hold a mass meeting at some neutral place in the city.[3]

A small group of Socialist union leaders, led by August Spies and Albert Parsons, decided the time was ripe for a mass uprising of laboring men; the moment seemed perfect for an expression of labor solidarity, when large numbers of people might be expected to rally to the cause as Spies and Parsons understood it—the growth of Socialist power. Haymarket Square was the obvious choice for a neutral site. Posters were printed in the early hours of the next day and spread throughout the city.

When Parsons and Spies mounted the speakers' rostrum the next night in Haymarket Square, they must have been appalled. Instead of vast crowds of militants, there were only a thousand or so people in the Square, and, as speaker after speaker took his turn, the crowd dwindled steadily. The audience was silent and unmoved as the explanations of the workers' role in socialism were expounded, though there was respect for the speakers of the kind one would feel for a friend whose opinions grew out of a different sphere of life. Yet as the meeting was about to die out, a phalanx of policemen suddenly appeared on the scene to disperse the crowd.

Why the police intruded is the beginning of the puzzle we have to understand. Their reaction was totally inappropriate to the character of what was occurring before their eyes; they ought rather to have breathed a sigh of relief that the meeting was such a peaceful fiasco. But, as the civil riots of a later chapter in Chicago's history show, it is sometimes more difficult for the police to "cool off" than the demonstrators. In any event, just as the Haymarket meeting was falling apart, the police moved in to disperse it by force, and thus brought back to life the temporary spirit of unity and of outrage against the violence at the McCormick Works that had drawn crowd and orators together.

The knots of men moved back from the lines of police advancing toward the speaker's stand, so that the police gained the area in front of the rostrum without incident. Then, suddenly, someone in the crowd threw a powerful bomb into the midst of the policemen, and pandemonium broke loose. The wounded police and people in the crowd dragged themselves or were carried into the hallways of buildings in the eastern end of Union Park. Drugstores, like Ebert's at Madison and Halstead and Barker's on West Madison, suddenly became hospitals with bleeding men stretched out on the floors, while police combed the residences and grounds of Union Park looking for wounded members of the crowd who had managed to find shelter, under stoops or in sheds, from the police guns booming in the Square.[4]

REACTION OF THE MIDDLE CLASS

As the news spread, small riots broke out in the southwestern part of the city, with aimless targets, but they were soon dispersed. By the morning of May 5, the working-class quarters were quiet, though the police were not. They, and the middle-class people of Chicago, especially those living in Union Park, were in a fever, a fever compounded of fear, a desire for vengeance, and simple bewilderment.

It is this reaction that must be explored to gauge the true impact of the Haymarket incident on the Union Park community. The first characteristic of this reaction was how swiftly an interpretation, communally shared, was formed; the middle-class people of Union Park, and elsewhere in Chicago, were moved immediately by the incident to draw a defined, clear picture of what had happened, and they held onto their interpretation tenaciously. Today it is easy to recognize, from the location of the meeting next to a police station, from the apathy of the crowd, from the sequence of events that preceded the bombing, that the Haymarket incident was not a planned sequence of disorder or a riot by an enraged mob, but rather the work of an isolated man, someone who might have thrown the bomb no matter who was there. The day after the bombing, these objective considerations were not the reality "respectable" people perceived. Middle-class people of Chicago believed instead that "the immigrant anarchists" were spilling out of the slums to kill the police, in order to destroy the security of the middle class themselves. "Respectable" people felt some kind of need to believe in the enormity of the threat, and in this way the community quickly arrived at a common interpretation.

The enormity of the perceived threat was itself the second characteristic of their reaction. The color red, which was taken as a revolutionary incitement, was "cut out of street advertisements and replaced with a less suggestive color." [5] On the day after the riot a coroner's jury returned a verdict that all prisoners in the hands of the police were guilty of murder, because Socialism as such led to murderous anarchy, and anyone who attended the meeting must have been a Socialist. Yet this same jury observed that it was "troublesome" that none of those detained could be determined to have thrown the bomb. Anarchism itself was generalized to a more sweeping level by its identification with foreign birth; the "agitators" were poor foreigners, and this fact could explain their lawlessness. For example, the *Tribune* reported that on the day after the Haymarket Riot police closed two saloons

> that were the headquarters of the foreign-speaking population, which flaunts and marches under the red flag, and heretofore they were the centers of a great throng of men who did little but drink beer and attend the meetings in the halls above.[6]

On May 5 and 6, the police were engaged in a strenuous effort to determine where the "anarchist" groups lived, so that the population as a whole might be controlled. On May 7, and this was the view to prevail henceforward, they announced that the residences of most anarchists must be in the southwestern portion of the city, the immigrant, working-class area.[7]

The assigning of the responsible parties to the general category of "foreigner" excited even more panic in Union Park. It was reported in the *Tribune* of May 7 that a fear existed in the community that lawless marauders would again erupt out of the proletarian sector of the city and terrorize people in the neighborhood of the riot.[8] These fears were sustained by two events in the next week.

First were reports of the deaths, day after day, of policemen and innocent bystanders who had been seriously wounded by the bomb on May 4, coupled with a massive newspaper campaign to raise money for the families of the victims. Second, and by far more important, fear of renewed bombing was kept alive by the phantasies of a Captain Schaack of the Chicago police who day by day discovered and foiled anarchist plots, plans to bomb churches and homes, attempts on the lives of eminent citizens. Such were the horror stories with which the middle-class people of Chicago scared themselves for weeks.

Some kind of deep communal force engendered in the people of Union Park an immediately shared interpretation of what objectively was a confused event; this same communal force led men to escalate the metaphors of threat and challenge involved in this one event. As events a year later were to show, the force that produced these two characteristics of response was also to prevent the men of Union Park from being able to deal with future violence in an effective way.

BURGLARIES AND MURDER

On Thursday, February 9, 1888, the *Chicago Tribune* gave its lead space to the following story:

> Amos J. Snell, a millionaire who lived at the corner of Washington Boulevard and Ada Street, was shot to death by two burglars who entered his house and made off with $1,600 worth of county warrants and $5,000 in checks. The murder was committed at about 2 A.M. and discovered by a servant at about 6:30 A.M.[9]

Snell had been a resident of the area since 1867, when he built a home in Union Park and bought up many blocks of desirable real estate around it.

The murder of Snell climaxed a tense situation in Union Park that had existed since the beginning of the year 1888. Since New Year's

Day, "between forty and fifty burglaries have been committed within a radius of half a mile from the intersection of Adams and Ashland Avenues," the Editor of the *Tribune* wrote the day after Snell's death. The police counted half this number; it appears that the burglars had a simple and systematic scheme: to loot any household goods, such as furs, silver plate, jewelry, or bonds left in unlocked drawers. Occasionally some of the property was recovered, and occasionally a thief was arrested who seemed to have been involved, but the operation itself was remarkably smooth and successful.[10]

How did people in Union Park react to these burglaries, and what did they do to try to stop them? The reaction of the community was much like the reaction to the Haymarket bombing: they felt involved at once in a "reign of terror," as the *Tribune* said,[11] that was none of their doing—they didn't know when the danger would strike again or who would be threatened. Most of all, they didn't know how to stop it.[12] Once again, the level of fear was escalated to a general, sweeping, and impersonal level.

Before the Snell murder, the citizens of the community had tried two means of foiling the robbers, and so of quieting the fears within their families. One was to make reports to the police, reports which the Editor of the *Tribune* claimed the police did not heed. The citizens then resorted to fortifying their homes, to hiring elderly men as private night guards, but the thieves were professional enough to deal with this: "somehow or other the burglars evaded all the precautions that were taken to prevent their nocturnal visits." [13]

AFTER THE MURDER: A CHANGE IN COMMUNAL ATTITUDES

The Snell murder brought public discussion of the robberies, and how to stop them, to a high pitch. Especially in Union Park, the vicinity of Snell's residence, the community was "so aroused that the people talked of little else than vigilance committees and frequent holdings of court . . . as a panacea for the lawless era that had come upon them." [14] Gradually, the small-town vigilante idea gave way to a new attitude toward the police, and how the police should operate in a large city. "It is no use," said one member of the Grant Club, the

West Side club to which Snell himself had belonged, "to attempt to
run a cosmopolitan city as you would run a New England village." [15]
He meant that the police had up to that time concentrated on closing
down gambling houses and beer parlors as a major part of their effort
to keep the town "respectable" and "proper." Thus they didn't deal
effectively with serious crimes like robbery and murder because they
spent too much time trying to clean up petty offenses; the main thing
was to keep the criminal elements confined to their own quarters in
the city. In all these discussions, the fact of being burgled had been forgotten. The search turned to a means of separatism, of protection
against the threatening "otherness" of the populace outside the community.

Such views were striking, considering the position of Union Park.
The community's own physical character, in its parks and playgrounds,
was nonurban, designed in the traditions of Olmstead and Vaux; the
people, as was pointed out repeatedly in the newspaper account, were
themselves among the most respectable and staid in the city, if not the
most fashionable. Yet here were the most respectable among the respectable arguing for abandoning the enforcement throughout the
city of a common morality. The petty criminals outside the community's borders ought to be left in peace, but out of sight. Union Park
existed in a milieu too cosmopolitan for every act of the lower classes
to be controlled; the police ought to abandon the attempt to be the
guardians of all morality and instead concentrate on assuring the basic
security of the citizens against outbursts of major crime.

What Union Park wanted instead, and what it got, was a garrison
of police to make the community riotproof and crimeproof. The police
indeed abandoned the search for the killers, and concentrated on holding the security of Union Park, like an area under siege. In this way,
the original totally suburban tone of the parks and mansions was
transformed; this respectable neighborhood felt its own existence to
be so threatened that only a state of rigid barriers, enforced by a
semimilitary state of curfew and surveillance, would permit it to continue to function.

The effect of the riot and the train of burglaries and murder was
to put the citizens in a frame of mind where only the closure of the
community through constant surveillance and patrolling would reassure them. Indeed, the characteristics of their reaction to violence

could only lead to such a voluntary isolation: everyone "knew" immediately what was wrong; and what was wrong was overwhelming; it was nothing less than the power of the "foreigner," the outsider who had suddenly become dominant in the city. Isolation, through garrisons and police patrols, was the only solution.

Union Park held onto its middle-class character until the middle of the 1890s; there was no immediate desertion by respectable people of the area in the wake of the violence: where else in a great city, asked one citizen, was it safe to go? Everywhere the same terror was possible.

The contrast between the limited character of civil disturbance and the immediate perception of that disturbance as the harbinger of an unnameable threat coming from a generalized enemy is a theme that binds together much research on urban disorders.

Until a few years ago, riots were taken to be the expression of irrational, and directionless, aggression. The "irrationality of crowds," and similar explanations of crowd behavior as an innate disorder, was first given a cogent interpretation in the industrial era in the writings of Le Bon,[16] for whom the irrational brutality of crowds was a sign of how the "psychology" of the individual becomes transformed when the individual acts in concert with other people. According to Le Bon, the crowd releases a man from the self-reflective, rational restraints that normally operate when a person is alone or with one or two other people. The anonymity of mass gatherings reinforces the desire each one has to cast off these rational, individual restraints, and encourages men to express more violent traits without fear of personal detection. It is the social psychology of the massive gathering to be unrestrained, Le Bon wrote, the psychology of the individual to prescribe rules for himself.[17]

This image of crowds was as congenial to many of the syndicalists on the Left (though not Sorel) as it was to the fears of bourgeois people like those in Union Park. The difficulty with the image is that, for the nineteenth century at least, it seems not to fit the facts of crowd behavior.

Thanks to the pioneering work of George Rudé and Charles Tilly,[18] it has been possible to ascertain that, in the urbanizing of English and French populations during the early nineteenth century, popular rebellions and crowd activities possessed a high degree of rationality; that is to say, the crowds acted to achieve rather well-defined ends, and used only as much force as was required to make their demands prevail. Though the work of Rudé and Tilly seems contradicted by the extensive researches of Louis Chevalier[19] on Parisian lower-class behavior during the nineteenth century, there are enough points of agreement, in looking at crowd behavior where violent coercion is involved, to rule out the "unrestrained frenzy" Le Bon saw in crowds that made them useless as a social tool to gain definite, common goals.[20] What is important in Le Bon's work, for the present purpose, was his *expectation* that this unrestrained frenzy would result from group action by the lower class.

For it is this same split between middle-class expectation of blind anarchy and the actual limitations on working-class disorder that characterized the Haymarket incidents, the same split between a reign of terror sensed during the later burglaries and the actual routine narrowness of these crimes.

The problem of the Union Park experience was the citizenry's inability to connect the facts seen to the facts as elements of what people knew was a correct interpretation. Expecting "seething passions" to erupt hysterically, the middle-class people of Chicago and their police were somehow immune to the spectacle they should have enjoyed, that of the workers becoming bored with the inflammatory talk of their supposed leaders. The expectations of a seething rabble had somehow to be fulfilled, and so the police themselves took the first step. After the shooting was over, the respectable people of Chicago became in turn inflamed. This blind passion in the name of defending the city from blind passion is the phenomenon that needs to be explained. A similar contradiction occurred in the series of robberies a half year later as well. As in the riot, the facts of the rationality of the enemy and his limited purpose, although acknowledged, were not absorbed; he was felt to be something else, a nameless, elusive terror, all-threatening. And the people reacted with a passion equal to his.

This mystifying condition, familiar now in the voices heard from the "New Right," is what I should like to explain, not through a sweeping theory that binds the past to the present, but through a theory that explains this peculiar reaction in terms of strains in the

family life of the Union Park people. What I would like to explore—
and I certainly do not pretend to prove it—is how, in an early industrial city, the fears of the foreign masses by a middle-class group may
have reflected something other than the actual state of interaction between bourgeoisie and proletariat. These fears may have reflected instead the impact of family life on the way the people like those in
Union Park understood their places in the city society.

Studies of overreaction to limited stimuli have centered, for the
most part, on the idea of a "frustration-aggression syndrome." This
ungainly phrase was given a clear definition in one of the early classic works of American social psychology, *Frustration and Aggression*
(1939). The authors wrote that

> aggression is always a consequence of frustration. More specifically
> . . . the occurrence of aggressive behavior always presupposes the
> existence of frustration and, contrariwise, the existence of frustra-
> tion always leads to some form of aggression.[21]

Applied in terms of social class, this frustration-aggression syndrome
implies that when a group fails to achieve goals it desires, or when it
is unable to maintain a position it covets, it becomes aggressive, and
searches out objects on which it can blame its failure. This simple,
clear idea Parsons[22] has applied to the formation of the Nazi party
in Germany: the fall in status in the 1920s of fixed-income, middle-
class groups breeding an aggressive desire to get back at their enemies,
without knowing, or really caring, who they were. Lipset[23] has incorporated elements of the same idea in his essay on working-class
authoritarianism in the United States after the Second World War.
And of course the concept is now used to explain the hostility of lower
middle-class whites toward blacks: the whites who have failed to rise
high in the economic system they believe in are said to make blacks
"aggression objects" of the frustration they themselves have suffered.[24]

If it is true, as this syndrome of frustration-aggression suggests,
that in the character one ascribes to one's enemy lies a description of
something in one's own experience, the nature of the fear of lower-
class foreigners among Union Park families might tell something about
the Union Park community itself. The Union Park men, during the
time of the riot and robberies, accused their chosen enemies of being,
first, lawless anarchists, which was transmuted, secondly, to being

pushed by their base passions outside the bounds of acceptable behavior, which resolved itself, finally, to being emotionally out of control. If the poor were reasonable, if they were temperate, ran the argument, these violent things would not have come to pass.

What about the Union Park people themselves, then? Were they
masters of themselves? A study I have recently completed on the family
patterns of the Union Park people during the decades of the 1870s and
'80s may throw some light on the question of stability and purposeful-
ness in their lives: it is the dimension of stability in these family patterns, I believe, that shaped sources of the reaction to violence.

INTENSIVE FAMILY LIFE

In 1880, on a forty-square-block territory of Union Park, there
lived 12,000 individuals in approximately 3,000 family units. These
family units were of three kinship types: single-member families, where
one person lived alone without any other kin; nuclear families, consisting of a husband, wife, and their unmarried children; and extended
families, where to the nuclear unit was added some other relative—a
brother or sister of the parents, a member of a third generation, or a
son or daughter who was married and lived with his spouse in the
parental home. The most common form of the extended family in
Union Park was that containing "collateral kin," that is, unmarried
relatives of the same generation as the husband or wife.

The dominant form of family life in Union Park was nuclear,
for 80 per cent of the population lived in such homes, with 10 per cent
of the population living alone in single-member families, and the remaining 10 per cent living in extended family situations. A father and
mother living alone with their growing children in an apartment or
house was the pervasive household condition. There were few widowed
parents living with their children in either nuclear or extended homes,
and though the census manuscripts on which my study of the year
1880 is based were inexact at this point, there appeared to be few
groups of related families living in separate dwellings but in the same
neighborhood.

Is this nuclear-family dominance a special characteristic of
middle-class life in this era? At the Joint Center for Urban Studies, I

was fortunate in working with other researchers in this field to co-ordinate census measures of class and family form that could be used comparatively across different studies.[25] Comparison with these other studies, as well as within the limited range of social groups in Union Park, convinces me that this kind of family form was not a middle-class phenomenon. Within Union Park, the 80 per cent dominance of the nuclear families held in lower social strata (of which enough ex-isted to measure and test statistically, since the population as a whole was so large—about 25 per cent of the community fell into a working-class category, excluding the servants in the homes of the other 75 per cent) and throughout the range of middle-class groups. In Lynn Lees' data on an Irish working-class district in London in 1860, it similarly appeared that about 80 per cent of her community's population lived in nuclear family configurations, 10 per cent in single-member families, and 10 per cent in extended families, virtually the same distribution as was found in Chicago's Union Park in 1880.

Again, the *outer* limits on the size of families in Union Park did seem to be the product of a special class condition. Contrary to the stereotype of the sprawling families of the poor, in Union Park the size of poor families was in its contours similar to the size of the wealthier ones: few families were larger than six members, among rich or poor. Similarly, comparison of family sizes in Union Park to the poor Irish of Lynn Lees' study or to the middle-class area of St. Pancras in London reveals the limits on family size in the three areas to have been the same.

Since family studies of nineteenth-century cities are at this date in a primitive stage, the body of future research may show these present examples to be "sports" or explainable by circumstances researchers do not now understand. Yet it does now seem more fruitful to concen-trate on the *function* of nuclear families or on the *function* of families of restricted size in middle-class communities in the great cities of the nineteenth century, rather than to try to locate the conditions of pecul-iarly middle-class life in the *structural* existence of these family types.

What I did find to be true in Union Park was the following: over the course of time internal conditions of family structure and of family size tended to lead to similar family histories. Nuclear families had characteristic histories similar to the experience of smaller families having from two to four kin members in the 1870s and '80s. Extended

families, on the other hand, had histories similar to the experience of
the minority of families with four to six kin members during these
decades. What made this process subtle was that nuclear families did
not tend to be smaller, or extended larger. Family size and family kinship structure seemed rather to be independent structures with parallel
internal differences in functioning.

Why and how this was so can be understood by assessing the
patterns of the generations of the dominant group of nuclear, small-
size families during the year 1880. These families were marked, in the
relations between husbands and wives, parents and children, by strong
patterns of family cohesion. Whether rich or poor, the young men and
women from such homes rarely broke away to live on their own until
they themselves were ready to marry and found families, an event that
usually occurred when the man was in his early thirties. The families
of Union Park, observers of the time noted, were extremely self-con-
tained, did little entertaining, and rarely left the home to enjoy even
such modest pleasures as a church social or, for the men, a beer at the
local tavern. The small family, containing only parents and their immediate children, resisted the diverse influences of either other kin
associations or extensive community contacts. This was the mode of
family life that dominated Union Park numerically. These families
can be called "intensive families," and their life histories contrasted to
families of larger size or more complex kinship. The intensive families
would seem to epitomize a defined order of stability among the people
of Union Park. Yet, Lynn Lees and I have found some functional differences between Chicago and London in families of this general
character.

INSTABILITY THROUGH
SEPARATION OR DESERTION

In most census collections in the United States and Britain, the
official tabulations of divorce are very low, because the formal breaking of the marital tie was considered a personal disgrace to both partners. But, as Talcott Parsons has demonstrated,[26] these official figures
are misleading, since a great deal of unofficial divorce through separation or desertion occurred, at a higher rate, Parsons thinks, than in

our own time. One means of detecting this hidden marital disorder in the census is to locate the individuals who were officially married but living without a spouse in the family. This measurement lets in a certain number of "beachhead migrants," men who have come to the city in advance of their families to establish a job and find a house, but in Union Park such men were less common in this category than spouses who were married, living with their children, but not with their husbands (or wives).[27]

In Union Park the number of families involved in such a break was about 10 per cent. But in London, in the middle-class district of St. Pancras, the incidence of such marital separation was one-half of this, or 5 per cent; in the lower-class Irish district Lynn Lees studied, there were less than a third as many marital separations of this type. In all three communities, of course, the official rate of divorce was nearly zero.

The explanation for this comparatively high incidence of marital break in Union Park is obscure, since there are now so few other comparative measures of family conditions behind the official statistics to use. In terms of these Chicago and London communities themselves perhaps the best thing to be said is the simplest: the higher incidence of marital break occurred in a city whose development was exclusively in the industrial era; the lower incidence of such a break occurred in a city for whom industrial production and large bureaucratic enterprises were but one chapter in a very long history.

WORK MOBILITY AND FAMILY STABILITY

Added to this kind of family instability in the community as a whole, my study of intergenerational mobility in work and residence from 1872 to 1890 revealed a complicated, but highly significant pattern of insecurity in the dominant intensive families when compared to the smaller group of less intensive families.[28]

In the nuclear-family homes and in the smaller families the fathers were stable in their patterns of job holding, as a group, over the course of the eighteen years studied; roughly the same proportions of unskilled, skilled, and white-collar workers of various kinds composed the labor force of these nuclear fathers in 1890 as in 1872. Given the enormous growth of Chicago's industrial production, its banking and financial capital, retail trade volume, as well as the proliferation of the population (100 per cent increase each ten years) and the greatly increasing proportion of white-collar pursuits during this time, such stability in job distribution is truly puzzling. Further, this pattern of job holding among the fathers of intensive families was not shared by the fathers in extended families or fathers of larger families living in Union Park. They were mobile up into exclusively bureaucratic, white-collar pursuits, so that by 1890 virtually none of these fathers worked with their hands. Within the range of white-collar occupations, the extended-family fathers and the large-family fathers gradually concentrated in executive and other lesser management pursuits and decreased their numbers in shopkeeping, toward which, stereotypically, they are supposed to gravitate.

Now the differences between fathers and sons in each of these family groups were even more striking. I found the sons in the dominant family homes to be, unlike their fathers, very unstable in their patterns of job holding, with as much movement down into manual pursuits over the course of the eighteen years as movement up within the white-collar occupations. Following the lead of Blau and Duncan,[29] we might be tempted to explain this pattern of dispersion simply as regression-toward-the-mean of higher status groups intergenerationally. But the sons of extended and large families did not move in this mixed direction. Rather, they followed in the footsteps of their fathers into good white-collar positions, with almost total elimination of manual labor in their ranks over the course of time. This pattern occurred in small-family sons versus large-family sons and in nuclear-family sons versus extended-family sons. The difference in the groups of sons was especially striking in that the starting distribution of the sons in the occupational work force was virtually the *same,* in the measure of family form and in those of family size. Thernstrom has pointed out in the conference discussions for this volume that economic aid between generations of workers ought to manifest itself more at the beginning point in the careers of the young rather than when the older generation has retired and the young have become the principal breadwinners. In Union Park, the fact that both extended-family and nuclear-family sons, both large- and small-family sons, began to work in virtually the same pursuits as their fathers, but then became distinctively different in their patterns of achievement, strongly suggests that something *beyond* monetary help was at work in these families to produce divergences in work experience in the city.

The residence patterns of the generations of the intensive and less intensive families also bear on the issues of stability and instability in the lives of the people of Union Park. Up to the time of violence in the Union Park area, the residence patterns of the two kinds of families, in both the parents' and the sons' generations, were rather similar. In the wake of the violence it appears that, within the parents' generation, there was significant movement back into the Union Park area, whereas for the half decade preceding the disturbances there was a general movement out to other parts of Chicago. It is in the generation of the sons that differences between the two family groups appeared. In the wake of the violence, the sons of large families and of extended families continued the processes of residential break from Union Park initiated during the early years of the 1880 decade. The sons from intensive families did not; in the years following the violence they stopped migrating beyond the boundaries of the community they had known as children, and instead kept closer to their first homes.

TWO THEORIES OF
INTENSIVE FAMILY STABILITY

In my study of Union Park,[30] I tried to explain these differences in work experience and in residence in terms of patterns of family life and child nurturance for bourgeois people in a new, immensely dynamic, disordered city. In so doing, my researches led me into a debate that exists between the work of the sociologist Talcott Parsons and the cultural historian Phillipe Aries.[31] For Parsons has argued that the small nuclear family is an adaptive kinship form to the industrial order; the lack of extensive kin obligations and a wide kin circle in this family type mean, Parsons has contended, that the kinship unit does not serve as a binding private world of its own, but rather frees the individual to participate in "universalized" bureaucratic structures that are urban-wide and dynamic.[32] Aries has challenged this theory by amassing a body of historical evidence to show

that the extended kinship relationships in large families, at least during the period he studied, were actually less sheltering, more likely to
push the individual out into the world where he would have to act
like a full man on his own at an early age, than the intense, intimate
conditions of the nineteenth-century home. In intensive homes, the
young person spent a long time in a state of independence under the
protection and guidance of his elders. Consequently, argues Aries,
the capacity of the young adult from small nuclear homes to deal with
the world about him was blunted, for he passed from a period of total
shelter to a state in which he was expected to be entirely competent
on his own.[33] Aries' attack has been supported for contemporary
American urban communities by a variety of studies, the most notable
being those of Eugene Litwak and Marvin Sussman, and it has been
supported for English cities by the work of Peter Wilmott and Elizabeth Bott.[34]

The data I have collected on Union Park during the early stages
of Chicago's industrial-bureaucratic expansion clearly are in line with
the argument made by Aries. The young from homes of small scale or
from homes where the structure of the family was nuclear and "privatistic," in Aries' phrase, had an ineptness in the work world, and a
rootedness to the place of their childhood not found to the same degree
among the more complex, or larger-family situations. (I have no desire
to argue the moral virtues of this rootedness to community or failure
to "make it" in the city; these simply happened to be the conditions
that existed.) But the context of these Union Park families as new
urbanites, in a new kind of city form, alters the meaning of stability
and shelter leading to instability in the next generation among the intense family households. For it is clear that the nineteenth-century,
privatistic, sheltering homes Aries depicts, homes Frank Lloyd Wright
describes in his *Autobiography* for his early years in Chicago, homes
that observers of the time pointed to as a basic element in the composition of the "dull respectability" of Union Park, could easily have
served as a refuge themselves from the confusing, dynamic city that
was taking shape all around the confines of Union Park. It indeed
seems natural that middle-class people should try to hold onto the
status position they had in such a disrupting, growing milieu, make
little entrepreneurial ventures outside their established jobs, and withdraw themselves into the comfort and intimacy of their families. Here

is the source of that job "freeze" to be seen in the mobility patterns of fathers in intense-family situations; the bourgeois intensive family in this way became a shelter from the work pressures of the industrial city, a place where men tried to institute some control and establish some comforting intimacies in the shape of their lives, while withdrawing to the sidelines as the new opportunities of the city industries opened up. Such an interpretation of these middle-class families complements, on the side of the home, the interpretation Richard Hofstadter has made of the middle classes politically, in the latter part of the nineteenth century. He characterizes them as feeling that the new industrial order was not theirs, but had passed them by and left them powerless.[35] It is this peculiar feeling of social helplessness on the part of the fathers that explains what use they made of their family lives.

CONFUSION IN THE DESIRE FOR STABILITY

What makes this complex pattern of family stability–instability significant for wider social orientations are the values about work to be found in the middle classes of this era. For here the idea of seizing opportunities, the idea of instability of job tenure for the sake of rising higher and higher, constituted, as John Cawelti has described it,[36] the commonly agreed-upon notion of how sure success could be achieved at this time among respectable people; in the same way, this chance-taking path was presented, in the Horatio Alger novels and the like, as the road into the middle class itself. One should have been mobile in work, then, for this was the meaning of "opportunity" and "free enterprise," but in fact the overwhelming dislocations of the giant cities seem to have urged many men to retreat into the circle of their own families, to try simply to hold onto what they knew they could perform as tasks to support themselves, in the midst of the upheaval of urban expansion.

This is deduction, to be sure, and perhaps it is characteristic of sociologists dealing with history that they speculate where historians would prefer to remain silent and let the ambiguities stand. Yet not only the body of Union Park data, but the memoirs, fictional portraits, and secondary studies of this period seem to me to indicate that such

an internally contradictory response to urbanization among the heads
of middle-class families is the means by which the differences in social
mobility between kinds of families can be explained. Conditions of
privacy and comfort in the home weakened the desire to get ahead in
the world, to conquer it; since the fathers of the intensive families
were retreating from the confusions of city life, their preparation of
their sons for work in Chicago became ambiguous, in that they wanted,
surely, success for their sons, yet shielded the young, and did not themselves serve as models of successful adaptation. The result of these
ambiguities can be seen directly in the work experience of the sons,
when contrasted to the group of sons from families which, by virtue
either of family form or size, were more complex or less intense. Over-
laid on these family patterns was a relatively high rate of hidden marital breakdown in Union Park—one in every ten homes—while the expectation was, again, that such breakdown must not occur, that it was
a disgrace morally.

These contradictions in family process gave rise, I believe, to the
characteristics of Union Park's reaction to violence during the years
1886 to 1888.

THE FEELING OF THREAT GENERATED
BY THE FAMILY EXPERIENCE

In the older version of the "frustration-aggression" syndrome it
was assumed that if a social group failed to achieve a certain goal, it
searched for an enemy to punish. But the goals of these middle-class
people in Union Park were themselves self-contradictory: they wanted
success in the work of the city and yet they didn't want it, given the
definition of success at that time as an entrepreneurial grasping of opportunities rather than the fruit of plodding and routine service. The
goals for the home were also contradictory: they wanted a stable shelter
from the confusion and terror of the city, yet somehow they expected
their sons, growing up sheltered, to be able to make it in that city
world, and the sons of the dominant family groups seemed unable to
do so. Divorce was a disgrace, yet there is evidence that one out of
every ten of the neighborhood families was involved in a marital
separation or desertion, a voluntary condition as opposed to the in-

voluntary break of widowhood. Thus, because the goals of these middle-class people were bred of an equal desire to escape from and succeed in the city, the possibility of a wholly satisfying pattern of achievement for them was denied. The contradictory nature of the family purpose and products was innately frustrating so that a family impulse in one direction inevitably defeated another image of what was wanted. This meant that the sources of defeat were nameless for the families involved; surely these families were not aware of the web of self-contradictions in which in retrospect they seem to have been enmeshed; they knew only that things never seemed to work out to the end planned, that they suffered defeats in a systematic way. It is this specific kind of frustration that would lead to a sense of being overwhelmed, which, in this community's family system, led easily to a hysterical belief in hidden, unknown threats ready to strike at a man at almost any time.

FEELING OF THREAT
AND PERCEPTIONS OF VIOLENCE

What I would like to suggest is that this complex pattern of self-defeat explains the character of the Union Park reaction to violence. For the dread of the unknown that the middle classes projected onto their supposed enemies among the poor expressed exactly the condition of self-instituted defeat that was the central feature of the family system in Union Park. And this dread was overwhelming precisely because men's own contradictory responses to living in such a city were overwhelming. They had defined a set of conditions for their lives that inevitably left them out of control. The fact that there was in Union Park a desire to destroy the "immigrant anarchists" or to garrison the neighborhood against them, as a result of the incidents of violence, was important in that it offered an outlet for personal defeats, not just for anger against lawbreakers. This response to violence refused to center on particular people, but rather followed the "path of hysterical reaction," in Freud's phrase, and centered on an abstract class of evildoers. For the fear of being suddenly overwhelmed from the outside was really a sign that one was in fact in one's own life being continually overwhelmed by the unintended consequences, or "latent consequences" as Merton calls them, of what one did.[37] By blaming the urban poor for their lawlessness, these middle-class people were expressing a passion for retribution that had little to do with riots or thefts. The retribution was rather in the nature of what Erikson calls a "cover object" for hostility, an expression of inability to deal with the issues of one's own life, of mobility and stability in the city: the fear in these middle-class people was that if they were to act entrepreneurially in the work world they might be destroyed, yet their desire was to make it big suddenly. The desire to escape to the safety of the simple home of father, mother, and children became, unexpectedly, a crippling shield when the sons went out into the world.

This dilemma, expressed in the terrible fear of attack from the unbridled masses, was also related to the fear of falling into deep poverty that grew up in urban middle-class families of this time. To judge from a wide range of novels in the latter half of the nineteenth century there was a dread among respectable people of suddenly and uncontrollably falling into abject poverty; the Sidwells in Thackeray's *Vanity Fair* plummet from wealth to disorganized penury in a short space of time; Lily Bart's father, in Edith Wharton's *Age of Innocence,* is similarly struck down by the symbol of entrepreneurial chance in the industrial city, the stock market. This feeling of threat from the impersonal, unpredictable workings of the city economy was much like the sense of threat that existed in the Union Park families, because the dangers encountered in both cases were not a person or persons one could grapple with, but an abstract condition, poverty, or family disorder that was unintended, impersonal, and swift to come if the family should once falter. Yet what one *should* do was framed in such a self-contradictory way that it seemed oneself and one's family were always on the edge of survival. In this way, the growth of the new industrial city, with its uncertainties and immense wastes of human poverty not all to be dismissed as personal failures, could surely produce in the minds of middle-class citizens, uneasy about their own class position, living out from the center of town, the feeling that some terrible force from below symbolized by the poor, the foreigner, was about to strike out and destroy them unless they did something drastic.

The demographic reaction among most of the families to the eruption of violence bears out this interpretation of events. With the exception of the upwardly mobile, extended-family sons, most family members did not try to flee the community as a response to the threats of riot and the organized wave of crime. The demographic movement mirrored a renewed feeling of community solidarity in the face of violence, a solidarity created by fear and a common dread of those below. Again, it is significant that the group that did not show this pattern of "sticking out the trouble" is the generation of young family members who lived in more complex family circumstances than the majority, and who achieved, on the whole, greater occupational gains than the majority.

The relations between family life and the perception of violence in this Chicago community could be formed into the following general propositions. These were middle-class families enormously confused in what they wanted for themselves in the city, considered in terms of their achievements in the society at large and in terms of their emotional needs for shelter and intimacy; their schema of values and life goals was in fact formed around the issues of stability and instability as goals in a self-contradictory way. The result of this inner contradiction was a feeling of frustration, of not really being satisfied, in the activities of family members to achieve *either* patterns of stability or mobility for themselves. The self-defeat involved in this process led these families naturally to feel themselves threatened by overwhelming, nameless forces they could not control, no matter what they did. The outbreak of violence was a catalyst for them, giving them in the figure of the "other," the stranger, the foreigner, a generalized agent of disorder and disruption.

It is this process that explains logically why the people of Union Park so quickly found a communally acceptable villain responsible for violence, despite all the ambiguities perceived in the actual outbreaks of the disorders themselves; this is why the villain so quickly identified was a generalized, nonspecific human force, the embodiment of the unknown, the outside, the foreign. This is why the people of Union Park clung so tenaciously to their interpretation, seemed so willing to be terrorized and distraught.

If the complex processes of family and social mobility in Union Park are of any use in understanding the great fear of disorder among respectable, middle-class urbanites of our own time, their import is surely disturbing. For the nature of the disease that produced this reaction to violence among the industrial middle classes was not simply a matter of "ignorance" or failure to understand the problems of the poor; the fear was the consequence, rather, of structural processes in the lives of the Union Park families themselves. Thus for attitudes of people like the Union Park dwellers to change, and a more tolerant view of those below to be achieved, nothing so simple as more education about poor people, or to put the matter in contemporary terms, more knowledge about Negroes, would have sufficed. The whole fabric of the city, in its impact on staid white-collar workers, would have to have been changed. The complexity and the diversity of the city itself would need to have been stilled for events to take another course. But were the disorder of the city absent, the principal characteristic of the industrial city as we know it would also have been absent. These cities were powerful agents of change, precisely because they replaced the controlled social space of village and farm life with a kind of human settlement too dense and too various to be controlled.

And it comes to mind that the New Right fears of the present time are as deeply endemic to the structure of complex city life as was the violent reaction to violence in Union Park. Perhaps, out of patterns of self-defeat in the modern middle classes, it is bootless to expect right-wing, middle-class repression to abate simply through resolves of goodwill, "education about Negroes," or a change of heart. The experience of these bourgeois people of Chicago one hundred years ago may finally serve to make us a great deal more pessimistic about the chances for reason and tolerance to survive in a complex and pluralistic urban society.

FOOTNOTES

1. Henry David, *The Haymarket Affair* (New York, 1936), p. 198.
2. See Foster Rhea Dulles, *A History of American Labor* (New York, 1949), *passim*.
3. *Chicago Daily Tribune*, May 4, 1886, pp. 1, 2.
4. See the full account in the *Chicago Daily Tribune*, May 5, 1886, p. 1.
5. David, p. 226.
6. *Chicago Daily Tribune*, May 6, 1886, p. 3.
7. *Chicago Daily Tribune*, May 7, 1886, p. 8.
8. *Ibid.*
9. *Chicago Daily Tribune*, February 9, 1888, pp. 1–2.
10. *Ibid.*, p. 4.
11. *Ibid.*, pp. 1–2.

12. See the statements of the Union Park fathers in *Chicago Daily Tribune*, February 9, 1888, p. 2.

13. *Chicago Daily Tribune*, February 9, 1888, pp. 1–2.

14. *Ibid.*

15. *Ibid.*

16. G. Le Bon, *The Crowd: A Study of the Popular Mind* (London, 1909).

17. It is interesting that Le Bon was led by this route into looking later in his life for a different set of psychological "instincts" in crowds than in individuals.

18. George Rudé, *The Crowd in History, 1730–1840* (New York, 1954) and Charles Tilly, *The Vendée* (Cambridge, Mass., 1964).

19. L. Chevalier, *Classes Laborieuses et Classes Danguereuses* (Paris, 1958).

20. I understand Chevalier is now more convinced of the "rationality" hypothesis. See, as one indication of this, the writings on Belleville in L. Chevalier, *Les Parisiens* (Paris, 1967).

21. J. Dollard, L. Boob, J. Miller, E. Mower, J. Sears *et al.*, *Frustration and Aggression* (New Haven, 1939), p. 1.

22. See "Democracy and Social Structure in Pre-Nazi Germany" in Parsons, *Essays in Sociological Theory* (rev. ed., Glencoe, Ill., 1954).

23. See Seymour Martin Lipset, *Political Man*, Pt. I, Chap. 4 (New York, 1960).

24. This theory, widely expressed in the press by amateur sociologists, explains the phenomenon neatly as a whole, but explains nothing of the particulars of class jealousy or fear.

25. Stephan Thernstrom and Richard Sennett, eds., *Nineteenth-Century Cities: Essays in the New Urban History* (New Haven, 1969). The measures are also relatable to the social class categories used by D. V. Glass in his study of integenerational social mobility in Britain; Part III of *Social Mobility in Britain*, D. V. Glass, ed. (London, 1954).

26. Talcott Parsons and Robert Bales, *Family*, Chap. 1 (Glencoe, Ill., 1955).

27. See Charles Tilly, *"Migration to an American City"* (unpublished manuscript on file at Joint Center for Urban Studies) for an excellent discussion of migration patterns.

28. There were, of course, no two-generation households in the single-member families.

29. P. Blau and O. D. Duncan, *The American Occupational Structure* (New York, 1967).

30. *Families Against the City* (Cambridge, Mass., 1970).

31. Phillipe Aries, *Centuries of Childhood* (New York, 1965).

32. Parsons and Bales, Chap. 1.

33. Bernard Wishy, in *The Child and the Republic* (Philadelphia, 1967), has material relevant to this idea for America in the late nineteenth century.

34. See Sennett, *Families Against the City*, Chap. 9, for a review of this literature.

35. Richard Hofstadter, *The Age of Reform* (New York, 1958).

36. John Cawelti, *Apostles of the Self-Made Man* (Chicago, 1965).

37. The Union Park situation was, in fact, a classic case of Merton's theory of latent consequences.

Index